"What a breath of fresh air to read this book, which offers essential history, sober analysis and courageous vision on how to take on antisemitism, directly from individuals who have been on the front lines of this work with the new generation of the Jewish Left. Lorber and Burley offer clear eyed lessons from our movements about how to keep Jews and all people safe, and timely alternatives to the failed approach of the pro-Israel American Jewish establishment. This book is a gift."

—Simone Zimmerman, co-founder, IfNotNow

"I don't think this book could come at a better time . . . *Safety Through Solidarity* is not just an appeal to avoid falling into a trap, it also recognizes how much stronger we all are when we do so. Most importantly, Burley and Lorber show how to build that strength against such odds. Everyone needs to read this book."

—Daryle Lamont Jenkins, founder, One People's Project

"In deconstructing the poisonous roots of anti-Jewish sentiment, Lorber and Burley show how antisemitism is not just a problem for Jews, but something that impedes social progress for everyone . . . at this dangerous moment for Jews around the world, *Safety Through Solidarity* is a book to rely on for real answers and solutions."

—Mike Rothschild, author, *Jewish Space Lasers*

"Antisemitism has again become a topic of intense conversation, and new books appear almost weekly analyzing what it is, why it is, and how to fight it. But none are quite like *Safety through Solidarity*. In their historically rich and deeply sophisticated analysis, Burley and Lorber view antisemitism as part of a larger phenomenon of hate and advocate Jewish solidarity with others in search of a society of equality and justice. This is a daring and provocative project, a desperately needed alternative to the phobic and sometimes shrill nature of the present discourse."

"Drawing on the experiences and insights of contemporary progressive activists, *Safety Through Solidarity* advocates an alternative approach to fighting antisemitism than that of the American Jewish establishment. At a time of rising antisemitism and white Christian nationalism, such a strategy is urgently needed . . . This book should be required reading for progressive activists."

"Burley and Lorber admirably and forthrightly explore the 'multitudes' of Jewish experience through a variety of voices and organizations. A timely book that avoids the 'cudgel' of antisemitism, 'cynically deployed to silence voices for Palestinian human rights.'"

SAFETY THROUGH SOLIDARITY

SAFETY THROUGH SOLIDARITY

A RADICAL GUIDE TO FIGHTING ANTISEMITISM

SHANE BURLEY AND **BEN LORBER**

MELVILLE HOUSE

BROOKLYN · LONDON

SAFETY THROUGH SOLIDARITY

First published in 2024 by Melville House
Copyright © 2023 by Shane Burley and Ben Lorber

All rights reserved
First Melville House Printing: March 2024

Melville House Publishing
46 John Street
Brooklyn, NY 11201
and
Melville House UK
Suite 2000
16/18 Woodford Road
London E7 0HA

mhpbooks.com
@melvillehouse

ISBN: 978-1-68589-091-9
ISBN: 978-1-68589-092-6 (eBook)

Library of Congress Control Number: 2024932506

Designed by Sofia Demopolos

Printed in the United States of America
1 3 5 7 9 10 8 6 4 2

A catalog record for this book is available
from the Library of Congress

CONTENTS

Part IV: How Do We Fight Antisemitism Today?

BUILDING SAFETY THROUGH SOLIDARITY

I t was one of the first nights of Hanukkah: a festival celebrating the Jewish people's right to maintain their traditions despite persecution. There was excitement everywhere as hundreds of people packed into the auditorium of a new Jewish Community Center in Virginia, the result of years of organizing and fundraising. Centers like these are core to any Jewish community: they bring together Jews beyond differences in religious observance (or lack of observance entirely), and are part of the vibrant web of American Jewish civic organizations that began, over a century ago, as a way to provide support to Jews excluded from state services.

But then a member of the board walked onstage and announced that the program that evening was being canceled. They had received a bomb threat.

The building was quickly evacuated. Dove Kent, then ten years old, dashed over to her mom, who whispered that since the building had been open, there had been a bomb threat every single day. This time, however, with hundreds there for one of the region's largest Jewish events, the safety of the entire community was at stake.

Dove didn't grow up around a lot of Jews. There were eleven Jewish students in her Virginia high school, and she had to insist to her skeptical teachers that Yom Kippur was the holiest day of the year, not just an excuse to duck her math exam.

That night, Dove joined the remaining attendees as they chanted that they would not be afraid.

"But they were clearly terrified and shaking," she told us, and it was definitely a formative experience for me to see the adults in my community so powerless and frightened . . . That was a really major moment that made me both feel committed, then and through my life, to my fellow Jews . . . But also in that moment, it was not specific to Jewish [people] . . . Why should someone with a bomb threat be able to just terrorize a community like this? No one should be experiencing this." That bomb threat wasn't the end of it: weeks later, swastikas were found scrawled on the side of the building. This harrowing December night sent Dove on her path to become a progressive community organizer, a leader of progressive Jewish organizations, and an active participant in Jewish communal life, uniting her desire for equality and justice with Jewish peoplehood. She inherited a long tradition of Jewish activism from ancestors who fought against antisemitism and for a better world for all, because those two fights are inextricably bound.

Antisemitism is on the rise today, alongside so many other forms of oppression. But the tangled mess of accusations and defenses we hear on the news every day makes it seem more challenging than ever to understand and confront.

Dove's inheritance is one we all share. In spite of a political culture that tries to divide us, Jews and other marginalized groups are realizing that when we rely on each other, we become stronger than the forces arrayed against us. Our book tells the story of the movements coming together to build safety through solidarity.

Crisis is the new normal. As economic and ecological catastrophe deepens, we are seeing a mass realignment—a select few are consolidating untold wealth and power, while the rest of us face permanent precarity, immiseration, or worse. The political center is collapsing, and radical instability demands radical responses. Fast-growing movements like Black Lives Matter and #MeToo, worker unionization, and the empowerment of queer, trans, and gender-nonconforming people are challenging injustice. But the far-right is growing at alarming rates, too, offering its own potent and electrifying story of white Christian dispossession and revolt.

People are scared, and looking for reasons why the world suddenly feels confusing and disempowering. A static society requires little explanation, but a world that is shedding its skin? That requires dramatic answers that move past our established narratives. "The old is dying but the new cannot be born; in this interregnum a great variety of morbid symptoms appear," wrote Italian Marxist Antonio Gramsci in 1930 from within a fascist prison: words that, nearly a century later, feel more prescient than ever.

Fascists march in the streets chanting "Jews will not replace us" and open fire at synagogues. Pundits spin conspiracy theories about George Soros, "globalists," and "elite cabals" on Fox News. Newspaper headlines continuously scream about antisemitism not only from Donald Trump but from Jeremy Corbyn, Linda Sarsour, Ilhan Omar: the list is endless. We hear that antisemitism is growing from all sides.

How can we make sense of this?

Antisemitism has not "reappeared" because, in truth, it never left us—the "crisis" is simply more visible in political life as exclusionary movements create a new populist narrative that provides alienated people someone to blame. Progressive movements have stood up against other forms of oppression, tracing the historic roots, and contemporary fruits, of white supremacy, colonialism, patriarchy, queerphobia, and many other ills plaguing our world. But we lack a similar framework for understanding what antisemitism is, and how to fight it.

This book is one attempt to put the fight against antisemitism back on the progressive agenda, where it belongs.

In the United States and around the world, progressive Jews

and our allies are building safety through solidarity: committing to fight antisemitism alongside all other forms of oppression, as we strengthen each other against the rising tide of white Christian nationalism, which threatens us all. We offer a justice-driven analysis of antisemitism, and a window into the social movements committed to taking it on and building a better world.

Antisemitism is an enduring thought form that distracts from structures of oppression and displaces attention onto a traditional bogeyman. It is particularly corrosive because it can hook into the most vulnerable and angry experiences, like losing a job or home, channeling resentment in a way that not only disempowers the survivor, but aims a weapon at another.

Like all forms of oppression, antisemitism is ingrained in our society. Anybody is liable to reproduce it, intentionally or even unconsciously, regardless of where they think their politics lie, simply by living in a world structured by white Christian supremacy.

But antisemitism is also not politically indifferent, as some would claim. In the battle of freedom, justice, and liberation, it "knows" which side it's on. Its foundational home is on the political Right, which remains the most direct threat to Jews and all marginalized people. Wherever it is mobilized, antisemitism serves the forces of division, repression, and Othering that foster inequality. It is part of the infrastructure of oppression, playing a vital role, alongside capitalism, white supremacy, anti-LGBTQ bigotry, anti-immigrant xenophobia, and Islamophobia, in reinforcing injustice.

Antisemitism doesn't harm only Jews; it holds all of humanity back in our shared struggle to build a better world. Antisemitism is not the exclusive province of the Right. At times it can also be a "go-to" narrative for some marginalized communities and ostensibly liberatory movements seeking a simplified explanation for structures of racism, inequality, and empire. In this way, it protects the powerful by telling the disempowered an inaccurate story about how to free themselves.

As the State of Israel deepens its brutal oppression of Palestinians, it's more important than ever to distinguish between principled criticism of that oppression on the one hand and antisemitism on the other. Contrary to what the Right insists, it is not inherently antisemitic to criticize Israel's unjust policies and the ideology of Zionism fueling those policies, or to support tactics like boycott, divestment, and sanctions that seek to hold Israel accountable. We see fighting antisemitism, and fighting for freedom, equality, and justice for Palestinians, as part of the same struggle for a better world.

This became all the more urgent as our book was completed in late 2023, when a surprise attack, and brutal massacre and kidnapping of Israeli civilians, by the militant Palestinian group Hamas was met with a genocidal Israeli bombardment, and displacement of nearly two million Palestinians across the Gaza Strip, dizzying and unprecedented in its violence and scope. Faced with a radically uncertain future, as both peoples bury their dead and the prospect of a protracted war looms on the horizon, the dire need for a truly just peace—one that interrupts the root causes underlying the cycles of violence, and reimagines a shared polity of full freedom and flourishing for all who live across the land—is clearer than ever. And faced with a rise in heinous antisemitism, Islamophobia, and anti-Arab bigotry in the United States and around the world, the need to build safety through solidarity is more dire than ever.

Too often, the fight against antisemitism is siloed from every other pressing political issue. Our book charts a new path: re-grounding that fight within the mass social movements fighting for justice for all people. Today, the loudest voices insist that Christian Zionists are the Jews' best friends; "radical" Muslims, people of color, and Leftists are our worst enemies; and only Israeli nationalism, and collusion with whiteness and state repression in the United States, will keep Jews safe. But the Jewish Left has another answer: safety through solidarity.

This means that forming alliances across differences, building bridges not walls, and striving alongside others for a future free from inequality, exploitation, and oppression in all its forms are the best strategies to fight antisemitism.

So who are we to make these claims?

As Jews and as Leftists, we have long been committed to this issue. For three years, Ben worked as a campus organizer at Jewish Voice for Peace, a Palestine solidarity organization. At universities across the country, he saw students and professors boldly stand for Palestinian justice and freedom and get smeared as antisemites, often with severe consequences. He saw Jews of all ages struggle for a Judaism beyond nationalism and build new rituals, communities, and identities celebrating that vision. He also saw the Left itself struggle to take antisemitism seriously, and shy away from rigorously confronting the ways it could show up in our own organizing. Now he works at Political Research Associates, a progressive think tank that monitors the far-right, where he researches antisemitic and white nationalist movements and helps activists understand and counter their reach.

Shane has long worked at the intersections of these issues. In college he formed a Palestine solidarity group, holding Israeli Apartheid Week and building campaigns in support of the Boycott, Divestment, and Sanctions (BDS) movement on his campus. For years he has worked as an organizer and journalist, documenting the rise of far-right groups like the Proud Boys and Patriot Prayer, and the antifascist movements that fight back, in the Pacific Northwest and across the country. These experiences have clashed profoundly—the centrality of antisemitism in motivating an insurgent far-right and conspiratorial worldview on one side, and the claims of antisemitism, often spurious, thrown directly at Jewish advocates for justice in Palestine on the other.

For us, the fight against antisemitism is clear. As Jews, our personal connection is undeniable: the fight for safety, acceptance, and liberation is our own. In our work researching and reporting on the far-right, Ben has faced torrents of antisemitic harassment from white nationalists online, and threats to his safety offline. Shane has faced threats as well—from stray texts from Proud Boys to emails from neo-Nazis and in-person confrontations with armed far-right vigilantes at protests.

As Leftists, we see the role that antisemitism has played in breaking apart movements to win true liberation. We have both experienced moments when antisemitism in Left spaces went unchallenged, and the call to take it seriously was met with dismissive silence. Like many others, we watched as controversies over antisemitism sent movements like the Women's March in the United States and the Jeremy Corbyn candidacy in the United Kingdom, under attack from the Right and unprepared to navigate the issue in their own ranks, into a tailspin. This is a blind spot the Left can't afford to ignore.

Safety through solidarity means we cannot truly end antisemitism by building higher walls, fortifying nation-states, hiring more police or militarized security at synagogues, or going along with politics that scapegoat activists of color and divide communities. It means we must fight antisemitism at its root by building powerful mass movements to transform society's underlying inequality, exploitation, and alienation. It means we must fight for a more just, more connected world where people no longer need to turn to conspiracy theories, scapegoating, or demonization to make sense of the fundamental brokenness they see all around them. It means we must recognize the intersectional links between antisemitism and capitalism, anti-Blackness, anti-LGBTQ bigotry, and other structures of oppression, and build relationships of co-resistance between Jews and other marginalized groups.

Antisemitism is *not* an "eternal hatred" plaguing humanity since time immemorial. It is not a virus, a plague, or some other "natural" phenomenon. It is not merely a private prejudice of the heart, not merely a symptom of "extremism" at the fringes, disconnected from broader political structures of the world we live in. Rather, antisemitism is a political project that reinforces structural inequalities in our white, Christian-hegemonic society and protects the most powerful.

We can defeat antisemitism, but it will require all of us. Too often Jews are tasked with leading this work within progressive movements, but antisemitism is fundamentally a problem of the non-Jewish world, and we need more non-Jewish accomplices in this struggle if we hope to win.

Time and again, the activists we interviewed told us that building genuine, deep relationships across communities is key to the approach to fighting antisemitism we explore in this book. "Solidarity is not easy," Dove Kent told an audience of Jewish activists in 2018. "It is difficult, it is trying, it is facing disappointments in each other over and over again—and reaching for each other over and over again. It's not walking away."[1]

Fear can be an important motivator to action, but a response driven solely by terror tends to build walls, not bridges. The Left-bashing strategy of organizations like the Anti-Defamation League (ADL) and right-wing Zionist groups thrives through a politics of perpetual fear. But understanding antisemitism requires a balancing act, recognizing the relative well-being many Jewish communities currently experience, while acknowledging the very real threats we face as well. As Jews we can refuse to define ourselves strictly in relationship to fear, trauma, and what scholar Salo Baron called the "lachrymose" story of Jewish history—instead committing to inheriting our traditions and peoplehood by living rich and full Jewish lives.

We live in radical times, and radical times call for radical solutions. The word "radical" is derived from the Latin root *radix*, meaning "root." We call our book "a radical guide to fighting antisemitism" because only by understanding the root causes of this form of oppression can we work to tear it out at its roots.

But just because our approach is radical does not mean it is fringe. Our vision for fighting antisemitism by building alliances across communities, and working together toward a more just world, is common sense—and it is shared by most Jews. If it is viewed as fringe or unrealistic by some of today's dominant voices on the topic, this only indicates how sorely needed the new approaches collected in this book have become.

The stakes are high. The far-right uses antisemitism to target Jews and drive a politics of exclusion while claiming to care about Jews and, with centrists and some liberals, convincing millions to look the other way and blame the Left for antisemitism. At the same time, progressive movements rarely know how to confront antisemitism with efficacy and nuance. Until we find a way to break out of this deadlock together, reactionary leaders will continue to capture the narrative and profit off scapegoating.

In this book, we uplift the voices and stories of frontline organizers and changemakers who are leading the way. *Safety Through Solidarity* begins by laying out the terrain of the problem, establishing our analysis of antisemitism, and examining why our current climate complicates the issue. We look at the central pillar of modern antisemitism, the conspiracy theory; unpack the conspiratorial worldview animating right-wing movements like MAGA and QAnon; and offer strategies for progressive changemakers to avoid conspiracy theories in our own work.

We then descend deep into the history of antisemitism. We examine its roots in European Christianity, and the ways that Christian demonization of Jews evolved, in the modern era, into conspiracy theories that imagined a hidden, all-powerful Jewish cabal behind capitalism and communism. We discuss how economic justice movements can avoid antisemitism in critiques of capitalism, and how the Right has used anti-communist antisemitism not just to harm Jews but to attack all marginalized communities and progressive movements.

Turning our gaze to the present, we analyze antisemitism in contemporary white and Christian nationalist movements, exploring the Right's bid to shore up authoritarian dominance in an era of dizzying change. We then offer a guide to today's explosive debates around Israel/Palestine, examining crucial differences between criticism of Israel and antisemitism, and telling the stories of Palestine solidarity organizers, past and present, who have navigated these differences in their work.

We go on to hear from activists who insist that healing from internalized antisemitism, and intergenerational Jewish trauma, is key to carving new pathways of solidarity. We also use the social justice framework of intersectionality to examine how antisemitism relates to anti-Blackness, xenophobia, queerphobia, and Islamophobia in today's world, offering new frameworks of shared struggle. Then we widen the frame, uplifting the often-overlooked experiences of Jews of color and Orthodox Jews and asking what it will take for white Jewish communities and non-Jewish communities of color to overcome cycles of conflict that entrench division between potential allies.

In our final chapter, we return to our critique of mainstream approaches to fighting antisemitism, and show how, for over a century, the Jewish Left has fought for a different strategy. We highlight how Jewish communities and social movements are building safety through solidarity, and call on the Left to integrate the fight against antisemitism into its vision of collective liberation.

Writing this book deepened our personal commitment to this fight. In the course of research, Ben discovered that in 1987, one year before he was born, his childhood synagogue, Shaare Tefila Congregation of Silver Spring, Maryland, won a landmark Supreme Court case against antisemitism. After white racists vandalized its building with antisemitic graffiti, the ADL advised Shaare Tefila to quietly scrub the walls, and avoid making waves.

Instead, Shaare Tefila decided to speak out. They rallied community support, fought alongside groups like the NAACP and the Arab American Anti-Discrimination Committee, and won a fierce legal case that expanded civil rights law to further protect Jews and other targeted minorities from such acts.[2]

Our work together also ran parallel to Shane's own journey into Judaism, something that was little more than an echo to his family's history. The process of writing this book was punctuated by holidays and Shabbat, debates over kashrut, and the memorization of Hebrew prayers—a deepening of Jewish identity that fundamentally changed the way that Shane related to the need for vibrancy and safety for Jews, and all people.

Ultimately this is just one intervention, collecting as many voices as we could. We introduce scores of leaders from around the world who have developed visionary approaches, and we encourage you to further explore their powerful work. As you read, we hope that you will be challenged and transformed as we were while writing, and that you will take the lessons learned into your work in the wider world, building the collective power that our troubled times require.

PART I

HOW DOES ANTISEMITISM WORK?

WHAT IS ANTISEMITISM? MAKING
SENSE OF AN EVOLVING DEBATE

"In 1982, I was a high school freshman in Olympia, Washington—one of the only Jewish students in the entire school," said Stosh Cotler, former CEO of Bend the Arc, a progressive Jewish organization.

> I found myself surrounded by a circle of cheerleaders in the busy hallway intersection just a few feet away from the principal's office. For what felt like an eternity, they held hands, bowed their heads, and solemnly prayed for my Jewish soul to be spared eternal hellfire and damnation . . . I could tell they really felt badly for me, like it was their job to save my Jewish soul. I remember feeling very conflicted—I didn't have a problem with being Jewish![1]

Antisemitism is part of Jewish education and identity—a memory of persecution handed down as the uncomfortable, intimate counterpart to the beauty of tradition. In moments like this, however, it becomes more visceral than the burnt edge of a scrapbook or family story of mourning—it explodes into reality with unmistakable force.

"I learned some of my earliest lessons about solidarity [in high school]," recalled Jewish activist and scholar Benjamin

Case. "Every single day, breakfast and lunch, you're being mocked for what you're eating and not eating . . . A lot of times I sat at lunch with the Muslim kids because they at least understood why I wasn't eating pork."

In a familiar process, what started as "casual" mockery quickly escalated.

"[At] one point I was getting dressed for gym and this kid from behind [shoved] me into a locker, hit me a couple of times, and [said], 'It's national fuck up a Jew day,'" he remembered. "Another kid [was] walking by in the background who I thought of as a friend of mine, snickering. 'Isn't that every day?'"

"Kids came up to me in school feeling my head . . . they were looking for my horns," remembered Rabbi Tom Gutherz. His father, a Holocaust survivor, moved his family to Cleveland, Ohio, hoping to find a refuge of tolerance, and growing up, they avoided walking through heavily Catholic streets on the way home from school.

"I've been called the N-word and the K-word at the same time," Robin Washington, a Black Jewish journalist and activist, told us. Growing up in Chicago in the 1960s, his school system de facto segregated Black from white students as well as Jews from Gentiles, and his civil rights activist family helped lead campaigns to battle these and other systemic injustices. Many Jews of color face antisemitism and racism in overlapping ways, and are forced to navigate the intersections of oppression across the interstices of communities.

When Rabbi Danya Ruttenberg was harassed by white nationalist trolls on Twitter for having a "Jewish nose," she encountered antisemitism and misogyny together. "[Calling me a Jew was] their way of telling me that I am ugly, because I do not conform to a Christian, 'Aryan' standard of beauty," she told us.

When these accounts harass Ben on Twitter, they will often share a picture of his face with the caption "groomer." Mocking his facial features as stereotypically Jewish, they are also linking Jewishness with pedophilia and sexual depravity, a common antisemitic trope.

Motti Seligson, a member of the Chabad Hasidic movement, recalled that "being raised in Crown Heights in the eighties and nineties, [antisemitism] was a part of life."

Antisemitism, he told us, is a constant presence for the visibly Jewish Hasidim, ranging from verbal slights to frequent physical attacks. Seligson, himself the grandson of three concentration camp survivors, noted that they lived in a congregation "without great-grandparents" because so many family members were killed by the Nazis. That led him to visit Poland to witness a piece of his family's history, and while riding on a train to visit the camp an angry passerby screamed for him to "go back to Auschwitz," another incident he said is not uncommon.

Hadar Cohen, an Arab Jewish artist and educator, moved to Los Angeles hoping to integrate with the Middle Eastern community there. "At first, people were really supportive and excited by the Palestine solidarity work I was doing," she told us. "An organization that uplifts the voices of Middle Eastern women even reached out to feature me in their work. I was honored by this but sadly they ended up not featuring me because, ultimately, they were scared to feature a Jewish person who was born in Jerusalem. They thought the community would not respond well, and they themselves were afraid. To me it is unacceptable to have a Middle Eastern organization that erases Jewish history and identity, as our identity was the bedrock of culture and belonging in the Arab world for millennia."

Seemingly endless ink has been spilled trying to answer the question "What is antisemitism?" Emily Tamkin, in her book *Bad Jews*, called antisemitism "the conviction that Jews are forever foreign or alien to whatever population they happen to be in, and often have designs on corrupting that population."[2]

In his landmark book *Anti-Judaism*, historian David Nirenberg suggests that for the early Christian communities in which anti-Jewish ideology first took root nearly two thousand years ago, Jews served as an antithesis to define oneself against: if followers of Jesus were holy and spiritual, then the Jews were carnal and procedural; if honest Christians were hardworking, then Jews were schemers looking to manipulate.[3]

His point is that these understandings of Jews did not require any *actual* Jews to function: an image of the Jew, usually denunciatory, served as a profanity against which to compare a society's alleged sacredness. This is why you find conspiracy theories in places where few or no Jews actually live: the idea of "the Jew" will suffice. Historian Brian Klug traces a distinction between Jews, as in actual Jewish people, and "Jews," the image of "the Jew" that antisemites project.[4] As with any bigoted stereotype, the fact that it does not correspond to reality does not stop it from carrying real-world consequences.

Sociologist Keith Kahn-Harris distinguishes between "consensus antisemitism," the kind that everyone can recognize, and "selective antisemitism," which is more subtle. The former, he explains, includes "open, unashamed, visceral hatred, disdain or abuse directed at Jews as Jews . . . It may be expressed through clear statements of hatred, through violence, through discrimination. It may take the form of conspiracy theories, fantasies of Jewish evil and the like."[5] The latter, on the other hand, can be trickier to pin down: it involves obsessive speculation about Jews, and the creation of a "good Jew/bad Jew" dynamic that allows, even celebrates, some types of Jewishness while scorning other types. The Right may profess love for Orthodox Jews or Israeli settlers while demonizing George Soros and Jewish liberals; the Left may cherish anti-Zionist Jews while heaping vitriol upon others. As with other bigotries, a person can resort to antisemitism in one instance, or hold a singular antisemitic idea, while recoiling in horror at other instances.

We will focus mostly on antisemitic *ideology*—a conspiracy theory about supposed Jewish power and wickedness. But we will also address the *institutional* discrimination that Jews have faced, the *interpersonal* harm done to Jews by Gentiles, and xenophobia directed at Jewishness. And we will describe how this is *internalized* by Jews themselves—what one Argentine resident described in the 1960s as "a daily experience; the uncomfortable feeling of being different which alternately included in me the desire to pass as a gentile or produced a reaction leading to an exaggeration of my Jewishness."[6]

WHAT'S IN A NAME?

The term "antisemitism," then written as "anti-Semitism," was introduced into our lexicon by German journalist Wilhelm Marr in 1879. Laundering older forms of Christian anti-Judaism into new racist pseudoscience, Marr alleged Jews were part of a non-European "Semitic" race, and that Jews introduced the corrosive effects of modernity into German society. To be "anti-Semitic," for Marr and others of his era, was to counter this foreign racial influence and restore holistic unity to "Aryan" Europe.[7]

Because "Semitism" is a pseudoscientific term, modern usage has dropped the hyphen. "If we say 'anti-Semitism' it means 'something against Semitism,' which there is not. That is an invented category," Kathleen Belew, a scholar who researches white nationalism, told us. Some contemporary scholars, such as David Engel, explain that the term may have too many conflicting meanings to be universally understood.[8] There are so many different forms of anti-Jewish oppression throughout history, they argue, with variable contexts and causes: Does it really make sense to speak of "antisemitism" as a unitary phenomenon?

We agree that it is important to ground patterns of anti-Jewish bigotry in their particular historical context. There are vast differences between medieval Jews facing marauding Crusaders in the Rhineland in the eleventh century, German Jews facing the rise of Nazism in the 1930s, Baghdadi Jews staring down the clash between Iraqi nationalism and Zionism in the 1950s, and American Jews facing white nationalism today,

Nonetheless, it is still useful to speak of "antisemitism" as a legacy emerging through Christian Europe and evolving into the present. "[Christian] society creates a certain self-perception against an 'Other,'" Magda Teter, author of *Christian Supremacy*, told us. "That is a powerful mental structure that you can't get rid of easily."

STRUCTURAL ANTISEMITISM: A BRIEF HISTORY

Christianity was for centuries the source of anti-Jewish attitudes. Early Christians were in a position of rivalry with Jews within the pagan Roman Empire, and texts like the Gospels and Acts of the Apostles framed faith in Jesus as "superseding" Mosaic law, and claimed Jews engaged in carnal malevolence. In the medieval period, as Christianity became largely hegemonic across Europe, Jews were falsely cast as "Christ killers"; Jewish ritual was denigrated as corporeal, materialistic, and legalistic; and accusations abounded that Jews used Christian blood in rituals (blood libel), "tortured" communion wafers since they are the literal body of Jesus (host desecration), and were up to all sorts of nefarious sorcery, immorality, and licentiousness. Christians established Jews as their archetypal opposite, and that distrust eventually turned lethal.

Over centuries, conspiracy theories about Jews etched certain persistent, deepening grooves in our collective consciousness. Antisemitism became what Ben Gidley, Brendan McGeever, and David Feldman labeled "a deep reservoir of stereotypes and narratives, one which is replenished over time and from which people can draw with ease."[9] We call this antisemitism "structural" since it is woven into the ideological fabric of Western civilization, utilized by generations of reactionary movements to fortify social hierarchies and manage the tensions of global capitalism.

As philosopher Bernard Harrison writes, those in power have often felt threatened by the historic Jewish resistance to assimilation: their refusal "to accept any of the grand offers . . . extended to them by Western civilization . . . [and] their consequent failure to dissolve into the majority community of the day and to cease, in doing so, to exist as a recognizably distinct group."[10]

For centuries, Jews were alternately insiders and outsiders: often dwelling apart from dominant society, often in communal dialogue with it, and often both simultaneously. Jews were barred from many professions and pushed to the edges of feudal society, and a few pursued moneylending and tax collecting (alongside many Christians). They found themselves wedged in between the ruling nobility, the exploited peasantry, and other social classes. When Christian clergy circulated stereotypes of Jewish economic perfidy, it allowed desperate peasants and others to take their rage out on Jews, leaving the broader inequities of the feudal system untouched.

The emergence of modern industrial capitalist society around the eighteenth century brought new tensions. Millions of Europeans experienced a "fish out of water" effect as they left the slow pace of traditional rural life and were sucked into the factory labor system. The new world of markets, nation-states, urbanization, migration, and mass production was immensely destabilizing for virtually all layers of society.

At the same time, new ideologies of Enlightenment social liberalism, democracy, and political radicalism rattled old hierarchies of power and privilege, and threatened to upend new ones as well. Before long, capitalist elites, church leaders, nationalists, and other power holders saw the benefits of spreading a new, secularized narrative to repackage the old Christian anti-Judaism: Jews, they claimed, had brought this strange and startling new world into being. New ideologies of race science led many to believe social differences were biologically determined, and so Jews became cast as a separate race, exerting a pernicious, demonological effect on society.

"[In] modern anti-Semitism . . . [Jewish power] is mysteriously intangible, abstract and universal," wrote Marxist scholar Moishe Postone, highlighting the centrality of antisemitism for right-wing explanations of capitalist modernity. "Because this power is not bound concretely, is not 'rooted,' it is [presumed to be] of staggering immensity and is extremely difficult to check . . . The Jews represent an immensely powerful, intangible, international conspiracy."[11]

The Left, at its best, points to real oppressive systems of capitalism, white supremacy, and patriarchy (to name a few) and offers a concrete way to confront them. The Right uses conspiracy theories of elite Jewish cabals to divert anger over oppression from actual systems of power responsible for making our world a difficult place, toward an imaginary, diabolic enemy instead.[12] Antisemitism mobilizes what Postone called a "foreshortened 'anti-capitalism,'"[13] a misguided attempt to attack a projected image of power that gets its targets wrong, combined with a virulent anti-communism, scapegoating the "Judeo-Bolshevik," or some analogue, as the hidden hand behind worker revolt, changing gender and social norms, racial justice movements, and other despised progressivism.

Most kinds of oppression tell a story of inferiority. White supremacy falsely claims that Black people are less intelligent, capable, and worthy than whites. Male supremacy insists that women are naturally subservient to men. Homophobia claims that LGBTQ people are abnormal, while straight families are virtuous.

Antisemitism draws from similar characterizations, but at root claims Jews are exceptionally clever and powerful, that a secret cabal of Jews lurks behind the heights of power, pulling the strings from behind the scenes. While many oppressions claim to "punch down," antisemitism claims that by "punching up" at all-powerful Jews, society can become more holy, more pure.

But this is a lie. There is no powerful, shadowy cabal at the root of the world's problems, and anyone who thinks so is punching at shadows.

"Whether or not you care about antisemitism specifically . . . to defeat fascism you must understand how they see the world and in many ways it hinges on antisemitism," scholar Benjamin Case told us. "Fascism requires a concealed ultimate enemy responsible for making the strong weak. It is the ultimate conspiracy theory, which is why a lot of the most popular conspiracy theories have an antisemitic architecture: the secret cabal behind the scenes running the show, bound by some evil, mystical lineage."

Historian Shulamit Volkov famously called antisemitism in *volkisch* Germany a "cultural code" of communal identity: by railing against the Jews, a person could show that they are anti-modern, traditional, and a good, upstanding member of the racial nation.[14] This cultural code continues today, as MAGA leaders rail against George Soros, "globalists," and "Cultural Marxist" cabals—all of which refer to historic tropes about Jews—to signal their supposed allegiance to *real* working-class Americans, rather than distant, out-of-touch elites.

Antisemitic conspiracy theories remain stitched into the fabric of a right-wing worldview that pines for the "good old days" of white Christian dominance, and directs wrath at all who they claim stand in the way of it. The white nationalist movement sees society as a corrupt plutocracy run by Jews who intend to destroy the white race. Some in this movement insist that to preserve whites, it will be necessary to have a catastrophic social collapse that brings on a race war. "A fascist simply looks at the evidence . . . jews [sic] have historically been a harmful influence on every society that hosted them," said one collectively written article on the accelerationist forum Iron March.[15]

The popular QAnon conspiracy theory movement posits that a secret cabal of pedophilic, blood-drinking satanists has undermined America, and only a strongman like Donald Trump can restore its greatness. Mike Rothschild, a journalist covering QAnon, explains that this is the historic antisemitic "blood libel on a grand scale. Except instead of one cadre of Jews drinking the blood of one child, it [is] a transcontinental network of elite pedophiles doing it to hundreds of thousands of children, aided by a media that's probably doing it too."[16]

As nationalists like Marjorie Taylor Greene become rising stars in the GOP, these tropes imagining shadowy, elite cabals grow increasingly foundational to a conspiratorial consensus, which casts suspicion on all minorities and blames marginalized people for the decline of America's white working class. The Right's rotating bundle of culture war targets, from "Critical Race Theory" to LGBTQ "groomers," recycles old European tales of Jews as nefarious political outsiders who prey on innocent children. In an era when these old antisemitic theories have been refashioned into a whole new lexicon, there are even sectors of the Jewish Right picking up the thread, from the Republican Jewish Coalition scapegoating George Soros to Israeli prime minister Benjamin Netanyahu's son Yair posting puppet master memes. This is a new world indeed.

As scholar Dan Berger told us, "antisemitism functions as a structuring apparatus" for the "racist political outlook" of Trump and the MAGA movement.[17] In addition to targeting Jews, MAGA antisemitism uses conspiracy theories to harm other marginalized communities, such as immigrants, racial justice movements, and trans kids. Movement messaging strategist Sharon Goldtzvik and Ginna Green call antisemitism "part of the machinery of division and fear created and used for specific political or material gain."[18] These narratives are built into our society's foundations, and those in power can pull on them even without knowing explicitly what they are mobilizing. They simply know what works, and what can divide the rest of us so we cannot unite and fight.

Antisemitism doesn't only appear on the Right in the form of conspiracy theories about Jewish power. Christian Zionist ideology, a core driver of GOP support for the far-right Israeli government with tens of millions of adherents in the United States and millions more around the world, largely holds that Israeli expansionism, and the violence and regional instability it spurs, is the necessary prelude to a cataclysmic End Times conflagration when Jews, and all non-Christians, will be forced to convert or perish. With friends like these, the oft-touted "Judeo-Christian" alliance on the Right offers cold comfort indeed.

And while antisemitism finds its most natural home on the white Right, it can also appear in ostensibly left-wing discourse, as well as in non-white communities across the political spectrum, where it plays a similar function: breaking the kind of unity working and oppressed people need to fight our common sources of oppression.

WHO ARE THE JEWS?

Antisemitism tells a false story about "the Jew." But what about actual Jews?

The word "Judaism" refers to the religion of the Jewish people: grounded in texts like the Torah and Talmud, traditions of piety, and an ever-evolving tapestry of religious practice. But the Jewish people are not simply "all those practicing the religion of Judaism." Nor are we a race, as antisemites claim, or one ethnic group—Jews hail from all over the world. Jewish peoplehood is more expansive than any one of these modern categories.

Jews are better understood as a multiracial, multiethnic, global diasporic people. Terms like "civilization" or "tribe" come close to capturing the way in which Jewish identity holds various religious, cultural, and ethnic components. For some, spirituality is paramount; others identify as proud atheists and cleave to Jewish cultural traditions and histories. Some were born Jewish, and some became Jewish later in life; some have two Jewish parents, some one, others none.

For nearly one thousand years before the Common Era, Jewish political civilization flourished in the land now called Israel/Palestine. In this time, Jewish communities also made their homes throughout the Mediterranean basin, and this diasporic process accelerated after the Roman occupation and expulsion of Jews from the Holy Land in 70 C.E. Since then, over millennia of voluntary as well as forced dispersion, Jews have built deeply rooted communities across virtually every part of the globe.[19]

Ashkenazi Jews, whose ancestors spoke Yiddish and lived for centuries across Europe and Russia, make up the majority of the American Jewish community, and form the dominant Jewish caste in the State of Israel. Mizrahi Jews hail from a diverse range of communities that lived often for millennia across Southwest Asia and North Africa, and make up an estimated 25 to 30 percent of the global Jewish community. Sephardic Jews, meanwhile, are those whose ancestors fled the Spanish Inquisition in the fourteenth and fifteenth centuries.[20]

Each of these communities, as well as communities of Jews from Africa, the Caribbean, and elsewhere around the world, carries distinct religious and cultural practices informed by the larger societies in which they have lived. "From the ancient community of Chinese Jews in Kaifeng," wrote Jews for Racial and Economic Justice in their groundbreaking 2017 pamphlet *Understanding Antisemitism: An Offering to Our Movements*, "to the B'nai, Cochini and Baghdadi Jews of India and the many Jewish enclaves of Latin America, Jews come from every part of the world, and look every kinda way."[21]

Over the course of time—especially in the second half of the twentieth century—many Jews of European descent were increasingly considered white in the United States, as discussed later in the book. Today, at least 12 to 15 percent of American Jews, around 1 million total, are Jews of color, according to a 2019 report.[22] As we will discuss, Jews of color face bigotry and exclusion from deeply ingrained white supremacy within Jewish communities, while Sephardi, Mizrahi, African, and other minoritized Jews face cultural erasure (and in Israel, systemic racism) from Ashkenazi dominance.

"We need to shift the thinking," April Baskin, a multiracial Jewish woman of color and Reform movement leader, told the *Forward* in 2017. "We're a Jewish global people. We've long been multiracial."[23] Many are surprised to realize that Jews only make up just over 2 percent of the US population,[24] and that includes people of literally every racial, gender, and class background. Jews don't live only on the coasts, we are not mostly Orthodox, we are not all Ashkenazi, and we are not majority wealthy.

Most mainstream understanding of antisemitism is pegged to a certain type of Ashkenazic experience: the pogroms faced by the shtetl communities of Eastern Europe, famously depicted by *Fiddler on the Roof*, are assumed to be a universal Jewish inheritance. And while the brutal demonization faced by Jews in Europe does form the ideological legacy of modern antisemitism, it's essential to remember that Jewish communities have experienced oppression differently across time, place, and context, and have drawn different lessons from those experiences.

Visibility, too, can impact how Jews experience antisemitism. Jews who wear ritual clothing or other items that visibly mark them as Jewish, such as a kippah, a tzitzit, or a Star of David necklace, often face more antisemitic harassment or threats than Jews who do not. Haredim—Jews who follow strict interpretations of Jewish law and often wear distinctive clothing, such as a black hat and coat for men and a hair covering or long sleeves for women, that promotes *tznius*, or religious modesty—

can be especially vulnerable to attack, scapegoating, and particular forms of prejudice. As we discuss later, it is essential to remain attuned to these and other differences of Jewish experience as we craft narratives and movements big and bold enough to include everyone.

HOW PREVALENT IS ANTISEMITISM, AND HOW THREATENING?

According to available data, antisemitic hate crimes have sky-rocketed. In 2021, the ADL tracked 2,717 antisemitic incidents: an average of more than seven incidents a day and a 34 percent increase over the previous year. This marks the highest number since the ADL began tracking in 1979.[25] In the FBI's hate crimes statistics, attacks on Jews rank as the most common form of religiously motivated bias crime, accounting for 51 percent in 2021—an extraordinary percentage, considering Jews are scarcely above 2 percent of the population.[26]

This data has problems, however. Federal hate crime data depends on local jurisdictions self-reporting. The national infrastructure is spotty, so large swathes of the country fail to report a single hate crime, even when they regularly occur. More fundamentally, for an incident to make it into the database, a community must trust going to law enforcement in the first place. It's no surprise why non-Jewish communities of color might not feel safe reporting hate crimes to racist law enforcement, or Muslim communities to an FBI that has surveilled and profiled them.

With the ADL's data, additional problems emerge. As journalist Mari Cohen at *Jewish Currents* has reported, the ADL routinely conflates incidents of criticism of Israel, or support for the BDS movement, with definite antisemitic incidents. The organization deploys inconsistent methodology, making it unclear whether a reported uptick merely reflects a change in the metrics used. Journalists' uncritical reliance on ADL

reporting has created an inaccurate picture of the threat, leading us to bad decisions based on problematic data.[27]

In the wake of the October 2023 Israel-Gaza war, for example, the ADL released a map and tally of antisemitic incidents
and anti-Israel rallies in the United States. As the *Intercept*
reported, by mapping Palestine solidarity rallies (including
many led by Jewish groups calling for a ceasefire) alongside
instances of anti-Jewish assault, vandalism, and harassment,
the ADL misleadingly suggested these rallies were part of the
rising threat to Jewish safety. The ADL also included rallies
where speakers used phrases like "from the river to the sea,
Palestine will be free" in its calculation of antisemitic incidents. This phrase is not an "antisemitic slogan," as the ADL
claims, but a call for Palestinian unity and liberation, which
many protesters intend as a demand for equality.[28] But politicians, media outlets, and pro-Israel groups uncritically echoed
the ADL's framing that ceasefire and solidarity rallies were a
threat to Jews, bolstering the climate of McCarthyite repression against activists.

The ADL's surveys of the public's antisemitic attitudes carry
similar complications. One January 2023 survey presented
plenty of troubling findings: 39 percent of Americans think
it "mostly" or "somewhat true" that "Jews are more loyal to
Israel than to America," for example, while 24 percent agreed
that "Jews have too much control and influence on Wall
Street." However, 46 percent agreed at least slightly with the
statement that "Israel is not a technology leader," and the ADL,
too, presented this as evidence of rising antisemitism.[29] Here
as elsewhere, the ADL's shoddy political analysis (which we
discuss later) makes it hard to draw reliable conclusions.

What about Jewish perceptions of rising antisemitism?
A 2020 Pew survey also found 75 percent of American Jews
thought antisemitism had increased during the previous
five years.[30] A 2021 poll by the American Jewish Committee,
a prominent communal institution, found that 24 percent of

American Jews reported they were the target of "antisemitic incidents—physical attacks, remarks in person, or remarks online" in 2021.[31]

But Jews themselves disagree on what constitutes antisemitism, and subjective experiences of "feeling less safe," while meaningful, can reflect a variety of factors—including the hyperbolic threat assessments of groups like the ADL that influence Jewish perceptions of "rising antisemitism." The same Pew survey found substantial majorities of American Jews reported high degrees of satisfaction and well-being in their neighborhood, family life, economic outlook, and other registers.[32]

Meanwhile, it remains common practice for leaders to signal their staunch opposition to antisemitism in the public square, even while trafficking in conspiracy theories and thinly veiled demonization. In fact, writes scholar Jacob Labendz, activists and politicians on both Right and Left regularly accuse their opponents of antisemitism, while touting their own defense of Jews. This reflects, not only a shared culture of anti-antisemitism (a legacy of the post-Holocaust and Cold-War periods), but also deeply contested understandings of Americanness and the place of Jews therein."[33]

These complexities notwithstanding, we cannot dispute that the rise of far-right nationalism and conspiracy theories, fueled by white grievance, has thrust antisemitism into the public spotlight, and amplified the threat to a degree unprecedented in recent decades, casting legitimate fear into the hearts of American Jews. The white nationalist mass shooting at a Pittsburgh synagogue in 2018 was the deadliest antisemitic attack in American history, and other attacks by white nationalists and other actors have been planned and carried out in years since from Poway, California, to Monsey, New York. High-profile celebrities and business leaders like Kanye West and Elon Musk have embraced, or edged closer to, open antisemitism, in a political climate where its expression is increasingly normalized. And the spike in antisemitic incidents in the United States and globally during Israel's genocidal attack on Gaza—when Jewish individuals and institutions were targeted with harassment, vandalism, intimidation, and even violence—serves as a grim reminder that antisemites are emboldened to spread their ideology, and put it into action, when the State of Israel commits shocking acts of violence in the name of world Jewry. Numerous studies have confirmed the correlation between Israeli military offensives with high Palestinian civilian casualties, and upticks in antisemitism around the world.[34] While Israel's behavior is not the root cause of antisemitism, the violence and tensions can reignite latent, preexisting bigotries.

Most American Jews remain clear on where the primary threat to our safety lies. A November 2022 poll found that 76 percent of American Jews held "Donald Trump and his allies in the Republican Party" responsible for "a rise in antisemitism," with 74 percent agreeing that "Donald Trump and the MAGA movement are a threat to Jews in America."[35] Similar polls have found American Jews more likely to locate the threat of antisemitism on the Right.[36]

And overt discrimination against Jews does still exist. According to a 2022 study, over a quarter of hiring managers are less likely to move forward with Jewish job applicants due to "negative bias" that "Jews have too much power" and make assumptions about the Jewishness of candidates based on appearance. A full 17 percent say they were told by leadership to avoid hiring Jews, and nearly a third say that antisemitism is common and acceptable in their workplace.[37] One 2022 study found that half of Jews say they experienced religious discrimination in the workplace.[38]

In the modern era, antisemitism has ebbed and flowed in severity. In the late nineteenth century, many Jews were highly assimilated into European society and it seemed that centuries of persecution had come to an end—but before long, the rise of nationalism and fascism proved otherwise. In Southwest Asia and North Africa, meanwhile, centuries of relative coexistence came to a startling end in the mid-twentieth century, and Jews were forced to flee the regions where their families had lived, in some cases, for millennia.

These recent memories have left many Jews understandably cautious, worrying that any period of seeming stability may be fleeting, and that heightened persecution lurks around the corner. What makes it so difficult today to separate signal from noise, and build consensus around where antisemitism comes from? How do we understand its stubborn persistence, and how, ultimately, do we fight it?

NEITHER ETERNAL NOR INEVITABLE: NEW PERSPECTIVES ON "THE OLDEST HATRED"

On August 19, 1991, Menachem Mendel Schneerson, the leader of the Chabad-Lubavitch Hasidic movement, was returning from a reverential visit to the grave of his father-in-law in the Brooklyn neighborhood of Crown Heights when a car from his motorcade accidentally struck and killed Caribbean American child Gavin Cato. The events that followed, later known as the Crown Heights riot, laid bare the long-simmering tensions between the mostly white Lubavitchers and the mostly non-Jewish Black and West Indian communities living side by side.

On orders from the NYPD, the Hasidic ambulance service picked up only the Jews hurt in the crash, and the crowd erupted in anger, both at their Jewish neighbors and the systems of racist violence permeating their lives. An emerging riot hit Kingston Avenue, the center of the Lubavitch community, where Yankel Rosenbaum, a visiting student from Australia, was stabbed to death.

The following days saw clashes between the communities, with much of the violence directed at Jews. Rioters raged through Crown Heights streets chanting "Heil Hitler" and "Kill the Jews," attacking Jewish businesses and passersby. The communities faced off in the streets, hurling rocks, bottles, and insults at each other. All in all, the Crown Heights riot became what historian Edward Shapiro called "one of the most serious incidents of antisemitism in American history."[1]

As the dust settled, community members and pundits alike sought to make sense of this crisis. Inside Crown Heights, there were real material disputes between some Hasidim and their neighbors, including employment and landlord disputes. Some Black residents felt the mostly white Hasidim received preferential treatment from police and state services, a charged observation liable to blend legitimate grievance with antisemitic fantasy.

Living in proximity meant that these communities interacted frequently, and yet, entrenched cultural differences limited the depth of cross-communal bonds. Like everywhere in the United States, capitalism maintained multigenerational poverty and disinvestment in Brooklyn's Black communities, while many Hasidim lived in poverty as well. "Without some redistribution of wealth and power," wrote Black radical philosopher Cornel West, reflecting on the riot, "downward mobility and debilitating poverty will continue to drive people into desperate channels."[2] These dynamics, of course, remain present today.

Cato's killing pushed simmering disaffection on many fronts into boiling anger, and Hasidim became the target. Whether or not particular Hasidim were to blame for these myriad tensions, and the events that sparked the riot, is debatable—but if they were, it was not due to their Jewishness. When Black leader Al Sharpton slandered Jews as "diamond merchants" at a rally, he played on long-established tropes of Jewish financial power, through a classic antisemitic redirection: the pain was real, but the bigotry made it harder to confront the underlying causes.[3]

While the Black community in Crown Heights compared the riots to the history of Watts and Detroit, the Hasidim, a community with many Holocaust survivors, called it a pogrom. They took out an ad in *The New York Times* declaring,

"This year Kristallnacht took place on August 19 right here in Crown Heights."[4] Channeling anti-Blackness, *Times* columnist A. M. Rosenthal railed against "Black pogromists" and "street thugs,"[5] while the Israeli paper *The Jerusalem Post* ludicrously claimed the riot had been "fed by Arab propaganda and financed by Arab sources," and the author urged Chabadniks to move to Israel.[6] Far from a clear-eyed analysis of the conditions that led to the conflagration, provocations like these only fueled the fire.

ESAU HATES JACOB?

For some in Chabad, the riot seemed to confirm an old lesson: Gentiles simply *were* this way, and so Jews have to fortify, protect, and fight back. As scholar Shaul Magid has recently observed, this logic draws on a lingering theological stream that lends antisemitism a God-decreed permanence: the biblical rivalry between Jacob and Esau.[7] "The voice of the blood of our brother Yankel Rosenbaum . . . is screaming to us," said Shmuel Butman, a Lubavitch rabbi speaking at a commemorative event five years later. "After the hands of Esau have committed this atrocious murder, on this very spot, the voice of Jacob—and in our case the voice of Jacob [the Americanized translation of Yankel] Rosenbaum—is calling out."[8]

In Genesis 25:21–34, Jacob and Esau are the sons of Isaac and Rebecca, grandchildren of Abraham and Sarah: the patriarchs and matriarchs of the Jewish people and indeed of monotheism itself. The Torah traces a long-standing rivalry between Jacob and Esau, who, it was said, were at odds from the beginning—they wrestled even in their mother's womb.

Shortly before Isaac passes, Jacob receives from his father a blessing that Esau believes should have been his: Jacob's children would be chosen for a special spiritual mission, while Esau's descendants were to be wracked with unholy jealousy. The Torah makes it clear that Jacob is the spiritual ancestor of the Jewish people, and later rabbinic commentators came to identify Esau as the ancestor of the Gentile world.

"Even in those places where the hatred of Jews is [apparently] unknown and it appears that they love us, know that this is just a lie and an illusion," said leading Haredi rabbi Moshe Feinstein in 1977. "For it is a halakhah [divine law] that Esau hates Jacob." Esau's hate, according to this interpretation, rings eternal—it was in his metaphysical essence, meaning there is something in the Gentile soul that perpetuates antisemitism.[9] What else could explain centuries of pogroms, mass murders, blood libels, and synagogue shootings?

"A symbolically charged picture of the children of Jacob and Esau thus emerges in canonical rabbinic literature and contemporary Hasidic discourse," wrote scholar Henry Goldschmidt, "an image of Jews and Gentiles as opposing peoples and principles, locked in eternal hatred and struggle."[10] For many, Esau's hatred represents a kind of preordained struggle, ultimately part of God's plan for the divine saga of creation, and so the goal is no longer to eradicate antisemitism: the most we can do is to create structures of maintenance. Any instance of communal conflict is transformed through this lens: antisemitism is at the core of all clashes.[11]

In many right-wing and Orthodox circles, this theology bolsters a distinctly pessimistic narrative about antisemitism. "Esau's hatred of Israel—Gentile anti-Semitism, is akin to a law of nature," states one article published by the Haredi outreach organization Aish HaTorah. "It is immutable. It is everlasting. It need not be rational to be. It just is."[12]

This perspective is embedded in some Zionist thought as well. Early Zionist thinker Leon Pinsker wrote in 1882, reflecting on recent Russian pogroms, that "Judaism and Jew-hatred [have] passed through history for centuries as inseparable companions." The only solution, he and others argued, was for Jews to have a nation-state of their own.[13]

Zionism's founder Theodor Herzl took a similar lesson

from the Dreyfus affair a few years later, as the Jews of France, convinced they had fully assimilated into enlightened European society, suddenly faced the first antisemitic mass political movement of the modern era after French Jewish army captain Alfred Dreyfus was accused of treason and dual loyalty by the nationalist Right. Reflecting on lessons learned from the affair in 1895, Herzl wrote in his diary: "I achieved a freer attitude toward anti-Semitism, which I now began to understand historically and make allowances for. Above all, I recognized the emptiness and futility of efforts to 'combat antisemitism.'"[14]

In the decades leading to Israel's founding in 1948, much of the Zionist movement saw antisemitism as an inevitable feature of the diaspora, and so *shlilat ha'galut*, "negation of the diaspora," they said, was necessary to revitalize Jewish muscle. The Holocaust seemed to confirm for many that liberalism or Left politics would not protect Jews against perennial antisemitism: only Jewish nationalism would. Today, as we will discuss, the false notion that the Israel/Palestine conflict is caused, at root, by perennial antisemitism holds sway in many Jewish communities, clouding the kind of sober, grounded assessment that could light the way toward a just peace.

After the Holocaust, the idea of perennial antisemitism found renewed focus on the Zionist Right. Meir Kahane was an American Orthodox rabbi who founded the far-right Jewish Defense League in 1968 in an effort, as he claimed, to defend impoverished urban Jews from neighboring antisemites. Kahane's program hinged on anti-Blackness, aggressive anti-communism, and what evolved into a rabid form of anti-diasporism that sought to build a "New Jew" on strength and survivalism.

Kahane helped perpetuate the idea that antisemitism was intrinsic to American Gentiles, and that long-standing Jewish support for liberal and Left politics left Jews vulnerable and misguided. "Jewish liberalism," explains scholar Shaul Magid in his 2021 study of Kahane, "was based . . . on the belief that Jewish integration into American society would decrease the depiction of the Jew as 'other' and thus dismantle anti-Semitic stereotypes." Kahane held, to the contrary, "that liberal Jews were fooling themselves into believing that anti-Semitism was not a constitutive part of gentile society."[15] His conviction, Magid wrote elsewhere, was that "[anti-Semitism] was part of what it meant to be a gentile and living with anti-Semitism was part of what it meant to be a Jew."[16]

Instead, Kahane offered violence as an "ethic" for Jews in their relationship to Gentiles.[17] The JDL fought Black Power activists on the streets, and attacked Jewish Left gatherings. Later, Kahane moved to Israel, won elected office, and led a movement calling for the wholesale expulsion of Palestinians, a formulation so extreme (at the time) that he was banned from serving in the Israeli Knesset in 1985. His legacy is explicitly celebrated by leaders of today's fascist Israeli Right, which has achieved a level of mainstream success Kahane only dreamed of.

In Magid's telling, while much of today's American Jewish world has repudiated Kahane, his calculation is flourishing. "Tacitly, it seems like a lot of the conversation about antisemitism today is acknowledging Kahane's basic approach," Magid told us. "[People] writing these popular books about antisemitism, they identify this or that incident of antisemitism—sort of like 'the greatest hits of antisemitism.' But there's never any real theorizing about why it happens or what it means . . . I think underlying it is this ontological claim that they never want to actually make. Which is that Gentiles are always going to be antisemitic, and there's nothing you can do about it."

Leading anti-antisemitism pundits like Deborah Lipstadt, appointed as President Biden's special envoy to combat antisemitism in 2022, take what's called an "eternalist" position: antisemitism is unique, distinct, and forever. "Medication may alleviate the symptoms, but the infection itself lies dormant and may reemerge at an opportune moment in a new incarnation, a different 'outer shell,'" writes Lipstadt in *Antisemitism: Here and Now*, showing that she largely agrees with alarmist antisemitism scholar Robert Wistrich's characterization of antisemitism as the "longest hatred."[18] Without a clear pathway to understand what antisemitism is, how it operates, and, ultimately, what to do about it, we are left with little more than echoes of biblical decree, the 614th commandment to make suspicion a mitzvah. What else could explain the "lethal obsession" or the "longest hatred"?

Many Jews interviewed for this book reported growing up with these messages. "The way I learned [about antisemitism] when I was growing up," Jewish activist Morriah Kaplan told us, "is that it's this ancient, baseless hatred, unconnected to anything. It's irrational and indelible, and it's a unique kind of hatred that is reserved for Jews." Kaplan helps lead IfNotNow, a Jewish Palestine solidarity group that educates its members to understand antisemitism as part of rising white Christian nationalism, and to fight it by developing solidarity between communities harmed by the Right's advance.

When Dove Kent attended Hebrew school, her character was commended on her report card as the "strength of a [Holocaust] survivor." The school's approach, she told us, was that "our Jewish past can be summed up in the Holocaust, and what we learned from that is 'don't trust any non-Jews.' That our neighbors will always turn on us." Famed Jewish historian Salo Baron warned against the "lachrymose" story of Jewish history, the tendency to see little more in the Jewish past than a long, unending string of persecution. The bomb threat Dove lived through was horrifying—but perhaps inevitable, if the lachrymose narrative proved to be our central one.

If we take the lachrymose narrative as our guide, we create a monster so overpowering that nothing can defeat it, and we never get closer to protecting Jews, or addressing the root causes of oppression. "Nobody is born antisemitic," Chabad rabbi Mordechai Lightstone told us, sitting in a popular kosher burger joint in Crown Heights a few blocks from where the riot began thirty years prior. "It's an effect of the brokenness of our world, the same brokenness that leads to all negativity and oppression."

Antisemitism remains an everyday part of the life of the Hasidim walking the neighborhood, he said, something they all have experienced as visible Jews. But it is far from inevitable, and Lightstone remained hopeful that by connecting with their non-Jewish neighbors to promote understanding and address shared concerns like communal disinvestment, progress could be made. "You can work across our different communities to solve these problems," he offered, "but it certainly is difficult."

ANTISEMITISM AS A POLITICAL FOOTBALL

If antisemitism, as adherents to the lachrymose narrative insist, is the world's oldest hatred, perennial and unending, then the only rational response is to fortify the barricades of Israeli nationalism—and any political challenge to that nationalism, and the repressive policies that flow from it, is ipso facto evidence of further antisemitism. Motivated by this logic, pro-Israel organizations often wield the charge of antisemitism as a battering ram against critics of Israel's policies. Pushed by Jewish and Christian Zionist NGOs as well as politicians and media figures, these accusations, and the consensus they generate, have led to the firing and blacklisting of progressive academics, the suppression of campus movements, and legislative restrictions on freedom of speech. The broader Right uses these accusations to demonize, divide, and disorganize left-wing movements as a whole, zeroing in on popular targets like the Women's March and Bernie Sanders in the United States, and Jeremy Corbyn and the Labour Party in the United Kingdom

In the decade following Israel's 1967 occupation of Palestinian territories, worldwide condemnation escalated. In response, pro-Israel organizations like the ADL pioneered a thesis they called "new antisemitism." While earlier discourses scapegoated Jews as the enemies of Christianity or the "master race," they argued, "new antisemitism" goes after Jewish national self-determination in the State of Israel.[19] In April 2022, ADL CEO Jonathan Greenblatt continued this legacy by bluntly proclaiming that "anti-Zionism is antisemitism," dispensing with nuance and effectively redefining the term into a political weapon.[20] The "new antisemitism" thesis has been taken up by Christian Zionists, Islamophobes, and fellow travelers across the political establishment, eager to use Jews as a shield and fig leaf for a broader agenda of imperial dominance.

In late 2023, as Israel's genocidal bombardment of Gaza claimed thousands of Palestinian lives and wreaked unprecedented destruction, Israel advocates and political leaders doubled down on the use of antisemitism charges to suppress widespread protest around the world. In the United States, politicians and groups like the ADL clamored to investigate activists with ludicrous claims of "material support" for terrorism, universities shut down Students for Justice in Palestine chapters, individuals were fired from jobs for pro-Palestine social media posts, and a climate of McCarthyism reigned across civil society.[21] Officials in France, and in cities across Germany, moved to ban all Palestine solidarity protests, while in countries like Great Britain and Austria, officials considered shutting down protests by falsely claiming that slogans like "from the river to the sea, Palestine will be free" represented threats to Jews.[22] None of this repression, however, was enough to stop one of the most vibrant and broad-based anti-war movements in decades from changing the national and global conversation.

One major tool that has been instrumentalized is the

"Working Definition of Antisemitism" adopted by the International Holocaust Remembrance Alliance (IHRA) in 2016. This definition originally sought to create consensus among political, civic, and educational institutions to aid in combating antisemitism. Beginning with the vacuous assertion that "antisemitism is a certain perception of Jews," it lists a number of examples, ranging from explicit conspiracy theories and Holocaust denial to "claiming that the existence of a State of Israel is a racist endeavor" and "applying double standards by requiring of [Israel] a behavior not expected or demanded of any other democratic nation."[23] As we discuss, these latter examples are highly dubious—but they have proven useful for those wishing to shut down criticism of Israel's unjust policies.

A concerted effort by the State of Israel and pro-Israel organizations has made IHRA's definition the guiding tool used by over one thousand institutions around the world by the end of 2022, including governments, universities, and NGOs, leading to serious and often unconstitutional restrictions on freedom of speech for critics of Israel.[24] The Trump administration attempted to use IHRA's definition to craft federal policy, and anti-BDS laws using or inspired by it have passed in at least thirty-one states.

Many of these bills, like Colorado's HB 16-1284 or Florida's SB-86 in 2016, blacklist companies allegedly supportive of the Israel boycott from receiving government contracts, and similar legislation in Germany creates a potential pathway to prosecution. Some universities have also adopted IHRA's definition of antisemitism, driving investigations into BDS activism on campus and threats to cancel events and speakers, shut down pro-Palestine student groups, block access to resources, and even expel students.

Critics argue that the overly broad language in the IHRA definition can rope in criticisms of Israel that are not actually antisemitic. The definition "radically departs from the traditional understanding of antisemitism," wrote Radhika Sainath, senior staff attorney at Palestine Legal, and is "fueling anti-Palestinian racism, whereby anything coded as Palestin-ian—even identifying one's Palestinian heritage—is deemed antisemitic (and thus punishable)."[25] Kenneth Stern, a primary author of the definition, has expressed his own misgivings, saying it was only intended to be a guide, not a legislative tool, and has been "weaponized" by the political Right.[26]

This redefinition of antisemitism is "a way of protecting the State of Israel," Antony Lerman, author of *Whatever Happened to Antisemitism? Redefinition and the Myth of the "Collective Jew,"* told us. "It uses the terminology of the 'new antisemitism' to defend Israel as a state against the kinds of criticism lots of states experience." Proponents of the definition suffered a setback in 2023, when the Biden administration released a much-awaited report outlining its national strategy to fight antisemitism that, rather than adopting IHRA's definition, merely mentioned it in passing.[27]

In 2021, over two hundred scholars released the Jerusalem Declaration on Antisemitism (JDA), a counter-definition they hoped would bring more nuance to the conversation. After de-fining antisemitism as "discrimination, prejudice, hostility or violence against Jews as Jews (or Jewish institutions as Jewish)," the declaration threads the needle with texture and care, pars-ing various examples of Israel/Palestine discourse that "on the face of it" are and are not antisemitic.[28] Crucially, it insists that tactics of "boycott, divestment and sanctions," "criticizing or opposing Zionism as a form of nationalism," or "support[ing] arrangements that accord full equality to all inhabitants 'be-tween the river and the sea,'" are not inherently antisemitic.

No definition can offer a "magic formula" that substitutes for the hard work of organizing to end antisemitism, and some are skeptical that a focus on definitions is the best approach. "I don't think the solution is another definition," scholar Sheryl Nestel, longtime activist and one of the coauthors of the JDA, told us, "because I think any definition privileges antisemitism within the antiracism struggle and that's a recipe for division."

JEWISH DISSENT

Pro-Israel advocates claim to speak on behalf of the Jewish community. But Jews are hardly a monolith when it comes to Israel.

"Guided by a vision of justice, equality and freedom for all people," wrote Jewish Voice for Peace (JVP), a leading U.S. Jewish Palestine solidarity organization, in a 2019 statement, "we unequivocally oppose Zionism because it is counter to those ideals."[29] They weren't the first—there is a rich history of Jewish anti-Zionism, ranging from the politics of Left activism to several strands of Orthodox theology and the centrist, assimilationist stance of the early Reform movement. "As Jews, we feel a deep responsibility to speak out against the ideology and practices of Zionism," read the statement of principles announcing the 1978 launch of the Jewish Alliance Against Zionism, a small US activist group. "We seek to help re-establish the clear distinction between anti-Zionism and anti-Semitism."[30]

These Jewish activists were horrified not only by Israel's rightward trajectory, but by the foundational ethnic cleansing of Palestinians and the chauvinistic attitudes they felt were capturing the beauty of their tradition. "[These] new Zionists who want only to establish a Jewish state . . . [are] the farthest thing from our religion," wrote Shmuel Alexandrov, an early twentieth century Hasidic mystic who, while celebrating the building up of Jewish culture in Eretz Yisrael, saw exclusivist nationalism as inherently antithetical to the healing vision of Judaism.[31]

Inevitably, a rift has formed between establishment Jewish organizations like the ADL and young Leftist Jews; organizations like Jews for Racial and Economic Justice, IfNotNow, Jewish Voice for Peace, and Independent Jewish Voices are advancing a different vision of what antisemitism is, and how to fight it. "I think when people like Greenblatt say 'antisemitism,'" writer Ari Brostoff told us, "what they really mean at this point is the forces that are threatening [their] political hegemony." As the broad upsurge in Jewish Left organizing in response to Israel's genocidal war on Gaza in late 2023 demonstrates, these groups are a vocal and vibrant part of the American and global Jewish landscape—and our claim on the Jewish future can't be ignored.

ANTISEMITISM AND THE LEFT

We count ourselves part of these new Jewish Left movements. But like many others, we have often found the Left's analysis of antisemitism, and commitment to fighting it, sorely lacking.

Part of the reason for this lack is that antisemitism, and Jewishness more broadly, scrambles many of the categories progressives commonly use to understand identity and oppression. The Left "uses a model of anti-Black racism as a way to analyze whether or not Jews are oppressed," Dove Kent told us, "and that completely ignores all the actual ways antisemitism operates." Being Jewish doesn't stop white Jews from experiencing white privilege, and at this historic moment, Jews do not face structural levels of police violence, poverty, and other commonly understood effects of state-sponsored, institutional racism *as Jews*.

Jews who wear visible markers of Jewishness are more vulnerable to certain types of bigotry, but the majority do not wear those markers, and are generally able to "blend in"—an option not available to many other marginalized groups. And while many bigoted ideologies, like anti-Blackness, tell a tale of group inferiority, antisemitic ideology imagines a cabal of all-powerful Jews pulling the strings from the height of society: a conspiratorial form of demonization the Left is not used to countering.

The result is that activists try to slot Jews into a series of ill-fitting categories, and some conclude antisemitism is little more than a "white people issue," not worth taking seriously.

This invisibilization is compounded when the Right and political establishment gin up antisemitism accusations to throw Leftists into a tailspin. "Repeatedly, I find that I am pre-occupied not with countering anti-Semitism, but with trying to prove that anti-Semitism exists, that it is serious," wrote Jewish feminist Irena Klepfisz in 1982, discussing her experience in some left-wing circles. "[The] truth is that the issue of anti-Semitism has been ignored, has been treated as either non-existent or unimportant."[32] Little has changed.

What Klepfisz and many others have described is an often subtle yet pervasive absence of care. Jewish marginality is rarely acknowledged in social movement spaces. As we discuss later, activists will often disbelieve Jews when they say they experienced something antisemitic, downplay the antisemitic components of conspiracy theories, and dismiss claims of antisemitism by assuming that they must inherently be disingenuous, even sinister accusations intended to shield Israel from accountability. Echoing broader narratives in popular culture, many Leftists reduce antisemitism to merely a problem of personal prejudice or "hate," a hangover from the Nazi past found mostly at the fringes of society, detached from the broader structures of oppression. This disregard was on full display in late 2023, when parts of the Left minimized (or even celebrated) Hamas's massacre of hundreds of Israeli civilians, and seemed to care little that this shocked and alienated most of the Jewish community, including many Jewish Leftists.

Organizations like the ADL, for their part, deepen confusion by reflexively labeling any instance of Jewish discomfort as antisemitism while refusing to acknowledge complex dynamics of power and privilege. The Right, meanwhile, vigorously denies its antisemitism, claims that accusations against it are disingenuous, and points, ironically, to its pro-Israel policies to name itself the greatest friend the Jews have ever had. This leads to a seemingly impossible dynamic to decipher, where antisemites pledge allegiance to Israel, left-wing Jews are tarnished as antisemites themselves, and even right-wing Jewish organizations track in antisemitic fearmongering.

"Whenever the Left is quiet about an issue that matters to people, it leaves a vacuum for the Right to walk into," wrote activist and scholar April Rosenblum. "They use it to their advantage, to draw in people worried about that issue, and as moral ammunition for their crusades." When the Left doesn't speak out on antisemitism, we leave Jews outside our circle of care—and we hand the Right one of its strongest rhetorical weapons against our movements.[33]

So, what does it mean to cut through the rhetoric, dive between the conflicting definitions and debates on what antisemitism is, root out its core, and fight back? "It's a good question," Shaul Magid told us. "I don't have an answer. But it's a good question."

PIGS AREN'T KOSHER

But the lachrymose narrative isn't the only one available to Jews seeking to understand and counter antisemitism. Throughout the centuries, Jews have proposed other interpretations of the biblical rivalry between Jacob and Esau—interpretations that stress not the inevitability of antisemitism, but the possibility of collective liberation. Grounding in these traditions can help break the deadlock, and light a way forward.

One tradition associates Esau not with Gentiles as a whole, but with powerful, oppressive state tyrants (sometimes Rome in particular). Esau was the ancestor of the ancient tribe of the Edomites, which eventually became the Romans—the imperial force that destroyed the Second Temple, exiled Jews from the Holy Land, and attempted, in other ways, to force Jews to give up their distinct identity and assimilate into the dominant culture.

"Why is [Rome/Edom] compared to a pig?" ask the rabbis in one of many passages associating the empire with the nonkosher animal. "Because, just as a pig when he lies down, displays his cloven hooves as if to say, 'I'm ritually clean,' so this wicked kingdom steals and commits violence, yet it appears as if they establish courts of law."[34] For an animal to be kosher according to Jewish law, it must have split hooves and chew its cud. Just as a pig pretends to be kosher on the outside (by displaying split hooves) but inside it is not (since it does not chew its cud), so the Roman Empire's systems of "justice," the rabbis charged, were ultimately hollow, a mask for structural injustice.

Rabbinic polemics against Edom, in the first centuries of the Common Era, served as proxy critiques of broader human traits of cruelty, exploitation, greed, and forced assimilation. Edom's wrath was a core obstacle holding back the coming of the messianic era, a vision which preserved hope of human redemption, peace, and justice for Jews and all people. As the Roman Empire steadily Christianized after the conversion of the emperor Constantine in the fourth century c.e., and anti-Jewish persecution took on a more foundational and brutal edge, rabbinic polemics increasingly identified "Edom" with Western Christianity.

In the eighteenth century, Hasidic leader Rabbi Menahem Nahum of Chernobyl wrote in *Me'or Einayim*, his homilies on the Torah, of Esau's symbolism for the spiritual darkness in the universe. "In order to lift something up, one has to lower oneself to go down to the place where it lies and grab hold of it," wrote Nahum. "The two of them had to be joined together to a single source with great intimacy, so that Jacob could raise up that holiness which lay in Esau."[35] Instead of being divorced from the Jewish people, Esau was ultimately bound to them through his brotherhood with Jacob. Esau's story is a call to confront the difficult places in all of us and to elevate our community toward justice.

For Chabad mystic Shmuel Alexandrov, writing in 1905, Esau represented the world of systemic violence and state power, while Jacob was Jewish spirituality, transforming swords into plowshares. Giving in to only an exclusivist nationalism, one that pulls us away from relationship with other peoples, would abandon the revolutionary revelation of Judaism, which Alexandrov saw as a cosmopolitan union of all people working for a better world.[36]

This is part of a deeper current in Jewish thought that uplifts the emancipatory potential of ethical monotheism against the brutal machinations of empire, colonialism, and militarism as well as the profit-driven forces of greed and corruption. Seen in this light, the Esau and Jacob story is not about the inevitability of community tensions, but about how we can meet oppression with liberation, the act of *freeing* ourselves and others. Instead of a purely particularist reading, one that pits Jews against Gentiles in an eternal dispute, this story has larger ramifications: the struggle of people to be free from systems of oppression that seem to be passed down between generations as an inheritance. The struggle against antisemitism gives Jews a shared mission with everyone fighting for a more just world.

Helplessness acts as a barrier to a new future, so the "eternal antisemitism" thesis leaves little room to actually address the problem. Instead, we can build a social movement that invites both Jews and Gentiles to actually confront the issue, taking part in a veritable "healing of the world." In building this movement, we can draw on earlier histories of Left struggle against antisemitism, as well as the entire social movement playbook.

To do this, we must first understand, and defeat, the most basic building block of modern antisemitism: the conspiracy theory.

PART 2

WHERE DOES ANTISEMITISM COME FROM?

THREE

THE CABAL: ANTISEMITISM AND CONSPIRACY THEORIES

> Everything seems impossible or terribly difficult without the providential appearance of antisemitism. It enables everything to be arranged, smoothed over and simplified.
>
> Charles Maurras, French nationalist leader, 1911

On August 22, 2020, hundreds of far-right protesters descended on downtown Portland, Oregon, to stage a Back The Blue rally supporting the police. This counterdemonstration to the powerful Black Lives Matter movement, sweeping the country after the police murder of George Floyd, saw the alt-right street gang Proud Boys, militia groups like the Three Percenters and Oath Keepers, and assorted conspiracy theorists converging on Portland's courthouse, a boarded-up behemoth that served as the center of the summer's clashes between masked protesters and militarized police.

One sign was visible behind the shields held by the front line of demonstrators, ready for battle: "S.O.S., Stop Operation Soros," referring to George Soros, a prominent progressive Jewish philanthropist.

"George Soros: he's one of the elites in politics to sway government decisions," a woman going by the name Avani Love told us. She believes the first building burned down during the protests in Minneapolis was owned by Soros, who ordered his own property torched to instigate further unrest. Across the

country, she insisted, Soros sent undercover agents provoca-
teurs to escalate protests.

"It's a very well-known tactic . . . George Soros operates the
Open Society Foundations, which funds antifa, funds Black
Lives Matter, and he's just a big instigator." The conspiracy
theories of the day flanked her on all sides: the shields displayed slogans from the QAnon movement, including "WW-
GIWGA," short for "where we go one, we go all," and "Save
the Children," a nod to QAnon's central theory that Democratic leaders and media elites are satanic, child-sacrificing pedophiles, and only the forces of MAGA can stop them.

"So the rumor mill is that George Soros is paying Black
Lives Matter and antifa to riot and do destruction and cause
division," a combat vet told us at a Vancouver, Washington
protest that October, holding an AR-15 with Three Percenter
militia patches covering his tactical vest. "He is the money behind the scenes . . . He's the puppet master. Nothing, of course,
is confirmed whether it's true or not. But that is the more logical reason things are going on."

Soros conspiracy theories proliferated throughout the volatile 2020 news cycle. As the COVID-19 pandemic escalated
that spring, far-right pundits insisted Soros had engineered
the deadly virus in a Wuhan, China, biolab and would use
vaccines to install microchips in the bodies of unsuspecting
Americans. That summer, the Right worked overtime to identify the hand of Soros in the George Floyd uprising, collapsing
Black Lives Matter and antifa, two autonomous social movements, into one formless enemy, with Soros pulling the strings.
If we could just arrest George Soros, they claimed, these protests would end in an instant; if we can just capture the puppet
master, the fighting and division would simply evaporate.

While the summer of 2020 is now in the rearview mirror,
Soros conspiracy theories are not. Whether it's Elon Musk
claiming Soros "wants to erode the very fabric of civilization" and "hates humanity," Donald Trump accusing Soros

of engineering his criminal indictment, or GOP leaders slamming progressive district attorneys as "Soros-backed" for their criminal justice reform efforts, the Right remains fixated on its favorite bogeyman.[1]

WHO'S AFRAID OF GEORGE SOROS?

Why has George Soros become an obsession for the Right? The billionaire investor has long donated to an assortment of liberal causes, from refugee resettlement and public health projects to criminal justice reform and democracy initiatives, through the charitable gift-giving of his Open Society Foundations. While Soros is far from the only deep-pocketed political donor—and his overall influence pales in comparison to right-wing movement funders, like the Koch brothers—the broad scope of his liberal philanthropy makes him an easy target for conservative outrage.

Unlike Soros, the Koch brothers (who are Christian) are rarely portrayed by their detractors as satanic tricksters who puppeteer world government, financial, and media systems, undermine traditional values and healthy nationalism, and enslave humanity, squeezing the world dry in a vampiric embrace. That's because George Soros is Jewish, and antisemitism is central to right-wing conspiracism.

Molded in the image of modern antisemitism, Soros becomes a proxy figure for conspiracy theorists to project their most dire fears. As a billionaire hedge fund tycoon, Soros seems, for them, to reflect the "Jewish banker" trope, manipulating world economies for profit. As an unapologetic liberal, he embodies the much-feared "Judeo-Bolshevik" power lurking behind progressivism. With the global reach of his investment and philanthropy, he is easily cast, by nationalist and populist movements, in the mold of antisemitic tropes: as a foreign outsider, simultaneously everywhere and nowhere, subverting national borders in a slippery, sinister crusade.

Soros conspiracy theories have circulated across the Right since at least 2010, when media personality Glenn Beck ran a three-night report on his Fox prime-time series called "Exposing George Soros: The Puppet Master?" claiming Soros was "notorious for collapsing economies and regimes all around the world" and that his "next target" was the United States.[2] In the Trump era, these narratives became a fixture of right-wing discourse. In October 2018, as the November midterms neared, Trump, leading Republicans, and Fox News anchors fearmongered about a "caravan" of migrants creeping toward the southern border, insinuating that this caravan was funded by Soros in order to "replace" white Americans with brown immigrants.

Barely a week after its emergence, the conspiracy reached an estimated audience of over 100 million on Facebook and Twitter alone. On the morning of October 22, a Trump supporter delivered a pipe bomb to Soros's mailbox, tweeting that "the world is waking up to the horrors of George Soros." And on October 27, white nationalist Robert Bowers murdered eleven Jews at the Tree of Life–Or L'Simcha synagogue in Pittsburgh, Pennsylvania. Bowers believed the Jews at that synagogue, and elsewhere, were part of a conspiracy to replace American white people with non-white immigrants—what white nationalists call the "great replacement"—and that the caravan, too, was part of the Jewish plot. Buoyed by a media climate awash in antisemitism and xenophobia, Bowers was encouraged to act.

With ethnonationalism on the rise the world over, Soros is a familiar target for nationalists from Poland to Brazil and Israel. In his native Hungary, Soros has become the perfect villain for an increasingly far-right government rolling back progressive gender education from universities and closing the country's southern border to refugees. "We are fighting an enemy that is different from us," Hungarian dictator Viktor Orbán insisted in a 2018 speech largely focused on Soros, utilizing the key themes of modern antisemitism. "Not open, but hiding, not straightforward but crafty; not honest but base; not national but international; does not believe in working but speculates with money; does not have its own homeland but feels it owns the whole world."[3] Orbán has pioneered a series of "Stop Soros" laws, threatening to criminalize a range of humanitarian initiatives supporting refugees and asylum seekers.[4]

"BACON-WRAPPED PROTOCOLS AND BLOOD LIBEL FOR BOOMERS AND WINE MOMS"

Once a Soros conspiracy makes an appearance on the Right, it's not long before you encounter two other antisemitic dog whistles—"globalists" or "Cultural Marxists." In their worldview, the "globalist elite" describes a transnational cabal of elite urban financiers, cosmopolitans, and journalists hellbent on destroying sovereign borders and engineering a "New World Order" through free trade, unfettered immigration, and rampant liberalism. While not everyone who condemns "globalists" means Jews, sometimes the association is clear. In Atlanta, Georgia, at a November 21, 2020 Stop the Steal rally dedicated to Trump's election fraud conspiracy theories, flyers were found strewn outside the Capitol Building with the word "Globalists" surrounded by Stars of David.[5]

Similarly, "Cultural Marxism" refers to an imagined conspiracy of left-wing intellectuals who, for the past several decades, have supposedly radically reshaped Western society, undermining gender, race, and other hierarchies in order to institute a sinister reign of feminism, LGBTQ rights, and other liberal causes. Some of the Right's most maligned "Cultural Marxist" intellectuals, such as the critical theorists of the Frankfurt School, are Jewish, but conservatives insist the theory is not antisemitic. However, its conspiracy structure remains intact, leaving a giant Soros-shaped hole in popular ideology—and all it takes, in many cases, is a slight prodding to move believers toward explicit antisemitism.

These conspiracy theories are reshaping right-wing politics. Increasingly, right-wing supporters of QAnon are running as candidates in US elections, including at least 107 in the 2020 election season,[6] and 73 in 2022.[7] QAnon adherents were among the mob that stormed the US Capitol on January 6, 2021, flooding congressional chambers to overthrow the blood-drinking pedophile cabal that, they are convinced, controls US and global affairs.

The Q narrative has taken on a life of its own since its 2017 emergence. One 2020 survey found that more than half of Republicans believe the theory was "mostly or partly true."[8] While the conspiracy has lost some momentum during the Biden presidency, its core accusations of elite pedophilia have now moved mainstream into the GOP's moral panics about supposed "groomers," a crusade that has inspired harassment and violence against LGBTQ communities across the country.

"The basis for QAnon is just bacon-wrapped *Protocols* and blood libel for boomers and wine moms," cult expert Sarah Hightower told us, referencing the influential antisemitic conspiracy forgery named *The Protocols of the Elders of Zion*. Accusations of ritual child sacrifice were core to the "blood libel" myths motivating anti-Jewish scapegoating over centuries in medieval Europe and into the modern era. "Maybe I'm naive, I'm just struck by the number of people whose suburban Aunt Susan was ready to believe in blood libel," antifascist activist Molly Conger, who organized to confront the far-right during the Trump presidency, told us. "It's not just in the far reaches of Telegram anymore. It's in boomer memes on Facebook. If you just gently scratch the surface, it's blood libel."

QAnon's user-generated universe acts as a clearinghouse for every conspiracy under the sun, making it no surprise that familiar antisemitic narratives about the wealthy Jewish Rothschild banking family and the Elders of Zion freely appear in their forums. In the wake of the Capitol insurrection, as the Right seethed over its failure to subvert democracy and deliver

Trump a second term, the antisemitism in QAnon spaces grew even more pronounced, with major influencers railing more openly against Jews to hundreds of thousands of followers.

"If somebody came up to you on the street and said, 'Hey, did you know the Democrats are running a secret cabal, blood-drinking, children-stealing pedophilia ring?' you'd go 'Fuck you. That's absurd' . . . but you don't start there," explained Shannon Reid, a criminologist who studies far-right gangs. "And so, as you get deeper, you become more susceptible to the conspiracy theories . . . I think they give people a reason to feel like their disenfranchisement or their inability to attain what they want is somebody else's fault."

"A CLUE TO THE MODERN MAZE"

"The more you look at the history of the far-right, there is a core conspiracy theory scaffolding," Cynthia Miller-Idriss, a researcher tracking white nationalism, told us. "And that conspiracy theory is always antisemitic, and that is the idea of orchestration." And one conspiracy narrative, in particular, forms the core of the modern scaffolding. "*The Protocols of the Elders of Zion* are certainly the modern-era ur–conspiracy theory," David Neiwert, a journalist who has spent decades covering the far-right, told us. "The *Protocols* became the architecture of the narrative of conspiracism—and that architecture has never really gone away."

The Protocols of the Elders of Zion was first printed in imperial Russia in 1902 or 1903 by Pavel Krushevan, a journalist aligned with the ultranationalist Black Hundreds and partially responsible for the devastating 1903 Kishinev pogrom. The book was a forged, fictional account of a secret meeting of an all-powerful Jewish cabal exerting secret control over politics, media, and the economy in an effort to establish a Jewish dictatorship across the planet. Conservatives hoped that propaganda like the *Protocols* would convince workers and other oppressed people to distrust movements for revolutionary change then sweeping Russia—movements in which Jewish workers played a crucial role—and would build opposition, among the general public, to widespread modernization programs rapidly transforming Russian society.[9]

The myth at the heart of the *Protocols* repackages many centuries of Christian anti-Jewish polemics we explore later: Jews as demonic emblems of pure evil, all-powerful, secretive, and scheming, embodiments of the Antichrist, and driven by primordial hostility against the Gentile world in general, and the Christian faithful in particular.

After the 1917 Russian Revolution, members of the newly deposed czarist nobility and the counterrevolutionary White Army fled the new Soviet state with copies of the *Protocols* in hand, spreading the message that the Jews were to blame for the advance of Soviet communism that many feared would soon sweep the globe. By the early 1920s, American auto manufacturer Henry Ford was mass publishing commentaries to the *Protocols* in his newspaper, *The Dearborn Independent*, and the anthology *The International Jew: The World's Foremost Problem*. At the peak of Ford's antisemitic campaign in 1924, his paper had grown to seven hundred thousand subscribers nationwide, with Ford instructing his car dealerships to push subscriptions alongside sales of Ford's Model T.[10]

In the United Kingdom, meanwhile, the conservative *Morning Post* published more than a dozen articles on the *Protocols* in 1920 alone, while then-politician Winston Churchill opined in the *Illustrated Sunday Herald* that "international Jews" were engaged in a "world-wide conspiracy for the overthrow of civilisation."[11] As aristocratic nobility, business magnates, and major statesmen obsessed over the growing threat of workers' revolution, they propagated conspiracy theories like the *Protocols* with increasing ferocity, determined to maintain the status quo by redirecting anger away from those responsible for society's misfortunes and onto a specter.

A flurry of articles soon proved the *Protocols* to be a forgery, the original "fake news" of the modern era. But before long, *The International Jew* was translated into sixteen languages, its growing reach due in no small part to Ford's celebrity endorsement. It influenced Nazi ideologues such as Alfred Rosenberg and Julius Streicher, and the Nazis released twenty-two German editions of the *Protocols* between 1929 and 1938.[12]

At first glance, it appears strange that the *Protocols* became one of the most influential conspiracy texts of the twentieth century. The text itself is jumbled and disorganized, switching haphazardly between a broad array of topics, presenting little in the way of clear argumentation. It reads like a partial transcript of a committee meeting, a series of dictates snatched hastily from some hidden file cabinet. It is precisely this inaccessibility of the text that grants the forgery a seemingly irresistible allure for believers, certain they possess a text not intended to be read, privy to a glimpse into the private world of absolute power. "There is almost the tone of a tradition or a religion in it all," marvels the pamphleteer of Ford's *The International Jew*. "Nothing like [the *Protocols*] in completeness of detail, in breadth of plan and in deep grasp of the hidden springs of human action has ever been known."[13]

The Elders claim to exert control over a panoply of mass media institutions in order to "gain control of the Gentile society to such an extent that it surveys the world's affairs through the coloured glasses which we put over its eyes."[14] They have engineered a dizzying array of hyper-partisan, polarized voices while staffing the world with faceless technocrats. Their ideologies of liberalism and democracy are "eating, like so many worms, into the well-being of the Christians," and all of this is meant to confuse, and ultimately enslave, Gentiles.[15]

The Elders claim to have established "the despotism of Capital, which is entirely in our hands," instituting a world of cold, rapacious greed in which "lust of gold will be [the Gentiles'] only guide" so that "all the nations will be striving for their own profits, and in this universal struggle will not notice their common enemy."[16] These Elders have also orchestrated radical Leftist social movements as false saviors, meant to redirect Gentile anger away from their true masters.

While it's easy to mock such a paranoid conspiracy, the *Protocols* successfully won millions of devotees for over a century because it can seem to many that, by rebelling against the Elders of Zion, they are struggling for a better world. For workers resentful of economic exploitation yet suspicious of revolutionary fervor; or small businesspeople, anxious to preserve fast-vanishing privileges yet resentful of elites and bureaucracies; or devout, tradition-minded believers frightened by creeping secularism; or disgruntled urban intellectuals, left alienated by liberalism and dreaming of "revolt against the modern world"—for these and many others, the *Protocols*, in the words of Ford's pamphleteer, can "give a clue to the modern maze."[17] It can furnish desperately needed proof for the gut conviction, as he later put it, that "distrust and division are everywhere. And in the midst of the confusion everyone is dimly aware that there is a higher group that is not divided at all, but is getting exactly what it wants."[18]

The circumspect vagueness of the schemes in the text, as well as the Elders' eagerness to adopt any ideology in pursuit of their goal, lends the *Protocols* an elastic ability to reflect a changing world. Today, the *Protocols* circulates among white nationalists and conspiracy forums and has appeared in grade school textbooks in Qatar,[19] television broadcasts in Jordan,[20] and doomsday cults in Japan.[21] In the United States, a 2021 survey found that 49 percent of respondents who believe in QAnon, and 32 percent of right-leaning adults overall, agree "with the Protocols of the Elders of Zion, which claims that the rise of liberalism has equipped Jews to destroy institutions, and in turn gain control of the world," while nearly 80 percent of *Protocols* adherents likewise believe in QAnon.[22] Birds of a feather, it seems, flock together.

OUR COUNTRY OF CONSPIRACY

While plenty of ink has been spilled analyzing today's rise in right-wing conspiracism, this is nothing new. The United States is a conspiracy country, and many of its major political movements have carried conspiratorial tones. During the centuries-long Indian Wars, European settlers accused Indigenous tribes of conspiring with the devil. In the late nineteenth century, agrarian populist movements won adherents by railing against big-city gilded cabals. During the red scares of the 1920s, 1950s, and beyond, the US Right and business elites imagined traitorous communists plotting takeovers in tenement basements, union halls, and Hollywood studios. Indeed, conspiracy theories are America's traditional folk narrative for reckoning with change, threat, and power.[23]

In his famous 1964 essay "The Paranoid Style in American Politics," author Richard Hofstadter reflected on the potent blend of white grievance and anti-communism that helped Barry Goldwater capture the Republican presidential nomination that year. "I call it the paranoid style simply because no other word adequately evokes the sense of heated exaggeration, suspiciousness, and conspiratorial fantasy that I have in mind."[24]

With the fall of the Soviet Union in the early 1990s and the triumph of neoliberal globalization, right-wing paranoia fixated on an imagined New World Order. Millions bruised by economic dislocation and frightened by social change imagined that the United Nations, with its fleet of unmarked black helicopters, was preparing to seize their guns and strip them of land and sovereignty. This fueled the rapid growth of the militia and sovereign citizens' movements and, later, the Tea Party, laying the groundwork for Trump's rise. "The Trump era," wrote journalist Anna Merlan in *Republic of Lies*, "has merely focused our attention back onto something that has reappeared with reliable persistence: the conspiratorial thinking and dark suspicions have never fully left us."[25]

Conspiracy theories, wrote scholar Michael Barkun, attempt to "delineate and explain evil" by positing a "universe governed by design" where "nothing happens by accident," "nothing is as it seems," and everything is connected."[26] They pivot around the "us versus them" distinction, where a band of heroic rebels unite against impossible odds to defeat a wicked and all-powerful enemy. "The paranoid spokesman," wrote Hofstadter, "sees the fate of conspiracy in apocalyptic terms—he traffics in the birth and death of whole worlds, whole political orders, whole systems of human values. He is always manning the barricades of civilization."[27] And when nationalist, populist leaders need an enemy to name and a movement to mobilize, they turn to conspiracy theories: with deadly results.

A THREAT TO US ALL

The Right's arsenal of conspiracy poses a threat to all marginalized communities and, indeed, to multiracial democracy itself. The far-right builds momentum, bases of supporters, and political power with a narrative that "punches up" at imagined elite cabals, which are demonized as all-powerful threats to tradition, order, beauty, and the "common man." When the Right brings its friend-enemy distinction into the highest halls of power, catastrophe follows.

During the first years of the COVID-19 pandemic, to name just one example, right-wing leaders insisted the all-powerful Chinese Communist Party engineered the virus to subvert American dominance, and that a cabal of "globalist" elites in the West worked hand in hand with the CCP to open the borders, terrorize the public with draconian mask and vaccine mandates, and usher in a dystopian New World Order. The anti-China conspiracy proved very flexible—during the 2020 Black Lives Matter uprising, for example, conspiracists claimed the protests were a CCP-driven plot to destroy America. "It's just following the script of antisemitic conspiracy theories,"

Tobita Chow, an organizer campaigning against anti-China militarism, told us. "They took that model and swapped out the names." These scapegoating narratives have inspired acts of violence against Asian American communities, and added fuel to a dangerous uptick in anti-China militarism.

Our society has now jumped headfirst into a new world of "alternative facts" and parallel realities. With Trump's ascension, conspiracism became official state narrative, establishing what Barkun labels "stigmatized knowledge" as the foundation of MAGA's political consciousness.[28] Conspiracy mythologies gave Trump an advantage: If you don't like the world you're in, why not just invent a new one? There doesn't even need to be a coherent theory to back up the conspiracy: unvalidated rumor will suffice.

As the Capitol insurrection showed us, years of mass radicalization and entrenched conspiracism, bolstered by an insular media ecosystem, have summoned for the Right a veritable army. Now, that army can be deployed against the government, vulnerable minorities, and progressive leaders, and its foot soldiers are increasingly convinced that violence might be the only way to wrest "freedom" from the clutches of the cabal.

Conspiracism jettisons our grip on reality as we confront vital issues. As the COVID-19 pandemic raged, right-wing media networks and QAnon forums convinced millions of Americans that the virus was either far less deadly than suggested or manufactured out of whole cloth. A network of rallies to reopen, often organized by Tea Party groups and supported by Republican leaders, insisted the government was lying about the crisis and using public health measures to exert despotic control over Americans. These conspiracy theories became one of the "strongest and most consistent predictors of vaccine hesitancy," as one 2021 study put it.[29]

As with all large-scale conspiracy narratives, the antisemitism was hard to miss. White nationalist Telegram channels exploded with allegations that the Jews were behind the coronavirus, working in concert with other named enemies, like the Chinese government, either to spread the virus itself or to engineer the "lockdown regime." A 2020 British study found that 79 percent of anti-vaccine social media networks contained antisemitism.[30] Right-wing leaders compared public health measures to Nazi policy, a form of Holocaust trivialization bordering on denialism.

Meanwhile, while onlookers were being distracted by such conspiracy theories, the one percent actually took advantage of the crisis to orchestrate one of the greatest upward wealth transfers in history. Instead of uniting to demand our political leaders provide families with the resources we needed to weather the pandemic, conspiracism kept working people fragmented, confused, and "punching up" at imaginary targets.

Today, these trends have only deepened. An August 2023 survey found that 60 percent of teenagers, and 49 percent of adults, agreed with four or more conspiracy statements. Among teenagers who self-reported spending four or more hours a day on social media, 54 percent agreed with the statement "Jewish people have a disproportionate amount of control over the media, politics and the economy."[31]

THE DANGEROUS APPEAL OF EASY ANSWERS

Conspiracism is alluring to many because it offers easy answers to pressing existential questions and deeply felt crises of political agency. Movements like QAnon, like the *Protocols* a century earlier, tap into the alienation, frustration, and rage felt by millions still reeling from two debilitating market crashes in just over a single decade, and living in one of the most vastly unequal societies in human history. The prospect of open revolt against a distant, larger-than-life cabal of diabolical elites can lend purpose, resolve, and hope when many are used to disempowerment. The world is chaotic and cruel, and so a shadowy cabal must be pulling the strings. What else could explain it?

In a sense, far-right conspiracy theories agree with the political Left that things are not as they seem, that beneath the unassuming veneer of business-as-usual lies the truth of injustice. The Left, after all, has its own critique of mainstream media as a producer of a kind of "fake news," pushing support of US overseas wars, upward wealth redistribution, and other elite propaganda in order to "manufacture consent," as Noam Chomsky famously put it. The conspiracists' fiery charges of elite decadence, fever dreams of societal decay, and pining for apocalypse hold a mirror up to a broken society, begging for release from its clutches.

But that's where the resemblance to Left social change ends. Conspiracy theories bypass the hard work of grappling with nuance and complexity, instead championing a cosmic battle between good and evil, with clearly named absolute enemies and ironclad certainty of the virtues of "our side." Conspiracy theories often misleadingly hook on to small grains of truth, so that if one squints hard enough, reality can be "made" to appear like the conspiracy. For example, the 2018 revelations that liberal financier Jeffrey Epstein had long engaged in child sex trafficking, and that an array of elites may have been involved, dominated the news cycle, convincing many that QAnon's broader narrative was surely true.

Tellingly, QAnon's push to "save the children" rarely leads adherents to support meaningful policies to combat child sex trafficking, such as funding foster care and housing initiatives. This world of patient, grounded policy advocacy can be less viscerally thrilling than envisioning yourself as part of a small band of holy warriors, hot on the trail of an all-powerful Antichrist-cabal. Conspiracism usurps what fascism scholar Robert Paxton calls "mobilizing passions," the emotional energies that lend social movements their force.[32] When combined with the politics of resentment, white rage, misogyny, and other bigotry, the result can be explosive. But while conspiracy theories may promise to put you back in the driver's seat, ultimately, nothing could be more disempowering. They leave you chasing shadows, rather than changing the world.

While conspiracism is central to the right-wing political arsenal of white resentment, it can also show up in pseudo scientific health cures and "wellness" communities, New Age spirituality, or anywhere people are desperately looking for "forbidden knowledge" and answers not provided by our society's institutions. Conspiracy theories are, at root, a stunted attempt to make sense of the world, and popular allegations about the Rothschilds and the New World Order are deeply ingrained in cultural consciousness, liable to show up wherever frustrated and fed up people are desperate to understand unjust conditions—including on the Left.

In the Occupy movement, for example, conspiracy films like *Zeitgeist* and 9/11 "truther" myths circulated widely. As discussed later, Occupy's polemics against "banksters" and the one percent channeled real resentment against finance capitalism, but its broad populist messaging, while effective, left the door open for fuzzy caricatures of elite cabals. On a few occasions, protests at encampments mobilized antisemitism, and right-wing conspiracy actors found opportunities to get involved and claim common ground.[33]

As we discuss later, conspiracism hampers the ability of marginalized communities to understand material conditions and build social movements to confront injustice, dismantle power dynamics, and transform society. "Illuminati theory helps oppressed people to explain our experiences in the hood," explained *How to Overthrow the Illuminati*, a popular 2013 radical pamphlet that unpacks the fight against conspiracy theories in Black communities.[34]

But the conspiracy theories peddled by reactionary Black nationalist groups like the Nation of Islam, they explain, are ill-equipped to help oppressed people truly become free. They view every incident as carefully orchestrated by elites, leaving no room for coincidences or mistakes; make the enemy out

to be all-powerful; fail to make basic logical or scientific arguments; are impossible to disprove; lead to a closed-off, cultlike
elitism among adherents; and offer no real solutions to the
problems they attempt to explain. What we are left with, the
pamphleteers explain, is "no strategy, no game plan, no way
out for billions of oppressed people on this planet."[35]

The realities of injustice and power are both more complex
and simpler than conspiracy theories would suggest. It's true
that, in our era of rampant inequality and alienation, interest groups wield unchecked influence, financial systems are
deliberately opaque, and powerful government and business
elites routinely hide their political agendas. But power is ultimately distributed in our society across vast and complex systems, and even with deepening inequalities, there is no single
group of rulers pulling the strings. "Most capitalist plans for
economic and foreign policy," the authors of *How to Overthrow
the Illuminati* remind us, "are printed openly in the pages of
the *Economist* and the *Wall Street Journal*. We can see them dis-
agreeing publicly, and we can see that sometimes their plans
don't work out."[36] As a stunted effort to confront inequality,
the myth of the shadowy cabal prevents us from addressing
actual conspiracies, those of capital, which rarely hides fully
from view.

To fight the root of conspiracy theories we need robust
social safety nets and well-resourced communities, and an
end to inequality, so people no longer face conditions of desperation in their everyday life and are less eager, in turn, to
blame scapegoats. We need a political system where people
feel truly empowered to participate meaningfully in the
democratic process, so they are no longer plagued by cyni-
cism and powerlessness.

In short, the surest antidote to conspiracism is the Left's
project of human emancipation itself—which, after all, is why
conspiracy theories are so central to the reactionary attack
on positive change. In our era of dizzying tumult, the wide-

spread embrace of conspiracy theories means the Left hasn't yet fully figured out how to reach enough people with a concrete analysis of what's actually wrong with the way our world is structured, who's to blame, and what we can all do about it, together. We've got our work cut out for us.

Antisemitic conspiracy theories didn't pop up overnight. They evolved from the fertile soil of European Christianity, with its centuries-old demonization of Jews. It is to this history that we now turn.

FOUR

A CHRISTIAN HISTORY: ANTISEMITISM
IN CHRISTIAN EUROPE

Today, the loudest voices on the Right insist that the bulk of anti-Jewish ideas emerge from Islam, and that the Muslim world is the primary threat to Jews. "The difference between Islamic fanatics, or Jew haters, and Hitler is that Hitler hid the Final Solution, and the Iranians and Hezbollah shout it from the rooftops. And the whole Muslim world accepts it," proclaims "counter-jihad" activist David Horowitz, echoing the kind of unhinged Islamophobia common across the far-right.[1]

Mizrahi Jewish author Bat Ye'or propagates the "Eurabia" conspiracy theory that alleges European elites are conspiring with Muslims to "Arabize" the West. "To be pardoned and loved by Muslims," wrote Ye'or in 2016, "European leaders went as far as seeking to 'Islamize' Europe and collaborating with radical and terrorist movements."[2] Europe, she wrote in the 2005 book *Eurabia: The Euro-Arab Axis*, has degenerated into a "post-Judeo-Christian civilization that is subservient to the ideology of jihad and the Islamic powers that propagate it," thanks to "faceless networks" of European Union bureaucrats managing a "Kafkaesque world functioning as a totalitarian anonymous system . . . [of] political correctness and censorship."[3]

This racist worldview suggests Islam is an inherently intolerant, aggressive ideology, particularly against Jews (and

Christians as well), and that the opposition to Zionism felt by millions across the Middle East is primarily driven, not by solidarity with Palestinians or anger against the harmful regional impacts of US- and Israeli-backed imperial dominance, but rather by perennial anger toward Jews for daring to challenge the subservient "dhimmi" status ordained by Islam. This has filtered through the scholarship of various "antisemitism institutes" led by scholars like Robert Wistrich, who helped introduce terms like "Eurabia" and "dhimmitude" to the lexicon of antisemitism studies.[4] This scholarship closely tracks the antisemitism of Muslim-majority countries and Muslim immigrants to Europe, implicitly casting immigration as a great threat to Jews by associating Muslim migrants with supposedly rampant antisemitism.

There are certainly some anti-Jewish passages in classical Islamic sources, and traditions that are less than charitable to Jews. Much like Christianity, Islam views the Jewish tradition as a precursor to its own, and early Islamic sources sometimes portray Jews as "betrayers" of the true voice of God: they chose something other than the path offered by Muhammad. At the same time, Jews were considered fellow travelers on the shared path to monotheism, and Muslims, therefore, had a duty to protect Jews.[5] This cast Jews as subordinate, which is where the category "dhimmi" emerged, meaning a non-Muslim "person of the book" residing as a distinct class in Muslim society: to be neither singled out for special persecution nor treated equally to Muslims.

Jews and Christians shared this status in much of the classical Islamic world, where they faced restrictions on clothing, transport, and more. Jews also experienced long arcs of peace, stability, and prosperity in many Muslim-majority societies, and periods like the "golden age" of Muslim Spain are widely recognized as high points for tolerance and pluralism across centuries of Jewish diaspora. The clash-of-civilizations narrative favored by right-wing scholarship flattens this texture and nuance in favor of a unidimensional portrait of perennial Muslim hostility toward Jews.

While Jews may not have had equal rights in Muslim countries, they were tortured, expelled, and murdered across Christian Europe. If Muslim sources are said to be intolerant of Jews, Christian sources demonize Jews in sometimes near-genocidal terms. In some Islamic contexts, Jews, like other dhimmi groups, were considered with contempt and condescension as a lower caste—a form of xenophobia, for sure—but they were not, as in Christian Europe, vilified as a uniquely malevolent incarnation of supernatural evil.

"Anti-Judaism is patently built into the New Testament and the Quran. They are set up as counterpoints to Israel [a biblical term for the Jewish people]," Steven Wasserstrom, a scholar who researches early Islamic responses to Judaism, told us. "But that's different from what happened, particularly in [Christian] Europe, where it became pathologized, which did not happen in the Muslim world until the twentieth century."

To be sure, the tendency for xenophobic leaders to utilize religious ideas as cover for their sordid agendas is a tale as old as time. There are potentially problematic, and potentially liberatory, ideas inside of all religious traditions, but that does not mean that all are equally culpable in the two-thousand-year-old development of antisemitism.

Whether we look at the features of Islamist antisemitism, neo-Nazi antisemitism, or any other variety, we have to acknowledge the common root: European Christianity, the religious ideology of the civilization that, with the onset of modernity, would come to think of itself as "white" and "the West." Today, with white Christian nationalist movements on the rise, it's more important than ever to understand the early roots of antisemitism in Christian Europe, as we continue to combat its bitter fruits.

"THE UNGODLY RACE OF CARNAL JEWS"

Christianity has not just been historically antisemitic; antisemitism is itself a Christian invention. That said, it was influenced by the political and regional context that existed before Christianity. As early monotheists, Jews were religiously different from their pagan neighbors across the ancient Near East, and as a small minority living amidst larger societies and groups, their reputation was shaped by the geopolitical rivalries around them.

Toward the end of the fifth century B.C.E., ancient Egyptian leaders accused local Jewish communities of allying with the Persians, who were seen as enemy oppressors of the Egyptians. This was one of the earliest accusations resembling later charges of Jewish "dual loyalty" and Jews as a dangerous fifth column. Instigated by these accusations, Egyptians destroyed an ancient Jewish temple at Elephantine, an island on the Nile, in 410 B.C.E. Egyptian historians and priests portrayed Jews as unclean lepers whose beliefs and customs clashed with others, who were "enemies of all gods," who ruled with a bloodthirsty streak and were consumed by misanthropy.[6]

These slanders spread across the Mediterranean basin during the period of Greco-Roman antiquity and were repeated by future chroniclers such as the second-century C.E. Roman historian Tacitus. Combined with larger tensions between widespread paganism and the new Jewish idea of monotheism, this led to episodic persecution and occasional violence, such as the Alexandrian riots in 38 C.E., commonly remembered as the first anti-Jewish pogrom in history. "From the cradle onward," wrote the early first-century Jewish philosopher Philo of Alexandria, "most people in Alexandria are taught that Jews are bad people. Children are instilled with hatred of Jews."[7]

When the new religion of proto-Christianity emerged from its beginnings as a Jewish sect and, led by the apostle Paul, began to proselytize to the pagan world, a new and potent form of anti-Judaism was gradually added to the mix. "Christianity absorbed pagan hostility to the Jewish people and utilized aspects of Pharisaic Judaism to distance itself from the faith from which it had evolved," wrote Rabbi Dan Cohn-Sherbok.[8]

Paul created a binary between believers of the spirit and those of the fleshly and fallen world, ascribing carnality to Jews and holy otherworldliness to Christians. By refusing to acknowledge Jesus as the longed-for Messiah promised by Jewish teaching, the Jews, he claimed, misread their own scriptures and were spiritually blind.

More than this, Paul, and the new religion he helped birth, rejected the theological claim that Jews specifically were a chosen people, and that the only way to access this relationship to God in its fullness was to follow Jewish laws and commandments, such as circumcision or the laws of kashrut (kosher), in one's everyday life. His goal was to expand beyond the Jews.[9] "Because of unbelief they [the Jewish people] were broken off," Paul said in Romans 11:20–25, "and thou [Gentile believers in Jesus] standest by faith . . . Blindness in part is happened to Israel, until the fulness of the Gentiles be come in."

Paul insisted that, through faith in Jesus, divine revelation was available to Gentiles as well, and that following Jewish law and commandment was unnecessary for Gentiles. Later commentators would go further—following Jewish law, they claimed, was a sinful, material obstacle to the true faith, which could only be found in one's heart.

The Pharisees, the Jewish sect that became Rabbinic Judaism after the destruction of the Second Temple in 70 C.E., were the ultimate foil in many of the Gospels. Pharisees, the Gospels claimed, were "hypocrites" using devious knowledge to confuse the Jewish masses. The Jews, so the story developed through the ages, were not the only victims of their folly; their perniciousness was boundless. Calling someone a Pharisee remains a criticism today, a testament to the legacy of Christian anti-Judaism in our speech and popular understanding.

The Gospel of John sets up what historian David Nirenberg, in his influential book *Anti-Judaism: The Western Tradition*, calls a "cosmic battle" between the "lower" earthly forces of the world, typified by the Jews, and the "higher" saved realm of the spirit, led by Jesus. "If Jesus and his followers do not belong to the world," writes Nirenberg, describing this position, "precisely the opposite is true of the Jew."[10] In a much-cited passage alleging Jewish treachery, John 8:44 reads, "You belong to your father, the devil, and you want to carry out your father's desires. He was a murderer from the beginning, not holding to the truth, for there is no truth in him. When he lies, he speaks his native language, for he is a liar and the father of lies."

Early Christianity was caught in a double bind. Its Jewish origin was necessary to establish the veracity of God's revelation, as promised in Jewish scriptures. However, the persistence of Jews in the present, who continued to refuse Jesus's divinity, threatened to unsettle Christian claims of absolute truth. The legitimacy of Christianity depended on "supersessionism"— the idea that the Christian church was the new, completed, and perfected Israel, the inheritor of the divine covenant, and that God's old covenant with the Jews was now invalid. This idea persists today, reflected even in commonly understood terms like "Old" and "New" Testament.

Anti-Jewish polemics often derived as much from intra-Christian sectarian conflicts over theology as from real-life interaction with actually existing Jews. As early as the formative period of the "church fathers" in the second through fourth centuries, Christian theologians slammed fellow Christian opponents within the church as "Pharisees" or "Judaizers" as a way of condemning supposed excessive legalism, literalism, hypocrisy, materialism, pride, or some other negative quality. Anti-Judaism, in short, became a central negative category against which generations of Christians came to understand themselves.

For a few centuries, Jews and Christians both competed

to win new adherents in the Roman Empire, and both were persecuted by pagan rulers. This changed with the conversion of the Roman Emperor Constantine in the fourth century c.e. Christianity quickly became the dominant faith across the Roman Empire, the creed of ruling elites and their subject populations alike, spread by persuasion and force of the sword. Constantine's conversion, wrote Nirenberg, "transformed a minority religion, still subject to periodic state persecution as seditious, into a public cult called to intimate association with imperial power."[11]

Writing nearly a century later, St. Augustine of Hippo instructed Christians, now dominant, to keep Jews poor and degraded, but not destroy them. Instead, their suffering and servitude should serve as "important testimony" to the truth of Christianity. "Not by bodily death shall the ungodly race of carnal Jews perish," Augustine wrote around the year 400. Rather, "the continued preservation of the Jews will be a proof to believing Christians of the subjection merited by those who, in the pride of their kingdom, put the Lord to death."[12]

This established the Christian relationship to Jews, which only accelerated into the Middle Ages and with mass Christianization across Europe. The systemic oppression of Jews in Christian Europe was not motivated by religious ideology alone. Rather, like all oppression, it was shaped by, and helped shape, the realities of social, economic, and political life. In towns and cities across medieval Europe, Jews were segregated into ghettos and often forced to wear special clothing to distinguish them from their neighbors, from pointed hats to red or yellow badges, a practice revived with the Nazi yellow star in the twentieth century.

As we discuss later, Jews were barred from owning land, joining Christian guilds, and pursuing many professions. Christian ruling elites pushed many Jews into jobs like moneylending and tax collecting, associated in the public imagination with usury, considered a sin by Christians. Rulers then spread the canard that Jews were sinful lenders and economic exploiters, directing popular hostility and violence against the Jews (and, conveniently, away from the ruling elite) and cementing the association of Jews with greed that continues to this day. Jews were formally expelled from dozens of lands across Christian Europe, and their property was seized, with a mixture of economic and religious justifications.

The aggression toward Jews hit new peaks during the First Crusade in 1096, when marauding armies massacred Jews across the Rhineland en route to capture the Holy Land from Muslims. Scholar Geraldine Heng calls medieval England "the first racial state in the history of the West" for its "church and state laws [that] produced surveillance, tagging, herding, incarceration, legal murder, and finally, the expulsion of English Jews."[13] These and other factors merged to keep European Jews—for centuries, the continent's primary internal Other—in a state of permanent vulnerability and precarity, where Jews were forced to constantly wonder when it would be time to flee.

The charge of deicide—the slander that the Jewish people killed Jesus—solidified in the European Christian imagination during the Middle Ages, and persists today. This myth serves as a convenient deflection to hide the fact that it was the occupying Roman Empire, not the Jewish masses, that condemned Jesus to death for his rebellious affront to the empire's imperial domination.

Over centuries in Christian Europe, these anti-Jewish tropes formed what researchers Ben Gidley, Brendan McGeever, and David Feldman call "a deep reservoir of stereotypes and narratives, one which is replenished over time and from which people can draw with ease."[14] Reverend Anne Dunlap, a minister in the United Church of Christ, recalls that during her Presbyterian upbringing, anti-Judaism "was ubiquitous." She was taught that "the Pharisees were exclusive, they were all antagonistic to Jesus, they were legalistic, hypocritical . . . It was a terrible thing to be a Pharisee." Hearing the church choir sing Johann Sebastian Bach's Passion cantatas, Dunlap remembers verses like "Let us crucify him!" at the thunderous climax of the performance, conveying the message that Jews as a whole—and, more broadly, all of humanity—were responsible for Jesus's death.

When she later critically studied the Bible at seminary, Reverend Dunlap developed more nuanced interpretations, seeing the Pharisees as simply one among many Jewish movements of that era, struggling to chart a religious future during great tumult. Blaming the Pharisees for Jesus's death, she realized, was a convenient narrative to absolve the Roman Empire of complicity. "The more that Christianity moves into the spaces of empire, and gets co-opted by empire," she told us, "the more it's actually the deflection—'the problem is the Jewish people, it's not Roman oppression, don't look over here'—that is the root of the problem." This pattern of deflection would persist—modern antisemitism, for example, offers the false scapegoat of an elite Jewish cabal to misdirect popular resentment over widespread alienation from the root causes of capitalism, as we will discuss.

Dunlap worked as a faith organizing coordinator with Showing Up for Racial Justice (SURJ). Founded in 2009, SURJ organizes white Americans against anti-Black racism and has played an important role, since the Trump presidency, in mobilizing support for Black Lives Matter. "Once you understand this deflection tactic," she told us,

> you'll start noticing it everywhere: liturgies, hymns . . . It serves to set Christianity up to be "the good ones," "the ones who figured it out" . . . How easy it is, then, to take that dynamic, and bend it towards even more malevolent ends like white Christian nationalism, where it's like,

"We are the good ones, and we are going to wipe you
out" . . . or the "us versus them" dynamic, which you
can base all the antisemitic conspiracy theories around.

DEVIL JEWS

In 1144 a new type of story emerged in Norwich, England,
when a twelve-year-old boy named William was found dead.
Christians in Norwich blamed the town's Jews for his death,
accusing Jews of using his blood in occult rituals. This "blood
libel" story was taken up by church leaders, and the false accusations that Jews ritually tortured pure, innocent children and
consumed blood in an act of sacred cannibalism spurred exe-
cutions, massacres, and other persecution of Jews across Christian Europe for the next several hundred years.

"[Once] you begin to focus on the suffering of Christ, then
Jews inevitably enter the picture," scholar Magda Teter told us.
Teter's 2020 book *Blood Libel: On the Trail of an Antisemitic Myth*
traces a history of the accusation, from its origins in the charge
of deicide to its emergence in medieval Christianity's growing
obsession over Jesus's suffering, and increasing suspicion of
Jews. "These became powerful tropes that were amplified in
the medieval period through liturgy that cast Jews much more
publicly as killers," Teter told us.

The blood libel myth appeared in regional histories, saint
canonization, historical works, and art that still adorns the
walls of churches to this day. For Teter, who is not Jewish, "the
memory of some of these beliefs were still present" in her Polish
town growing up, which itself had two famous cases of blood
libel accusations. "My father would recall the fear that was instilled in him and in children about Jews or about the blood libel,
because it was so present in the popular memory of the town."

The blood libel trope has held throughout the centuries,
and remained one of many demonizing accusations levied
against Jews during the widespread pogroms of the late nine-

teenth and early twentieth centuries in Eastern Europe and into the Nazi era. It influences today's QAnon movement, and groundless right-wing moral panics about LGBTQ "groomers" supposedly preying on vulnerable children.

Evil is easier to understand and fight when it is in human form, and European Christendom's image of "the Jew" rendered Jews not just suspect but distinctly threatening and abhorrent, a secretive and malevolent cabal built on sorcery. "Really I doubt whether a Jew can be human for he will neither yield to human reasoning, nor find satisfaction in authoritative utterances, alike divine and Jewish," said Peter the Venerable, a twelfth-century Benedictine abbot.[15]

The idea that the Jews were *literally* of the devil, that they had horns and tails, and that their religion was a form of dark magic was so deeply laid that the medieval lore of witchcraft, vampires, and assorted sorcery, which is still part of popular culture today, is shot through with anti-Jewish tropes. On the other hand, occultists misappropriated Jewish traditions, romanticizing Jews for their alleged secret knowledge, and this served as a foundation for Western occultism.[16]

Jews were accused of poisoning water wells to cause mass Christian death, of spreading sickness like the bubonic plague in the 1300s, and of "desecrating the host," vandalizing the wafers offered to worshippers as the literal body of Jesus during services, in an effort to enact a second suffering on the Christian savior.[17] Thousands of Jews were murdered as these fantastical accusations evolved from village to village, and pogroms and other violence against Jews often spiked around Christian holidays like Easter. Passages of Talmud were taken out of context, or wholly fabricated, to "prove" that anti-Jesus rage animated Jewish beliefs. Public "disputations" were staged between local rabbis and Christian theologians, often with ruling nobles in the audience—stubborn attempts to reinforce Christian truth claims and inspire Jewish conversion to Christianity, though deeper persecution ensued when no conversion came.

In 1517, according to legend, a reformer named Martin Luther nailed his Ninety-Five Theses to the door of All Saints' Church in Wittenberg, Germany, demanding an end to institutional corruption and other changes in the Catholic Church. Luther initially saw the mistreatment of Jews as abominable primarily because he reasoned that it dissuaded Jews from converting to the one true faith. But as it became clear that Jews refused to accept the Jesus narrative and continued to keep *mitzvot*, he became enraged, publishing tracts demanding that Jewish homes and synagogues be destroyed, Jews be expelled from Christian lands, and Jewish teaching be prohibited.

Luther's texts, such as the iconic *On the Jews and Their Lies* in 1543, were eventually distributed along with a 1574 broadsheet that showed a Jewish woman giving birth to piglets, an example of the *Judensau*, the obscene portrayal of Jews suckling female pigs, that still adorns many European churches.[18] Luther's antisemitism has remained influential for centuries—one Nazi propaganda poster from 1933, for example, read that "Hitler's fight and Luther's teaching are the best defense for the German people."[19]

Luther was calling for Jews to convert in an era when converts increasingly faced suspicion. In what became known as the Spanish Inquisition, Jewish and Muslim converts to Christianity were treated with intense scrutiny in Christian Spain, leading to their expulsion in 1492. Ruthless persecution of suspected "crypto-Jews" and "crypto-Muslims"—converts who, it was feared, continued practicing their prior religion in secret—persisted for centuries afterward. This is an early example of the "racialization" of Jews, whereby the evil taint of Jewishness could not simply be washed away in the baptismal waters of the Church, but instead was locked into the blood, then the ancestry record, and then finally in the genes. The conversion might hide them, but it could not cure them.

INTO THE MODERN WORLD

Beginning in the eighteenth century, with the European Enlightenment and its project of liberal, secular modernity, many of the formal structures barring Jews from full participation in civic life were gradually removed, and it seemed for a time that, with full citizenship and belonging no longer limited to Christians, a new spirit of tolerance and pluralism would reign.

Before long, however, conservatives and liberals alike modernized and retrofitted Christian anti-Judaism into new arguments. As we discuss, reactionary clergy, and masses of believers, played strong roles in the reactionary movements that targeted Jews across Europe, weaving theology into new discourses of nationalism, race science, and conspiracy theory. This fueled increasingly violent pogroms against Jews toward the end of the nineteenth century and fascism during the twentieth century.

After the horrors of the Holocaust, the Church, along with the West as a whole, started soul-searching. With reform initiatives like the 1962–1965 Second Vatican Council, Christian leaders around the world gradually repudiated antisemitism, sought atonement for the Church's role in it, and promised to build a new narrative for Jews in Christianity's story. Many spoke out forcefully against the long-standing conviction that Jewish piety was wicked or sinful, and rejected the long-standing practice of attempting to convert Jews. Some proposed foundational changes to Christian theology, attempting to redefine or leave behind harmful precepts such as supersessionism. As the twentieth century progressed, the so-called Judeo-Christian West geared itself up for a clash of civilizations against other specters: first communism, then Islamist terrorism. The two-thousand-year-old reservoir of Christian anti-Jewish animus, many concluded, had dried up for good.

The truth, however, is that deep reservoirs do not dry up overnight. As we discuss later, today's Christian Right is engaged in an overt, coordinated attempt to dominate politics, culture, and other societal spheres in order to overthrow democracy, enshrine white minority rule, and roll back human rights for those who don't conform and anyone who stands in the way. Antisemitism remains an animating principle across this emboldened white Christian Right, even while there are Jewish Right factions that are collaborating with it.

CHRISTIAN HEGEMONY

Over the last few years, Shane has decided to run an experiment. Walking the streets of Portland, he, like many others, is regularly accosted by Christian proselytizers. But what if, instead of avoiding eye contact and moving on, he told them "No thanks, I'm Jewish"?

Instead of putting a damper on their proselytizing, it often switched it to overdrive.

"That's great, so is the Messiah!"

"You still need to be saved!"

"The Hebrew prophets predicted Jesus!"

What Shane realized was that, in the eyes of these missionaries, his Jewishness was never treated as perfectly legitimate on its own. Rather, it was understood as an immature and temporary state to be "completed" by faith in Jesus. These Christian street preachers often presented themselves as admirers and friends of Jews; until, that is, those Jews decided to politely decline their entreaties, and instead to continue doing the very things that made them Jewish.

The United States is a Christian-hegemonic country. The patchwork of US Christianity is interwoven with numerous communities, sects, and denominations, with important differences in racial, class, and other positionality. Nonetheless, broadly speaking, the norms of Western Christianity have been a dominant cultural, civic, and political force in American life since its founding.

Until the mid-twentieth century, the US elite was composed almost exclusively of white, Anglo-Saxon Protestant men, and a matrix of laws and social customs barred non-Christians (and non-white men) from holding elected office or societal power. As historian Leonard Dinnerstein put it, "while by an absence of restrictive legislation all white men had equal opportunities in the United States, most Protestants regarded Catholics and Jews as inferior and adherents of these faiths often perceived themselves as outsiders in a Protestant nation, at best tolerated but not embraced."[20]

While antisemitism in the United States never became the central, guiding ideology of a mass movement (white Christians, after all, always had anti-Blackness and Indigenous genocide to serve that purpose), Jews faced varying levels of de jure and de facto restrictions on immigration, employment, housing, and political office, as well as other institutional discrimination and social stereotyping, harassment, violence, attempts at conversion, and simmering contempt from a majority determined to defend Christianity as the sole state and civil society religion in the United States.

Political movements of many stripes mobilized antisemitism infused with Christian themes, from the populist movements of the late nineteenth and early twentieth centuries that identified Jews with big-city finance capital and "usury" to Father Charles Coughlin and the hard-right Christian Front in the 1930s, which identified Jews with the specter of Asiatic Bolshevism.

Despite some diversification in recent decades, practicing Christians and those raised Christian continue to dominate society, wielding key levers of military, media, and governmental power. Acknowledging this is a helpful corrective to the core antisemitic conspiracy theory that rich, elite Jews control society—if any "one group" holds the most power in our society, it's rich, elite (and, we should say, white, straight, and male) Christians.

Even while religious affiliation and church attendance are declining, an analysis of 2020 census data by the Public Religion Research Institute shows that seven in ten Americans identify as Christian, and more than four in ten are *white* Christian.[21] Churches and other Christian institutions in the United States also receive billions in tax breaks and other privileges, and wield outsized economic and social power in shaping policy decisions about health care, education, and other parts of our social fabric.[22]

Many Jews have experienced firsthand the consequences that can come from living in a Christian country. Jewish scholar and activist Benjamin Balthaser recalls that growing up in a white, lower-middle-class evangelical town in rural California, antisemitism was "part of the texture of town life—if not the chorus, at least the melody." Phrases like "Jewing someone down" and questions like "Why are Jews so greedy?" were commonplace. His younger brother one day returned home from visiting a friend's evangelical church "to announce that the Jews deserved the Holocaust for rejecting Jesus." A group of Christian classmates once surrounded Balthaser in the schoolyard playground, praying for the "salvation" of his soul.[23]

Balthaser's mother worked as an organist in several churches and recalls regularly hearing preachers sermonize that "we must pray for the perfidious Jews," that Jews were "blind and stupid for rejecting Jesus," Jews "are the Pharisees and the Pharisees are hypocrites," and other themes. Balthaser once found a swastika carved into his high school locker and faced threats and attacks from local white nationalist skinheads. "I have no animus against Christianity," he wrote in 2016, soon after Trump's election,

and applaud the many churches that have been on the front lines of the struggle for racial justice since America's

violent foundation. Yet my experience with conservative
Christianity in rural America was to observe an institutional site of anti-Semitic thought, or at least a space in
which such thought is considered normal and acceptable.[24]

Chava Shervington told us that growing up in the South, "it
was more like religious expressions of antisemitism," including the threats of hell that she heard all around her in the dominant Christian society. "Religion is such an integral part of
how people organize themselves and their lives" in the South,
Shervington explained, and since few in those communities
knew Jews personally (or really knew anything about Jews),
a mix of stereotypes, rumors, and the rigidity of monolithic
Christianity served as a substitute. Who was "saved" and who
was "left behind" was predetermined, and Jews were expected
to answer for their difference.

"There's a profound amount of Christianness to the Midwest," Carin Mrotz, former executive director of Jewish Community Action in Minnesota, told us, "and this creates an
atmosphere where Jews are so Othered by definition, simply
by existing, that it feels easy to exacerbate." In the Twin Cities,
Mrotz told us, where Jews make up 2 percent of the population,
"my kids are the only Jews in the school they go to, and they
hear antisemitic things."[25]

Ignorant of Jewish holidays, school staff have often required
documentation before allowing her children an excused absence during the High Holy Days. Two years ago, Jewish parents across the Twin Cities protested when classes were slated
to begin during Rosh Hashanah, and only sustained pressure
convinced administrators to eventually change the schedule.
Many Jews, Mrotz explained, will not bother trying to take off
work during holidays. "There's an alienation, and a loneliness,"
she told us, "that makes us feel both invisible and more visible
at the same time."

Activists have used the term "Christian hegemony" to describe the all-pervasive background influence of Western Christianity on the shape of American life. Author and educator Paul Kivel defines Christian hegemony as "the everyday, systematic set of Christian values, individuals and institutions that dominate all aspects of US society. Nothing is unaffected."[26]

As Mrotz describes, the rhythms of American civic life remain dominated by the Christian calendar. Every December, when Jews and other non-Christians are inundated with wishes of "Merry Christmas" and invitations to join in cheery songs about Santa Claus, we are reminded that we live in a society whose core cultural scripts do not represent us, and we must evolve our own strategies to navigate this reality. This allows those of even a secular, culturally Christian background what researcher and former evangelical Chrissy Stroop calls "Christian privilege," an effect of personally aligning with the rhythm of the dominant culture.[27]

The influence of pervasive and unexamined Christian cultural norms runs deep. When elected officials or community leaders slander someone they disagree with as a "Pharisee" (as Democrat leader Pete Buttigieg labeled Mike Pence in 2019), they mobilize deep-seated Christian tropes associating Jews with sin, falsehood, and materialism. When we refer to the Tanakh as the "Old Testament" and Christian scripture as "New," we reinforce the notion that the "old" Judaism has been superseded by the "new" Christianity. Christianity's influence can be invisible since it is embedded across society, but it affects the "common sense" notions we hold about religion and spirituality, sin and salvation, and countless other categories.

Too often, Jews and others who exist as a non-Christian minority in our society are made to feel abnormal, and the pressure to assimilate has done much to erase the distinctiveness of Jewishness. We risk losing touch with distinctly Jewish theologies, rituals, and folkways, adopting Christian norms instead, which is why we need Christian political partners to help undermine this hegemony and to build a world where all of us can flourish.

And, of course, Jews aren't the only group impacted by dominant Christianity, in the United States and around the world. In the United States alone, Protestant Christianity has been used from the beginning to entrench brutal oppression of and dominance over Indigenous people, enslaved Africans, and a host of other minorities. The activist organization Soulforce uses the term "Christian supremacy" to describe "the parasitic relationship that is formed when Christianity is forced to serve systems of power and domination." Christian supremacy "uses the culture and sacred text of Christianity to moralize the violent actions of institutions, governments, individuals, and groups of people."[28]

In her 2023 study, *Christian Supremacy*, scholar Magda Teter examined the ways in which the anti-Jewish spiritual hierarchies and social prejudices of early Christianity laid the groundwork and "mental habits" for later forms of systemic oppression, such as anti-Blackness and colonialism, inflicted by white Christian Europe on other people around the world. She writes that this mental structure "developed first in a religious sense with regard to Jews and then transformed also into a racialized dominance, accelerating when Europeans expanded their political reach beyond Europe and established slaveholding empires."[29]

From the Crusades to the Spanish Inquisition, Jews, like many other people, know in our bones, in our *kishkes* (guts), that a society that proclaims and legally enforces chauvinist forms of Christianity is not a safe place for us for long. We also know that while Christian supremacist movements often single out Jews for acute persecution, Jews are never alone—Christian supremacy is a threat to the safety and survival of all religious, sexual, and cultural minorities alongside us. By tracing the shared roots of our oppression, the many different groups victimized by Euro-Christian supremacy can find a shared stake in struggle, and build a shared horizon of collective liberation.

Those with Christian privilege, of whatever background, have a role to play in this work. "I think it's difficult for Christians to grapple with Antisemitism," wrote Elizabeth Moraff, a Puerto Rican Jewish activist, after a Boston rabbi was stabbed outside a synagogue in summer 2021, "because most Christians haven't recognized that Christianity is a dominant, oppressive force in the U.S. that operates on its own axis."[30]

Well-meaning Christians can still perpetuate anti-Jewish stereotypes. Progressive Christians, explained Reverend Anne Dunlap, frame early Judaism in negative terms as a way of promoting a narrative that makes Christianity look superior. For instance, they might celebrate a

> progressive feminist Jesus who was welcoming women because Judaism was so misogynist—or Jesus as the outcast, because Judaism was so exclusive—or the liberator Jesus . . . liberating people from Judaism, not from the impacts of the Roman Empire . . . We just made up a version of Judaism that's not really true!

What countering this narrative requires is a form of conscious accountability where Christian leaders do not just avoid anti-Jewish rhetoric, they acknowledge and actively undermine the church's antisemitic legacy. "I really want Christian pastors to take seriously the ways in which New Testament texts, particularly the writings of Paul, can put antisemitism out into the world," Rabbi Rachel Schmelkin, who served at Congregation Beth Israel in Charlottesville, Virginia during the Unite the Right rally in 2017, told us, "and not just say that when somebody like the Poway synagogue shooter writes an antisemitic manifesto infused with Christian themes, 'That's not Christianity.' Well, I'm sorry, but that person put that manifesto in your name, [and] now you have to do the work of explaining why [or] how that was a misuse of the text."

When progressive Christians, or folks raised Christian, are challenged to confront these realities, they may be defensive, insisting "not all Christians" perpetuate such harms, for example, or that Christian nationalists are "not real Christians." But this isn't helpful. "The whole of Christianity is one long antisemitic story," Rabbi Danya Ruttenberg told us,

> alongside all the beauty of St. Francis and St. Theresa, [activists like] Thomas Merton and Dr. King, and [liberation theologists like] James Cone . . . It's both there, and we need our Christian allies to understand that "not real Christians" is a sort of gaslighting that implies that fake Christians murdered our ancestors—that does not help us. What helps us is an honest grappling with the true history of Christianity.

But we also should not ignore the hard work that has been done by Christian radicals and progressives, particularly since they have an active, and essential, role to play in undermining antisemitism and challenging Christian nationalism.

The church may have set the groundwork for antisemitic ideologies, but those ideas took new forms beginning in the eighteenth century, with the emerging modernity and its strange new world of capitalist exploitation and urban life. Drawing on those same notions of Jewish perfidy and conspiracy, antisemites spread one of the most lasting accusations: that Jews were responsible for the horrors of capitalism.

FIVE

THE SOCIALISM OF FOOLS: ANTISEMITISM AND ANTI-CAPITALISM

Allie[1] grew up living in affordable housing in New York City. "A lot of really basic issues didn't get resolved" in her neighborhood, she told us, "and we would just have to deal with them ourselves." But when the neighborhood started gentrifying, "suddenly, these issues were getting resolved—but it was clearly not for us. And a big root of my anger was asking myself, 'Why do we have to wait for people with money to move into our neighborhoods, in order for them to become livable?' It was completely about power."

Today Allie works as a tenant organizer in Brooklyn, helping mostly low-income tenants build collective power to win better housing conditions. "Whenever I'm organizing," she told us, "there's always going to be at least one person who's like, 'Oh, you know, the Jews are buying up all the buildings. That's the issue in the neighborhood.'"

Slumlords range in ethnicity, religion, and everything else, she explained. But the Jewishness of an Orthodox Jewish slumlord is visibly apparent, in a way that the "Greekness" of a Greek slumlord, for example, is not. And in a world where antisemitism teaches people to stereotype Jews as powerful oppressors, it's easy for that narrative to congeal.

In tight-knit apartment complexes, she told us, "one person will say some blanket statement about Jews, and then people just start regurgitating it. And then it just becomes this belief that people hold: 'I don't really know what a Jew is, but my neighbor told me that they're responsible here, and that makes sense.'"

As a Jew herself, these narratives disturb Allie. And as an organizer, she knows how dangerous they can be. "The second we start stereotyping power," she explained, "we lose the central thrust of what we're doing." When organizing against a slumlord, it's essential to clearly understand their real self-interest and the concrete power they hold, in order to figure out how to move them to accede to the demands of your campaign. Conspiracy theories and stereotypes only muddle the picture.

Allie isn't the first to notice this about antisemitism. For the last few hundred years, humans have faced widespread poverty and immiseration, instability and dislocation, inequality and exploitation generated by capitalism: an economic system that concentrates wealth and power in the hands of a few, while leaving most people struggling to make ends meet, vulnerable to the precarious whims of the market, and feeling alienated from the work they do for a living. During this time, people have sought answers to explain why the world got so damn hard, and what to do about it.

Antisemitism offers one easy answer: "It's the Jews." Armed with this belief, there's little need to grapple with the dizzying complexity of financial markets, the multilayered structure of economic fleecing, or the ways that systems like race- and gender-based oppression intersect to produce and reinforce class hierarchies. Instead, antisemitism allows someone to direct their rage at the simplified, and comforting, image of a demonic cabal nestled at the top of it all, pulling the strings.

"Antisemitism," economic justice organizer and educator Dania Rajendra says, "is a powerful explanation for a society looking for answers about why the richest nation in the history of the world often feels so terrible to live in, to work in, to be neighbors in."[2]

The problem is, this answer is wrong. There is a small minority of elites who regularly push through policies to enrich themselves and impoverish the rest, but it's not the Jews or any other shadowy cult—it's the rich.[3] No single racial or religious group controls the planet's wealth. As with any group, there are very rich Jews, there are very poor Jews, and most Jews fall somewhere in between. If it were as easy as uprooting a single cabal—rather than overthrowing an entire system—we would have defeated capitalism long ago and replaced it with something better.

Since it emerged, antisemites have claimed that Jews invented capitalism and used its levers to profit at the expense of the traditional societies and working classes. This libel stirred masses of Europeans, across the political spectrum, to imagine that by "punching up" at a Jewish cabal, they were liberating themselves from economic exploitation.

This myth was ridiculed by the European Left over a century ago as the "socialism of fools," a term popularized by German socialist August Bebel. The "socialism of fools" persists in our era of unprecedented wealth inequality, unchecked corporate monopoly and finance sector malfeasance, and widespread alienation. In the final closing television ad of his 2016 presidential campaign, broadcast into millions of homes a mere three days before election day, Donald Trump railed against "a global power structure that is responsible for the economic decisions that have robbed our working class, stripped our country of its wealth, and put that money into the pockets of a handful of large corporations and political entities" while the faces of three Jews—liberal financier George Soros, Goldman Sachs CEO Lloyd Blankfein, and Federal Reserve chair Janet Yellen—flashed across the screen.[4]

The myth persists in popular understanding, in widely held stereotypes that Jews are rich, greedy, good with money, and the like. Even when they are framed as "compliments," these stereotypes are false and harmful, and nobody is doing Jews any favors by spreading ignorance.

The Left, too, is not immune from antisemitic forms of anti-capitalism, often thought of as "punching up" because it alleges to direct its frustrations at the top. From "Google Jewish Bankers" signs at Occupy Wall Street to grumblings against "Jewish landlords" at tenant organizing meetings, these conspiratorial caricatures distract progressive movements from the concrete conditions we're up against in society, leading down a dead-end road.

Ending capitalism won't end antisemitism on its own—but it's an indispensable step. Because the suffering engendered by the system of economic exploitation provides such fertile soil for the growth of antisemitic ideas, we have to challenge that system at its core, and overcome the division it sows amongst working people, in order to build a world where Jews, and all people, can flourish. In this chapter, we'll look at how the "socialism of fools" evolved, how it has animated anti-capitalist sentiment on both the Right and Left, and how progressives can avoid conspiracy theories in our own organizing against economic injustice.

THE WEALTH OF NATIONS

To understand how the "socialism of fools" trap emerged, it helps to look back to how Jews, for centuries in medieval Christian Europe, were both manipulated by the empires they lived within, and misportrayed by the ruling classes lording over them. During the Middle Ages, Jews were banned from many different types of work across Europe. Many eked out a modest living at the edge of feudal economies, while a small number worked as moneylenders and tax collectors. Especially after the collapse of the Roman Empire and its centralized structures, elites and nobility sometimes relied upon networks of

Jewish moneylenders and merchants for long-distance trade, the lending of funds to finance projects, and other services across the far-flung European continent.

There were plenty of Christian moneylenders and merchants, too. "Just like Christians," writes scholar Kerice Doten-Snitker, "a handful [of medieval European Jews] were successful merchants and financiers, but the majority led economically mundane lives."[5] Over time, Christian theologians came to castigate moneylending as sinful, inventing a new term, "usury," to denigrate it. Even though Jews made up a small percentage of lenders, the stereotype of Jewish usury solidified.[6]

This dynamic pushed Jews into "middlemen" positions in between the elites and the peasants, encouraging the latter to project their anger onto the Jews rather than those Christian ruling classes truly responsible for widespread exploitation and mistreatment.[7] "Rulers used Jews for 'middlemen' jobs that put Jews in direct contact with the exploited, disgruntled peasantry," wrote April Rosenblum in her influential 2007 movement pamphlet *The Past Didn't Go Anywhere*, "shielding rulers from the backlash for their unjust policies. A peasant might live a lifetime without seeing the nobleman who decided her fate; it was Jews [who] were the face of power at her door collecting taxes and rent, Jews who seemed in control, and Jews who faced the violence when peasants in poverty decided to resist."[8] As Rosenblum has pointed out, this position of economic and political vulnerability is common to many diaspora communities around the world; European Jews were only one of what sociologists think of as "middleman minorities."

Jews were encouraged into these positions by Christian royals with ostensible legal protection, to serve as what Aurora Levins Morales calls "shock absorbers,"[9] visible scapegoats and outlets for the rage of an exploited peasantry. On orders from the nobility, Jews were confined to ghettos separate from their Christian neighbors. Within what historian Yosef Hayim

Yerushalmi calls this "vertical alliance" with state power, Jews were dependent on the monarchy or aristocracy for safety, and protection could be snatched away in an instant, leaving the nobility protected on the backs of Jewish vulnerability—a precarious safety strategy.[10]

Many pogroms can be tied back to incidents in which financial manipulation and crushing debt were caused by feudal lords, yet the Jews, forced to act on their behalf, bore the brunt of the rage. This protected those in power from riots from below. Jews rarely accumulated enough wealth or power to do anything other than maintain this unequal relationship to the rulers, who would frequently default on their loans and seize the assets of, and even expel, the Jews they claimed to protect, with few consequences. This locked in what became a familiar pattern for European Jews. "We are kept insecure by our history of sudden assaults," said Morales, "and as a strategy of survival, some of us accept the bribes of privilege and protection."[11]

Christian beliefs about usury added an economic dimension to earlier stories of Jewish wickedness. Before long, the image of the greedy, miserly Jewish merchant—a creature determined to amass worldly wealth—solidified. Figures like Shylock in Shakespeare's *The Merchant of Venice* and Barabas in Marlowe's *The Jew of Malta* came to represent an easily available trope. Each generation draws on antisemitic images to tell a new variation on an older tale. Each new image becomes fresh evidence for the next story.

The idea of a Jewish conspiracy has many sources, from Christian accusations of deicide to the claims of blood libel. The story of the Jewish cabal acting on the world stage can be traced back to the Middle Ages, yet more contemporary versions concerned secret societies like the Knights Templar, Freemasons, and Illuminati, who, legend says, conspired in secret to overthrow the natural order. By the early nineteenth century, the myth had evolved, suggesting these societies enacted the French Revolution, and, before long, reactionaries insisted the Jews were to blame.

Simultaneously, capitalism was developing rapidly in Europe, ushering in a new era of industrial development, urban expansion, massive wealth concentration, and novel instruments of exchange such as legal contracts, financial services, and endless speculation. These changes hit many traditional professions, like artisans and craftspeople, the hardest since they undermined the material bases of their occupations and left them few tools with which to understand the transformations. Rural elites felt the stable privileges they once enjoyed threatened by modernization, while peasants were forced from the countryside and faced horrific exploitation in urban factories and crowded, unsafe tenements.

"All fixed, fast-frozen relations," wrote Karl Marx and Friedrich Engels in *The Communist Manifesto* in 1848, capturing this widespread sense of dislocation and opportunity, "with their train of ancient and venerable prejudices and opinions, are swept away, all new-formed ones become antiquated before they can ossify. All that is solid melts into air, all that is holy is profaned, and man is at last compelled to face with sober senses his real conditions of life, and his relations with his kind."[12]

Cultural and scholarly elites worried that organic, "natural" ties of community had been replaced by those of impersonal, transactional modern society. Large masses of people grasped desperately to come to their "sober senses" and face the loss of more traditional ways of life, as well as the deep inequalities of society's emerging class structure.

Members of the clergy, nobility, and artisanal classes complained that capitalism stripped out traditional loyalties and strictly managed hierarchies, particularly those of family, faith, and nation, and instituted in their place a radically new, anarchic social order. Small businessmen and lower-middle-class workers and shopkeepers feared what little privileges they maintained would vanish in the upheaval.

"This was the true political function of anti-Semitism," wrote historian Michel Winock of nineteenth-century France, where "exploited workers [and] peasants forced to leave the countryside were shown [that] the Jew was responsible for all their ills." Now, with the use of conspiracy theory texts like the *Protocols of the Elders of Zion* (as we discussed), conservatives could take class conflict and refashion it as the result of pernicious Jewish influence, ultimately absolving the rich of reponsibility for their exploitation of the lower classes.[13]

Social conservatives criticized capitalism's allegedly "abstract" nature, based in the world of numbers, ideas, and manipulations, as a cursed counterpoint to the supposedly stable and sacrosanct world of work, crafts, and "organic" communities. This developed the meme of "producerism" that remains central to nationalist and populist movements (and occasionally appears on the Left) today, which claims that wealth accumulated through "concrete" means, such as physical labor or traditional industry, is sacred, while wealth produced through other "abstract" means, such as finance, interest, and speculation, is parasitic. This is ultimately a false dichotomy—both types of labor are integral parts of today's capitalist world system.

Jewish communities in Europe would eventually find themselves swept into the center of this political whirlwind. As feudalism transitioned to capitalism, ruling elites embarked upon large-scale nation building, and some again turned to Jewish moneylenders, who drew upon transnational networks for financing. Small numbers of Jewish banking families, including the Rothschilds and the Warburgs, became wealthy, while most Jews remained in poverty.[14]

At the end of the eighteenth century, in the wake of the French Revolution, the previous legal barriers separating Jews from Gentiles began to be gradually dissolved, and Jews were granted citizenship and a certain amount of civil equality in newly democratic Western and Central European nation-states. In a process called the *Haskalah* or Jewish Enlightenment, these Jews vigorously sought greater participation in civil society and its democratic institutions at the same time as sweeping changes to the economy and social fabric were taking place.

The traditional emphasis on literacy in Jewish communities, as well as the transnational mercantile relationships many had developed, meant that many newly emancipated Jews eventually became well represented in certain professions that required advanced education, ranging from banking to journalism and the arts, politics to commerce and law—especially as formal or informal barriers remained in other fields. A "perfect storm" commenced for European Jewry. Soon, critics of the social order accused newly emancipated Jews of "bringing" capitalism and its attendant social transformations, when the reality was simply that they were understandably eager, with their vigorous participation, to attempt to integrate into society considering the new (and, as they would seen discover, fleeting) promise of social equality.

Catholic nationalists and others in the emerging romantic movements looked to older antisemitic stories about Jews to explain society's changes. If the Jews (they imagined) had historically been responsible for ruining the lives of feudal peasants through usury—and if this new capitalist society felt, in its exploitative, debt-ridden sting, remarkably like usury—then perhaps, they reasoned, the new social structures were a Jewish invention.

Unlike the Right, the early European Left tended less to look backward at restoring a nostalgic past, and more to look forward, to the building of a more equal society. But they, too, often propagated antisemitism in misguided attempts to "punch up" at the root of capitalism, and the "Jewish question" was a fiercely common debate among Leftists. In the mid-nineteenth century, influential anarchist theorist Mikhail Bakunin railed against "the whole Jewish world, which consti-

THE SOCIALISM OF FOOLS

tutes a single exploitative sect, a sort of bloodsucker people, a collective parasite, voracious . . . every popular revolution is accompanied by a massacre of Jews: a natural consequence."[15] Anarchist Pierre-Joseph Proudhon went further, insisting that "the Jew is the enemy of the human race. One must send this race back to Asia or exterminate it."[16] Distinguishing between "rich Jews" and "poor Jews," as some socialists attempted, did little to blunt the antisemitic assertion that Jews were somehow distinctly predisposed to capitalist behavior.

As they articulated critiques of capitalism, social conservatives and progressive reformers alike made use of a powerful new fantasy storming the European consciousness—the conspiracy of the nefarious Jewish banking cabal.

ROTHSCHILD SPACE LASERS

Conspiracy theories about the Rothschilds trace to 1846, when a pamphlet was circulated, signed by "Satan," peddling the false claim that Nathan Rothschild, an English banker, observed the total defeat of French forces at the Battle of Waterloo in 1815, and exploited that knowledge to gain millions of francs on the stock exchange before word reached the British coast. With the development of industrial capitalism in the mid-eighteenth century, this fabrication fell easily into the well-worn lines of antisemitic conspiracy storytelling, making the Rothschilds an easy target, a stand-in for harmful ideas about Jewish ruthlessness and greed.[17] The fact that there were many more Christian bankers than Jewish ones did little to dissuade people's antisemitism because the European imagination was already primed for such a story.

Since then, antisemitic conspiracy theories have placed the Rothschilds at the center of practically every major historical event. MAGA congresswoman Marjorie Taylor Greene accused "Rothschild Inc." of using laser beams from space to spark deadly California forest fires in 2018.[18] Patriot militias increasingly spread the conspiracy that Alexander Hamilton married into the Rothschilds and created the national Bank of the United States (a precursor to the Federal Reserve) under the request of his new familial overlords to exploit a "central bank."[19] Lurid tales paint the Rothschilds as the puppet masters of the world's economy, who (the story goes) bankrolled Hitler and killed Abraham Lincoln, manipulated world affairs to create Israel, or, for reasons of devious hatred and Machiavellian enterprise, actively caused stock market collapse.

The Rothschild conspiracy theory serves a few ends, which is why the far-right continues to utilize it. On the one hand, it combines populist anger with convenient circumstances. There *really are* wealthy banking families, their fortunes really are the plunder of working people, and they did accumulate these resources through, in some sense, the "open conspiracy" of capital. The Rothschild narrative then tacks that anger on to a particularly demonized outsider, who, legend has it, has been manipulating markets for centuries. "Usurping the language of class struggle it negates the very idea of class struggle and replaces it with anti-Jewish struggle," wrote Steve Cohen, author of *That's Funny: You Don't Look Antisemitic*, an influential book, first published in 1984, that critiqued antisemitism in the UK Left.[20]

AGAINST THE MODERN WORLD

With the dawn of the twentieth century, as capitalism and imperialism continued to ravage the world, and ideologies of nationalism and race science were in full swing across Europe, right-wing movements found new languages to capture widespread alienation. They offered partial critiques of capitalism that—as in previous centuries—weren't about creating a world free from economic exploitation.

Instead, nationalists, social conservatives, and fascists set out to oppose a modern world that, in their view, uprooted traditional values such as the patriarchal family, white superiority, and the dominance of the Church, and brought morbid symptoms of modernity such as feminism, racial equality, and queer acceptance in their place. Adopting producerist narratives, they opposed some "rootless" aspects of capitalism, such as financial speculation—which they associated with Jews—and valorized "native" industrialists, small businessmen and farmers, and other, supposedly more "rooted" participants in capitalism.

Instead of confronting the permanent crisis of inequality generated by capitalism, they bemoaned people's "artificial" alienation from the supposedly organic national community, and blamed some mysterious force (perhaps the Jews?) that ripped us from premodern harmony. But this is a mirage: premodern societies were far from egalitarian utopias, and imagining we can return to them to escape the hardships of modernity is a fantasy. These reactionaries promised a different future for society, a comforting retreat from the malaise of the modern world, where the racial *volk* could enjoy harmonious, unbridled wealth within a moral economy—but they failed to deliver, building more brutally exploitative societies instead.

These theories about modernity—some of which can be alluring to Leftists as well—disguise the real antagonism at play, between the rich and the rest of us. Instead of seeking economic equality between classes, the nationalist promises a certain equality of belonging to the racial collective.

A false binary is then created, between the "good" capitalism that supports a "national community," and "bad" capitalism that is cosmopolitan and "globalist," and erases national identities. All the negative qualities of capitalism, and the alienating effects of the world it creates, get projected onto the image of the Jew, who is imagined as miserly, greedy, rapacious, rootless, materialistic, cold, and calculating. These tropes persist to this day in popular phrases like "Jewed you down," and stereotypes that Jews are greedy, stingy, good with money, and the like.

"It is the invention of the 'Jew' as the Other, the one that deviates from, and is not allowed to participate in, the community of blood and soil, who serves to provide equality where class conflict and struggle rages," writes critical theorist Werner Bonefeld.[21] Bonefeld presents this emerging rage, directed at Jews (or whatever the antisemites think is "Jewish") as almost a safety valve for capital: it is a type of anti-capitalism that gets its methods and targets wrong, misunderstanding the problem and thinking it is caused by the "character and the power of the Jew."[22]

According to historian John Ganz, antisemitism "allowed for the preservation of capitalism while indulging in anticapitalist rhetoric and themes: the problem was not the system as such, just this particular race."[23]

This can be seen in the way that Nazi propaganda used antisemitism to manipulate the desperation felt by Germans in the wake of the economic crisis of the Great Depression. In 1938, the publishers of the Nazi newspaper *Der Stürmer* released *Der Giftpilz*, or *The Poisonous Mushroom*, a popular children's book using vivid, simple illustrations to teach Nazi antisemitism to young audiences. One page depicted a slovenly businessman, marked as Jewish by a large nose and a Star of David, sitting outside a stock exchange atop an enormous bag of gold.

"Money is the god of the Jews," the caption read. "He commits the greatest crimes to earn money. He won't rest until he can sit on a great sack of money, until he has become king of money."[24] Money and greed, personified in the figure of the Jew, were presented as intrinsically evil, but capitalism itself was not.

ENEMIES OF CAPITAL

Shortly before the rise of fascist movements, early twentieth century Left organizing was making tremendous strides in building more just and equal societies. More Jewish radicals enthusiastically joined revolutionary movements, and the na-

tionalist Right steadily adopted antisemitism as a central ideological plank. But in the Left's historic upsurge, antisemitism
remained in the mix.

In 1917, when communist revolutionaries in Russia over-
threw the old czarist regime, they decisively rolled back some
of that regime's most bitter antisemitic policies. The movement firmly declared its opposition to antisemitism, with Soviet leader Vladimir Lenin declaring in 1919, for example, that
it served the interests of "capitalists [who] strive to sow and
foment hatred between workers of different faiths, different
nations and different races."[25] At the same time, the deep reservoir of antisemitic ideology, present for centuries, was not
fully drained overnight. "Popular anti-bourgeois sentiment,"
wrote historian Brendan McGeever in his book *Antisemitism
and the Russian Revolution*, "on the one hand a crucial reservoir
of revolutionary socialism, was at the same time a resource of
antisemitic mobilization."[26]

While most revolutionaries saw defending Jews as part of
their liberatory mandate, a few saw the Jews not as oppressed
but as agents of capitalism. The reactionary, czarist opposition
was responsible for the most extensive antisemitic brutality,
committing the overwhelming majority of pogroms during
the civil war of 1918–1921, when over one hundred thousand
Jews were slaughtered and six hundred thousand were forced
to flee. But around 8 percent of these pogroms occurred in
areas controlled by the revolutionary Red Army. As they
climbed across Ukraine, a few revolutionaries even chanted
"Smash the Yids, long live Soviet rule!"[27]

In Weimar Germany, the economic crisis created further
impetus to target Jews with the "socialism of fools." Many
Leftists, most notably the German Communist Party (KPD),
adopted forms of German nationalism themselves. While
they certainly understood that fascism and big business had
found an alignment, they often understood this through an
antisemitic lens. Allegations abounded that rich Jews were

funding Nazism to crush communism, spreading the idea that the "Nazis help Jewish capital," as one 1932 socialist newspaper article put it.[28]

Many communists at this time failed to recognize the potentially deep appeal of Nazi antisemitism, with its racialized populist anti-capitalism, to the disgruntled German masses. They tended to minimize it as secondary, arguing that fighting antisemitism distracted from the most important battle against "monopoly capital," or to explain it away as just a relic of the past. Some repeated the producerist error of separating out "productive labor" from "capitalist parasitism," leaving the door open to ideas of conspiratorial cabals.

"(((GLOBALIST)))"

One of the things that the far-right most loathed about Jews was that they were a transnational community, which fascists believed threatened their sacred national borders. The claim that Jews represent a "globalist" or "cosmopolitan" force aimed at crushing national distinction has always been an essential part of modern antisemitism, often tied to the alleged role of Jews in international finance.

In the post–World War 2 era, radical Right movements still turned to the "socialism of fools" to articulate their faulty critiques of changing patterns of capitalist exploitation. An example of this is the "farm crisis" of the 1970s–'80s, when neoliberal profit-driven international trade forced widespread foreclosures on family farms across the United States. Earlier, when socialists had a strong base in Kansas, Leftists would have explained the causes and offered concrete solutions for shared prosperity and economic redistribution. But the Left had all but abandoned rural America, and white power groups like the newly formed Posse Comitatus—a white nationalist militia that served as a precursor to the present-day militia and constitutional sheriffs movement—were eager to capitalize on the crisis, latching on to the grassroots farmer activism to spread antisemitism and win recruits across the country.

The populist message they offered to desperate farmers was built on Christian Identity theology that posed Jews, and an imagined Jewish "Zionist Occupation Government" as responsible for the crisis. This was not an analysis of the Israeli government; it was a fantasy of Jewish global control. As one bankrupt farmer told *The Denver Post*, in a stew of antisemitic anti-capitalism and anti-communism that is not uncommon, "We're prepared right now for the outcome of the battle that's being waged for this country by the Rockefeller cartel and the international Jew-Bolshevik cartel."[29]

The Left, again, was not immune from the "socialism of fools" during these years either. As the Cold War ramped up, the U.S.S.R. and satellite states like Czechoslovakia conducted hyped-up show trials accusing high ranking party officials, usually Jews, of colluding with Western elites to undermine communism from within. Throughout this period the term "Zionist" was usually simply a code word for "Jew," and this covered what were actually anti-Jewish campaigns. In the 1970s, for example, Soviet propagandists railed against a Zionist-capitalist global conspiracy, with writer V. Bolshakov claiming in a 1972 state-published pamphlet that "the international Zionist corporation . . . its countless branches and subsidiaries . . . is one of the most powerful units of finance capital . . . Economic conferences of Jewish millionaires are capital united on a world scale, used to exert pressure on states and governments in a series of capitalist countries in pursuit of political goals."[30] As we discuss later, a principled criticism of Israel's oppression of Palestinians or the ideology of Zionism is not antisemitic—but fever dreams accusing Jewish financial elites of using Zionism to dominate the world are.

Far-right polemics against "globalists" are another example of these dynamics. For the last several decades, neoliberalism has hollowed out communities, outsourced good jobs, and plunged millions of working people into poverty and permanent precarity. The Right falsely insists it can restore prosperity by doubling down on nationalism and conspiracy theories, on one hand "punching down" at immigrants, and on the other hand "punching up" at an imagined "globalist" cabal of liberal urban elites deemed responsible for the crisis.

On the Right, the "globalist elite" often refers to a loose assemblage of "deep state" government bureaucrats, Silicon Valley technocrats, Wall Street billionaires, cosmopolitan jet-setters, United Nations functionaries, liberal media influencers, and other figures. The fuzziness of this conception latches on to small grains of truth about the way today's globalized economy works and, like most conspiracy theories, paints a larger-than-life portrait of a sinister cabal behind it all, pulling the strings.

Tobita Chow directs Justice Is Global, an organization campaigning for structural reforms toward an equitable global economy. In recent years, Chow has watched the spread of "anti-globalist" antisemitism on the Right with alarm, recognizing it as a harmful narrative that makes it harder for progressives to challenge the global reach of corporate power.

"Antisemitic conspiracy theories," he told us, tell a manufactured story "about how the global economy works. They imagine this shadowy force exerting power over the nation, which is fundamentally a global and cosmopolitan force," concentrated in "abstract" sectors like finance and media, which operate across national borders, over and against "concrete" manufacturing and domestic industries. This narrative "redraws the map," he explains, and imagines that native-born workers can unite with "good patriotic capitalists," drive immigrants out of the country and globalists "out of the halls of power," and restore national greatness in competition against other nations.

But the truth is that without a fundamental redistribution of wealth and power, "native" capitalists are just as likely to exploit workers, whether immigrant or native-born. Instead of an America First framing that scapegoats immigrants, conspiratorial cabals, and enemy nations, we need an inclusive, pluralistic vision of community where all are welcome, and a global economy that works for everyone. Narratives of economic nationalism, Chow told us, "deflect us away from that struggle."

Antisemitism, then, "is one of the chief competing theories of how the world works to a real analysis of global capitalism." The real capitalist elite—from billionaire CEOs like Elon Musk and media titans like Tucker Carlson to political leaders like Donald Trump—are eager to redirect the anger of millions against George Soros and "globalist elites," while the overwhelmingly white and Christian titans of big business, heavy industry, oil, the weapons industry, finance, and more are happy to stay behind the scenes in their corporate boardrooms, raking in mega-profits undisturbed. "If you can get on the right side of the nationalist battle lines that get drawn up, and that antisemitism organizes people to support," Chow told us, "you can not only get protected from criticism—you can actually profit from it."

"(((BANKSTERS)))"

The destructive and irrational power of neoliberalism was on full display as the global economy imploded spectacularly in 2007. The liberalization of the finance sector crashed into a subprime mortgage scandal decades in the making, with derivative markets turning people's retirement funds into mush. For almost half a century, workers had seen falling real wages and were now living in a world of constant borrowing and accumulating debt, all while those running hedge funds and banking empires presided over one of the largest transfers of wealth in history. This led to the Left populist Occupy Wall Street movement, a grassroots network of encampments that at its best sought to confront not only income inequality and the mass displacement of the housing crisis, but the core inequalities of capitalism itself.

There is always a flip side to popular mobilizations. On the one hand, movements like Occupy won the support of millions with broad and flexible messaging, without requiring participants to agree on all the details. At the same time, precisely because Occupy was decisively "anti-banker," yet eschewed ideological clarity and discipline, conspiracy theories about banking families multiplied. Conspiracy theorist Alex Jones, far-right militia groups like the Oath Keepers, supporters of libertarian candidate Ron Paul, and other Rightists used Occupy circles around the country to mobilize followers, spinning lurid conspiracy theories about the Federal Reserve, which Jones called "the central organization empowering this world government system."[31]

Many white nationalists greeted Occupy with enthusiasm. David Duke railed against "Zionist thieves at the Federal Reserve" and "the most powerful criminal bank in the world, the Zionist Goldman Sachs," telling other white nationalists, "OWS is an opportunity . . . grab this opportunity!"[32] The first day that Shane arrived at the main Occupy Wall Street encampment at Zuccotti Park, he was greeted by a man holding a "Google Jewish Bankers" sign, offering his own answer to the financial crisis. Though, other protesters did surround him with signs disavowing his message.

Chow remembers encountering antisemitic propaganda about the Rothschilds in popular Occupy videos like *Zeitgeist*. This propaganda, Chow remembers, "offered a quasi-populist critique of finance that was appealing to a set of people who did have progressive instincts and sentiments."

The conceptual categories popular in Occupy, while powerful, helped leave the door open for right-wing infiltration. Movements like Occupy and trade unions often fall back on a producerist binary, juxtaposing the rooted virtues of "Main Street" over and against the rootless, parasitic predations of Wall Street. This kind of campaign messaging can be important. In our neoliberal economy, small businesses, local communities, and families are indeed getting screwed by a ruthless and out-of-control finance sector. At the same time, we need to remember that the root causes of poverty and wealth inequality under capitalism run right through the heart of "Main Street" as well, in the core, undemocratic, and exploitative relationship between bosses and workers.

Activists continue to grapple with how to discuss the rapidly accelerating debt crisis and attacks on workers' rights and wages while rejecting conspiratorial framings or imagery sourced from antisemitism like the octopus, vampire, or parasite. Housing organizers in places like Brooklyn, where Hasidic landlords are particularly visible, can face similar challenges. "I have to constantly remind people," Allie told us, that "Judaism doesn't impact whether or not somebody is going to be a slumlord." We should interrupt antisemitism whenever we hear it and remind people that your slumlord isn't exploitative because he's Jewish—he's exploitative because he's a slumlord, and ultimately, the problem is the broader system of developers, institutional investors, and policy and market forces driving housing injustice, independent of the greed of any individual actor within the system.

When the Left fails to recognize and condemn antisemitic conspiracy theories of capitalism, it puts Jews in danger and weakens sorely needed movements for social change. In 2018, controversy erupted in the United Kingdom when media revealed that longtime activist and then–Labour Party leader Jeremy Corbyn expressed support for an antisemitic mural, *Freedom for Humanity* by artist Mear One. The mural depicted a "New World Order"–style portrayal of global financial leaders, many with caricatured Jewish features, seated around a table, deciding the fate of the working classes.

In case any doubt remained about Mear One's antisemitism, an early draft of the mural even depicted some of these leaders wearing religious skullcaps, called *kippot*. When the artist was criticized, he responded by reinforcing antisemitic ideas, posting that "some of the older white Jewish folk in the local community had an issue with me portraying their beloved #Rothschild or #Warburg etc [sic] as the demons they are."[33]

Already facing a relentless campaign of antisemitism accusations from the Right and Center related to his Palestine solidarity activism, Corbyn initially doubled down and defended the mural, seemingly oblivious to, or unwilling to consider, the possibility that its conspiratorial depiction of elite power could in fact be antisemitic. Later, journalists uncovered another glaring mistake—in 2011, Corbyn had written an enthusiastic and uncritical foreword to the reprinted edition of John Atkinson Hobson's 1902 left-wing tract *Imperialism: A Study*, which included an antisemitic analysis blaming a global Jewish conspiracy for finance capitalism.[34] This further damaged his credibility, and made it even less likely for British Jews to trust that the Left was actually committed to their safety and liberation.[35]

"THE SHADOW OF CAPITAL"

The critique of capitalism is a critique of class and domination by a system that directs power to the one percent. Some on the Left may be tempted to ignore or excuse conspiracy theories that ostensibly oppose capitalism, thinking that any kind of populism works in our favor. The mistake can be forgiven, they reason, if the anger is directed upward.

But antisemitism makes Jews less safe, and it also undermines any movement clamoring for liberation. Social movements cannot win if they are focused on occult cabals rather than those in power. "People who try to change the world using Illuminati theory are boxing with shadows," claim the authors of the movement pamphlet *How to Overthrow the Illuminati*. "The shadow is the shadow of capital, the real alien created by all of us, through the social relationships we participate in every day."

Any organizer will tell you that rhetoric must remain concrete. Human beings don't work on abstractions; we need targets with names and faces. When we talk about multilayered economic injustices, such as rising wealth inequality or the global financial crisis, it is sometimes necessary and appropriate to blame a recognizable "bankster" or executive for the larger issue. But it is also important to remind people that the entire system of capitalism, not just its leaders, is the real problem. Our tendency to personalize these structures, systems, and processes is part of what opens the door to conspiracism and antisemitism. "The problem isn't so much that Jeff Bezos is greedy," Dania Rajendra, inaugural director of Athena, a national coalition challenging Amazon's antidemocratic influence, monopoly power, and worker abuse, told us:

> The problem is that our governing systems have allowed any individual to amass that much money and that much power. The business decisions that someone like Jeff Bezos makes are the same whether he is Jewish or not Jewish. They are the same logics I would need to use, if I were in charge of Amazon.com. It is simply not a function of who they are as people.

This balance is tricky since, while the root causes of economic oppression are systemic, there actually *is* an elite caste in the world; they are driven in no small part by greed and callousness, and they don't have our best interests at heart. But conspiracy theories mystify the elite as larger-than-life, supernatural, and, therefore, impossible to beat. The "hidden truth" these theories promise is not only wrong—it's profoundly disempowering. Avoiding conspiracism requires discipline around characterizing our opponents, explaining issues, and crafting strategies for mobilizing our potential base. "There's a huge need to connect the malfeasance of a single corporation, or a single executive, with the fundamental system that creates the incentives to malfeasance," Rajendra told us.

As we discussed, the actual world of power is often more transparent, and less all-knowing, than the fables conspiracy theories tell about it. Seeing those in power as fallible, beatable, is the cornerstone of enabling change.

"One of the great mistakes of conspiracy theorists is to take these everyday machinations [of power] as evidence for some grand conspiracy at the societal and historical levels," said G. William Domhoff, who conducts "power structure" research into the way that the wealthy try to build consensus, exert influence, and control capital. Rather, it is best, he suggests, to "study visible institutions, take most of what elites say as statements of their values and intentions, and recognize that elites sometimes have to compromise, and sometimes lose. Conspiracists study alleged behind the scenes groups, think everything elites say is a trick, and claim that elites never lose."[36]

For Dania Rajendra, building broad-based movements to transform our economy is a crucial way to fight antisemitism. "There's only one nonviolent, anti-Nazi strategy worth spit," she said in a 2018 speech to progressives in Minnesota. "It's shared prosperity. It's new rules for companies, it's providing for people's human needs, it's reducing the number of times a day a person thinks, 'Why do I feel so poor? Why do I feel so powerless?' And while we are fighting for those policies, it's giving better and more true explanations to those questions, as well as 'here's what we can do about it, together.'"[37]

Movements to end oppression have long understood that their freedom will ultimately require ending capitalism. It's no surprise, then, that alongside the "socialism of fools," those who benefit from the unjust status quo have also used another powerful trope to beat back revolutionary movements for change—the "Judeo-Bolshevik."

THE RED MENACE: ANTISEMITISM
AND ANTI-COMMUNISM

When James Green[1] first saw online attacks against him escalate, he couldn't fathom why they were mentioning his Jewishness. Green had maintained little connection to his Jewish identity, and it didn't feature in his public-facing scholarship or activism.

"I grew up in an environment where blatant antisemitism just wasn't a thing," Green, who was a tenured philosophy professor at a rural Midwestern university, told us. Green had never hidden it, or any other part of his life: he was an anarchist with a history of outspoken activism. Green had twelve years of spotless employment with the university, but suddenly an outrage was brewing that he had little context for.

In June 2020, as Black Lives Matter protesters were flooding cities around the United States, Green joined an activist effort to take down a local Confederate monument. Before long, a crowd of neo-Confederates, Proud Boys, and members of the alt-right came to defend the statue.

Local right-wingers discovered Green had changed his Facebook cover photo to a black banner that read, "abolish the police." They inundated his university with phone calls and emails, accusing him of being a Marxist operative indoctrinating their kids, an antifa member with violence on the brain.

But also, a Jew. "I don't know how these people got it into their head that I was Jewish in the first place," said Green, but to the far-right, a white professor lingering around antiracist protests and calling to abolish the police had to be a Jew; it was the only way this made sense. To them, the Jew is less a person than a category, an archetype that distorts an otherwise harmonious world.

"From the beginning, a lot of the death threats and hate mail I was receiving had antisemitic content," Green told us. Anonymous harassers promised to come to campus and shoot him or bomb his office. "It became all about Jew this, kike that, and then stuff like 'we're going to throw you in the oven.' Jewish Marxist, Jewish antifa, and then others, like '[N-word] lover' and 'race traitor.'"

National right-wing groups like Turning Point USA and pundits like Rush Limbaugh amplified the attacks on a larger stage. Across the street from Green's house, a protest encampment formed, filled with an organized stream of right-wing agitators looking through binoculars and yelling at him to come over whenever he glanced outside.

It all escalated even further that fall, when Rightists circulated a video of a speech Green gave at a rally on campus. They started going through his social media posts, and finally found what they were looking for: a Facebook comment where Green allegedly advocated for violence against police. Then all hell broke loose.

The death threats avalanched by the hundreds. Green described bullets sent to the university with his name written on them, rape threats against his family members, and two break-ins at his home where the word "kike" was spraypainted alongside a swastika and "antifa." When a reporter came out to cover the attacks, he asked Green why the word "kike" was included. "Because I'm Jewish," Green responded. "Yeah, but I don't get it," the reporter continued, stumped. It just didn't make sense. What does being Jewish have to do with anything?

Antisemitism isn't always expressed in this blunt, explicit

form. Often, it anchors itself to some other type of accusation: communist, capitalist, banker, conspirator, elitist. One
category bleeds into the other, compounding into an odd-
shaped tumor, until the accusations are indistinguishable
from one another. The "antifa" accusation was just the new-
est incarnation of "Judeo-Bolshevik," a subversive actor running underneath America's racial order, looking to dethrone
that which we hold most sacred. "For them it's all a hetero-
clite combination. So, they think [the Jewishness and Left-
ism] are totally inseparable," Alexander Reid Ross, a Jewish
antifascist journalist, told us, describing similar slurs against
him by the online far-right.

By December, Green was living in perpetual fear and had
to leave. He packed his car in the middle of the night and
skipped town, staying with his parents. He filed for emergency
leave and, facing a bout of suicidal ideation, checked into a
psychiatric hospital.

After offering little support and publicly condemning
Green's speech, the university demanded he return to the
classroom. With the danger taking a toll on his mental health
and his Americans with Disabilities Act request to teach re-
motely denied, he resigned his tenured position, effectively
destroying his academic career and leaving him in a spiral of
metastasizing debt. His ideation became more real, and he
attempted suicide, leaving him back in the hospital. He had
nothing left.

Green eventually moved on and tried desperately to put the
past behind him, as he started a yearlong visiting appointment
at another university. But his tenure was a thing of the past,
and the trauma would remain.

The persecution Green faced reflects the latest chapter in
the long history of the antisemitic trope of "Judeo-Bolshevism."
This is the idea that "the Jew" is responsible for communism, a
revolutionary firebrand, sparking global insurrection in order
to undermine the "natural order" and institute some totalitar-

ian nightmare in its place. This fear has haunted the reactionary imagination throughout the modern era, and remains one of the strongest, and most deadly, sources of antisemitism. In this chapter, we will look at how this fear has animated right-wing politics for over a century and into the present, in open and coded ways.

RED SCARE

Accusations that the Left is little more than a vast, well-organized Jewish conspiracy have been lobbed by the Right ever since the first cries of "liberty, equality, fraternity" echoed across revolutionary France in the late eighteenth century. These claims picked up steam throughout the nineteenth century, as radical movements swept across Europe and North America. After the 1917 Russian Revolution, with the circulation of texts like *The Protocols of the Elders of Zion*, the specter of "Judeo-Bolshevism"[2] gripped the imagination of millions of Rightists and centrists, convinced that communism represented a vast Jewish plot, an aggressive racial threat to Western civilization, much like the specter of "radical Islam" for Islamophobes today. In the middle of the twentieth century, Nazism presented itself as an immense, organized pan-European crusade against "Judeo-Bolshevism"—resulting in the genocide of a third of all Jews in the world—that began in the heart of the "civilized" West.

After the war, while explicit antisemitism fell out of favor, militant anti-communism carried conspiratorial and antisemitic undertones during the era of McCarthyism and continuing for decades afterward. Today, three decades after the fall of the Berlin Wall, fever dreams of "Cultural Marxists," "globalists," antifa, George Soros, and other Jewishly inflected bogeymen continue to serve as core organizing tools for the Right.

To be sure, plenty of Jews have enthusiastically contributed to movements for social change throughout the modern era,

In revolutionary Russia, in countries like Germany and France, throughout the United States, and in parts of the Middle East and North Africa such as Algeria and Egypt, Jews faced entrenched social ostracism and discrimination, and many flocked to movements promising a new social order wherein humans could transcend old divisions and encounter each other anew on a plane of true equality. Many already lived in cities, where radical ideas tended to proliferate, either because ruling elites had long confined them to urban ghettoization or because, in places like Eastern Europe and Russia, they had recently been forced, alongside so many other proletarians, to move from the countryside and work and live in crowded urban factories and slums.

We Jews are a radical people, and the authors of this book count ourselves among the proud inheritors of the living legacy of the Jewish Left. We draw strength from the memory of Jewish socialists, communists, anarchists, and other organizers such as Emma Goldman, Leon Trotsky, Alexander Berkman, and Rosa Luxemburg; the active involvement of many Jews in the American labor and civil rights movement; and the continued participation of Jews in social justice activism. The influential role of Jews in Leftist social movements is the result of a confluence of factors, none of which require conspiratorial claims of Jewish power or the assumption that all Jews must hold the same political opinions: Jews faced widespread systemic oppression, thus leading many to join social movements to remake the world, and the stories that define our religious tradition put human liberation at their center.

"One of the deepest strains in Jewish life is the moral injunction 'to become,'" wrote author Vivian Gornick in *The Romance of American Communism*, profiling twentieth-century American Jewish communists. "This strain runs with subterranean force through most Jewish lives regardless of what other aspects of experience and personality separate them. Thus, Jews 'became' through an intensity of religious or intellectual or political life. In the highly political twentieth century they became, in overwhelming numbers, socialists, anarchists, Zionists—and Communists."[3]

But the way that the racist Right has tried to tell this story is to recast the Jewish experience in the most pernicious, diabolical, and hyperbolic ways possible, alleging that Jews are inherently subversive and that we use left-wing politics to exploit non-Jews for our own benefit. As always, they speak not of actual, existing Jews, in all our diversity and complexity, but of "the Jew," the all-powerful figment of their antisemitic imagination.

The Right aims "Judeo-Bolshevik" conspiracy theories as weapons against revolutionary movements, hoping to fracture the wider unity progressives need to build in order to win. By portraying progressive movements for change as driven not by a grassroots rejection of conditions of brutal inequality and immiseration, but rather by a top-down secret cabal bent on world domination, these false stories help to undercut the possibility of solidarity. They block the ability of millions to find common cause with movements for change, to see their own struggles and interests reflected there, and to join and help build a better world.

JUDEO-BOLSHEVISM: A VIRAL MEME

In France at the end of the nineteenth century, a scandal that came to be known as the Dreyfus affair helped inaugurate a new era in the growth of antisemitism's appeal. French society was reeling from prolonged political crisis, economic instability, and the trauma of military defeat, and nationalism and antisemitism were on the rise. When Captain Alfred Dreyfus, a French Jewish artillery officer, was falsely convicted of treason, nationalist pundits like Édouard Drumont as well as social conservatives, royalists, military and Church leaders, and others rushed to support the accusation.

For many of his accusers, Dreyfus served as a symbol for Jewish "dual loyalty" and perfidy. Liberals, socialist parties, trade unionists, and a section of the French cultural elite leapt to defend Dreyfus as a symbol of the Republic and its Enlightenment promise that, they insisted, could not be abandoned. For social conservatives, accordingly, attacking Dreyfus became a way to express their deep skepticism, or outright hostility, toward liberalism in the century since the French Revolution. While Dreyfus was ultimately exonerated, monarchist groups like Action Française held antisemitic riots in cities across France, and the episode served as what Hannah Arendt, writing after the Holocaust, called "a huge dress rehearsal for a performance that had to be put off for more than three decades."[4] The battle lines had been drawn, and antisemitism "knew" which side it was on.

Across Europe, rising nationalist movements did not invent their antisemitism from scratch. Modern antisemitism, as scholar Paul Hanebrink writes of the "Judeo-Bolshevik" peril, "was constructed from the raw materials of [Christian] anti-Judaism, recycled and rearranged to meet new requirements."[5] Ideas of Jews as the demonological Antichrist, emblem of Evil, the embodied "Other" of the community of pure Christian believers, continued to hold sway over the minds of millions across Europe.

Antisemitic pseudo-critiques of capitalism, which we also discussed previously, were in the mix as well. In turn-of-the-century Russia, for example, pro-czarist armed bands like the Black Hundreds "pretended that Jews formed a capitalist-revolutionary conspiracy," as author Norman Cohn put it, "and that in order to prevent this conspiratorial body from establishing a monstrous tyranny the workers and peasants must stand firmly by the 'native' ruling class."[6]

The growing popularity of race science allowed many to understand the Jewish community in a new way, not as a religious community but rather as a separate racial group. The

Jews' attempts to integrate into Western societies, nationalists argued, were a ruse: While seeming to blend in, Jews remained strangers to the racial community of Europeans. Germany was for the Germans, they insisted, and France for the French—but Jews, forming a distinct minority in country after country, belonged fully to no European land.

All these trends—nationalism, race science, the "socialism of fools," anti-communism, and, underneath it all, a deep reservoir of Christian anti-Judaism—eventually converged in the idea of "Judeo-Bolshevism," allowing millions to "racialize" communism as a Jewish plot. For a Right wing that saw nationalism as healthy, communism was an internationalist conspiracy, pushed primarily by a foreign tribe. Much like the Right's crusade against "wokeism" today, this narrative was fashioned by politicians, religious leaders, journalists, and tastemakers into what scholar Shulamit Volkov called a "cultural code": a shared collective modality of viewing the world and orienting oneself and ones group within it.

At the dawn of the twentieth century, the Right was terrified by growing revolutionary movements in Russia, across Europe, and around the world. At a time when millions of workers, peasants, and other oppressed communities were casting their lot with revolutionary movements, the many opponents of these movements—such as industrialists, bankers, aristocrats, political elites, church leaders, and nationalist movements—needed propaganda tools to beat back this threat to their status quo. The myth of the Jewish conspiracy, it was hoped, could help lure the masses away from the Left by spreading a lie about its malevolent intentions.

Bolstered by texts like the *Protocols*, the "Judeo-Bolshevik" myth first took root in czarist Russia, where it was used by the czarist secret police and leaders of the aristocracy and Russian Orthodox Church. "The efforts to replace the autocracy of the divinely appointed Tsar by a constitution and a parliament," read one of many proclamations that appeared in villages across Russia, "are inspired by those bloodsuckers, the Jews, the Armenians, and the Poles. Beware of the Jews! All the evil, all the misfortune of our country comes from the Jews."[7]

The success of the 1917 Russian Revolution inspired a surge of triumphalist worker organizing across Europe, with many on the Left convinced that revolution would soon sweep the continent and usher in a new era of international peace, good-will, and fraternity. The Right made the "Judeo-Bolshevik" meme go viral in response, seizing upon the relatively high number of Jews in Bolshevik leadership to tell their twisted tale. Similar to present-day Islamophobia and anti-China saber-rattling, the new "Judeo-Bolshevik" Soviet government was often depicted in Orientalist terms as a diabolical power in the East, threatening the survival of European Christendom in a "clash of civilizations."

This conspiracy theory was not solely the preserve of avowed right-wingers. In February 1920, future British prime minister Winston Churchill, then serving in the Liberal gov-ernment, penned an op-ed in the *Illustrated Sunday Herald*, "Zionism Versus Bolshevism: A Struggle for the Soul of the Jewish People," in which he expressed his deep opposition to the Russian Revolution in starkly antisemitic terms. Churchill condemned "the schemes of the international Jews" and a Jewish "world-wide conspiracy for the overthrow of civilisa-tion" that began with Karl Marx and "has been steadily grow-ing," and insisted that the Bolsheviks aimed for nothing less than a "world-wide communistic State under Jewish domina-tion."[8] That such a screed was penned by the politician who less than two decades later would help lead the world's war effort against Nazi Germany shows just how unquestioningly these tropes were accepted by the political center (much like Islamophobia today).

The "Judeo-Bolshevik" conspiracy theory was, until the mid-twentieth century, a viral meme, easily transplanted across many different contexts to fit smoothly within a broader worldview. As Hanebrink notes, the myth "had power in particular contexts to crystallize a wider set of political and cultural anxieties in ways that other antisemitic stereotypes did not."[16] The "Judeo-Bolshevik" menace, in the Right's view, wasn't just organizing workers at the workplace—it was a broad cultural, spiritual, and civilizational threat.

"Judeo-Bolshevism" was the force responsible for sexual liberation and the emancipation of women; for new, threatening cultural formations like jazz and Hollywood; for the empowerment of Black Americans; for rapid advances in technology; and paradoxically, as discussed previously, Jews could simultaneously be blamed for the power of finance, speculation, debt, and the other "abstract," impersonal machinations of global capitalism.

Like today's far-right acolytes, many of the myth's most enthusiastic proponents argued for a wholesale rejection of modernity, claiming a desire to "turn back the clock" to earlier eras of aristocratic feudalism, religious traditionalism, and more. While in truth, these movements were as "modern" and contemporary as what they claimed to oppose, they nonetheless were savvy in portraying themselves as the "authentic" preservers of a mythical premodern past.

"WHOEVER IS NOT WILLING TO TALK ABOUT CAPITALISM SHOULD ALSO KEEP QUIET ABOUT FASCISM"

The myth of the "Judeo-Bolshevik" menace also held sway in America. In the late nineteenth and early twentieth century, as millions of Eastern European Jewish immigrants came to America fleeing persecution, nativists spread xenophobic narratives that these immigrants were a subversive threat to the American way of life, bringing "foreign" ideologies like communism that threatened the sanctity of faith, flag, and family. As discussed earlier, automobile magnate Henry

Ford, fearful of worker unrest and cross-racial solidarity in his factories, eagerly spread conspiracy theories of an imminent "Judeo-Bolshevik" takeover of America with his printed anthology *The International Jew*, handed out to customers in Ford dealerships nationwide and serialized in his newspaper, *The Dearborn Independent*.

America was experiencing its first Red Scare, with suspected communists chased out of labor unions and publishing houses and often deported. Antisemitism played a prominent role. "Practically the whole world knows," ran one Polish-language periodical in Chicago in 1924, "that the Jews direct socialism, Jews who through socialism are trying to stir up in various countries ferment and social unrest . . . [which] always results in harm to Christian society and in profit and gain for the Jews."[10]

Nativist elites such as Madison Grant, Burton J. Hendrick, and Lothrop Stoddard insisted that Jewish immigrants were "Asiatics," whose continued arrival, alongside Asian Americans and other minorities, threatened the racial integrity of white Anglo-Saxon Protestant America and whose supposed Bolshevik tendencies represented the threat of cultural subversion as well. The restrictionist immigration laws passed by the US Congress in 1921 and 1924 banned most immigration from Eastern Europe and Asia, and greatly inspired the Nazi movement in Europe. Today, the American far-right cites them as inspiration for their own calls for an immigration moratorium.[11]

With the onset of the Great Depression in 1929, millions of unemployed workers across the United States and Europe were left destitute and desperate for an alternative to the instabilities of capitalism. Leftists kicked into overdrive, insisting a world of equality and justice was possible and engaging in deep grassroots organizing across factories and fields, street corners and union halls, ballot boxes and militant marches to try to bring that world into being.

Radical movements on the Right got busy too, and business and political leaders were eager to make common cause with fascists rather than risk the overthrow of the entire capitalist system. Recognizing the ways in which fascists and capitalists worked hand in hand to beat back the Left, German Jewish refugee and critical theorist Max Horkheimer wrote in 1939 that "whoever is not willing to talk about capitalism should also keep quiet about fascism . . . Fascism solidifies the extreme class differences which [the capitalist system] ultimately produced."[12]

While these fascist movements were anti-communist at the core, they also mimicked its revolutionary energy. Benito Mussolini, a former militant socialist, called his fascist movement a "revolution against revolution,"[13] and it was precisely in this pseudo-revolutionary quality of fascism—its claim to "punch up," on behalf of the downtrodden, against an all-powerful communist conspiracy poised to overtake the world—that the antisemitism proved most useful.

In the first decade of its rise, the Nazi Party channeled anti-capitalist antisemitism, which they hoped would help mobilize the masses and win recruits away from the Left. But by the mid-1930s, they had violently purged these racial socialists, called "Strasserites," from party leadership. The Nazi Party solidified its power in Germany through an alliance with big business, and Nazism, more than most fascist movements, gave communism a Jewish face. "It was the Jew," thundered Nazi propaganda minister Joseph Goebbels in a 1935 speech, "who discovered Marxism. It is the Jew who for decades past has endeavored to stir up world revolutions through the medium of Marxism. It is the Jew who is today at the head of Marxism in all the countries of the world. Only in the brain of a nomad who is without nation, race and country could this Satanism have been hatched."[14]

While the Left proposed working-class solidarity as the solution to the market crash, the radical Right proposed the solidarity of the master race. The "socialism of fools" helped fascist movements capture energy from the Left, while their "Judeo-Bolshevik" myth demonized the Left. Whether it cast them as capitalists or as communists, antisemites insisted the Jews had uprooted the organic racial *volk*, or community, from its ties to blood and soil, and that by removing the parasite, the *volk* would reclaim its vitality. Much like contemporary "great replacement" conspiracy theories, the Nazis believed that Jews used Soviet communism to transform millions of racially inferior Slavic peoples into their foot soldiers, in order to swarm the Aryan West.[15]

While fascism gained ground in Europe, US reactionaries mobilized antisemitism as well. Opponents of President Roosevelt's massively popular New Deal slandered the social uplift programs as a communist "Jew Deal" and referred to Roosevelt as "Rosenfeld," falsely insinuating he was Jewish or controlled by Jews. In the late 1930s and 1940s, organizations deeply sympathetic to Nazi Germany, such as the Silver Shirts, German American Bund, and the Christian Front held rallies and marches, desecrated Jewish cemeteries, vandalized Jewish-owned businesses, and attacked Jews on the streets in New York, Boston, and elsewhere across the country.[16]

After the 1938 Kristallnacht pogrom in Germany shocked the world, far-right Catholic preacher Father Coughlin used his widely popular radio program to blame Jews for the persecution they faced under Nazism. Coughlin told listeners that Nazism "evolved to act as a defense mechanism against the incursions of Communism," suggesting that the communist movement was almost solely the invention of Jewish minds.[17] At this time, at least forty-five radio stations carried Coughlin's program, and millions of Americans listened regularly. His office reportedly received eighty thousand letters a week from concerned citizens around the country, requiring the effort of 105 staff members to read them.

On February 20, 1939, an estimated nineteen thousand fascist supporters, including over 1,700 New York City policemen, crammed into Madison Square Garden for a rally organized by the German American Bund in honor of George Washington's birthday. As Nazi flags dotted the crowd and cries of "Heil Hitler!" reverberated, banners read "Wake Up America! Smash Jewish Communism" and "Stop Jewish Domination of Christian America!"[18]

By the time the dust settled in mid-1945, Nazi crusaders against "Judeo-Bolshevism" had slaughtered one-third of the Jewish people worldwide, and two-thirds of the Jewish population in Europe. Fascist movements had bid for power in dozens of countries around the world. Millions of trade unionists and Leftists, Soviet citizens and Poles, as well as members of Roma communities, LGBTQ people, and swaths of other marginalized groups were killed by the Nazi menace. But the story was not over.

When the United States entered World War II, many of its homegrown fascist movements, which had argued for military nonintervention, faced state repression and lost some popularity. Then, as the horrors of the Holocaust became widely known after the war, explicit antisemitism became largely discredited in Western discourse. In response to these changes, Holocaust denial, the claim that the Nazi genocide was a Jewish hoax, started to percolate on the radical Right.

As the Cold War ramped up in the 1950s, the American anti-communist witch hunts led by figures like Senator Joseph McCarthy carried currents of conspiracism. "How can we account for our present situation," insisted McCarthy in a 1951 speech, "unless we believe that men high in this government are concerting to deliver us to disaster? This must be the product of a great conspiracy on a scale so immense as to dwarf any previous such venture in the history of man."[19]

While Jews comprised less than 2 percent of the American population, they made up two-thirds of those questioned by McCarthy's Permanent Subcommittee on Investigations in

1952. McCarthyist antisemitism played upon an associative link between Jews and communism deeply ingrained in the American public. A 1948 survey by the American Jewish Committee found that 21 percent of Americans believed that "most Jews are Communists," and more than half associated Jews with spying on behalf of the Soviet Union.[20] On the Senate floor, Senator John Rankin repeatedly "unmasked" the "true" Yiddish names of Hollywood figures brought in for questioning, mirroring tactics of the Soviet Union's antisemitic "anticosmopolitan" campaigns of the same period.[21]

The crusade peaked with the heavily publicized trial and execution of Ethel and Julius Rosenberg, accused of Soviet spying, in 1953, which sent waves of terror throughout the American Jewish community, still reeling from the horrors of the Holocaust less than a decade earlier. "Thousands of Jews," wrote contemporary Jewish Left organizer Yotam Marom, "wondering if they were still in the midst of the genocide many of them had barely escaped, gathered outside Madison Square Garden in breathless silence as the state executed the Rosenbergs."[22]

Unsurprisingly, the anti-communist crusade at the heart of the Rosenberg case was enthusiastically backed by big business. The conspiracist anti-communist John Birch Society, for example, was formed and led by board members of the National Association of Manufacturers, what scholar Matthew Dallek called "the nation's most influential pro-industry lobbying group."[23]

All in all, by spreading anti-communist antisemitism, these capitalists got a high return on their investment. McCarthyism decimated the fighting Left in the United States, sundered ties of solidarity between white Jewish and Black non-Jewish organizers, and helped to pressure the labor movement, then at the peak of its powers, to adopt a more quietist, reformist orientation toward business. It convinced a generation of Jews to tamper down their progressive activism and assimilate more heavily into white American cultural codes as survival strategies to avoid persecution.

"In many Jewish households and organizations," wrote activist and scholar April Rosenblum in 2006, "it was felt that the Rosenbergs were singled out not only as Communists but as Jews . . . In the post-Holocaust, anti-communist era, Jews had compelling reasons to want to blend in to the crowd. Both the 'carrot' of upward mobility and the 'sticks' of antisemitic violence and red-baiting motivated American Jews to avoid seeming too foreign, too visible, too 'ethnic.'"[24] Like today, antisemitism wasn't only targeting Jews—it bolstered white supremacy by fracturing social movements and dividing potential allies.

The authors carry this legacy in our own family histories. In the early 1950s Ben's grandmother, Kate Lorber, was a public school teacher in Harlem. "I definitely felt socialism strongly," she told us. The daughter of working-class Jewish immigrants, Kate attended Paul Robeson concerts, supported civil rights causes, and, like most other American Jews of the era, moved in a left-wing cultural milieu. But she decided not to join the heavily Jewish teacher's union and Socialist Party, because these institutions were targeted so severely by antisemitic McCarthyism at that time. "Of course my heart was in it, but I was afraid. After McCarthy I didn't want to join anything." Nonetheless Kate maintained a commitment to activism, later marching against the Vietnam War and supporting other causes.[25]

Despite fears of McCarthyist repression, American Jews continued to support liberation movements. Many lent an active hand in the growing struggle for Black civil rights, and groups like the KKK, desperate to preserve Jim Crow apartheid, cast Jews as the secret communist force behind the movement to unseat the established order. "Jews behind race mixing!" championed one circa-1950 flier by the Atlanta-based Christian Anti-Jewish Party. "It is the Jews who are leading the fight to destroy segregation in Atlanta schools . . . America must awaken to the Jew attack against White People!"[26] In 1957 and 1958, at least eight synagogues were torched or fire-bombed across the Jim Crow South, amidst a wave of attacks against Black churches.[27]

"WHO STOLE OUR CULTURE?"

On April 27, 2019, a white nationalist walked into a Chabad synagogue in Poway, California, during Shabbat services and opened fire with an AR-15, killing one and injuring three others. In the shooter's manifesto, he listed a litany of crimes he attributes to Jews, stretching all the way back to the blood libel myth and culminating in the canard that Jews are responsible for "the meticulously planned genocide of the European race," as he put it. Among these supposed crimes of the Jews, one stands out. Nearly thirty years after the fall of the Berlin Wall, he still blamed Jews, in his words, "for their role in cultural Marxism and communism."[28]

Even while the Cold War ended in capitalism's favor, with the rise of illiberal nationalism in the twenty-first century, conspiracy theories about communism and Jews (or their analogues) again loom large as bogeymen across the Right. The "Cultural Marxism" conspiracy theory was the brainchild of William Lind, a conservative strategist who played a key behind-the-scenes role in building the institutions of the contemporary US Right. After the fall of the Soviet Union, Lind and others realized that anti-communism might no longer serve as a reliable glue to unify their movement, and they needed a new civilizational enemy for their Manichean narrative.

"Sometime during the last half-century," Lind explained in a 2012 article,

> someone stole our culture. Just 50 years ago, in the 1950s, America was a great place. It was safe. It was decent . . . Where did it all go? How did that America

become the sleazy, decadent place we live in today—
so different that those who grew up prior to the '60s
feel like it's a foreign country? . . . Incredible as it may
seem, just as the old economic Marxism of the Soviet
Union has faded away, a new cultural Marxism has
become the ruling ideology of America's elites. The
No. 1 goal of that cultural Marxism, since its creation,
has been the destruction of Western culture and the
Christian religion.[29]

Lind found his new nemesis in the Frankfurt School, a group
of German Jewish critical theorists who fled Nazi Germany in
the 1930s and established the New School for Social Research
in New York City. In the mid-twentieth century, writers like
Theodor Adorno, Herbert Marcuse, and Max Horkheimer
used the tools of Marxism, psychoanalysis, sociology, aesthetics, and critical theory to interrogate authoritarian trends in
American consumer capitalism and popular culture. In real
terms, the influence of the Frankfurt School theorists has
mostly been limited to the realm of academia, where classic
works such as Adorno's *The Authoritarian Personality* and Marcuse's *One-Dimensional Man* have given intellectuals analytical
tools and frameworks to analyze mass society.

In Lind's story, however, the influence of the Frankfurt
School has been vast, warping and corroding nearly every
nook and cranny of American life. The "Cultural Marxist" plot,
so the story goes, is responsible for the spread of feminism
and LGBTQ identity and rights movements, sexual liberalism,
changing gender roles, secularism, multiculturalism, and political correctness across American society. These Frankfurt
School theorists, the Right claims, have stealthily embedded
their ideology within American news media, entertainment,
popular music, academia, and other spheres of cultural influence in order to engineer a sinister, top-down revolution and
undermine the foundations of the West.

Lind's narrative is fast moving mainstream. Reports published by leading conservative think tanks like the Heritage Foundation,[30] speeches by politicians like Florida governor and 2024 presidential hopeful Ron DeSantis,[31] and briefings prepared by former President Trump's cabinet[32] cast "Cultural Marxism" as America's ultimate enemy within.

In public, Lind and many other proponents of the "Cultural Marxism" conspiracy theory insist it has nothing to do with antisemitism. When speaking to certain audiences, however, their mask slips a bit.

In 2002, Lind spoke at the annual conference of the Barnes Review, a Holocaust-denial organization founded by stalwart white nationalist Willis Carto. "I do want to make it clear," Lind told the assembled audience, "that we [Lind and his organization, the Free Congress Foundation] are not among those who question whether the Holocaust occurred." That being said, when discussing the Frankfurt School, Lind made a point of stressing to the audience that "these guys were all Jewish . . . Their whole plan," he elucidated, shifting into the present tense, "is the destruction of Western culture."[33]

Conservative fearmongering against liberal Jewish financier George Soros, "globalists," antifa, and more tells a similar tale of the imagined sinister elites behind Black Lives Matter, non-white immigration, LGBTQ rights, and other named evils of the Left. "I think there's a great argument that the origins of political correctness and cultural Marxism was Jewish," said Proud Boys founder Gavin McInnes to his thousands of viewers. McInnes typically ducks behind the fact that the Proud Boys welcome Jews[34] (and even had a chapter in Israel), but antisemitism runs underneath these movements and it only takes a mild nudge for them to say the quiet part out loud.

From George Soros to "Critical Race Theory," "globalists" to "gender ideology," the Right's fearmongering about an elite liberal conspiracy clustered in the media, educational institutions, and social movements, can be wielded against almost any movement or social group that threatens power. This conspiracy theory narrative is intersectional, allowing believers to connect the dots between every progressive cause and marginalized community under the sun by imagining a single enemy behind it all. It helps white nationalists, Christian Rightists, and the MAGA mob come together under the banner of a powerful victimhood narrative. By imagining themselves as frontline defenders of Western civilization against Soros-financed Black Lives Matter protesters in the streets and "Cultural Marxist" professors in the classrooms, they tap into a cultural code, a powerful sense of belonging in the community of "real Americans."

This narrative is inherently demeaning to Black, LGBTQ, and other communities, since it assumes they cannot possibly be capable of winning their own liberation—rather, there must be some hidden hand behind the scenes. It is also a clear and present danger to Jews today. When political leaders repeat these narratives ad nauseam, they prime millions to see the world through an antisemitic frame, inspiring a few to take matters into their own hands.

While the Right is most adept at deploying the "specter of Judeo-Bolshevism," the liberal center has its own conspiracy theory culture. Historian Barnaby Raine has analyzed the ways that liberal fearmongering blaming "Kremlin hackers" for the rise of Trumpism, or scapegoating China as a civilizational enemy, tells a similar story of shadowy, foreign elites who are misleadingly blamed as the "hidden hand" behind deeper, structural problems.[35] As we discuss later, when Rightists, centrists, and some liberals team up to demonize the Left as a sinister, subversive den of antisemites, this functions as a new kind of McCarthyism—though this time, ironically, they're claiming to protect and defend Jews.

Business elites get in on the game as well. In 2018, Facebook hired a right-wing opposition research firm to tar activists who criticized the company's monopolistic abuses by associating these activists with George Soros. "This narrative has really dangerous antisemitic undertones," Rashad Robinson, executive director at Color of Change, a racial justice group targeted by these attacks, told *The Guardian*. "It's also deeply anti-black—the idea that our strategies, our ideas, our vision are somehow built off some puppet master."[36]

ANTISEMITISM'S HOME ON THE RIGHT

Antisemitism finds its most natural home in the ranks of the Right. Whenever there arises a vigorous, determined, and successful movement for human emancipation, its opponents can rely on antisemitism as a central plank and organizing principle.

A century ago, the "Judeo-Bolshevik" meme went viral across the Euro-Atlantic world amidst a protracted economic crisis and the possibility of revolutionary upheaval in its wake. Similarly today, the rise of antisemitism is part of a powerful current of right-wing populism that has emerged worldwide in response to the 2008 economic crash—the worst since the Great Depression. In an era of dizzying precarity, people are looking for answers, and these conspiracy theories are happy to provide.

At the same time, the Left in the United States is making powerful gains. Movements like Occupy Wall Street, Black Lives Matter, the Bernie Sanders campaigns, trans visibility and empowerment, worker unionization, and antifascism have reconfigured the landscape, delivering powerful challenges to power.

Right-wing fearmongering reflects the anxieties of the powerful in an era of palpable threats to their dominance. Like a cornered animal, white supremacy is growling and baring its teeth, and these conspiracy theories are part of its deadly roar. This growing fear testifies, in its ferocity, to the advances progressives have already made, and the very real possibility of our continued success. And it is in the white nationalist movement—the deadliest threat to Jews in American history—that the Right's roar is loudest.

PART III

WHAT DOES ANTISEMITISM
LOOK LIKE TODAY?

SEVEN

A RACE APART: ANTISEMITISM AND THE
WHITE NATIONALIST MOVEMENT

When the alt-right burst onto the national scene ahead of the 2015 presidential campaign of Donald Trump, many were shocked that such an openly supremacist and bigoted movement could still find legs in the United States. While it was a surprise to many, some antifascists and careful observers of the far-right were noticing something happening. For decades, they had seen the white nationalist movement grow increasingly energized and bold.

"After the 2016 presidential election, I decided to get organizing," Mimi Arbeit, a Jewish scholar and activist, told us. She joined the Charlottesville, Virginia, chapter of Showing Up for Racial Justice (SURJ), a national group that organizes white communities against racism.

In May 2017, after the Charlottesville city council vote to remove the city's Confederate monuments was blocked by lawsuits, alt-right leader Richard Spencer organized flash mobs at the statues.[1] In July, the Ku Klux Klan had a rally in the city, and alt-right organizer Jason Kessler had also filed for an August 12 permit for a protest he called Unite the Right. Arbeit joined the intense counter-organizing across those months, building a media strategy and coordinating with community networks to oppose the feared alt-right onslaught.

"The answer is we need twenty thousand people there to tell these people to fuck off," Ben Doernberg, an IfNotNow activist who grew up in Charlottesville, described the prevailing mood among activists. "People just don't understand how big this is going to be." Dedicated antifascists knew Unite the Right would be a crescendo for the white nationalist movement, weaving its many strands into one cohesive, and potentially violent, show of force. Doernberg was hoping to mobilize a large Jewish contingent to take the streets, as part of the counterdemonstration that local activists were organizing. Instead, he got the message that many Jewish community leaders, taking advice from the ADL, would be staying home.

"A local activist messaged me a screenshot of the permit and was like, 'you should know this is happening . . . next door to your synagogue,'" Rabbi Rachel Schmelkin, who served at Congregation Beth Israel, the only synagogue in Charlottesville, told us. She and her congregants faced difficult questions. What kind of security should Congregation Beth Israel have? Should Congregation Beth Israel join the counterprotest—or would squaring off with the alt-right merely provide the white supremacists the attention they desperately craved?

Rabbi Schmelkin started organizing with the Charlottesville Clergy Collective, which is an interfaith network formed after the 2015 white supremacist shooting at the Emanuel African Methodist Episcopal Church in nearby Charleston, South Carolina. When the KKK showed up in July of 2017, she joined the counterdemonstration alongside many congregants and joined another faith-based activist group that was formed in that event's wake called Congregate C'ville.

"People were scared," Schmelkin told us, "and the truth is that not everybody was aligned on what exactly to do . . . We had elderly congregants and people who had parents who were Holocaust survivors. Being out on the front lines was not the answer for everybody. So, we were trying to walk this line, saying that ignoring that this is happening was not the right option . . . [and] the community members chose to take various approaches to the presence of the alt-right and the KKK."

As the day of the alt-right rally approached, a large coalition of antiracist activists prepared to take the streets. This included some activists from IfNotNow, as well as a group of folks that would later form the Jewish Solidarity Caucus of the Democratic Socialists of America (DSA), and members of the Muslim-Jewish Anti-Fascist Front (MuJew Antifa), which had organized against Trump's Muslim ban and found a natural alliance, fighting Islamophobia and antisemitism across the MAGA movement.[2] "It felt extremely personal," Moishe Ben Marx, an organizer with MuJew Antifa who had come down from New York City and connected with Charlottesville's Jewish community, told us. "It felt like I was in the middle of a potential pogrom in the making, and I just felt the presence of my ancestors in a real way—[those] who had survived pogroms, or [those who] had not survived the Shoah."

The night before the rally, the now-infamous alt-right torch-lit march paraded through the University of Virginia campus, and chants of "Jews will not replace us" echoed across the campus. Counterdemonstrators were attacked as they desperately tried to hold their ground, and were supported by antifascists from out of town who came to support the community. "I was scared for my life. My chest started tightening up, and there was a ringing in my ears," remembers Diane D'Costa, a UVA student living on the quad the alt-right marched through. "I took off my Hamsa necklace . . . and my Shema ring . . . I just tried to hide any part of my Jewish identity." As she walked out of her room to leave, a man walked by with a swastika on his arm.[3]

"I've heard those chants, I've seen those marching, but they were always in these black-and-white movies," Tom Gutherz, senior rabbi at Congregation Beth Israel, told us. Gutherz's shock was eclipsed by anger, as congregants then asked if it was safe to bring their kids to preschool the next day, when the rally was scheduled to occur. "We had to explain to our kids why these people hate us . . . What do you say to an eight-year-old?"

Rabbi Gutherz is the son of a Holocaust survivor, and grew up, he told us, with the casual antisemitism of slurs and "pennies thrown." But this time, violent antisemitism was banked up not just against him, but his entire congregation and community. The alt-right rally would occur during Shabbat, and Congregation Beth Israel, Gutherz told us, knew they would not back down—they would continue their services *davka*, Hebrew for "specifically because," of this threat. They refused to let the Nazis undermine Jewish living.

On the day of the rally hundreds of white nationalists stormed the city, decked out in fascist insignia, waving Confederate flags, and carrying battle shields. Many Congregation Beth Israel congregants showed up to *daven* (pray) that morning and went to join the counterdemonstrations after services. Gutherz and others in the Clergy Collective had planned to hold hourly prayer services, but that plan went out the window in the ensuing chaos. With "roving bands of Nazis walking down the streets," the situation was dangerous, and some activists had set up care, medical, and food stations in neighboring parks, while Gutherz and others maintained a safe space in a nearby church where community members, often injured, could escape the expected violence.

Arbeit helped handle national media requests, while Doernberg ran the protest's live streams and antifascists hit the streets. Alan Zimmerman, president of Charlottesville Congregation Beth Israel, helped stand guard in front of the synagogue as the fascists marched by. "[I'm] appreciative of the fact that these [antifascists] are willing to get out into the street and fight these neo-Nazis," he told us, "and I think that history has shown that meeting forces like this in the streets is a part of the response that needs to be made."

Violent skirmishes took place in front of onlooking news cameras, and long after the fascists had seemingly pulled into retreat, one of them slammed his Dodge Charger into what had become a victory demonstration, killing antifascist protester Heather Heyer and injuring thirty-five others. Everyone was in shock, and it was unclear if more attacks were to follow. Word circulated that some alt-righters were planning on heading to Congregation Beth Israel to torch the synagogue, so the rabbis had to ensure it was clear, canceling later services.

Three days later, as news of Heyer's murder shocked the nation, then-president Trump gave a major boost to the white nationalist movement with his now-infamous remark, at a press conference at Trump Tower, that there were "very fine people on both sides" of the battle of Charlottesville.[4]

What happened there changed the entire community, everyone involved, and echoed throughout the country as people tried to understand where the violence had come from and why so many people felt unprepared for it. Like other marginalized groups, Jews felt fear—and it pushed them into action. "There was a sense that things are continuing to escalate, [that] the Jewish community is under attack and is not prepared to counter the attack," Moishe Ben Marx told us, "and we felt like we needed an organizational home for the Jewish antifascist Left in New York City." This led to the creation of Outlive Them, an NYC-based Jewish antifascist group, just weeks before the Pittsburgh synagogue shooting in October 2018.

After Unite the Right, "Congregation Beth Israel and the Jewish community there, and really Charlottesville in a larger way, started to take antiracism really seriously in a way that they never had before," Rabbi Schmelkin told us. The lesson had been clear—an organized response is necessary to push back on the advance of white supremacy.

"There were physical threats to my safety," Arbeit told us, noting how frightening the climate had gotten in advance of the rally. "But I felt that I had people in my corner. I didn't feel alone. I had people who were organized together to keep each other safe and to keep the community safe."

The battle raging that day in Charlottesville was a microcosm of the war waged every day on Capitol Hill, in classrooms, at school board meetings, and on the streets across the country: between those who think the United States ought to remain a country dominated by white Christian men, and those who fight for a truly pluralist, multiracial democracy. And in this contest over the contours of "we, the people," the American Jewish community finds itself in the crosshairs, alongside other groups. By understanding the white nationalist movement, and the antisemitism at its core, we can fight back.

WHITE NATIONALISM: AN AMERICAN MOVEMENT

White nationalism is a patently American phenomenon. The United States was founded as a settler-colonial society, built on the enslavement of Black people and the genocide of the Indigenous inhabitants of Turtle Island. Driven by the profit motive of racial capitalism, the inequalities of white supremacy have structured the institutions and social relations of American life. Some of the core "virtues" championed by today's white nationalist movement—like white racial purity and demographic dominance, racist segregation, patriarchal norms, and social traditionalism—were not uncommon among many white Americans until the mid-twentieth century. In the following decades, movements for racial, immigrant, feminist, and LGBTQ justice rattled these unjust foundations, and attempted to build a more equal society. Today's white nationalist movement is a desperate reaction to the very real successes of these movements for change.

White nationalists see themselves as beleaguered underdogs, brave, persecuted race rebels, raging heroically against a mammoth, overpowering anti-white system. They give this system a Jewish face, and imagine that, by overthrowing Jewish power, they can build a radically new social order of unbridled white dominance.[5]

White nationalism isn't only expressed through tiki-torch marches and neo-Nazi rallies. It also wears a suit and tie, sitting at the highest echelons of power. Donald Trump tapped nativist fearmongering, white resentment, and conspiracy theories to win the presidency. The Trump administration was stacked with advisers and organizations with close ties to white nationalists and far-right populists, from Steve Bannon and Stephen Miller to nativist groups like the Federation for American Immigration Reform and Center for Immigration Studies.

White nationalism has also crept deeper into the heart of mainstream conservatism. Leading GOP politicians, and prime-time pundits like former Fox News host Tucker Carlson, routinely warn against the "great replacement" of white Americans by non-white immigrants, at the hands of scheming liberal elites like George Soros and "globalists." Recently, white nationalists have been exposed as staffers at conservative Beltway institutions, media outlets, and electoral campaigns. Notable Republican politicians and celebrities have spoken at white nationalist conferences, and in November 2022, former President Trump even dined with Nick Fuentes, one of the country's leading white nationalists.

If systemic white supremacy is at the root of so many problems plaguing our society, the white nationalist movement is one bitter fruit, warping American politics to reflect its dystopian vision. We can't assume these organizations and actors will simply "go away" or treat them merely as a sideshow. They have been a core part of the American story long before the alt-right, and they will grow unless they are countered.

A WHITE ETHNOSTATE

We use the term "white nationalism" to describe a movement emerging after World War II, as white supremacists worldwide found a new language to articulate their key demand: a society for whites only.

White nationalists believe that race is not a social construct, but a biological and/or spiritual fact. While you often find beliefs in racial superiority, they tend to couch these ideas in the language of difference or other coded distractions.

As census data predicts that by 2045, non-Hispanic whites will fall below 50 percent of the US population,[6] an important political concern for white nationalists is what they call the "great replacement," the extinction of the white race in the United States and Europe through non-white immigration and miscegenation. And they're convinced "the Jews" are behind the "great replacement," and all other threats to white dominance.

Racists had to rethink fascism's presentation after the catastrophic defeat of Axis powers and the total delegitimization of Nazism as the realities of the Holocaust shocked the conscience of the West. To reclaim fascist politics from the burned-out cities and war tribunals of Europe, a new message was needed.

Francis Parker Yockey was a significant figure in this process, an American organizer who cocreated a neofascist network called the European Liberation Front. Yockey's ideas were preserved in his magnum opus *Imperium*, a rambling screed demanding a pan-European civilizational unity that would reestablish the greatness of the white West against the dominating subversion and degeneracy advanced by Jews. "In this period of history," wrote Yockey in 1948, "America and Jewry form a Symbiosis. The head of the organism is the Jewish entity, the body is America."[7] For Yockey and others, America was under Jewish control, and its postwar ascension as a geopolitical superpower was yet another front for Jewish world domination.

Willis Carto would inherit Yockey's crusade. Born in 1926 in Fort Wayne, Indiana, Carto visited Yockey shortly before his suicide in a San Francisco prison in 1960, and would carry on his teacher's legacy for the ensuing decades.

Carto pursued what researcher Leonard Zeskind called a "white supremacist realpolitik," dressing his radical views in suit and tie in an attempt to influence mainstream politics.[8] In 1958 he founded the Liberty Lobby, establishing it as a Capitol Hill advocacy outfit across the 1960s. He organized groups like the Youth for Wallace organization, which went on to become the National Youth Alliance, a prelude organization to the neo-Nazi National Alliance.

Through sponsorship of the Institute for Historical Review and, later, *The Barnes Review*, Carto almost single-handedly built the infrastructure of late-twentieth-century Holocaust denial in the United States. By blending explicit antisemitism within a broader slate of nativist, anti-government and anti-communist ideas, Carto found a wider audience for his fascist radicalism. At Carto's peak in the 1980s, Liberty Lobby commanded a mailing list of four hundred thousand, while circulation of his newspaper *The Spotlight* was said to surpass three hundred thousand.

In the 1950s, Black-led freedom movements gained new momentum in their struggles against Jim Crow segregation, terrifying white supremacists. Like their Nazi forebears, these white supremacists used antisemitism to explain how the world went so wrong, and what to do about it. Since they believed that Black people are less capable than white people, they needed an outside deus ex machina to explain why the Black freedom struggle was succeeding. They concluded that the Jews built Black movements as a battering ram against white interests. While the Western world welcomed Jews into the covenant of whiteness, white nationalists held on to "the Jew" as a primary enemy combatant.[9]

In their view, Jews remained not simply a subhuman race, but almost a type of "anti-race," as critical theorists Max Horkheimer and Theodor Adorno described—one whose biosocial foundations led them to undermine, and ultimately destroy, other races and peoples so as to ensure their own survival. They were clever, in a way, but not industrious, creative, or honest, and so they manipulated the racial taxonomy to appear white, in order to dismantle the white race from within. As we discuss, groups like the Ku Klux Klan and White Citizens' Councils claimed Jews were behind the growth of the civil rights movement in the Jim Crow South, and firebombed multiple synagogues as part of their campaign of violence and terror.

In the 1950s another figure carried the mantle of Nazism into postwar America. With his American Nazi Party, George Lincoln Rockwell used the shock of the swastika to garner attention while exploiting white opposition to civil rights to garner support. In 1961, as the Freedom Rides registered disenfranchised Black voters, Rockwell and his storm troopers traversed the South in his "hate bus," intimidating Black activists—one of many racist stunts.

The Jews engineered the Black freedom struggle, Rockwell told Alex Haley in a 1966 *Playboy* interview, by turning Black Americans "into a psychological bomb . . . They're just natural-born agitators. They just can't help coming in and getting everybody all stirred up."[10] Though Rockwell's American Nazi Party scarcely had over one thousand members and ran a shoestring budget, his white power slogans, neo-Nazism, and Holocaust denial carried an outsized impact for future generations of white nationalists.

Rockwell and others built international forums like the World Union of National Socialists for like-minded fascists to collaborate and share ideas.[11] Issues like the defense of apartheid in South Africa gained new significance, framed through a shared language of global white survival.[12] Highly publicized agitation like the infamous National Socialist Party of America march on the Chicago suburb of Skokie in 1978, home to thousands of Holocaust survivors—called off after a thousands-strong antifascist coalition put pressure on the Nazis—underlined the centrality of antisemitism for this new generation of neofascists.

In 1974 William Pierce, a close associate of both Rockwell and Carto, founded the National Alliance as a fascist vanguard with revolutionary aspirations (and its own pantheist spirituality). Pierce's 1978 novel *The Turner Diaries* depicted a cataclysmic race war in an apocalyptic future, during which a band of white guerrillas overthrows the Jewish-controlled US government, kills billions of non-white people worldwide with nuclear weapons, and institutes an Aryan republic on American soil. The novel inspired generations of white nationalist violence, including Timothy McVeigh's bombing of the Oklahoma City federal building in 1995, and remains influential today.

In the 1970s and '80s, radicalization deepened as disgruntled, traumatized Vietnam veterans entered the movement, the victories of the civil rights struggle continued to bear fruit, and white nationalists, convinced that political reform was a lost cause, focused on paramilitary training and violence. Clandestine organizations like The Order carried out bombings against federal targets, armed robberies, and the assassination of Jewish talk radio host Alan Berg.

The Klan also entered its own post–civil rights era when a new leader, David Duke, reinvigorated it, making antisemitism a centerpiece of the worldview. Throughout the 1970s, 1980s, and 1990s, Duke ran electoral campaigns for various Louisiana and national offices that garnered national attention (including his successful 1989 legislative run for Louisiana's District 81), employing diatribes against Black welfare recipients, school bussing, and non-white immigration that channeled racist grievance, fears of dispossession, and the growing sense of victimization among white voters.

While rural white nationalists traded apocalyptic fantasies and prepared for a race war, the urban movement saw white power skinheads escalating the violence. The skinhead movement arose in late 1960s Britain as a multiracial coalition of youth united by their working-class identity and love of Jamaican ska and rocksteady. In the 1970s, the fascist National Front began recruiting them, eventually splitting the scene into competing racist and antiracist factions (the split became more pronounced in the 1980s). This influenced racist groups in America, which became famous for gang-style attacks on interracial couples, Jews, and queer folks. Cities like Portland, Oregon, became beset by violent teenage Nazis supported by a neo-Nazi organization, White Aryan Resistance (WAR).

WAR saw skinheads as the rank-and-file storm troopers of the white revolution. They often carried out attacks against minorities, and when WAR was sued for its association with the 1988 murder of Ethiopian immigrant Mulugeta Seraw, the group's leader, Tom Metzger, pushed toward the "lone wolf" model of racist violence pioneered by white supremacists like Louis Beam and James Mason so that they could better avoid government infiltration.[13] While militant antifascist groups like Skinheads Against Racial Prejudice (SHARP), the Baldies, Anti-Racist Action (ARA), and Red and Anarchist Skinheads (RASH) existed prior to Seraw's murder, this tragedy became a rallying point that pushed the growth of antifascist organizing that would, decades later, lead to the modern antifa movement.

MAINSTREAMING RACIST HATE

Amidst this world of chaotic ultraviolence, "suit-and-tie" white nationalism was seeing a revival, and started moving into the mainstream. At the edges of mainstream conservatism, a new "paleoconservative" movement supported traditionalist values and defense of "Western civilization," was suspicious of "globalist" foreign intervention and free-market neoliberalism, and often showed sympathy to the segregationist South. When running for president in 1992, paleoconservative leader Pat Buchanan closely followed David Duke's Louisiana electoral strategy.[14] "The way to deal with Mr. Duke," Buchanan noted after Duke won a surprising 55 percent of Louisiana's white vote in the 1991 gubernatorial runoff election, "is the way the GOP dealt with the far more formidable challenge of George Wallace. Take a hard look at Duke's portfolio of winning issues and expropriate those not in conflict with GOP principles."[15]

Adopting a framing that is common across the radical Right, Buchanan critiqued US support for Israel using America First conspiracy theories, claiming malicious "Zionist" infiltrators covertly controlled US foreign policy.[16] Other paleoconservative leaders Joseph Sobran and Sam Francis spoke at Holocaust denial and white nationalist conferences[17] and became a leading white nationalist, respectively.[18] Many of those in the MAGA orbit or among the burgeoning National Conservatives can count the paleocons as their ideological forebears.

Some white nationalists jumped headfirst into pseudo-academia. Publications like *American Renaissance,* launched in 1990 by Jared Taylor, insist intelligence is racially determined, white people are more evolutionarily advanced than other races, and racially homogeneous societies are the only pathway to human flourishing. Eager to lend an academic sheen to bigotry, Taylor and others coined pseudoscientific terms like "race realism" and "human biodiversity" (HBD), inspiring an entire blogosphere that explains the world through long-discredited race science and advocates for eugenics.

DENYING REALITY

"Those numbers you always see are overblown, probably invented entirely."

It was the year 2000. Shane, sixteen at the time, was browsing a string of Cheetah Chat message boards, a vestige of the heyday of early Internet chat rooms, when he stumbled into a political debate forum.

"The Zionist lobby manufactures these horror stories about Auschwitz because they think no one will notice if they change the numbers. There weren't even that many Jews in Europe at the time."

The conversation revolved around some heady mix of Federal Reserve policy and the first Iraq War, nothing he could make heads or tails of—what did any of this have to do with Jews, Israel, and the Holocaust, as commenters kept insisting? He grabbed a couple quick search terms and plugged them into Yahoo. Did other people think key facts about the Holocaust were falsified, and the Jews were to blame? And why?

Holocaust denial had been a feature of the global far-right since before the true magnitude of the Nazi genocide was even in full view, and in the years after the war figures like Austin J. App, Arthur Butz, and Robert Faurisson sought to challenge the facts. At its core, the assertion that Jews have falsified the Holocaust, or deliberately exaggerated its core details, is a massive conspiracy theory, impossible to accept without the underlying premises of global Jewish power and control over media, government, and society. Further, it is used by the radical Right as a core recruiting tool. If the Holocaust was inflated, they say, then maybe Nazi ideology got a bad rap, and perhaps the moral barriers now in place against extreme nationalism and antisemitism can be lifted.

As Shane headed to college and started to engage in organizing and politics, he heard of something called the Pacifica Forum. Created by University of Oregon professor emeritus Orval Etter, the Forum brought controversial speakers to campus, including some Leftists. At least in the early years.

"There is a man inside that building who is absolutely possessed by his hatred of Jews," shouted a visibly upset woman as Shane walked out of the journalism school after another late afternoon of classes. The man was Mark Weber, a former member of the National Alliance and major figure in the Institute for Historical Review, which projected an academic veneer onto Holocaust denial. The Pacifica Forum was now hosting these sorts of speakers regularly.

Holocaust denial had popped up on campus life in many places, as fascists sought to exploit the university's role as a space for young minds to question their most basic assumptions. The Committee for Open Debate on the Holocaust was launched in 1987 by Bradley Smith as an affiliate of the Institute for Historical Review. The committee tried to take out ads in student newspapers questioning the facts. The project was a win-win for them: either the ad ran and they reached potential recruits, or the ad did not run and they claimed censorship.[19]

David Irving, a formerly respected historian of the Third Reich, was one of the few credentialed figures in their scene. He became the face of the effort to reform Hitler's image, both by trivializing and denying key aspects of the Holocaust, and by subtly shifting historical responsibility for it onto the Jews themselves.[20]

Around the same time as Shane and his friends were organizing against a new movement called the "alternative Right" led by the "suit-and-tie" fascist Richard Spencer, Irving was touring the United States once again, giving talks in private venues. Just like with the Committee, an Irving appearance was a test: either he would be allowed to speak, thus indicating communal sympathy, or he wouldn't, and he could claim censorship. He was visiting a hotel in the nearby city of Syracuse, and an antifascist bloc was organizing to stop it. Community members got together and organized a call-in, with participants on both coasts phoning the manager and demanding the event be canceled. But despite the fact that one of the most notorious Holocaust defenders in the world was inviting neo-Nazis and antisemitic militants to convene in their hotel, management refused to cancel the talk and threatened the antifascist demonstrators with the police.

Denialism—whether of the Holocaust or any genocide or historical atrocity—has long served as a pathway to expressing deeper bigotries that dare not be named. But it is also used to ignore the consequences of dystopian political and social ideas, to mask the brutality of ethnic nationalism. It is, in effect, yet another grasping after easy answers, to point at scapegoats and distract from real answers for society's ills.

THE RISE OF THE ALT-RIGHT

For many decades, the white nationalist movement's mainstream reach remained relatively limited. This would change in the twenty-first century, when the rise of illiberal right-wing nationalism around the world granted the movement an opening that previous generations could only dream of.

Beginning in 2008, white nationalist Richard Spencer and paleocon author Paul Gottfried popularized the term "alternative Right." Their big-tent reactionary movement rejected mainstream conservatism for its supposed capitulation to liberalism, and asserted that a more authentic Right must reject the notion of human equality in any form.

Spencer was influenced by the growing "identitarian" movement championed by the European New Right (ENR). Started by French philosopher Alain de Benoist in the late 1960s, the ENR attempted to reframe fascist politics away from obvious racism and toward a cultural renaissance that pushed their noxious political vision through the social back door.

The ENR helped to spawn the "identitarian" movement, which believes that growing rates of immigration from the Global South (including from refugee resettlement and especially from Muslim countries) represented an existential threat, deemed the "great replacement" by French writer Renaud Camus,[21] carried out against white Europeans by a sinister and malicious (and for many, a Jewish) elite. Many of these far-right activists demanded some kind of ethnically and/or culturally homogenous region, something that they believed manifests the alleged historic continuity of their national identity. In the mid-2010s, the alt-right Americanized the ENR, roping together racist pagans, men's rights activists, neoreactionaries, "radical traditionalists," paleocons, and others into a tacit coalition whose defining features were racial thinking.

Antisemitic conspiracy theories were core to the alt-right worldview, providing a scaffolding for the movement's male supremacy, anti-Blackness, xenophobia, and other bigotries. "I don't think that you can have a full understanding of the world without addressing the question of Jewish identity and Jewish power," Richard Spencer told us in 2016.

Kevin MacDonald, an evolutionary psychology professor who taught for many years at California State University, Long Beach, built the intellectual architecture for alt-right antisemitism. In a series of books beginning in the 1990s, MacDonald cast centuries of Jewish theology, and practices such as kashrut (kosher foods) and endogamy, as part of a pernicious "group evolutionary strategy" to preserve Jewish genetic material from contamination through intermarriage with non-Jews. "From an evolutionary perspective," he writes,

> this Jewish sense of moral and religious idealism, which results in genetic segregation, is in fact a mask for a self-interested evolutionary strategy aimed at promoting the interests of a kinship group that maintains its genetic integrity during a diaspora.[22]

Once the formal structures separating Jews and Gentiles were dissolved during the European Enlightenment, MacDonald argues, these liberal and emancipated Jews created ethnically driven networks among political, media, and literary elites, thus controlling modernity's core, and progressive activism itself became the "group evolutionary strategy" for these assimilated Jews. Modern Jews, he insists, have used psychoanalysis, critical theory, and racial justice movements to pathologize and undermine the healthy hierarchies of white Western society. In the end, MacDonald's views won and have become largely ubiquitous, in one form or another, across the white nationalist movement.

MacDonald justifies antisemitism as merely another "group evolutionary strategy" conducted by Gentiles to "push back" against an alien enemy seeking to undermine their ethno-racial integrity. His writing retrofits centuries of antisemitism into a coherent, unified twenty-first-century theory with a pseudoscientific veneer. There is no *Protocols*-style cabal necessary to explain its functioning, except perhaps metaphorically. Instead, "Jewish power" is engendered by evolution itself, the predictable consequence of Jewish genes.

Once he was forced into academic retirement due to widespread protest in 2014, MacDonald doubled down on his white nationalist activism. Today, even while many followers lack the patience to comb through his tomes, his underlying theory about Jews has become a near-consensus belief for white nationalism and conspiracists looking for a totalizing theory to explain "Jewish power."

BECOMING MAINSTREAM

The growth of social media allowed alt-rightists to enlarge their digital footprint and adopt online troll culture while participating (often anonymously) in a user-generated content mill and community.

But it took the 2015 presidential campaign of Donald Trump to energize the movement, and bring it beyond the world of conferences, journals, podcasts, and 4chan, and into the streets. "Hail Trump! Hail our people! Hail victory!" thundered Spencer in a now-infamous speech to a crowded room of white nationalists, many of whom responded with Hitler salutes, in a Washington, D.C., conference center days after Trump's election victory. Groups like Identity Evropa, Vanguard America, and Patriot Front began recruiting whites across communities and campuses, and within conservative institutions.

These groups brought antisemitism with them. "We do not see Jewish people as European because they themselves consider themselves Semitic, which is Middle Eastern, mixed-race population," Identity Evropa founder Nathan Damigo told us in 2016, channeling long-discredited "Semitic" categories of nineteenth-century European race science. "And they have hundreds of organizations, many of which are hostile to European interests and have been for a very long time."

The deadly violence at the Unite the Right rally—and President Trump's assertion afterward that there had been "very fine people" on both sides—was further indication that the fight was escalating, and the fascists had friends in power. "Many of us that have been dealing with [fascists] for generations were kind of used to it," Daryle Lamont Jenkins, founder of the antifascist One People's Project, told us, "but when they really started to become a little more intensified because they felt they had a safety net provided them by the White House, we realized that we needed to reconfigure how we approached things."

The alt-right's crescendo was in Charlottesville, and afterward, pressure from antifascists resulted in heavy deplatforming and the inability of alt-right groups to keep a stable "IRL" presence. By the time a second Unite the Right was planned one year later, the alt-right was a shadow of its former self—but white nationalism wasn't going anywhere.

In the fallout, groups like Atomwaffen and the Base introduced recruits to "accelerationism," the belief that acts of violence are necessary to trigger the collapse of the system. A series of mass shootings, celebrated on 4chan and targeting Jewish, Muslim, Black, Latinx, and LGBTQ communities, underscored the movement's eliminationist intent.

Others remained convinced white nationalism could find widespread appeal among millions of Trump voters and disaffected white Americans by working alongside them on campus or by speaking their language: American patriotism, conservative Christianity, and traditionalism. The Gen-Z America First/groyper movement, led by virulent antisemite

Nick Fuentes, sought to lead Republican student organizations, embed themselves within GOP electoral campaigns, network at conservative conferences, and otherwise influence the establishment Right. By using Christian nationalist rhetoric, the groypers hope to appeal to a wider base of MAGA supporters.

"This is about the satanic globalist elite," Fuentes yelled into the megaphone to a crowd of hundreds at the December 2020 Million MAGA March in Washington, D.C., naming ubiquitous Jewish targets of right-wing anger, such as George Soros, "versus us, the people of Christ."[23]

Today, while its on-the-ground organizing has decreased relative to the heyday of Unite the Right, the white nationalist movement has succeeded in reshaping mainstream conservatism in its image. During the Trump presidency, GOP politicians like Steve King faced severe consequences for promoting white nationalist ideas. But now the Overton window has shifted so sharply that those consequences are no longer ensured. Leading MAGA politicians like Paul Gosar and Marjorie Taylor Greene have spoken at groyper conferences, and in late 2022, Fuentes even sat down for dinner with former president Trump himself.

As America becomes more racially diverse, and growing racial justice movements mount powerful challenges to systemic white supremacy, millions of white Americans are terrified of losing their dominant status. Right-wing leaders are using white nationalist ideas to channel their reactionary grievance. In an era when Fox News anchors and GOP politicians warn incessantly against the "great replacement" and a supposed endemic of anti-white hatred, movements like the groypers have arrived right on time.

White nationalist views on immigration, demographics, race, and even Jews have diffused across the base of the MAGA movement. An April 2021 study at the University of Chicago found that supporters of the Capitol insurrection were highly likely to subscribe to core tenets of the "great replacement" theory, and that arrested insurrectionists were six times more likely to live in a county where the percentage of non-Hispanic white people has decreased in recent years.[24]

A June 2022 YouGov poll found 61 percent of Trump voters think that "in the U.S., a group of people is trying to replace white Americans with immigrants and people of color who share the group's views" (the number increased to 73 percent when "Democrats" were named as the group in question), and 12 percent agreed that the Jews were behind this plot.[25] Another 2022 study by researchers at Harvard and Tufts University found the "epicenter of antisemitic attitudes is [found with] young adults on the far right," with this population two to three times more likely than young far-leftists to hold overt antisemitic attitudes.[26]

White nationalism is an ever-present force in American politics, but it does not function alone. Its politics of exclusion are closely tied in with Christian narratives of triumphalism and dominance, used by the West to justify centuries of colonization and repression. An increasingly volatile Christian nationalist movement is trying to repeal the foundations of liberalism and multiculturalism, and institute a fundamentalist dystopia that would disenfranchise not only Jews, but most marginalized communities who challenge its theocratic vision.

EIGHT

A CHRISTIAN NATION: ANTISEMITISM
AND THE CHRISTIAN RIGHT

"If we are going to have one nation under God, which we must, we have to have one religion! One nation under God, and one religion under God!"

It was November 13, 2021, and retired US Army general Mike Flynn, a prominent Christian nationalist, QAnon promoter, and Trump acolyte—and briefly, Trump's national security adviser—thundered this proclamation from the pulpit. Flynn spoke at a rally at Cornerstone Church, a congregation led by influential Christian Zionist pastor John Hagee, in San Antonio, Texas.[1] That afternoon's rally was part of ReAwaken America, a nationwide tour featuring a who's who of pastors, politicians, media celebrities, and far-right influencers trumpeting a toxic mix of Christian nationalism, QAnon, COVID-19 conspiracy theories, and election denial. Nobody in the jubilant audience had any doubts which "one religion" Flynn was referring to.

At tour stops across the country, leading election deniers like Roger Stone and MyPillow CEO Mike Lindell took the stage alongside far-right 2022 midterm candidates like Doug Mastriano and "apostles" and "prophets" from the New Apostolic Reformation, the country's leading Christian nationalist movement. In San Antonio, conspiracy theory–monger Alex Jones warned the crowd that the "New World Order" was "meeting right now, plotting the next bioweapon released, plotting the next big cyber crash . . . [and to] collapse the Third World into the United States!" Audience members blew shofars, spoke in tongues, and cheered for the Rapture, convinced they were on the front lines, squaring off against elite Democrat pedophile cabals in the final battle between good and evil—the battle, they were told, to turn America into a Christian nation. Less than a year into the Biden administration, the MAGA base was readier than ever for holy war.

While it is easy to mock Christian nationalist crowds like these for their wacky tales of vaccine microchips and their kitschy religious triumphalism, the threat they pose to the safety and thriving of trans and queer folks, to the reproductive choice of millions, to the religious freedom of Jews, Muslims, and other religious minorities—and to the very foundation of multiracial democracy—is deadly serious.

Since the 1970s, the Christian Right has mobilized thousands of churches, nonprofits, think tanks, legal foundations, and advocacy organizations into a powerful movement, bent on reshaping the United States to reflect its fundamentalist interpretation of Western Christianity.

Today's Christian Right remains what writer Sean Quinn called in 2008 "the organizing engine of the Republican Party," a battering ram mobilizing millions with an endless barrage of anti-feminist, anti-LGBTQ culture war campaigns.[2] One of their crowning achievements remains the election of Donald Trump, who won with the support of 80 percent of white evangelicals, his most devoted constituency.[3] Another is, of course, the repeal of *Roe v. Wade*, the culmination of forty years of conservative legal strategy. And if Christian nationalists succeed in building their longed-for "Christian nation," it will turn Jews—and anyone else who fails to conform—into second-class citizens at best.

THE CHRISTIAN RIGHT'S ANTISEMITISM

White grievance has long animated the Christian Right. While many assume the movement first sprang into action after the passage of *Roe v. Wade* legalized abortion in 1973, in fact, defense of segregation provided the initial impetus, as Professor Randall Balmer has documented. By the late 1970s, Southern Christian leaders were incensed by mounting court orders to desegregate, and turned to conservative operatives like Paul Weyrich for help. Weyrich, determined to deny Democratic president Jimmy Carter a second term, was looking for the hot-button issue that could mobilize millions of white evangelicals. But since publicly opposing integration was a political dead end, they turned to abortion instead.[4] "When political power is achieved," Weyrich wrote in the mid-1970s, the "Moral Majority" he sought to build "will have the opportunity to re-create this great nation."

As discussed, the United States is a Christian-hegemonic country, animated by strong currents of Christian supremacy that have long been oppressive to Jews and many other marginalized groups, here and around the world. It's little surprise then that from its beginnings, the Christian Right, despite fervently declaring love for "Judeo-Christian values" and the State of Israel, carried more than a whiff of antisemitism. Movement leaders, bankrolled by big business and channeling Cold War anti-communism, have long appropriated thinly veiled conspiracy theories against "secular humanist" liberal elites who, they claim, dominate media and academia in order to erode traditional morality.

While Christian Right leaders like Jerry Falwell, Billy Graham, Pat Robertson, and Tim LaHaye rarely brought explicit antisemitism center stage, they couldn't always hide it either.[5] Over the decades, their lurid associations of Jews with money, media, pornography, and even the Antichrist made headlines.

At a rally for the Christian Right's Moral Majority in August 1980, Reverend Bailey Smith, then president of the thirteen-million-member Southern Baptist Convention, drew gasps for remarking that "God Almighty does not hear the prayers of a Jew."[6] Reverend Jerry Falwell, head of the Moral Majority, met with Jewish leaders shortly after to reaffirm his commitment to religious freedom and the separation between church and state. "America is a pluralistic republic," Falwell reassured them. "It cannot survive if we allow it to become anything else."

The year before, he struck a different tone—*The Washington Post* quoted Falwell expressing his desire to "turn [the United States] into a Christian nation."[7] The Christian Right is now poised to dispense with even the pretense of Falwell's 1980 assurances. Christian nationalists want to drastically reconfigure US civic and political life according to the dictates of an ultra-patriarchal, traditionalist, and intolerant version of Christianity.

The United States "is steadily becoming less Christian and less religiously observant," as a 2019 Pew report put it, and Christian nationalists know their agenda is supported by an ever-shrinking minority.[8] Much like white nationalists, they are terrified of losing their traditional dominance, and committed to an antidemocratic strategy of securing permanent minority rule, in order to preserve that dominance at any cost. "Christian nationalism," writes researcher Frederick Clarkson, is "not so much about moral purity as it is about power—the kind of power to defend and to deliver the Christian nation that never was."[9]

Millions of charismatic, Pentecostal, and evangelical Christians are part of a decentralized movement called the New Apostolic Reformation, which charges followers to capture the "Seven Mountains" of societal influence—education; religion; family; business; the government and military; arts and entertainment; and the media. Christian nationalists aim to steadily change societal attitudes while simultaneously reshaping law and public policy toward their exclusionary vision.[10] This is happening not only in the United States, but also in Latin American countries like Brazil, Eastern European countries like Poland and Hungary, and elsewhere around the world, making the Christian Right a backbone of rising authoritarianism globally.

The movement has increasingly lobbied for, and won, discriminatory religious exemptions allowing Christian institutions receiving state funding to deny adoption and foster services to LGBTQ couples, and reproductive health and other health care to women and LGBTQ people. We can now see how this agenda might target Jews as well. In January 2022, a Jewish couple filed a lawsuit against Tennessee's Department of Children's Services, after a Christian adoption agency receiving taxpayer funding refused to help them foster a child because they are Jewish. The agency advertises itself as "committed to Christian biblical principles," and it was able to discriminate because of a 2020 law likely inspired by Project Blitz, a Christian nationalist initiative shaping state-level legislation across the country. "I felt like I'd been punched in the gut," said Liz Rutan-Ram, one of the plaintiffs in the lawsuit. "It was the first time I felt discriminated against because I am Jewish."[11]

A 2019 survey by the Public Religion Research Institute found that 19 percent of Americans—including 24 percent of Republicans, and 24 percent of white evangelicals—agreed that small business owners should be allowed to refuse services to Jewish patrons, if doing so violates their religious beliefs. The survey found even higher levels of support for such discrimination against LGBTQ people, atheists, and Muslims.[12]

The Christian nationalist movement's decades-long attack on abortion rights, which finally succeeded in overturning *Roe v. Wade* in 2022 and triggering state-by-state abortion bans and restrictions across the country, is a major threat to Jewish religious freedom. The classical rabbinic tradition locates the beginning of life not at conception, nor during the gestation of a fetus, but during the birthing process—and even during child-birth, if the pregnant person's life is in danger, saving their life takes precedence. This all stands in stark contrast to Christian Right theology, and where that theology becomes state policy, it can leave Jews literally unable to follow religious law.

"The fundamentalist Christian position is the exact opposite of the halachic approach to abortions," stated Ephraim Sherman, an Orthodox nurse practitioner, in a May 2022 op-ed. "The success of this Republican-Christian strategy should strike terror in the hearts of frum [traditional Orthodox] communities across America. It should also motivate us to action."[13]

For Dania Rajendra, a Jewish organizer and educator, this became strikingly clear when she received emergency, life-saving surgery to end an ectopic pregnancy. "My deepest, most intimate experience of antisemitism," she told a Minnesota audience in a 2019 speech,

> isn't someone calling me horrible names, or threatening me or my family—though that happens, sometimes. Antisemitism, to me, is the idea that at my absolutely most vulnerable, I might be denied the means to save my life, because someone else's religion says my fetus is as important as I am, even though my tradition says otherwise . . . [We] need to start recognizing antisemitism even when people are not calling us names, and when they are "just" limiting our secular freedoms—to have an abortion, to join a union, to go to public, secular school. Those rights protect us as Jews.[14]

Christian nationalism has been normalized across the MAGA movement and American society. A 2023 survey found that over half of Republicans, and 29 percent of Americans overall, are adherents to or sympathizers of Christian nationalism, and while the bulk are white evangelical Protestants, Hispanic and other Protestants and Catholics of color are well represented as well. This group shows significant support for statements like "[because] things have gotten so far off track, true American patriots may have to resort to violence in order to save our country" and "I would prefer the U.S. to be a nation primarily made up of people who follow the Christian faith."

Where these views predominate, antisemitism is more commonly found as well. The survey found 23 percent of Christian nationalist adherents, and 19 percent of sympathizers, agreed with the statement that "Jewish people hold too many positions of power."[15] A 2021 analysis of survey data found voters who endorsed statements like "the federal government should declare the United States a Christian nation" were much more likely to support statements like "Jews are more loyal to Israel than to this country" and "Jews killed Jesus." Christian nationalists who held QAnon beliefs, in turn, subscribed to twice as many antisemitic tropes as those who did not. "These are not independent forces operating in American politics," explain the authors, "Christian nationalism and QAnon support work together to drive up anti-Semitism."[16]

Inside the conservative movement, the standard had been to slightly veil this Christian nationalist agenda, but the veneer has peeled away as the ideology moves mainstream. Far-right Georgia representative Marjorie Taylor Greene, one of the most popular and influential GOP politicians, declared, "We should be Christian Nationalists," at the July 2022 Turning Point USA Student Action Summit, and later insisted "I am being attacked by the godless left because I said I'm a proud Christian Nationalist."[17]

CHRISTIAN ZIONISM

Today, tens of millions of conservative Christians are staunch and active supporters of the far-right Israeli government—so much so that Israeli leaders count them as a more reliable base of support, even, than the often-critical American Jewish community. Yet counterintuitively, Christian Zionism is one of the largest and most powerful, if slow-burning, antisemitic movements in the United States.

The core theological belief of Christian Zionism is that the "ingathering" of Jews and the creation of a Jewish state in the Holy Land is part of a divine plan that will trigger the long-awaited End Times. In this apocalyptic scenario, Jesus will return to the Earth, humans will become embroiled in a cataclysmic war, the Christian faithful will be raptured to heaven, and finally, all Jews and other non-Christians will either convert or burn in eternal hellfire.[18]

This supremacist eschatology has been maintained by generations of Christian Zionist leaders in one form or another, and is deeply troubling, to say the least. While movement leaders appear to offer warm and heartfelt support to Jewish political ambitions, this is undergirded by longing for the eventual negation of Jewish peoplehood.

The United States' most active Christian Zionist group, Christians United for Israel (CUFI), claims 10 million members—3 million more than the entire American Jewish population. Major Christian Zionist leaders have amassed unprecedented political power in pursuit of their goals. Trump administration officials like Vice President Mike Pence and Secretary of State Mike Pompeo were Christian Zionists, and the movement took credit for some of the administration's most hard-right Middle East policy moves, including moving the US embassy to Jerusalem and the cancellation of the Iran nuclear deal.

The Christian Zionist agenda is a major obstacle to prospects for a just peace in Israel/Palestine, and stability in the Middle East region. Based on a selective interpretation of biblical verses, most Christian Zionists support the Israeli Right's agenda of permanent occupation of the West Bank, Gaza Strip, and East Jerusalem, believing these lands were given to the Jewish people by God (international law, however, does not recognize such a divine arrangement).

Christian Zionists aggressively lobby against common sense measures for peace like the Iran nuclear deal because, in their fantasy, escalating war, unrest, and instability in the Middle East are prophetic signs of the coming End Times. Thus, they eagerly goad the conservative movement and Israeli Right to pursue more aggressive, expansionist policies that make the prospects for meaningful peace ever more remote.

In the wake of Hamas's October 7 attack and Israel's bombardment of Gaza, Christian Zionists clamored for total war. "America should roll up its sleeve and knock the living daylights out of Tehran for what they have done to Israel," Pastor John Hagee, leader of CUFI, announced to roaring applause at CUFI's annual "Night to Honor Israel," held days after Hamas's October 7 attack. "Hit them so hard that our enemies will once again fear us and our friends will again trust us." Sharing the stage that evening with Israeli ambassador Gilad Erdan as well as numerous GOP representatives, Hagee insisted a two-state solution is "not a reality . . . there is [only] a one-state solution—Israel today, Israel tomorrow, Israel forever." Channeling End Times fervor, he declared "when Messiah comes . . . he's going straight to the city of Jerusalem, [to] put his foot on the Mount of Olives, and establish the eternal kingdom of peace."[19] Later, Hagee spoke before an audience of tens of thousands at the March for Israel in Washington, D.C., along with hard-line Christian nationalist and House Speaker Mike Johnson, who declared that "this is a fight between good and evil, between light and darkness, between civilization and barbarism. The calls for a ceasefire are outrageous."[20] Clearly, an end to bloodshed for Palestinians and Israelis was not on the Christian Zionist agenda.

"Christian Zionism and, more broadly, Christian nationalism affect us all," Jonathan Brenneman, a Christian Palestinian American activist, said in 2022. "And if people who are working for justice, and particularly working for Palestinian rights, don't understand the amount of power and influence that Christian

Zionists have, they're going to be missing a key dynamic in what is perpetuating the oppression of Palestinians."[21]

Christian Zionism is older even than the Jewish political movement of the same name. Since at least the time of the Crusades, a significant portion of European Christendom has turned toward Jerusalem as the supposed site of apocalyptic End Times scenarios, and beginning in the late sixteenth century, many British Protestant theologians accorded Jews a central role in this process. Decades before Theodor Herzl convened the First Zionist Congress in 1897, many English church leaders and statesmen were clamoring to deport European Jews to Palestine, where the building of a Jewish commonwealth would trigger the End Times. This would have the added benefit of bolstering their colonial ambitions while emptying the metropole of Jews.

One 2017 poll found that 80 percent of evangelicals think the "the modern rebirth of the State of Israel in 1948 and the regathering of millions of Jewish people to Israel" were "fulfillments of Bible prophecy that show we are getting closer to the return of Jesus Christ."[22] Not every Christian Zionist leader or follower holds the fiery End Times scenario closest to heart. Many adhere more to the "prosperity gospel," according to which God promises wealth and success to Christians who support Israel, based on the loose translation of Genesis 12:3, "he who blesses Israel shall be blessed, while he who curses Israel shall be cursed."

But even at its least eschatological, Christian Zionism is suffused with the supremacist paternalism of traditional anti-Judaism.

"The Jews are returning to their land of unbelief," Jerry Falwell exclaimed in his 1980 book *Listen, America!* "[Jews] are spiritually blind and desperately in need of their Messiah and Savior. Yet they are God's people, and in the world today Bible-believing Christians are the best friends the nation Israel has."[23]

The movement instrumentalizes Jews and Israel as characters in a Christian drama, what scholar S. Jonathon O'Donnell calls "overdetermined . . . fetish objects invested with supernatural power."[24] It is impossible to show respect and allyship to Jews as Jews if that support merely reinscribes us as pawns in a Christian narrative of sin and salvation.

Most movement leaders effusively condemn antisemitism—which they mistakenly claim, of course, to be equivalent to criticism of Israel. At the same time, they view antisemitism as divine punishment for Jewish sinfulness, and a cosmic stimulus to goad Jews to leave the diaspora and return to the Holy Land.

"It was the disobedience and rebellion of the Jews," Pastor John Hagee, leader of CUFI, said in his 2006 book, *Jerusalem Countdown*, "that gave rise to the opposition and persecution that they experienced beginning in Canaan and continuing to this very day." The reason for the Holocaust, Hagee said in a 2005 sermon, was "because God said, 'my top priority for the Jewish people is to get them to come back to the land of Israel.'"[25]

Jews deserve better allies in the fight against antisemitism.

NAMING THE JEW

After the Holocaust, most Christian denominations worked hard to purge open antisemitism, yet their success in doing so has remained uneven. The rise of the global far-right has bolstered reactionary currents within Christian denominations worldwide, and antisemitism is part of this toxic upsurge.

Within the Catholic world, a growing movement of traditionalist Catholics, or "trad Caths," rejects the liberal, modernizing reforms of the Second Vatican Council. They focus on maintaining the traditional Latin liturgies, including prayers regarding "Jewish perfidy," and enforce strict gender roles and sexual prohibitions. While not every adherent is an antisemite, "the historical association," wrote the then editor of *National Catholic Reporter* in 2009, "between some strains of traditionalist Catholicism and anti-Semitism runs deep"—a legacy stretching back from conservative opposition to the French Revolution in the late eighteenth century to the Dreyfus affair in the late nineteenth and the rise of hard-right preacher Father Coughlin in 1930s America.[26]

In the late 1980s, English bishop Richard Williamson of the Society of Saint Pius X (SSPX), one of the largest and most prominent traditionalist Catholic branches, was revealed to be a Holocaust denier. SSPX remained ambivalent regarding Williamson throughout his years of open antisemitism, and has continued to promote antisemitism and support other far-right theologians.[27] In 2013, a commemoration of the Nazi pogrom of Kristallnacht at the Metropolitan Cathedral of Buenos Aires was disrupted by young members of SSPX who demanded that "followers of false gods" be removed and that "the Jews killed Jesus."[28]

"Trad-Cath" aesthetics, and similarly reactionary forms of Eastern Orthodoxy, Mormonism, and other Christian movements are increasingly popular with the online far-right. For example, the Gen-Z America First/groyper movement, led by Unite the Right attendee Nick Fuentes, combines militant "Christian futurism" with antisemitism and white nationalism, and has built coalitions with far-right Christian groups such as Church Militant.

At the groypers' 2022 conference, which featured GOP representatives Marjorie Taylor Greene and Paul Gosar, Gab CEO Andrew Torba railed against the "synagogue of Satan," a phrase from the Book of Revelations that features prominently in the antisemitism of movements like Christian Identity, and was met with loud applause from the mostly Gen-Z audience.[29]

As discussed earlier, US white supremacist organizations and leaders have long interwoven antisemitism with Christian doctrines, from the second-era Ku Klux Klan of the 1920s to demagogic preachers like Gerald L. K. Smith in the 1940s. In the 1980s, groups like Aryan Nations and leaders like Richard Butler adhered to an ideology called Christian Identity, which took Christian supersessionism to a radical, racist conclusion. White Aryan Christians, they claimed, were the "true" genetic and spiritual descendants of the ancient Israelites, while present-day "Jews" were diabolical, scheming imposters: a mongrel tribe hell-bent on defiling the "real Jews" with race mixing, and perverting the true Israelite religion by mixing it with demonic practices. People of color were not fully human, perhaps lacking a soul, and were the "beasts of the field" named by Adam in Genesis. The End Times would take the form of a race war and the longed-for extermination of the "fake Jews."[30]

Christian Identity initiated some of the most militant and bloody episodes in contemporary US white nationalism. Identity compounds like Elohim City in Oklahoma, or the Aryan Nations near Hayden Lake, Idaho, became centers of revolutionary militia activity, aimed against the "Zionist Occupation Government," and Identity theology was influential amongst populist proto-militias like Posse Comitatus in the rural heartland. Identity adherents committed murders and orchestrated bomb plots across the 1980s and 1990s, including the 1999 shooting of five at the Los Angeles Jewish Community Center by an Aryan Nations associate.[31]

As scholars like Alex DiBranco have noted, beginning in the 1980s, as Christian Right leaders ramped up anti-abortion rhetoric on the national stage, Christian Identity groups like Aryan Nations and Phineas Priesthood, as well as neo-Nazi skinheads, linked up with militant movements like Operation Rescue to target abortion providers with assassinations, bombings, and other acts of terror.[32]

These white nationalists weren't the only antisemites in the anti-abortion coalition. The Catholic anti-abortion organization Human Life International charged that "American Jews have been leaders in establishing and defending the efficient destruction of more than 30 million pre-born children in this country," and its leader, Father Paul Marx, once said it was a "strange thing how many leaders in the abortion movement are Jewish."[33] The murder of Dr. Barnett Slepian by Catholic militant James Charles Kopp in 1998 helped to highlight that Jewish abortion doctors could be particularly vulnerable to attack, with one report noting that four of five abortion doctors shot during this period were Jewish.

Other white nationalists take the antisemitism forged in centuries of Christian anti-Judaism and focus on it so completely that they eclipse Christianity itself. For neo-Nazi pagan or heathen movements like Wotanism or the Vinlanders Social Club, the Jewish conspiracy is so totalizing that Christianity itself becomes a millennia-old Jewish plot to take down European whites.[34] Christianity is reframed as worship of a foreign, Semitic ethnic God, which colonizes European white people with a deceptive message of weakness rather than strength. Its "turn the other cheek" message, they claim, runs counter to the nationalist warrior ethos, and the universalism of Christian claims to salvation undermines sacred boundaries between races.

Christianity is then, as the fascist neo-pagan Odinist movement frequently calls it, "Cultural Marxism," a universalizing force that paved the way for materialism, the Enlightenment, and modernity, a virus destroying Germanics, subsuming them in degeneracy and mass immigration. Instead of reading the Jewish scriptures as a metaphor and precursor, pointing the way toward "New Testament" salvation (as Christians do), they reject "Old" and "New" Testaments alike as twin symptoms of Jewish malfeasance. Instead, groups like the Asatru Folk Assembly claim to revive pagan folk traditions, and appropriative interpretations of Eastern mysticism, cast in racist glaze.

"Post-Christian" white nationalism, in various forms, has influenced the European New Right and "identitarians" like

France's Generation Identity, as well as US alt-right leaders like Richard Spencer and Greg Johnson, offering a supposedly more authentic spiritual foundation for their seething racist rage. It carries a long history in modern European romantic and far-right movements, championed by fascist intellectuals like Julius Evola and Savitri Devi and movements like Nazism.

"JUDEO-CHRISTIAN" VALUES

The Christian nationalist movement feels for Jews like storm clouds on the horizon. We can almost see distant cracks of lightning and hear peals of thunder. It is disorienting, however, that even as these dark clouds gather, Jewish-Christian relations can appear friendlier than ever. Christian politicians and pundits speak forcefully against antisemitism (as they understand it) and in support of Israel, and wax rhapsodic about the supposed "Judeo-Christian values" at the heart of the American idea.

A dizzying inversion has occurred—Jews have now been refashioned as a stalwart part of, even core guardians of, the (white) Christian West, which used to be the chief source of antisemitic persecution. "Europe's post-war rehabilitation," wrote scholar Gil Hochberg, "the desire of Jews to assimilate, and various US political parties' interests all came together to generate a powerful myth: an always already existing Judeo-Christian civilization, synonymous with 'Western Culture.'"[35]

In popular discourse, "Judeo-Christian" functions as a floating signifier, defining not so much who we *are*, as who we *are not*. In the decades of the Cold War, the freedom and openness of the "Judeo-Christian West" was counterposed to the closed authoritarianism of the U.S.S.R. and the broader communist menace. More recently, during the "War on Terror," the enemy of the "Judeo-Christian West" has become radical Islam, which threatens "our" way of life with its wholly barbaric

Otherness. "In the post-9/11 world of the Bush presidency," wrote scholar Shalom Goldman in 2011,

> American Islamophobia flourished and "Judeo-Christian" has become a term of exclusion, rather than inclusion. The implication in the current context is that the U.S. can accept Jews into the social contract (or at least those Jews who embrace "traditional values"), while Muslims, who "killed us on 9/11" in Bill O'Reilly's phrase, are permanently excluded.[36]

In the political center "Judeo-Christian values" are evoked to prop up a status quo of American exceptionalism, free-market neoliberalism, and pervasive Islamophobia. On the Right, although the term signals "a message of cooperation and ecumenicism," in Goldman's words, it has come to signify cultural conservatism and chauvinistic nationalism, and is "really a cover for an attack on the values of the Enlightenment; the very values that enabled Jews to enter Western societies."

Meanwhile, around 22 percent of US Jews stake their political loyalties within the Republican coalition.[37] Prominent Orthodox figures like Ben Shapiro and organizations like the Coalition for Jewish Values stand alongside Christian Rightists, and insist upon a shared biblical framework of traditionalism. A 2023 survey found that 7 percent of US Jews are adherents to or sympathizers of the core tenets of Christian nationalism.[38] When General Flynn's "one nation, one religion" comment went viral in late 2021, Jewish hard-right Ohio Senate hopeful Josh Mandel tweeted "We stand with General Flynn" and "America was not founded as a secular nation."[39]

Many Jewish Rightists misleadingly insist that Jewish religious teaching is aligned with the Christian Right agenda on issues like abortion. This kosher stamp of approval helps the Christian nationalist movement lend its supremacist project a veneer of pluralism.

The Jewish Right's visible alliance with the Christian Right also provides ample cover for antisemitism. There is, of course, a long history, in modern antisemitism, of demonizing liberal, secular Jews as existential threats to faith, flag, and family—and persecuting them on that basis.

Today's rhetoric provides a twist—the Right demonizes these Jews not as embodiments of "the Jew," but rather of "the anti-Jew." They are seen as "not really Jewish" at all, in contrast to more "authentic" Orthodox and right-wing Jews. "It is precisely [the Christian Right's] staunch support for certain kinds of Jews and certain forms of Judaism that makes possible their attacks against, or at the very least disregard for, defending the rights of other types of Jews," wrote scholar Eliyahu Stern. "If progressive Jews are not really Jews and if left-wing Jewish values are not really authentically Jewish, then it follows that opposing these types and values does not indicate any particular anti-Jewish animus."[40]

Channeling this dismissiveness, the Catholic Trump über-ally Rudy Giuliani rambled in a 2019 interview that "Soros is hardly a Jew. I'm more of a Jew than [George] Soros is. I probably know more about—he doesn't go to church, he doesn't go to religion—synagogue." Giuliani also called Soros an "enemy of Israel."[41] Giuliani's word mush offers a telling window into this mindset, misinterpreting Soros's Jewishness under the weight of Christian categories (church, religion) before denying it outright, while Othering him as secular and insufficiently pro-Israel.

Jewish scholar and activist April Rosenblum calls this "crude, coercive and conditional 'love' for Jews" a product of "a world where centuries of Christian rulers have been invested in what the symbolism of Jews means for them—and [are] much less interested in the fate or needs of real, flesh-and-blood Jews."[42]

The Jewish Right is also eager to back the Christian Right for its fervent support for the hard-right policies of the contemporary Israeli government. And here, too, they are providing cover for increasingly open antisemitism against liberal diaspora Jewry.

In October 2022, former president Trump took to social media to warmly praise US evangelicals and Israeli Jews who supported his far-right policies on Israel, and sharply castigate liberal American Jews who did not. "U.S. Jews have to get their act together and appreciate what they have in Israel—before it is too late!" Trump concluded with a barbed threat.[43]

One week later, with midterm elections fast approaching, Christian nationalist Pennsylvania gubernatorial candidate Doug Mastriano was asked by a Jewish reporter to explain his widely reported connections to antisemites like white nationalist Gab CEO Andrew Torba. In response, his wife, Rebbie Mastriano (also a fervent Christian nationalist), retorted with thinly rebranded Christian supersessionism. "I'm gonna say as a family we so much love Israel," she sneered with contempt, "in fact I'm gonna say we probably love Israel more than a lot of Jews do."[44]

Far-right politicians like Mastriano peddle antisemitism with one hand while accusing left-wing critics of Israel of antisemitism with the other. It's no surprise that authoritarian Christian nationalists in the United States see their Jewish counterparts in Israel as worthy allies, and it's easy to expose their hypocrisy. But how, exactly, can progressives ensure that when we criticize Israel or Zionism, we avoid antisemitism? Questions like these are some of the most vexing and controversial in contemporary political discourse, and it is to them that we now turn.

NINE

LOOKING AT ANTISEMITISM
AND ISRAEL/PALESTINE

One balmy August night Ben was packed into a crowded room with over one hundred activists fighting for Palestine. Most of them were young and supported the Boycott, Divestment, and Sanctions (BDS) movement for Palestinian rights and were putting that commitment into action with powerful campaigns challenging Israeli apartheid. They were there to make a difference.

Riveted by powerful speakers who presented over the weekend, Ben and the others sat hunched over, scribbling into battered notebooks. One speaker explained the "deadly exchange" trips between US and Israeli police. On these trips, sponsored by groups like the Anti-Defamation League, police officials share cutting-edge tactics and technologies of repression used against oppressed people in both countries. These "deadly exchanges," the speaker warned, highlight brutal resonances between structural racism in the United States and Israel/Palestine, underscoring the need for international solidarity.

Then the talk took a strange turn. The speaker alleged that if a US police car had the words "internationally accredited" across its side, this meant the department was trained by the Israel Defense Forces (IDF). "Your cops on campus," the speaker told the student activists in the room, "are trained by the IDF." But that was just the beginning of the big reveal. The speaker went on to claim that "Zionist capital" underdeveloped Africa, then suggested that Martin Luther King Jr. was potentially murdered for criticizing Israel.

They painted a picture of an immensely powerful, multi-tentacled global Zionist adversary, working behind the scenes to stir up anti-Blackness and global repression. The audience's eyes widened, heads nodding in approval. A grim acknowledgement passed through the room, as if Ben and the other activists had been ushered into a terrible secret: *this is how deep it goes; Israel's brute, repressive power stretches across the globe, extending to our own backyards.*

Ben's body froze, the hairs standing on the back of his neck, as he heard this grandiose, conspiracy theory–laden reimagining of the actual US-Israel relationship. He understood that the structural problems of economic underdevelopment and exploitation plaguing the African continent were the result not of "Zionist capital" (whatever that means), but many interlocking systems of Western-backed economic oppression in which Israel-related geopolitics plays no central role. Later, he pored over documentation and confirmed that police departments in the United States can apply for international accreditation. But not from Israel: instead from the Commission on Accreditation for Law Enforcement Agencies (CALEA), a domestic agency evaluating departments on metrics including field statistics, management procedures, personnel policies, and interagency coordination. A few campus police departments across the country have sent officers on Israel trips—though not necessarily IDF training—and even visits remain uncommon.

In a flash, the speaker had transitioned from grounded political education to a paranoid conspiracy theory where Israel's hidden hand lurked in the fine print on neighborhood police cars, pulling the strings behind cops everywhere, and engineering global financial and political domination. If you've made it this far in our book, you will recognize that such an outsized conception of hidden, global, and scheming Jewish power—in this case, concentrated in the Jewish state—is a hallmark of antisemitism.

More disturbing still, the audience didn't seem to notice. This crowd would hopefully have recognized, and called out, subtle Islamophobic, queerphobic, or racist claims, but they didn't have that same intuitive guardrail when it came to understanding antisemitic conspiracy theories packaged as criticism of Israel. The crowd would have balked at suggestions of antisemitism, yet here they were, lingering in coded language.

The moment passed; the presenter continued. It didn't put Ben in any immediate danger as a Jew; but it was lodged in his mind, as such moments often remain for Jews. He wished he had challenged the misinformation, named why we need to avoid antisemitism, and initiated a generative conversation. Instead, he shrunk in his seat, remaining silent. Ben worried that if he named antisemitism, he would be accused of defending Israel's oppression of Palestinians. It could jeopardize his organizing relationships, and if word about the antisemitism he had heard hit the political Right it would be used to delegitimize the movement's demands for Palestinian liberation. *And*, Ben thought, overcome with internalized shame, *who knows, maybe I'm too sensitive?*

After the presentation, he discovered other Jewish attendees felt similarly. Shaken, they walked under the night sky, processing what had happened. Grateful for each other, they nonetheless felt profoundly lonely, betrayed by a movement they had called home.

Ben heard later that somebody did, in fact, share a concern privately with the speaker—which wasn't received well. The dreaded whisper campaign had, in fact, come to pass—Ben was told that this Jewish activist was "problematic" for suggesting these assertions were antisemitic. Again, he kept his head down.

What if more people in that room had a nuanced understanding of antisemitism, and had spoken up? What if non-Jews, especially, had led this charge, so the Jews in the room weren't isolated? What if in-depth political education on antisemitism had long been standard for activists—so rather than reacting defensively and dismissively, the group was equipped to critically analyze the material and explore hidden biases?

Over the years, the Palestine solidarity movement has repeatedly expressed a real commitment to fighting antisemitism. And yet, moments like these serve as stark reminders that this commitment needs to deepen. What if we took more seriously the possibility that antisemitism may sometimes show up in criticisms of Israel, and did something about it?

THE ONGOING NAKBA

Israel's oppression of Palestinians remains one of the central human rights crises of our time—and its history stretches back over a century.

The Jewish Zionist movement emerged in the late nineteenth century as a variety of European ethnic nationalism. It sought to respond to the threat of rising antisemitism in Europe through the creation of a Jewish nation-state in historic Palestine.

The State of Israel was formed in 1948 through ethnic cleansing, the violent dispossession of hundreds of thousands of Indigenous Palestinians in what is called the Nakba—a process that continues to this day. In fact, long before 1948, the Zionist project was recognized by Palestinians, and described by certain Zionist leaders as an unfolding process of settler colonialism.[1] The waves of Jewish settlement in the pre-state community called the New Yishuv served to displace, disenfranchise, and ultimately expel Palestinians through land acquisition and seizure,[2] the expansion of civil society institutions designed to be exclusively or primarily for Jews,[3] and other measures aimed at the creation of a majority-Jewish society.[4]

During most of this time, Britain was the imperial sponsor for Zionism, hoping to secure a regional foothold for its vast empire, and employed a divide-and-conquer strategy between Jewish settlers and Indigenous Palestinians in order to prevent powerful alliances that could challenge its colonial authority.[5] Over the decades before and since the creation of Israel, minority currents within the Zionist movement sought, to varying degrees, to resist the dispossession of Palestinians and strive instead for coexistence. However, this was never the dominant trend, and most Palestine solidarity activists today use the word "Zionism" to refer not to what could have been, but to what actually occurred.

Today, millions of Palestinians worldwide remain barred from returning to their lands,[6] and many continue to live in overcrowded, under-resourced refugee camps,[7] denied opportunity and freedom of movement in countries like Lebanon to which they were expelled or fled.[8] Israel, meanwhile, maintains racist laws and policies to explicitly preserve a Jewish demographic supermajority—an ethnonationalist project that violates core principles of human rights and democracy.[9]

The status quo in Israel/Palestine constitutes what human rights organizations like B'Tselem and Amnesty International call apartheid—a system of entrenched inequality that privileges Israeli Jews over Palestinians in citizenship, housing, wealth, community investment, access to land and water, freedom of movement, and more.[10] This systemic, multilayered oppression of Palestinians is the core obstacle to a just peace.

Since 1967, Israel has maintained an illegal military occupation over the West Bank, East Jerusalem, the Gaza Strip, and the Golan Heights. In the West Bank and East Jerusalem, hundreds of thousands of Israeli settlers live in ever-expanding settlements in direct violation of international law, while Palestinians live under Israel's discriminatory regime of walls, checkpoints, land seizure, military surveillance, and mounting human rights violations.

In the Gaza Strip Israel confines millions of Palestinians to an open-air prison, subjecting them to chronic malnourishment, strangling economic blockades (also maintained by Egypt), lack of resources and opportunity, compounding trauma, and periodic rounds of deadly bombardment.[11] As our book was completed in late 2023, Israel's bombardment of Gaza reached genocidal levels, while many described Israel's mass displacement of nearly 2 million Gazan civilians as akin to a second Nakba.

Moreover, even within Israeli Jewish society, deep structural racism persists as well. In its first decades, Zionist colonization in Palestine was mostly carried out by European Ashkenazim, but Zionist leaders quickly realized that in order to maintain a Jewish demographic majority, they needed to recruit hundreds of thousands of Jews from across the Middle East and North Africa as well. From the beginning, Mizrahi Jews in Israel were marginalized as second-class citizens, or what Mizrahi scholar Ella Shohat called a "semi-colonized nation-within-a-nation" by the dominant, Orientalist Ashkenazi caste.[12] Derided as savage and "undeveloped," Mizrahim were segregated into shantytowns, denied access to vital resources, education, community investment, and opportunities for advancement, and systematically disenfranchised across Israeli society.

Their Arab Jewish histories and identities were denied and repressed, in a brutal process of enforced assimilation to Eurocentric norms. "The cultural affinity that Arab Jews shared with Arab Muslims," wrote Shohat, "in many respects stronger than that which they shared with European Jews, threatened the Zionist conception of a homogeneous nation modeled on the European nationalist definition of the nation-state." An exploited Jewish underclass, they were slotted into a role, explained Shohat, both as "dominated and dominators; simultaneously disempowered as 'Orientals' or 'blacks' vis-à-vis 'white' Euro-Israelis and empowered as Jews in a Jewish state vis-à-vis Palestinians."[13]

Today, Mizrahi Jews outnumber Ashkenazim in the Jewish state, and continue to face pervasive discrimination. While movements like the Israeli Black Panthers in the early 1970s fought to build Mizrahi-Palestinian solidarity—a powerful alliance that could have rattled the Zionist project at its foundations—today that horizon appears more remote than ever. Alienated by the Ashkenazi-dominated, largely secular, and often racist Israeli liberal camp, most Mizrahim have cast their lot squarely with the Right.

Israel's oppression of Palestinians is maintained in major part thanks to US support. The "special relationship" the United States touts with Israel is not driven by any genuine solidarity it holds toward Jews—rather, the United States uses Israel to anchor American geopolitical dominance in the Middle East. Israel is "the best three-billion-dollar investment we make," remarked then-senator Joe Biden in a 1986 congressional hearing. "Were there not an Israel, the United States of America would have to invent an Israel to protect her interests in the region." Biden has repeated that formulation as recently as 2022.[14]

Today, the ethnonationalist far-right has taken over Israeli politics. Neo-Kahanists set state policy and help lead governing coalitions while attempting to dismantle already deeply flawed democratic institutions and inciting escalating anti-Palestinian violence across Israeli society.

The Israeli Right is a key player in the global far-right, building close alliances with ethnonationalist leaders and regimes across the world, from Donald Trump in the United States to Viktor Orbán in Hungary and Narendra Modi in India. Many Christian far-rightists support Israel because they see it as a frontline defender of the "Judeo-Christian West" in its Islamophobic "clash of civilizations" against the Muslim world. This setup fulfills the Orientalist vision of Zionist leader Theodor Herzl one century earlier that the new Jewish state be, as he put it, "the portion of the rampart of Europe against Asia, an outpost of civilization as opposed to barbarism."[15] Not only is this geopolitical role disastrous for Palestinians, and for the broader Middle East—it's also dangerous for Jewish safety and generates its own brand of "philosemitic" antisemitism, as we will discuss.

Both of us have each devoted more than a decade to supporting the Palestinian struggle for freedom from Israeli occupation, apartheid, settler colonialism, and ethnic cleansing. We stand for full equality for all inhabitants of the Holy Land, regardless of religion, nationality, or race. We support bi-nationalism, including the right of return for Palestinians, and a future that welcomes Jews, Palestinians, Druze, Samaritans, and others to flourish in a cooperative society. We support the Palestinian call to boycott, divest from, and sanction Israel for its ongoing oppression, and we reject any notion that this call, or principled opposition to Zionism, is inherently antisemitic.

POLITICIZED CHARGES OF ANTISEMITISM

Israel's policies are demonstrably unjust. The country's defenders have given up on defending these policies on their own terms. Instead, they redirect the conversation with antisemitism accusations. Not only does this threaten to derail Palestinian rights advocacy—it also harms efforts to fight antisemitism, and confuses what antisemitism even means.

Activism for Palestinian rights is routinely labeled antisemitic by political leaders from across the spectrum, including liberals. As discussed previously, these misleading accusations have been levied since at least the late 1960s, when groups like the ADL propagated the "new antisemitism" thesis. Their claim was that mounting criticism of Israel, in the wake of its 1967 occupation, represented a novel and dangerous form of global Jew hatred.

These accusations gained momentum alongside the rise of the BDS movement in the early 2000s. BDS raised crucial awareness on college campuses, within religious institutions, and in other communities of conscience, and was quickly recognized by Israel as a major threat to international support.

The infuriating truth is that today, antisemitism accusations are often a cudgel cynically deployed to silence voices for Palestinian human rights. The authors saw this firsthand in our own organizing on college campuses. For example, when students launch a campaign urging their university to divest from corporations complicit in Israeli apartheid, the backlash is often swift and severe. Off-campus pro-Israel organizations like StandWithUs mobilize hundreds to flood administrators with angry phone calls and emails, publish op-eds in local newspapers, and even lobby city and state officials to release public statements, raising alarms about alleged dire threats to Jewish safety on campus.[16]

Before long, student and professor activists—often first-generation Palestinian, Arab, and Muslim American students—find a flurry of posters on their campus quad, emails in their inboxes, phone calls to their employers, and social media posts slandering them as vile terrorists and antisemites. They have been targeted by Canary Mission, a website, maintaining a blacklist doxing thousands of activists and accusing them of antisemitism and terrorism. As a result of this pressure, professors have been fired, and students have been unjustly disciplined, kicked out of graduate programs, fired from jobs, and even pulled out of class by the FBI and questioned about social media posts.[17]

These racist and Islamophobic attacks can have a chilling effect on activism, making many hesitant to speak out for fear of being targeted. Students targeted by these attacks, Liz Jackson, an attorney at Palestine Legal, told us, have suffered "the effects of extreme stress on their body," failed or dropped out of school, and even had family members visited by the FBI, with "all the ripple effects of the trauma that comes from that—losing your sense of belonging, feeling the gaze of the police state following you everywhere, and being truly afraid for your freedom."

At first, these opportunistic antisemitism allegations were largely targeted at campuses, liberal churches, and other sites of BDS organizing. Beginning during the time period of Trump's presidency, Israel advocates and political leaders seized upon opportunities to paint a broader range of opponents as antisemites or enablers of antisemitism, from Jeremy Corbyn and the Labour Party in the UK to the Women's March, Bernie Sanders, and the Democratic Socialists of America (DSA) in the United States. Palestinian, Arab, Muslim, and Black leaders—such as Linda Sarsour, Ilhan Omar, Rashida Tlaib, Angela Davis, and Marc Lamont Hill, in recent years—get hit with accusations most frequently, a testament to the racist dynamics driving political anger.

Thanks to a concerted campaign by the Israeli government and pro-Israel organizations, laws, resolutions, and other policies have been advanced by government leaders in countries like Germany and France and in at least thirty-one states in the United States to penalize and discourage support for Palestinian rights, BDS, and anti-Zionism. These laws often utilize the faulty International Holocaust Remembrance Alliance (IHRA) definition of antisemitism, as discussed earlier. This has become a template for how to beat back other protest movements. The fossil fuel industry and gun lobby have modeled their own legislative efforts after state laws barring companies or individuals that boycott Israel from receiving government contracts.[18]

Politicized antisemitism accusations reached a fever pitch in late 2023, as millions took to the streets around the world in protest against Israel's genocidal bombardment and displacement in Gaza. Groups like the ADL smeared Palestine solidarity organizations as "hate groups," and called on the government to baselessly investigate them for material support for terrorism. Elected officials demanded the "deactivation" of Students for Justice in Palestine campus groups, and university administrators complied. The Biden White House, and elected officials across the aisle, repeated the canard that Palestine solidarity protests were hotbeds of bloodthirsty Jew hatred, often by misportraying chants like "from the river to the sea, Palestine will be free" as calls for the ethnic cleansing of Israeli Jews. Individuals were fired from jobs across media, tech, and other industries, including within Jewish organizations, for expressing support for Palestinian rights, and protests were banned in France and in cities across Germany.[19]

The Right's "selective outrage" on antisemitism amounts to what Jewish writer Elad Nehorai calls a "disinformation campaign."[20] Like George Soros conspiracy theories, false antisemitism claims are mobilized to discredit opponents as sinister and beyond the pale. Whether the wielders of these accusations think of themselves as sincerely concerned about Jews or not, the effect is to instrumentalize Jewish pain, Jewish fear, and public sympathy to attack justice movements. The "'new antisemitism' is not about Jews per se, any more than old antisemitism was," writes Jewish scholar Benjamin Balthaser. "It is a transnational modality of power and governance used to shore up the legitimacy of Western state power and attack its critics."[21] This wielding of Jews as "mute props to use as cudgels in a war of escalating rhetoric," as writer Talia Lavin called it, is itself a form of antisemitism, homogenizing our identity while isolating us from potential allies.[22]

Unsurprisingly, many far-right accusers have their own track record of antisemitic statements and maintain relationships with antisemitic political movements, from Donald Trump and Marjorie Taylor Greene to Christian Zionists whose End Times fantasies culminate in eternal hellfire for most Jews and the wholesale destruction of Jewishness through conversion to Christianity for a "lucky" few.

In an ironic twist, some Christian commentators have even claimed to experience antisemitism when their pro-

Israel positions are challenged. "They're weaponizing [the term antisemitism]," Eli Valley, a left-wing Jewish cartoonist who satirizes Zionist political figures, told us. "They're changing the meaning of antisemitism not to mean hatred of Jews, but to mean negative attitudes toward Christian Zionists, which is the most ultimate ludicrous endpoint of where we're headed." Valley himself faced accusations from Christian conservative pundit Meghan McCain, a disorienting reversal that erased his own Jewish identity and the intensely Jewish nature of his work.

Valley's experience is not uncommon. In fact, one of this book's authors has a lengthy Canary Mission profile, accusing him of "promoting antisemitism" through Palestinian rights activism. Some Jewish anti-Zionists are frequently targeted for being the "wrong kind of Jew," oftentimes by non-Jewish conservatives whose "love for Jews" is opportunistic and selective. According to one report, Jewish anti-Zionist activists within the UK Labour Party were up to thirty-five times more likely than non-Jews to be targeted by disciplinary procedures during the Right's attacks against Labour and former leader Jeremy Corbyn.[23]

Meanwhile, the broader media ecosystem, buoyed by profit-driven sensationalism, takes the lure, devoting endless attention to these attacks while saying comparatively little about white nationalist violence and pervasive conspiracy theories on the Right.

"I feel really frightened as a Jewish person, by how the Zionist Right has captured the conversation, making it so much harder for all of us to challenge the real antisemitism at its root," Liz Jackson of Palestine Legal told us.

Politically I just see what a convenient wedge and distraction tool it has been, for figures like Trump to use [these antisemitism accusations] as a cloak to hide his white supremacist policy, not to mention the white supremacist movement underneath him—it's really dangerous politically for the whole Left and for every marginalized community on the planet.

The seemingly endless discourse generated by these controversies distracts from the ongoing and vital need for justice for Palestinians. "I sometimes find myself thinking that Palestinians are just the canvas against which Jewish psychodramas play themselves out," Tareq Baconi, Palestinian analyst and scholar, charged at a 2022 conference on Holocaust memory in Berlin where, ironically enough, he was later targeted with false accusations for his speech. "We, as Palestinians, refuse to be singled out to defend against accusations of antisemitism."[24]

HOW THE LEFT RESPONDS

Caught in this cross fire, the Left remains frozen. Exasperated by the barrage of allegations, many activists bristle with defensiveness, refusing to take any discussion of antisemitism seriously, convinced the issue is entirely manufactured. Assuming all charges of antisemitism are dishonest and false, however, is a mistake.

Some criticism of Israel can be animated by antisemitism, or mobilize an antisemitic framing unwittingly. Not only can this harm Jews—it leads to faulty analysis and practice. Just as antisemitic conspiracy theories of Jewish banker cabals block a sharp perspective on capitalism, antisemitic anti-Zionism masks the root causes of Palestinian oppression by distracting our attention with lurid tales of innate Jewish wickedness and global Zionist power. And numerous studies have confirmed that Israeli military offensives with high civilian casualties are often accompanied by an uptick of antisemitism around the world—a correlation confirmed by the spike in antisemitic incidents during Israel's genocidal attack on Gaza beginning in late 2023.[25]

Many Jews have legitimate and understandable concerns that certain criticism of Israel or Zionism could be antisemitic or help foster a climate that endangers Jews. Discounting their perspective from the outset as brainwashed by pro-Israel propaganda and therefore not worth taking seriously (or to assume that they are lying, in a sinister Israel-backed scheme to silence criticism) is disrespectful at best, and at worst, functions as its own conspiracy theory of perpetual Jewish duplicity.

There is no one-size-fits-all formula to avoid antisemitism when advocating for Palestinian rights. As with any oppression, fighting antisemitism isn't a simple matter of remembering which words or "tropes" to avoid. We need a thoughtful analysis of antisemitism and Israel/Palestine, grounded in collective liberation. We can't provide all the answers, but we hope we can help ask the right questions.

We oppose Israel's oppression of Palestinians for the same reason we oppose antisemitism—we stand against reactionary nationalism and racist oppression in all its forms. We demand a world without exclusionary borders, where humans encounter each other in dignity and equality. Wherever it occurs, antisemitism weakens movements for positive change and strengthens forces of oppression and division. This is particularly evident in the case of Israel/Palestine—whether mobilized by Israel's supporters or its critics, antisemitism harms Palestinian solidarity, and reinforces the most reactionary elements of the United States, Israeli, and global Right.

On one level, the question of how to criticize Israel's injustices while avoiding antisemitism is similar to other situations where we might criticize human rights abuses committed by a state while avoiding bigotry against a group of people associated with that state. We strive to critique human rights violations committed by the Chinese government without an Orientalist frame that contributes to Sinophobic harassment against Asian Americans. We recognize it is valid to criticize the Saudi government for its oppression of women, while checking ourselves for Islamophobia.

An additional layer is at play when it comes to Israel: Israel is an oppressive agent of control for millions of Palestinians. And antisemitism presents itself as a challenge to oppressive power structures. Antisemitic conspiracy theories remain our collective cultural inheritance. Just as other forms of bigotry can arise despite our intentions, antisemitism can emerge unexamined.

The establishment of the modern nation-state of Israel in 1948—a mere three years after fascists accomplished the near-total destruction of European Jewry—opened a new era in the dialectic of Jewish power and powerlessness. Israel represents the first time in nearly two thousand years in which a Jewish collective wields sovereign state power, pursuing what it defines as self-determination. At the same time, the Jewish identity of the State of Israel—and the concrete, structural privilege and power afforded Israeli Jews (and any diaspora Jews who immigrate or, to some degree, even travel there)—is maintained through Palestinian dispossession.

It is of course possible, as the "new antisemitism" thesis alleges, for the State of Israel to embody the larger-than-life fantasy of what historian Brian Klug called the "collective Jew" in the antisemitic imagination.[26] But Israel is an actual, existing nation-state, maintaining real policies that affect the lives of millions within and beyond its borders. It is perfectly legitimate to forcefully criticize it on those grounds, including to call for structural changes that would secure justice and equality for all.

The world has changed for Jews outside of Israel, too. During the twentieth century, white Jews in many countries, including the United States, became integrated into structures of white privilege, and many (though certainly not all) became middle or upper class. As we have discussed, many on the Left wonder why antisemitism should receive attention when, from the looks of it, Jews as a group today are not facing material disempowerment, whether in Israel or elsewhere.

To complicate things further, there is a history of antisemitic, anti-Zionist ideology connected to the Left that many are unaware of. Beginning in the 1950s, as the new State of Israel gradually formed geopolitical alliances with the capitalist West, the U.S.S.R. reversed its initial pro-Israel stance, and began enthusiastically propagating "anti-Zionist" conspiracy theories as part of its Cold War campaigns. Much of this propaganda drew upon antisemitism, portraying Zionism as a global cabal of parasitic, bloodthirsty capitalists and imperialists in tones that replicated conspiracy theories of sinister Jewish world domination. In the U.S.S.R. and Soviet satellite states like Czechoslovakia and Poland, antisemitic purges and show trials, such as the Slánský trial in 1952, scapegoated prominent Jews, accusing them of dual loyalty, Zionism, and "cosmopolitanism" while channeling nationalism.[27] In an era when many anti-capitalist and anti-colonial movements looked to the U.S.S.R. for inspiration and material support, this propaganda, couched in left-wing, albeit Stalinist, language and sensibilities, sometimes influenced anti-Zionist rhetoric.[28]

AVOIDING CONSPIRACY THEORIES

Anti-Zionism can mobilize antisemitism, knowingly or otherwise, when fantastical portrayals of outsized, shadowy "Zionist" power take the place of grounded criticism of Israel's injustices, or concrete assessment of the actual political influence wielded by the state or its supporters.

For the time being, support for Israel's oppression of Palestinians remains hegemonic for dominant state, media, corporate and civil society institutions across the Global North. These institutions support Israel's oppression because they reflect and uphold the broader ideological consensus of Western imperialism. Their support is also reinforced by the advocacy and lobbying efforts of pro-Israel organizations and actors, such as the American Israel Public Affairs Committee (AIPAC) and Christians United for Israel (CUFI) in the United States.

In recent years, the Israeli government and affiliate institutions, eager to attack the Palestine solidarity movement, have stepped up *hasbara* (public relations) and advocacy campaigns, and they sometimes collaborate with pro-Israel organizations around the world which are not formally tied to the Israeli state. This kind of collaboration is mirrored by other repressive regimes looking to build support abroad. For example, affiliates of the far-right Hindu nationalist regime in India collaborate with groups like the Hindu American Foundation to foster American support.[29] These Hindu nationalists have been supported in their efforts by Israel advocates, and even adopt similar tactics, such as accusing critics of Hinduphobia.[30]

Some Israel advocates claim to represent Jewish, Christian or other communities, while others do not. Regardless, like other repressive actors, many prefer to avoid public scrutiny or accountability. The concrete influence of their efforts should be exposed—but not misportrayed as the spear's tip of a globe-trotting cabal plotting subversive, omnipotent control.

As UK activist Daniel Randall puts it, an antisemitic critique of Israel advocacy can misleadingly frame it "not as a mundane expression of the lobbying, interest-promotion, and soft-power building that international cultural and political milieus attached to nearly every state on earth conduct, but as a project for world domination."[31] The relations of power and influence wielded by Israel advocates are concrete and contingent, and are pursued by limited and fallible real-world actors. Seeing Israel advocacy in this way—as we've also discussed, for example, in relation to capitalist exploitation—is essential to strategically assessing its actual influence, identifying tensions and weaknesses, and countering its anti-Palestinian agenda.

Many diaspora Jewish organizations, communities and individuals currently support Israel, and some communal institutions, such as The Jewish Federations of North America or The Board of Deputies of British Jews, pursue Israel advocacy as one part of their broader work. This does not mean these actors hold some duplicitous "dual loyalty" (a classic antisemitic trope), nor that the Jewish communities these institutions claim to represent should be held collectively responsible for Israel's actions.

Far from revealing some sinister foreign allegiance, Western Jewish establishment support for Israel aligns with the dominant anti-Palestinian, imperialist consensus of the broader societies in which Western Jews live. And these organizations' political priorities are opposed by many of the Jews they claim to represent—a familiar story for many unrepresentative communal institutions in our undemocratic era.

Diaspora Jews hold an array of textured relationships, ideas, and agendas regarding Israel, just as they do with every social issue. Homogenizing pro-Israel Jews as monolithic fronts or pawns of Israel—or caricaturing their Israel advocacy as Zionist "subversion" or "infiltration"—robs them of agency and full belonging in the countries they call home. It relies on an antisemitic conflation between Jews and Israel, and can promote a hyperbolic, conspiratorial conception of global Zionist power.

In a parallel manner, explained Randall, some U.K. mosques have alleged "links to repressive states" like Saudi Arabia. "But to assume everything those mosques do is merely an enactment of those states' drive for power, or that Muslims who worship in them are effectively state agents or complicit in the crimes of those states, would be both a bigoted calumny and a facile misunderstanding of how power works."[32]

"(((THE LOBBY)))"

For example, some discussions of the "Israel lobby" can carry this conspiratorial framing. The term was popularized by the controversial 2007 book *The Israel Lobby and U.S. Foreign Policy* by prominent academics John Mearsheimer and Stephen

Walt. They argue that unwavering US support for Israel is not chiefly due to the United States' own strategic pursuit of geopolitical dominance—rather, pro-Israel movements and actors have hijacked US foreign policy at the highest levels, riding roughshod over the United States' best interests.

"Other special-interest groups have managed to skew foreign policy," Walt and Mearsheimer argue, "but no lobby has managed to divert it as far from what the national interest would suggest, while simultaneously convincing Americans that US interests and those of the other country—in this case, Israel—are essentially identical."[33]

As an overall analysis of US foreign policy, this "tail wagging the dog" argument gets it backward. The US political establishment supports Israel because it serves as what professor Noam Chomsky called a "military offshoot of the United States"[34]: it benefits the United States' own imperial interests, it lines the pockets of weapons manufacturers and war profiteers, and it fulfills the End Times fantasies of Christian Zionists, whose base of support and influence far outpaces anything the American Jewish establishment musters. "The seeming success of the Jewish Israel lobby," writes author and activist Benjamin Balthaser, should be "rooted in the fact that it travels with the current of Western states and their ideological and geopolitical interests, not against it."[35]

Any demand to rescue an American "national interest" from the clutches of some sinister, foreign "Israel lobby" rings of far-right America First nationalism, and overlooks that the United States itself, like Israel, is a settler-colonial project, born through the ethnic cleansing of Indigenous peoples and maintained through racial supremacy. We should redirect the over $3.8 billion in annual US military aid to Israel toward health care, public education, and social services not because American citizens deserve it more than residents of a foreign country, but because all people everywhere deserve a robust social safety net. In fact, the United States requires that Israel use most of its military aid to purchase weaponry manufactured by US corporations, underscoring the driving role of the military-industrial complex in the "special relationship" between the countries.[36]

For the far-right, polemics against the "Israel Lobby" are a perfect fit for their antisemitism. On his website, white nationalist David Duke rails against "the Zionist Treason of ZOG ['Zionist Occupation Government,' a white nationalist conspiracy theory term] driving America into the Ultimate Catastrophe of War for Israel Against Iran," explaining that "Zionist Jews run our foreign policy not for the benefit of Americans but for Israel."[37] If this lobby is torn out by its Jewish roots, they insist, white Christian America can reclaim its organic interest. In late 2023, white nationalist leaders like Nick Fuentes and groups like the National Justice Party exploited widespread outrage over Israel's horrific bombardment of Gaza to spread this type of anti-Zionist antisemitism, and some even attempted to join Palestine solidarity rallies across the country, where they were quickly rebuffed.[38]

This framing can show up, in muted form, in left-wing Palestine solidarity circles as well. In 2015, leading solidarity organizations circulated statements disavowing campaigner Alison Weir and Weir's organization, If Americans Knew (IAK), which had been accepted in some circles. Critics charged that Weir had recycled medieval blood libel conspiracy theories, demonized Jewish theology, and associated with white nationalists, but less attention was paid to the structural antisemitism undergirding her broader argument. IAK's website promises to reveal "the hidden history of how the United States was used to create Israel," claiming that in the first half of the twentieth century, a cabal of influential American Jews, such as Supreme Court Chief Justice Louis Brandeis, infiltrated US politics to covertly steer it toward support of Israel.[39]

Other pages fixate on reports of Israel spying on the US government (a practice common to many governments), or incidents like Israel's accidental 1967 attack on the US warship the USS *Liberty* (also frequently mentioned by white nationalists) in order to claim the Israel lobby causes "profound harm to the United States."[40] The picture that emerges is that a sinister, shadowy, and almost exclusively Jewish cabal has brainwashed Americans—and if citizens uproot this cabal they can restore their destiny.

"Our movement cannot flourish and achieve its aims," wrote the US Campaign to End the Israeli Occupation (now named the US Campaign for Palestinian Rights) in a 2015 statement disavowing Weir, "if we tolerate the same biases and bigotry against which we fight."[41]

The term "Israel lobby" is not always problematic. When many pro-Israel institutions visibly collaborate to defeat a progressive politician, or on the national stage to squash the Iran nuclear deal, to name two examples, it may make sense to speak of an "Israel lobby," just as one might condemn the "gun lobby" or the "Cuba lobby." Yet, in other cases, it flattens the political landscape, conflating actors who in fact have conflicting interests and dulling our strategic interventions with shades of conspiracism. "A more comprehensive approach," wrote organizer Jonah Boyarin, "can assuage Jewish concerns about antisemitism and sharpen Left analysis around U.S. foreign policy regarding Israel by emphasizing the larger network of financial and strategic interests sustaining the U.S.-Israel relationship. It would also link Israel/Palestine to other important progressive concerns, from bloated Pentagon budgets to U.S. support of autocratic regimes to the political dominance of the Christian right."[42]

Israel's crimes result from the realpolitik of Western imperialism, of which Israel is just one player rather than the entire system's architect. Instead of vague claims of lobbying or influence, focusing on specific actions, organizations, and relationships is best. Don't avoid naming names when applicable but avoid hyperbole or rampant speculation: these are real-world actors engaging in documented abuses. In short—do a rigorous "power analysis," a process activists use to figure out who is in charge and how they can be pressured and frame the real power that pro-Israel actors (Jewish and non-Jewish) hold within broader structures of exploitation.

"ZIONISM IS NOT JUDAISM"

A central way activists guard against antisemitism in Palestine solidarity work is by affirming that "Zionism is not Judaism." We don't deny that Israel defines itself as a "Jewish state," that the majority of Jews today support Israel in some form, or that its supporters, Jewish or non-Jewish, often mobilize arguments drawn from Jewish theology, history, and identity. But our critique should be directed toward Zionism as a political ideology and the actions of the Israeli state, not with Judaism as a religion or Jews as a people. By the same token, we insist that the supremacist Hindutva movement in India does not represent all Hindus, or that Saudi Arabia's oppression of women does not reflect some unsavory truth about Islam. To insist that Judaism or Jewishness itself is the cause of Israel's mistreatment of Palestinians misunderstands the colonial and imperial history of the country, and relies on antisemitic misinterpretations of Jewish life.

Israel doesn't oppress Palestinians because Jews are naturally oppressive, or Judaism is inherently chauvinist. Instead, we point to concrete geopolitical actors and interests, from US imperialism to the military-industrial complex, to explain the persistence of injustice. Israel's occupation, apartheid, and settler colonialism hold a distinct local context, but its core features are also observable elsewhere. Settler colonialism has been practiced in places like North America and Australia, while apartheid was best known in South Africa, for example.

Over time, the Palestine solidarity movement has rooted out many propagandists who made antisemitic equations between

Zionism and Judaism. In 2012, organizers circulated open letters disavowing Israeli British writer Gilad Atzmon, who argued that Israel's oppression of Palestinians resulted from specifically Jewish pathologies, such as ethnocentrism and anti-Gentile hostility, encoded in Jewish theology. "The never-ending theft of Palestine in the name of the Jewish people is part of a spiritual, ideological, cultural and practical continuum between the Bible, Zionist ideology and the State of Israel," wrote Atzmon. "Israel and Zionism . . . instituted the plunder promised by the Hebrew God in the Judaic holy scriptures."[43]

The US Palestinian Community Network circulated a collective letter, signed by leading Palestinian activists, calling Atzmon's words "immoral and completely outside the core foundations of humanism, equality and justice" that drive the struggle for a free Palestine. "Our struggle was never, and will never be, with Jews, or Judaism . . . We reaffirm that there is no room in . . . our struggle for any attacks on our Jewish allies, Jews, or Judaism; nor denying the Holocaust; nor allying in any way shape or form with any conspiracy theories, far-right, orientalist, and racist arguments, associations and entities."[44]

Sometimes, criticism of Israel can channel the tropes of Christian anti-Judaism, even if unintentionally. We see this, for example, in depictions of Israelis as bloodthirsty vampires who sadistically prey on children, or as Satanic embodiments of pure evil—repackaging medieval blood libel and demonology, respectively.

People are often unaware that this imagery is rooted in antisemitism, and because antisemitic images and conspiracy theories filter widely throughout our culture, they can be reproduced without consciously connecting the dots. Many Jews, including us, share the unnerving experience of encountering at a Palestine solidarity rally, alongside plenty of inspiring signage, an image of the Star of David[45] dripping in blood, a vampiric Benjamin Netanyahu feasting on a Palestinian child's organs, or a hook-nosed and swarthy Israeli soldier.

Those who are receptive to feedback will quickly apologize and lower their sign. This is, however, not always the case, and sometimes they counter by accusing their critics of being Zionists.

At a 2014 London rally contesting Israel's attacks on the Gaza Strip, UK organizer Daniel Randall saw a sign reading "Research: The Babylonian Talmud, The Protocols of the Learned Elders of Zion," below which a Star of David sat with the number "666" inside, dripping with blood. He challenged the sign holder, and was met with a scoff: "You're blinded by your bias because you're a Jew." Instead of finding support, Randall experienced defensiveness from those nearby.[46] "More people in our immediate vicinity took his side than supported me," Randall told us, adding that he has encountered other types of antisemitism in organizing spaces. "[I've heard] conspiracy-theorist ideas about Zionism, massively overinflated claims about the power and influence of Israel, claims that Israel is somehow a singular and quintessential expression of racism and imperialism."

Randall's experience at the London rally was not ambiguous. There are situations, however, where it's possible to mistake legitimate criticism for coded antisemitism. For example, traditional antisemitism frames Jews as thieving and duplicitous—but it's not inherently antisemitic to condemn the Israeli government or settlements for stealing land belonging to Palestinians (typical of settler colonialism) and covering it up (typical of bad state actors).

To further complicate it, Israel, and its supporters, including many Jews themselves, often insist the Jewish state is global Jewry's representative. This false belief gets used as a support for the antisemitic logic equating Zionism and Judaism, and even risks charging Jews living elsewhere with implicit "dual loyalties." "When the state of Israel claims Jews as its own," explains historian Brian Klug, "and when Jews en masse proclaim Israel to be theirs, it is not surprising if others fail to make the distinction between Jewish state and Jewish people."[47] While progressive Jewish activists work within our communities to disentangle Jewish identity from Zionism, our allies can support these efforts by consistently rejecting the notion that Jews, or any other people, are a homogenous unit, synonymous with a state.

Tagging a random synagogue with "Free Palestine" graffiti, demonstrating outside a synagogue or Jewish center to express generalized opposition to Israel's injustices, harassing random Jews on the streets with condemnations of Israel—these detestable acts betray an inescapably antisemitic logic, holding diaspora Jews collectively responsible for Israel's government. During widespread protests against Israel's 2021 war on Gaza, at least two synagogue buildings in the United States and United Kingdom were attacked and defaced,[48] respectively; individuals drove through a predominantly Jewish neighborhood in London blaring antisemitic messages from a loudspeaker.[49]

Jews in Leftist spaces sometimes face "litmus tests" from non-Jewish comrades who position them as implicated in Israel/Palestine, or pressure them to weigh in for little reason other than their Jewishness. "What I've found so often is this nervous, tentative game of 'we're gonna bring this up, and see how you react!'" Rabbi Danya Ruttenberg explained to us.

> I express my true feelings, which is that I desire an end to the occupation and support Palestinian human rights and self-determination—and there's this sigh of relief! And it's uncomfortable. I'm aware that I'm being tested . . . What I really should do is name it as a litmus test, and have that conversation, rather than just moving on.

The assumption that every Jew is a Zionist until proven otherwise, or the notion that Jews' loyalty to the movement must be tested, can result from antisemitic assumptions. Even when those ideas are not motivating the questioning, the indifference to impact suggests a troubling distrust of and disregard for Jewish experiences.

TAKING JEWS SERIOUSLY

While it's true that Zionism is not Judaism, sometimes problematic conclusions are drawn from this in Palestine solidarity circles. If Zionism is not Judaism, some argue, this means most Jews worldwide who currently identify as Zionist must be brainwashed, ignorant, or "doing Judaism wrong." Their personal attachment to Zionism, then, is simply racist, reactionary false consciousness, and little more needs to be said. "After all," this perspective continues, "some Jews share our politics and are part of our movements!"

This sets up a toxic "good Jew/bad Jew" binary where the minority of Jews who identify as anti- or non-Zionist are celebrated (sometimes tokenized), while the rest are belittled as unworthy—a dynamic in which Jewish Leftists, too, can certainly participate, and which is mirrored, in inverted form, on the Right. The Left's understanding of Zionism as a nationalist movement that has wreaked settler colonialism, occupation, and apartheid is true—but it's not the whole story.

The majority of the world's Jewish people currently support Zionism because they relate to Israel, quite understandably, as a life raft in a cruel, stormy ocean. For them, Israel embodies Jewish resilience, survival, and pride, and the nonnegotiable demand that, so long as antisemitism exists, Jews must maintain a safe place, backed up by the assurance of force, somewhere on Earth. The creation of a Jewish state in 1948, a mere three years after Nazi genocide, was experienced by *most* Jewish people as nothing short of a miracle.

Most Jews did not arrive in the Holy Land as willful colonizers eager to serve as the shock troops of Western imperialism.

Rather, they were flung there atop the storm-tossed waters of the twentieth century, fleeing the wreckage of pogroms and genocide across Europe (when anti immigrant nativists in the United States and elsewhere, it must be remembered, refused to take them in, even after the Holocaust), and state repression and expulsion across the Middle East and North Africa, the U.S.S.R., and elsewhere around the world. Once they arrived, they and their descendants, reeling from unhealed intergenerational trauma, facing continued violence and socialized into militarist nationalism, have known little other option than to cling to the Zionist project as if fighting for their very lives.

"A man once jumped from the top floor of a burning house in which many members of his family had already perished," explained Marxist historian Isaac Deutscher in June 1967, offering a powerful metaphor dramatizing this tragic aspect of the conflict:

> He managed to save his life; but as he was falling he hit a person standing down below and broke that person's legs and arms. The jumping man had no choice; yet to the man with the broken limbs he was the cause of his misfortune. If both behaved rationally, they would not become enemies. The man who escaped from the blazing house, having recovered, would have tried to help and console the other sufferer; and the latter might have realized that he was the victim of circumstances over which neither of them had control. But look what happens when these people behave irrationally. The injured man blames the other for his misery and swears to make him pay for it. The other, afraid of the crippled man's revenge, insults him, kicks him, and beats him up whenever they meet. The kicked man again swears revenge and is again punched and punished. The bitter enmity, so fortuitous at first, hardens and comes to overshadow the whole existence of both men and to poison their minds.[50]

Today, the State of Israel contains nearly half the world's Jewish population, at least half of whom are Mizrahim.[51] Most Jews worldwide feel a deep spiritual, familial, and/or communal connection to the Land of Israel and the Jewish civilization that exists there, intimately bound up with their concern for its safety and thriving. While we take care to separate our critique of Zionism from critiques of Judaism or Jewishness, we must also recognize that contemporary Jewish identity and peoplehood remain bound up with Israel and the traumas that helped form it.

As long as Israel's oppression continues to intensify, it would be unrealistic, even problematic, to demand historical empathy and compassion from Palestinians as a precondition for peace and justice, especially absent even the slightest parallel gesture from their oppressors. But for most non-Palestinians, a refusal to seriously grapple with Jewish attachment to Zionism represents a colossal blind spot, undermining the Left's aspirations to meet marginalized communities where they are at. If our approach isn't informed by a deep understanding of the underlying trauma and fear that has led so many Jews to put their faith in nationalism, we limit ourselves to a regrettably partial view of the full picture, and our attempts to transform the hardened status quo won't be as effective or strategic. We cannot dismiss broad swathes of any marginalized community as a priori enemies, unworthy of relationship and solidarity if they do not immediately agree to a radical critique that runs counter to their entire socialization. To do so would be to abdicate our responsibility to transform that community, ceding territory to the Right. Activists must meet people where they're at, treat them like they are worth more than just their political agreement, and work to move them along issues that matter.

With these principles in mind, progressives should unequivocally welcome the Jewish community in our big-tent coalition of belonging, co-resistance, and care. As we continue building the movement for Palestinian rights, we should model generative, uncomfortable debate, inviting in as many people as possible and not writing people off for their mistakes or lack of understanding. We should insist upon the basic humanity of Israeli Jews, even in the face of a brutal occupation that dehumanizes everything it touches.

We must affirm that our vision for a just future in Israel/ Palestine is one where Israeli Jews will enjoy safety and collective flourishing while Palestinians finally reclaim the same as well. We must fight for pluralistic societies across the Middle East where Jews, Palestinians, and other minorities can live free from persecution.

Unfortunately, in the wake of Hamas's brutal massacre and kidnapping of hundreds of Israeli civilians on October 7, 2023, parts of the Left took the opposite tack, and the entire movement suffered as a result. On social media and at rallies across the country, some activists uncritically celebrated Hamas's overall attack as "resistance," minimizing Israeli civilian victims into a homogenous category of "settlers", unworthy of solidarity or support. This callous and unprincipled stance horrified and alienated many Jews, leftists, and members of the general public who were or might have been otherwise supportive of the Palestine solidarity movement's goals and aims.[52]

When the Left misses the mark here, our movements are weaker and more vulnerable to attack. Many progressive Jews who might otherwise align with, or be open to, the message of Palestine solidarity keep their distance, because they encounter ignorance and insensitivity to Jewish identity, history, and trauma in movement spaces. Pro-Israel organizations claim Palestine solidarity activism creates a "hostile" or "unsafe" climate for Jews on campuses and in communities. They organize pressure campaigns that weaken and marginalize activist coalitions, deepen divisions, and stifle free speech.

These *hasbara* campaigns are usually hyperbolic—for example, Jewish students often insist they do not face a "hostile" or "unsafe" climate on campus, even if they find Palestine solidarity activism to be deeply offensive.[53] But the campaigns enjoy easy momentum and a veneer of credibility, so long as the Left lacks an established track record of taking Jewish subjectivity seriously.

It's also important for Jews grappling with these issues to distinguish between feeling uncomfortable and being unsafe, between encountering challenging perspectives and experiencing antisemitic harm. Sometimes, the line between insensitive microaggression and legitimate critique is fuzzy, and it's easy to mistake one for the other. Confronting hard truths about Israel should unsettle us, and there is nothing inherently "hostile" or "unsafe" about this.

"Political speech does not have to be measured, proportional, tempered, or reasonable to be protected" as free expression, states the Jerusalem Declaration on Antisemitism, and "unreasonable" speech is not necessarily antisemitic.[54] The demand that activists exercise "civility," and refrain from forcefully criticizing Israeli oppression, is itself deeply oppressive. "The disciplining of language," wrote Arab scholar Lara Sheehi while facing a firestorm of weaponized attacks in 2023, "is an old misogynist cudgel by which Black, Indigenous, and women of color, especially, are expected to, at best, reply to racism, sexism, and xenophobia with a gentile and 'civil' reply."[55]

Even in cases where the antisemitism is clear-cut, calling on state and administrative power to punish a few "bad apples" does little to tear out antisemitism at the root. "This is anti-racism as procedure," wrote author Michael Richmond, noting the inadequacies of widespread campaigns to expel activists from the UK Labour Party in the wake of its antisemitism controversies, "a search for legal and bureaucratic fixes to a localized outbreak, so that a never-clean institution can be given a clean bill of health again."[56] On the Left, too, it's not enough simply to "purge" our movements of obvious antisemites like Gilad Atzmon or Alison Weir. We need grassroots political education in our movements, strong relationships to navigate difficult moments together, and systemic change to transform the inequitable world where conspiracy theories thrive.

An unwillingness to take Jewish Zionism seriously does not mean that the Left is a simmering hotbed of antisemitism-in-waiting, with fanatical conspiracy theories of Jewish world domination and demonizing views of Jews as Satanic baby killers brewing just below the surface. The truth, as we see it, is both more nuanced and banal than that. The Left is often just ambivalent about Jewish issues. Warmth, curiosity, and openness mix in with patches of resentment and microaggressions in a broader stew of ignorance. This is a far cry from the threats Jews face on the Right, but it nonetheless remains an obstacle.

The Left is a deeply imperfect work in progress, with all too human tendencies to blur the world's messy details into broad generalities, oversimplistic binaries and too-easy hero-villain narratives. The embrace of nationalism as a safety strategy by much of world Jewry in the twentieth century and into the present reflects the Left's ongoing failure to take antisemitism seriously, and resolve to fight it. We're entering a period of flux in American Jewish support for Israel, with widespread opposition to the occupation and the Israeli Right's assault on democracy, and the Left must prove that solidarity is a surer bet than nationalism.

TEN

A SAFETY OF NATIONALISM? ANTISEMITISM
AND THE HISTORY OF ZIONISM

> The tradition of all dead generations weighs like a night-
> mare on the brains of the living.
>
> > Karl Marx, "The Eighteenth Brumaire
> > of Louis Bonaparte," 1852[1]

The handful of detestable street attacks against Jews in the
United States and United Kingdom during Israel's bombardment of Gaza in 2021 were quickly condemned in the Palestine solidarity movement. A few voices, however, blamed
Israel for what occurred. "Every time they bomb Gaza," asserted Tariq Ali, a leading left-wing intellectual in the United
Kingdom, "*that* is what creates antisemitism . . . Stop the occupation, stop the bombings, and the casual antisemitism will
soon disappear."[2]

At best, this flawed logic overlooks, as author Keith
Kahn-Harris put it, that "no social phenomenon is simply 'reversible.' Racism has its own dynamic that persists beyond its
origins."[3] Even if it were true that Israel's oppressive actions
were the initial impetus for a spike in antisemitism, there's
no guarantee that ending Israel's oppression would end the
antisemitism, which takes on a life of its own.

At worst, however, it's a perverse form of victim-blaming.
While Israel's oppression can inflame latent antisemitism, it does
not *cause* antisemitism. Antisemitic scripts had been circulating
for nearly two thousand years before Theodor Herzl put pen to

paper. They remain deeply ingrained in societal consciousness, available as a reservoir that Israel's critics can draw upon, knowingly or otherwise. Both phenomena—antisemitism, and Israel's oppression of Palestinians—merit condemnation on their own terms, and neither "causes" the other.

This theme is familiar. A 2013 book by prominent Left theorists Alain Badiou, Éric Hazan, and Ivan Segré argued that attacks on Jews by Black and Arab French youth were not caused by antisemitism per se, but rather were misguided responses to Israel's oppression of Palestinians. "The hostility of these young people toward Jews is fundamentally bound up with what is happening in Palestine," the authors write, and when they see pro-Israel public interventions from leaders of French Jewish community institutions, it "can lead them to believe all the Jews in the world, here and elsewhere, are their enemies."[4]

But just because anger at Israel's actions is real and valid, does not make the actions, beliefs, or intentions that feed off that anger inherently justifiable. Holding all Jews worldwide collectively responsible for Israel's actions, and attacking them on that basis, is antisemitic and this antisemitism must be condemned, not explained away. Israel is not the root cause of antisemitism, but Israel's oppression of Palestinians does radicalize tensions, which more easily feed on existing antisemitic ideas. In many countries throughout the northern Africa and Southwest Asia region, antisemitism is espoused by opportunistic political leaders and circulated across broad social and class strata. These policies and rhetoric from above shape attitudes at the grassroots, as seen in Europe, where antisemitic attitudes are present in some immigrant communities.[5]

Where did this antisemitism come from? The assumption, championed by the Zionist Right, is that it reflects some foundational flaw within Islamic theology, or Muslim and/or Arab civilization, itself. This racist and Islamophobic view "contributes to that false notion that [Israel/Palestine] is an inherent conflict between Muslims and Jews," Deanna Othman, Palestinian American journalist and educator, told us, "so therefore there's nothing we can do to fix this."

Mystifying this antisemitism as an inherent, eternal quality of an entire religious civilization only clouds our understanding. Ironically, many of the far-right voices that claim to locate the roots of this antisemitism in the Muslim world and its hoary past would be better served examining their own Euro-Christian civilization instead.

Much of the antisemitism in the Middle East was originally introduced by European nationalist, colonialist, and fascist movements. And throughout the region, it is nationalism that keeps antisemitism locked in place—including, counterintuitively, within the Zionist movement itself. In this chapter, we will dig at some of these roots, in order to glimpse the possibility of a world beyond antisemitism and the religio-nationalist Othering on which it stands.

ANTISEMITISM IN THE MIDDLE EAST

One century ago, European fascist leaders sought to spread antisemitism not only across Europe, but into the Middle East as well. They hoped to use antisemitism to exploit growing opposition to British colonialism and increasing Jewish settlements in what would become the State of Israel, and build their own global base of support.

Starting in the 1930s, the Nazis looked, often with little success, to build coalitions with reactionary Arab leaders to block Allied influence. "Together," writes scholar Jeffrey Herf, "the Nazis and the pro-Nazi Arab collaborators produced a cultural fusion, a synthesis that brought together the anti-Western, antidemocratic, and vehemently antisemitic currents of National Socialism and radical Arab nationalism infused with an equally radical Islamist reading of the traditions of Islam."[6]

As historian Matthias Küntzel has documented, Nazi leaders shared texts like *The Protocols of the Elders of Zion*, and even established an entire radio station outside of Berlin, equipped with what was then one of the world's most powerful short-wave transmitters (which Nazi propaganda leader Joseph Goebbels proudly called their "long-range gun in the ether") to broadcast antisemitic ideology aimed at Arab listeners across the region.[7]

Meanwhile, European colonizers tried to use antisemitism as a tool to keep anti-colonial anger under control. Nationalists in countries like France, meanwhile, exported antisemitism to the Arab Muslim streets of overseas colonies like Algeria, hoping to redirect the anger of colonized peoples away from the colonial metropole and onto their Jewish neighbors instead. While the Nazis pursued the Holocaust in Europe, antisemitic agitators simultaneously targeted Jews across the Middle East and North Africa, helping to propagate attacks, such as the horrific pogrom known as the Farhud in Baghdad in June 1941 or the smaller series of anti-Jewish riots in Egypt in November 1945.

During this time, growing Arab nationalist movements organized to throw off the yoke of European colonialism, and win independence. They were sharply anti-Zionist, opposing the imperial British and, later, American backing of the Zionist project. While the majority of Arab Jews were not Zionist at this time, many Arab nationalists nonetheless suspected them of harboring dual loyalties, especially as the Zionist movement worked intensively to court Arab Jewish support.

"The Zionist view that Arabness and Jewishness were mutually exclusive," wrote Mizrahi scholar Ella Shohat, "gradually came to be shared by Arab nationalist discourse." Mizrahi Jews found themselves "on the horns of a terrible dilemma," increasingly seeing little future for themselves in the places some of them had called home for millennia.[8] Propelled by these and other factors, hundreds of thousands of Jews departed from countries across the region in the following decades, and many arrived in Israel, where, as discussed, they continue to face pervasive discrimination from the dominant Ashkenazi caste.

Growing Islamist religio-nationalist movements, which rose to power in many countries in the latter decades of the twentieth century, fused the antisemitic conspiracy theories introduced earlier by European nationalists, using barbed interpretations of classical Islamic texts to create a novel twist on an old story. "[Zionists use] wealth to stir revolutions in various parts of the globe in order to fulfill their interests and pick the fruits," stated Hamas's old 1988 charter, reproducing classic antisemitic conspiracy theories of Jewish secret control to explain the suffering, and channel the rage, of Palestinians. "They aim at undermining societies, destroying values, corrupting consciences, deteriorating character and annihilating Islam."[9] It is hardly surprising that these Islamist movements would make ready use of antisemitism, since they share many far-right characteristics: opposition to modernity and liberalism, regressive gender hierarchies, longing to restore an imagined "golden era" of civilizational purity, and conspiracy theories about pernicious Western elites.

Marxist scholar Moishe Postone has argued that contemporary antisemitism in some Islamist movements functions as a kind of "foreshortened anti-imperialism," channeling widespread anger at US imperialism in order to "punch up" at an imagined Zionist Jewish cabal controlling global economies, subverting Arab national sovereignty, and engaging in anti-Muslim perfidy. Where conservative Islamist leaders have state power, he writes, they use antisemitism as a "nationalist lightning rod to deflect popular anger and discontent" against their own domestic policies, and "attribute the *misère* of the Arab masses and, increasingly, the educated middle classes, to evil external forces."[10] This helps corrupt autocrats portray themselves as heroes of the people, often, ironically enough, while quietly collaborating with the very Western forces they claim to oppose.

MY ENEMY'S ENEMY

The fight for Palestine requires broad coalitions, but this has not always meant that we all share the same political motivations. Some anti-Zionists practice what has been called "campism," the tendency to support nearly any actors in the broad "camp" of anti-Zionism, regardless of their larger politics. At times, activists in various contexts have lent unqualified support to Islamist regimes such as the Iranian government, political parties like Hezbollah in Lebanon, or resistance movements like Hamas in Gaza, despite those groups' reactionary beliefs.

"Rather than analyzing this reactionary form of resistance in ways that would help support more progressive forms of resistance," writes Postone, "many on the Western Left have either ignored it or rationalized it as an unfortunate, if understandable, reaction to Israeli policies in Gaza and the West Bank."[11]

There is an understandable hesitancy in many Western activist communities to criticize the ideology or tactics of Global South resistance movements, since such criticism is regularly weaponized by our political opponents in pursuit of noxious agendas. But championing groups with reactionary ideologies as progressive vanguards—or overlooking, even celebrating detestable tactics such as violence against noncombatant civilians—betrays our moral principles and blurs the clear vision necessary to win justice. The Left's shortcomings here became painfully obvious in late 2023, when the massacre of hundreds of Israeli civilians by Hamas received little condemnation, and even occasional applause, across much of the Palestine solidarity movement. Some embraced Hamas uncritically as a flagship resistance movement, abandoning moral principles and strategic grounding in the process.[12]

We should challenge antisemitism in the Middle East, and call for pluralist and tolerant societies across the region where Jews and other religious minorities live in safety and freedom,

while we work toward justice in Israel/Palestine and an end
to US imperialism. We also cannot hope to end these ideologies or tactics in a vacuum, overlooking the root cause of the
conflict: over seven decades of exile and dispossession, occupation and apartheid, humiliation and subjugation of Palestinians that is only deepening. "It is true that two wrongs don't
make a right, as we love to point out to the people we have
wronged," wrote James Baldwin in 1967, checking those who,
in his day, moralized against militant resistance to apartheid
in South Africa:

> But one wrong doesn't make a right, either. People
> who have been wronged will attempt to right the
> wrong; they would not be people if they didn't. They
> can rarely afford to be scrupulous about the means
> they will use. They will use such means as come to
> hand. Neither, in the main, will they distinguish one
> oppressor from another, nor see through to the root
> principle of their oppression.[13]

ZIONISM'S "JEWISH QUESTION"

While the Zionist Right endlessly fixates on the antisemitism
that, in their view, underlies anti-Israel animus, little attention is paid to the antisemitism that, counterintuitively, has
appeared in Zionism itself.

Many Jews who emigrated to Palestine before World War
II were fleeing Russia, where Jews were periodically terror-
ized by pogroms. These mob attacks against Jews could be
obscenely violent. "[They] forced unfortunates to eat their
excrement. They shoveled earth over them and buried them
alive," wrote Scholem Schwartzbard about the pogroms he
witnessed in Russia between 1918 and 1920.[14]

One of the most famous of these massacres occurred in the
city of Kishinev, in 1903. "Behold on tree, on stone, on fence, on

mural clay, the spattered blood and dried brains of the dead," wrote esteemed Jewish poet Hayyim Bialik in his 1904 poem "In the City of Slaughter."[15] Bialik's tortured words memorialize the victims of the Kishinev pogrom, a mass slaughter of Jews committed by ultranationalist forces in imperial Russia that, determined to beat back revolutionaries, used antisemitism to blame the country's instability on Jews. These tropes inspired barbaric attacks on Jews, in which non-Jews—often their neighbors and with encouragement by state officials—channeled a kind of sacrificial rage.

People forget, however, how Bialik's poem also chastises the victims. "They are too wretched to evoke thy scorn. They are too lost thy pity to evoke, so let them go, then, men to sorrow born, mournful and slinking, crushed beneath their yoke." In a different poem, Bialik criticizes Orthodox Jewish men, who, he suggests, were not manly enough, and too religion obsessed to sufficiently protect their communities.[16]

The Jews, he insisted, had been degenerated by diaspora life—cleaving to religious texts, passively submitting to the oppression they faced, and hiding from the world of strength, power, and self-determination. This prognosis, by Bialik and other early Zionists, centered the idea of *shlilat ha'galut*, negation of the diaspora, a central Zionist tenet that called for liquidating the Jewish diaspora and building a "new Jew" in the Land of Israel: the kind of Jew they could finally celebrate.

These Zionists' arguments reinforced some of the claims antisemites made about Jews. In his classic 1882 text *Auto-Emancipation*, Leon Pinsker, one of the earliest Zionists, lamented that "Judaism and Jew-hatred [have] passed through history for centuries as inseparable companions . . . What a pitiful figure we do cut! . . . We shall forever continue to be what we have been and are, parasites, who are a burden to the rest of the population, and can never secure their favor."[17]

In 1897, Zionist figurehead Theodor Herzl penned an article titled "Mauschel"—a German epithet for a haggling Jewish trader, used by Herzl to caricature those Jews in fin de siècle Europe who rejected the Zionist movement. Herzl's Mauschel was a "spineless, repressed, shabby" figure, "a distortion of human character, something unspeakably low and repugnant" who "carries on his dirty deals behind the mask of progress and reaction alike."[18] Zionism is "the only cure for a sickness," wrote journalist Arthur Koestler, and the Zionist effort to normalize the Jews by turning them into a nation *"ke-khol am ve'am"* or "like any other nation," as Israel's declaration of independence would put it, was the cure in action.[19]

The idea, for many leading Jewish Zionists, was that Jews required an almost imperial quality to restore their dignity, to become a new nation, modeled off European masculinist ideals, where power and military strength determine our fate. Even ostensibly left-wing figures like the eco-anarchist Aaron David Gordon saw in Zionism a way to "regenerate" the Jewish soul through labor, a kind of *volkisch* mysticism, echoing some strains of European racial thinking prevalent at the time (while challenging others), that would anchor Jews to the land instead of the cosmopolitan exilic world of books and ideas.[20]

This strain of muscular-nationalist thinking—with its contempt for a warped image of diaspora Jews, partially blaming Jews for their alleged perpetual victimhood, and its desire to sculpt a "new Jew" in the image of European nationalism—mirrored right-wing antisemitic, patriarchal tropes of the era.[21] It influenced Israeli society from its beginnings, and was reinvigorated by the post-1967 occupation and the increasingly dominant role played by the Israeli far-right.

From the beginnings of the Zionist movement, a few leaders sought to make pragmatic alliances with antisemitic European movements. After all, many antisemites wanted Jews out of Europe, and readily supported Zionism in pursuit of that shared goal. In one 1895 diary entry, reflecting on lessons learned during the antisemitic Dreyfus affair in France, Herzl concluded, "I achieved a freer attitude toward anti-Semitism, which I now began to understand historically and make allowances for. Above all, I recognized the emptiness and futility of efforts to 'combat antisemitism.'"

In another entry that year, he optimistically noted that as the Zionist movement succeeds, "the anti-Semites will become our most dependable friends, the anti-Semitic countries our allies." Antisemitic Europeans, he hoped, would happily assist the Zionist movement in transferring Jewish property and persons outside the borders of Europe.[22]

Some antisemitic leaders of Herzl's era seemed to share his hope. In 1897, the far-right French nationalist publication *La Libre Parole* cheered that year's First Zionist Congress, sneering that "not only does [*La Libre Parole*] offer, freely and enthusiastically, publicity for the [Zionist] colonists," but they would also provide money to export the Jews from France.

One decade later, the paper's editor, Édouard Drumont, whose polemics during France's Dreyfus affair helped shape modern antisemitism, wrote that Zionism represented the "future of the Jewish Question and, consequently, the future of humanity as a whole," speculating that, were the Jews transferred from Europe to Palestine, "this Jewish Question, which . . . dominates all human affairs, including the Social Question, would be resolved, at least for the time being, and the world would finally know a period of calm and relative security."[23]

Antisemitic liberal European leaders saw Zionism as a solution to their concerns. Statesmen who feared that "Jewish Bolshevism" was a growing threat, such as Arthur Balfour and Winston Churchill, eagerly supported Zionism as an alternative. Other non-Jewish leaders, equally antisemitic, courted Zionist Jewish leaders because they thought these figures possessed immense, world-shaping power and were eager to ally with this imagined power.[24] Many Christian Zionist leaders of the era, moreover, played an important role in forming and supporting the Jewish Zionist movement due to their own antisemitic End Times fantasies, as we discussed previously.

With the growth of fascism, many Jewish Zionist leaders, wrote historian Enzo Traverso, "tried to 'use' antisemitism as a chance for increasing Jewish emigration to Palestine instead of fighting [antisemitism]." Many Jewish Leftists of the era condemned the defeatism and escapism of this approach.[25]

Today, much of the European and US far-right is fiercely Zionist, even while their own movements are deeply antisemitic. Across the far-right, a "new philosemitism," as researcher Hannah Rose puts it, positions Israel as a garrison outpost defending the West against supposed Islamic barbarism.[26] This conflation between Israel and world Jewry (itself antisemitic) offers *conditional* protection to Jews or the Jewish state, and functions as its own "good Jew/bad Jew" dynamic, demanding that the "right kind of Jew" must be Zionist and Islamophobic, and that the Muslim world writ large is the site of the only antisemitism worth mentioning.

Fighting anti-Zionism has become a proxy, for much of the Western far-right, for absolving the guilt of participating in antisemitism, while at the same time advancing their own imperial interests. "As Zionism mirrored anti-Semitism in the past," explains historian Barnaby Raine, "so the mainstream Right mirrors anti-Semites now, sharing a distorted image of Jews as representatives of the status quo but *finding new love for them on that basis*, rather than objecting to it."[27]

Many right-wing Jewish organizations and Israeli political leaders, unfortunately, are all too willing to embrace these erstwhile "allies." For example, Netanyahu and other Israeli Rightists have forged numerous alliances with antisemitic European ethnonationalist leaders, while in the United States, the far-right Zionist Organization of America hosted Steve Bannon for a fiery address at their 2017 awards gala.[28] In late 2023, after one-time Twitter CEO Elon Musk was widely condemned for endorsing an antisemitic white nationalist tweet that Jews are responsible for "dialectical hatred against whites," Israeli leaders invited him to tour the Gaza border and meet with Prime Minister Benjamin Netanyahu—a grotesque attempt to repair Musk's reputation by casting him as a stalwart defender of Israel as it relentlessly bombed Gaza.[29]

Meanwhile, the Israeli far-right traffics in antisemitic conspiracy theories, much like their European counterparts. Netanyahu and allies frequently rail against George Soros as the all-powerful mastermind behind liberal opposition to their ultranationalist project. Netanyahu has even dabbled in Holocaust revisionism,[30] while his son Yair once shared an antisemitic meme depicting Soros alongside reptilian and Illuminati puppet masters behind global affairs, imagery common across 4chan.[31]

Birds of a feather, it seems, flock together. Wherever far-right religio-nationalism rears its head, antisemitism is likely to follow—even in the "Jewish state."

A FUTURE BEYOND NATIONALISM

Zionism was founded on the certainty that antisemitism is inescapable and that we can only mitigate, but can never destroy, it. But today, it's clearer than ever that the Zionist project has failed in its supposed mission to ensure Jewish safety. More and more Jews are realizing that a nuclear-armed, ultra-militarized garrison state, founded on the unjust oppression of another people and condemned to the endless cycles of bloodshed necessary to maintain that oppression, wedged in the tightening contradictions of empire, sliding deeper into outright fascism and allying with far-right nationalist antisemites, is a dangerously precarious vehicle for our people to seek dependable safety—and is certainly a far cry from the moral "light unto the nations" many of us imagined Israel to be.

Zionist hegemony dominates Jewish scholarship, civic life, and religious discourses, making non-Zionist political solutions appear unrealistic or impossible. There may be understandable reasons why some cling to this belief, but we now have a choice about whether we want to reproduce this mentality or search for new strategies for combating antisemitism.

As we will discuss, we can also look to past generations of Jewish revolutionaries to lead the way. Over a century ago, while Zionists proposed their nationalist answer to the "Jewish question," massively popular left-wing groups like the Jewish Labor Bund in Eastern Europe countered with their ideology of *doikayt*, or "here-ness." They viewed Zionism as a reactionary, bourgeois nationalist movement and insisted, as one translation of a 1931 song put it, that "we'd rather stay in the diaspora, and fight for our liberation."[32] Jewish progressives and Leftists pursued similar strategies throughout Southwest Asia and North Africa, the United States, and even in Mandate Palestine itself. Today's movements for safety through solidarity build from this legacy as we look toward a horizon of collective liberation and justice for all.

PART IV

HOW DO WE FIGHT ANTISEMITISM TODAY?

ELEVEN

GENERATIONS OF TRAUMA: HEALING
FROM ANTISEMITISM'S SCARS

Growing up in northern Virginia, Jo Kent Katz was one of the only Jews in her elementary school. She remembers hiding her matzah in the cafeteria during Passover, embarrassed that it marked her as different from her peers. Her mom, she told us, would come into her classroom every year "to quote-unquote 'do Hanukkah,'" giving an educational presentation meant to raise awareness of cultural and religious diversity among the student body.

Jo was grateful for her mother's offering, she told us, but these visits felt "excruciating." She remembers "consciously holding my breath until she left," when a classmate would

> come and tell me that they thought my mom was either "beautiful" or "nice" . . . And that's when I would exhale. [Now I understand] I needed to know . . . that even though we were highlighting this difference, I was still going to be acknowledged as being part of this kind of whiteness that I was trying to make my way through.

Later in high school, students would sometimes throw pennies on the floor, and tell everybody to wait for the Jewish students to go and pick them up. "I didn't understand the historical context," of antisemitism, Jo explained. "I just knew that it was unkind, and made me feel really uncomfortable."

In her graduating class of six hundred students, Jo was one of only twelve Jews. "I knew who they were," she explained, "and I mostly didn't speak to them by choice—but I remember that my senior year of high school, the table that I sat at for lunch, in this huge sea of a cafeteria, was all the Jews. We all sat together at lunch. And I didn't want to sit with them . . . but it felt like that was the spot for me to fit."

In college, this charged tension between proximity and distance remained. She chose to attend her university for its high proportion of Jewish students—she wanted, for the first time, to be around a lot of other Jews. "And I remember specifically getting there, and people asking me if I was Jewish, and I said 'my family is.' Not 'I am.'"

She felt alienated from the Jews she met who grew up in places with large Jewish communities with greater access to wealth and cultural practice, and so moved with a kind of social capital that was foreign to her. "I didn't like who they were, they felt stereotypical to me in a way that wasn't familiar. And I could feel the things that I was taught to feel about them."

It wasn't until her twenties, as she developed a deeper analysis of racism, that Jo explored ways in which internalized antisemitism may have influenced her identity, and her relationships with other Jews. Living in Seattle, Jo co-facilitated antiracism training sessions with other white activists. But she found little room to explore the particularities of her Jewishness. "There were moments," she explained, "when I felt the starkness of how the group was talking about 'white families,' 'white culture,' 'white socialization,'" and other supposedly universal white American experiences, "and I was like 'hmm, no, that's actually not my experience.' But I felt very strongly that I wasn't allowed to talk about that."

"[Seattle's] political landscape, at the time, didn't allow for the kind of intersectionality that I needed in order to hold the whole of me. So these were secret thoughts that I was having."

Jo began to meet discreetly with another white Jewish

activist to probe these "secret thoughts." Armed with a tape recorder and a bottle of wine, "I remember locking my door— why did I have to lock the door?" and began, finally, to explore the ways in which internalized antisemitism, and inherited trauma, shaped their Jewish lives.

Katz's story is not universal: it is specific to her own identity as a white, raised-upper-middle-income, Ashkenazi Jewish ciswoman. But it offers one window into what it *feels* like for many Jews navigating a society in which antisemitism is subtle yet persistent, marked by pressure to assimilate and consequences for refusal, or inability, to do so—where negative messages and stereotypes can be directed inward, internalized by Jews themselves.

Katz now works as an intuitive healer and social justice educator, helping Jews of all identities process experiences like these, unlearn harmful societal narratives, and reclaim empowered, holistic Jewish identities. This kind of healing work, Jo and many others insist, is an act of Jewish liberation—and it is an essential piece of building movements sharp enough to win a better world for all.

INTERNALIZED OPPRESSION

Like earlier generations, contemporary activists are drawing attention to the ways in which systems of oppression are not merely "external" to an individual or social group, embedded in societal disparities of power, wealth, housing, and education. They are also internalized by members of the oppressed group themselves, living in our bodies, shaping the way we think and feel about ourselves and our place in the world. "Internalized oppression," writes Katz in her web project, Transcending Jewish Trauma, is a term that describes "the ways that oppression is observed, absorbed, and accepted into the minds and practices of those of us targeted by oppression, assuming the role of the oppressor from the inside."[1]

Penny Rosenwasser, activist and author of the 2013 book *Hope into Practice: Jewish Women Choosing Justice Despite Our Fears*, recounted growing up in a white, middle-class, majority Christian suburb of northern Virginia in the 1950s–'60s. "I remember people saying to me, 'gee Penny, you don't look Jewish!'" she told us, "and I would shrug my shoulders and say 'thank you,' because that's what I thought I was supposed to say. I think that's an indication of the antisemitism I absorbed in that place, at that time."

Ari Brostoff, author of *Missing Time* and senior editor at *Jewish Currents*, recalls that growing up as a white Jew, they were sometimes coded as "pushy" by their peers—many of whom were also Jewish—and marked by what they called a subtle yet palpable difference of "ethnicness."

"You're too loud. You're too weird," Brostoff would hear from others. "I got teased for having a big nose . . . It was moments like that where I was being told that I was like a bad, old kind of Jew and why couldn't be I be like a normal Jew . . . I often felt like I failed the process of assimilation."

Rosenwasser explained that in her thirties she developed an awareness of "the role that Christian hegemony plays in making a lot of us feel like, as Jews, that there's something wrong with us." For her doctoral work, Rosenwasser met with a diverse group of other Jewish women for a year, "really sharing our stories and realizing that there's nothing wrong with us—the problem is the systems of oppression." Rosenwasser is confident that "when you start noticing it, you can start working on healing from it, recovering from it."

INTERGENERATIONAL TRAUMA

Antisemitism is a living legacy of our world. It is not just "in the past"—it shapes what Jews carry in our bones and face in our daily lives.

"I remember taking the Torah scrolls out of the synagogue

because of a bomb threat," Rabbi Ariel Stone, whose Portland, Oregon, congregation, Shir Tikvah, had itself faced antisemitic vandalism, told us. She began her rabbinic career in
Ukraine, helping to rebuild a progressive Jewish community,
and there, she discovered the scars of the twentieth century
were far from healed.

"I put a mezuzah up on my door and my community members said to me 'don't you think you should put that inside your
door? Babi Yar is just down the road,'" she recalled.

As part of her work there, she put together a retreat for Jewish kids, and after one Shabbat, as she lined up the children at
the phones to call home, she caught a glimpse into how rele-
vant Ukraine's history of antisemitism remained.

> I got within earshot [of non-Jewish Ukranians waiting to
> use the phone] and I heard them saying things [about the
> children] that just were shocking to hear. Even worse
> was the look in the eyes that made me feel like a cock-
> roach. And it was very strong. It was the first time I had
> understood what real Eastern European antisemitism
> was, the kind that meant Ukrainians were more than
> happy to help the Nazis.

Ilana Lerman is an organizer, educator, and founding member of the Jewish anti-occupation group IfNotNow. "I grew up
with a lot of stories in my family of recent ancestors who made
the right or the wrong decisions that either led them towards
life or death," she told us.

> I always had a lot of intense feelings around decisions.
> Decision-making was hard, but there were extra layers
> to it—the feeling in my body was, if I do or don't go
> to this party, it might lead to euphoric or catastrophic
> things! . . . I started to realize that I was carrying an in-
> grained need to take decision-making extraordinarily

seriously, and an ingrained need to be extremely useful. The way my grandfather survived Auschwitz was by making hats for Nazis, knowing Polish, and helping a wide variety of people. I love helping people! I love being useful! And, there's a way in which sometimes it can start to move outside of a rational place and into more of a reactive survival place.

In 2016, Lerman was part of a core of organizers launching If-NotNow. The movement began as a series of public Jewish ritual actions in protest against Israel's bombing of Gaza during Operation Protective Edge two years earlier. Lerman and IfNotNow channeled the urgency of that moment into the momentum of a movement they hoped would be powerful enough to end American Jewish support for Israel's occupation.

Gathered around kitchen tables with laptops open and sheets of paper taped to walls, scrawled with notes and diagrams, Lerman and the other activists shaped a strategy to reach their Jewish community. The movement for Palestinian rights was stronger than ever, and the national progressive consensus was shifting toward greater support for Palestinians, but the institutions of the American Jewish establishment continued providing support for Israel's occupation. In order to spark a sea change in Jewish opinion, they realized they needed to truly win hearts, minds, and souls. To do this they needed, like any good organizing campaign, to meet their people where they were at.

Lerman reflected back on the heavy inheritance of fear and trauma she received from her ancestors, and pondered, not for the first time, the ways in which this inheritance impacted her community's ingrained discomfort with mobilizing against the occupation. Across years of conversations with her family and Jewish community, she observed, "I would see over and over again that the clinging to Israel was a trauma response, an ancestrally ingrained fear of not being safe."

The Jewish community is so "stuck" around Israel, as she put it, "because people are scared. People can think rationally about oppression, but when it comes to Israel, they lose the rational thinking . . . That's because of trauma, because of fear that stems from a long line of ancestors having to figure out keeping themselves, and their most beloveds, safe in times of existential danger."

Narratives of generational trauma are now mainstays of public discourse and understanding, though fierce debates remain over whether the inheritance is primarily social, epigenetic, or some combination. "I was scared of things I didn't have a reason to be scared of . . . I was just starting to feel a very acute sense that the pain I was carrying wasn't just mine," Ami Weintraub, rabbinic student and organizer, told us. "And then I started to see in my family, what are the patterns that we are stuck in as a family? Maybe [it's] related to the fact that most of our ancestors who didn't come to America were murdered by fascists and we don't talk about that."

The predominant Jewish communal narrative around antisemitism—that it is a permanent feature of non-Jewish society; that Jews cannot expect to rely on non-Jewish allies, but must fight it alone; and that, therefore, seeking proximity to power, including in the form of a militarized Israel, is the only safe strategy—can be understood, on one level, as a response to unhealed intergenerational trauma, forged prominently (though not exclusively) from the wreckage of twentieth-century Europe.

Many argue that, precisely because persecution ebbed and flowed—with periods of relative stability punctuated by escalating violence—it has left Ashkenazi Jews in particular with a lasting unease. "Because it didn't happen 24/7," explained Rosenwasser, "it can leave Jews feeling uncertain, like you never know when the ax is going to fall. I still have friends that keep a suitcase packed so that they can flee."

Understanding this can help Jews and non-Jewish allies see, as Rosenwasser put it, how "the uncertainty that devastation and violence could happen very quickly" animates seemingly outsized responses to perceived antisemitism today, and can help us "not dismiss Jewish fear as ridiculous, [but] to take it seriously and understand there's a real reason for it. Then as Jews we need to have the courage to face our fears—but not act on them—to choose justice despite our fears."

In order to transform the hearts of American Jews, Lerman and the other activists realized, IfNotNow needed to address this trauma head-on. What was "absolutely crucial for IfNot-Now's success," she explained, "was to create a space at the very beginning, baked into the core of what IfNowNow is, for people to both grapple with what antisemitism is, and to dedicate themselves towards ending it."

The founding members of IfNotNow incorporated education around antisemitism into their membership training. In 2016, with the alt-right on the rise, it was an opportune time. The training traced deep connections between rising antisemitism, inherited intergenerational trauma, and Jewish communal support for Israel. The goal, she told us, "was to build a lot of compassion for why the Jewish community is frozen around Israel . . . We have to build a muscle of being able to face that and meet that fear with love."

For Mizrahi Jews—whose ancestors often experienced less acute forms of antisemitism, at least until the mid-twentieth century—the legacies of intergenerational trauma are complicated. For many, the pain of exile from countries across the Middle East and North Africa is compounded by the erasure of cultural memory and connection to the Arab world, a rupture that resulted not only from political events in Arab countries, but also from the actions of racist Ashkenazi elites in Israel and the Ashkenazi-dominant American Jewish community.

Hadar Cohen, an Arab Jewish artist and educator, told us that "many Mizrahim, like my parents, were trying to assimilate into Israeli culture and identity, in a similar way that many immigrants in the US try to assimilate into whiteness or an Americanized identity. In Hebrew there is a word *lehishtaknez*, meaning to 'become Ashkenazi'—many Mizrahi communities including my family attempted this to feel a sense of belonging that was robbed of them. Still to this day, there is much racism towards Mizrahim from Israeli society." That racism becomes internalized, Cohen explained to us, and can often lead Mizrahim to deny their Arab identity and connections to the Arab world.

Keren Soffer-Sharon, a Mizrahi educator and organizer, recalled attending a Jewish day school with mostly Mizrahi peers whose parents had moved from Israel/Palestine to the United States. The day school, she explained, was led by white Ashkenazi Jews. "And the dominant narrative [on Jewish history and antisemitism] that we grew up with was, of course, a right-wing, incredibly Ashkenazi narrative. The only allusion to non-Ashkenazi history related to antisemitism in my Jewish history textbook growing up was one paragraph about the Spanish Inquisition—which is still Europe!"

As they struggle to reconstruct what Soffer-Sharon called "critical and alternative histories of our families," many Mizrahim are confronting the very real trauma their ancestors have faced in recent memory, while also parsing with nuance the complex stew of factors that led to the twentieth-century expulsion of Arab Jewish communities across the Middle East. "Many of our Mizrahi grandparents are the last generation living" with deep connections to life before the traumas of expulsion, Keren Soffer-Sharon explained to us.

> Their experience was one of real fear during a specific and modern period of heightened antisemitism that caused many of them to flee. Our families continue to be haunted by their experiences of forced migration and displacement. But the story of why those things happened

isn't as simple as constant and ever-present antisemitism throughout the entire history of Jews in that region, culminating at that point. That's the powerful propaganda that's been superimposed on our rich and layered history. The truth is much more complicated than that.

"OUR GRIEF CONNECTS US TO OTHERS' GRIEF"

Virtually every Jewish community carries trauma from persecution, displacement, and exile in recent memory. Struggling to stay afloat in the storm-tossed waters of the twentieth century, many Jews, as Ilana Lerman realized in conversations with her family, came to see the State of Israel—a nation-state of, by, and for Jews, where Jews could chart a sovereign political course as a nation defended by force of arms—as a life raft, the only possible safety in a hostile world.

Across the Jewish world, the tendency is too often to replay collective trauma in ways that do not promote resolution and healing, but that reinforce messages of isolation, fear, distrust, and a belief in the eternal nature of persecution. The annual March of the Living, held on Yom HaShoah (Holocaust Remembrance Day), brings young Jews from Israel and around the world to witness Israeli fighter jets flying over the ruins of Auschwitz, a visceral reinforcement of the conviction that only strength and dominance—embodied in a tough, militarized Israel—can protect Jews from a perennially hostile world.

In another yearly ritual, many American Jewish summer camps hold simulation exercises where young Jews reenact harrowing episodes of persecution and combat drawn from recent Jewish memory—running from Nazi captors, for example, or battling Palestinian militants. Exercises like these reinforce a broader worldview that terror, hostility, isolation, and the need for combat are fundamental features of Jewish identity and peoplehood. "It's very intentional the way the Jewish community is steeped and inculcated in the trauma narrative," Jewish feminist scholar and activist Sheryl Nestel told us. Nestel is wary that the impulse to "protect one's innocence," as she puts it, encourages some to refuse to face the ways in which Jews can be implicated both as oppressors and as oppressed, depending on the circumstance.

"I come from a family that I think has a very legitimate claim to Holocaust trauma," Rowan Gaudet, an activist with Independent Jewish Voices, told us. Gaudet's father was a concentration camp survivor who eventually died by suicide. "There's constructed trauma [and] there's real trauma in the Jewish community, and both of those are being manipulated."

There is a danger, wrote Arielle Angel, editor in chief of *Jewish Currents*, in a 2022 essay, that "to take the pain for granted as a constant is also to will it into being, to deaden an awareness of the present in favor of a reenactment of the past."[2]

To be sure, remembering the trauma of the past is important. For thousands of years, Jews have used embodied ritual, storytelling, and other instruments of collective memory to recall legacies of persecution, mourn, and imagine a better future.

Indeed, this element of Jewish culture has helped to inspire many activists. "Our grief connects us to others' grief," Dove Kent said. "Our terror connects us to others' terror. The trauma Jews have experienced does not make us separate from other Peoples; it connects us to other Peoples."[3]

What would it look like, in the twenty-first century, to honor and heal from our inherited, intergenerational trauma in a way that builds bridges of solidarity—connecting our pain with the experiences of persecution faced by other groups, and imagining a better future together—rather than doubling down on isolation, fear, and distrust? "What would it mean to metabolize those feelings," as Angel put it, "instead of chewing them like a bitter cud?"[4]

THE WORK OF HEALING

A sensitivity to Jewish trauma can help Jewish organizers who seek to transform our communities from within. "If I want my beloved community to end the occupation of Palestine," Dove Kent told us, "then I need to understand why they are holding on to the occupation of Palestine with the death grip that they are. And if I don't understand that grip, then I'm not going to be able to understand how to undo it . . . We have got to engage with that fear, we have got to battle with that fear if we're going to be changing this stuff."

Engaging with that fear, Dove was quick to clarify, does not need to mean diluting your message, softening your radical critique, or compromising core principles. "Do not lay off, do not back off," she told us. "Do not let any oppression go uninterrupted. But understanding the conditions that are leading actors to act enables us to be significantly more effective organizers."

Non-Jews can help Jews heal from intergenerational trauma. For non-Jews of Christian heritage especially, this can be seen as a responsibility, as part of repair for the harm their communities have perpetrated. When non-Jews take a vocal stand against antisemitism, it can powerfully challenge the internalized narrative that Jews are isolated, bereft of allies—a story that feeds into support for a dominant, militarized Israel as the only guarantor of safety in a perennially hostile world.

When progressives acknowledge and validate Jewish trauma, speak out against antisemitism, and offer a hand in shared struggle, it helps Jews heal and commit to forging safety through solidarity. Hannah Freedman, a Jewish organizer in Boston, told us that after the Pittsburgh synagogue shooting in 2018, activists from Muslim, white anti-racist, and other communities "came through and held grief space and ritual space" for Jews processing the trauma of what had just occurred. "It felt really powerful for me, to see and feel non-Jewish friends at our backs and with us as we were going through the whole range of emotions."

Unfortunately, the opposite sometimes occurs. "There's a way in which antisemitism and Jewish trauma is belittled, or seen as not real, in movement spaces," Hadar Cohen told us. "There's a real lack of understanding around Jewish peoples' experiences, and what we carry in our bodies." The reigning assumption, Hadar explained, is that from the United States to Israel/Palestine, "Jews are now in an oppressor category, so we shouldn't engage with anti-Jewish oppression anymore."

After a 2021 Proud Boys rally in Portland, Oregon, many progressive activists were sharing a video of local Proud Boys engaging in Holocaust denial and threats against Jews, seeking to expose the bigotry. Some Jewish activists raised concerns that this was unintentionally helping spread a deeply triggering message. There had recently been a string of threatening far-right and antisemitic incidents in the city, and some Jews felt the activist community had not meaningfully addressed it.

"Where's your actual support for the fucking Jewish community? . . . This is trauma porn, everyone," an activist using the name Dog from Matzah Bloc, a Jewish mutual aid group in Portland, told us. "How scary that this kind of stuff is allowed to happen and the impacts and generational trauma that comes along with this is just completely lost on anybody but the Jewish community."

The same dynamic can play out in what is often termed a type of "soft Holocaust denial" or "trivialization." "The Holocaust is mostly an invention of Zionists to justify the creation of the State of Israel on top of Palestine," an activist explained to Shane many years ago, amidst a cloud of Camel cigarette smoke. Growing up in a small coastal town in Oregon meant that Shane regularly bumped into college students on spring break, and after running into a crowd buying beer at a local convenience store he joined their party at a rental house near the dunes. "The term 'antisemite' is sort of inaccurate since

Jews are just one of the Semitic people," the guy continued. "And I'm not against the rest of them."[5]

Clearly, there is a lot going on here beyond mere insensitivity. But underneath the layers of antisemitic conspiracism, borderline Holocaust denial, and linguistic manipulation in comments like these is a smoldering contempt, a refusal to take Jewish pain, or Jews' right to name their oppression, seriously.

Similar dismissal of Jews' experiences take place in movement spaces, albeit more subtly. Casandra Mae, a Jewish mutual aid organizer in Salem, Oregon, told us that she stepped away from some of her organizing work because of the constant disinterest from non-Jewish comrades in trying to learn about antisemitism.

"Because Jews are white and therefore in a place of privilege," so their reasoning went, "it's punching up even when [antisemitism] does exist, and therefore not worth taking seriously . . . I don't think any of [the people I was organizing with] understand why I quit . . . They weren't willing to take the time to understand antisemitism happening around us."

All these trends were glaringly obvious in late 2023, when some on the Left minimized or even celebrated Hamas's massacre and kidnapping of hundreds of Israeli civilians on October 7, and even spun revisionist theories holding Israel primarily responsible for Israeli civilian death, while also saying little about the spike in antisemitism worldwide. This dismissive posture shocked and traumatized Jews, including many Jewish Leftists, who found themselves unable to trust that their comrades had their backs. Some, wrote Arielle Angel, are "asking themselves how they can be part of a left that seems to treat Israeli deaths as a necessary, if not desirable, part of Palestinian liberation."[6]

Hadar Cohen's experience as a somatic healer tells her that this attitude of dismissal among some non-Jewish Leftists is "incoherent . . . because if you look at the majority of Jewish people's bodies from a somatic perspective, there is profound

terror and trauma that is unrecognized and unacknowledged . . . The denial of Jewish trauma and oppression amplifies the trauma that is stored in the body, especially when the
world gaslights and erases our stories."

Some on the Left, Hadar told us, demonize her Mizrahi
Jewish community—who are the majority-Jewish population
in Israel/Palestine—as little more than privileged oppressors,
without taking into account that most fled to Israel as refugees from state-sponsored antisemitic repression and expulsion, and once in Israel, Mizrahim faced, and continue to face,
deep structural racism at the hands of the country's dominant
Ashkenazi caste.

"The trauma that we've been through is deep and heart-
breaking," Hadar told us. "We need trauma-informed activism to truly transform systems of oppression. Critique and
judgment do little to change political realities. Mostly, it just
pushes people to curl up into a ball of terror and fear, and
shut down."

RADICAL HEALING

The Jewish Left is growing, and taking on antisemitism with
new boldness. This wasn't always the case.

"For a lot of Jews that were part of the social movement Left
over the last many years," Dove Kent explained to us, "it felt
disgusting to get together and talk about antisemitism." Some
of this, Dove said, was due to the traumatizing and isolating
forms of antisemitism education many Jews experienced in
childhood, combined with outrage at Israel's ongoing oppression of Palestinians and the harm caused by weaponized antisemitism allegations. Still, a deeper discomfort was palpable.
"People actually had to get beyond this certain level of disgust
to engage in the conversation . . . And that tells us something
about the oppression—there's something about the oppression that says, 'Jews are disgusting.'"

Writing in 2016, organizer Yotam Marom diagnosed this difficulty, and offered a rousing call to action. "Our inability, as young Jews in the movement today, to talk about anti-Semitism is a product of internalized anti-Semitism itself," he proclaimed in his popular movement manifesto. "Toward the Next Jewish Rebellion . . . and it is killing us. It puts us and our families at risk, weakens the political struggles of which we are a part, denies us our full agency, and makes it impossible for us to ask for help from our would-be allies."[7]

Overcoming this internalized oppression, and claiming the space to gather as Jews on the Left to take on antisemitism, is itself liberatory and healing. This work strengthens progressive movements to fight against antisemitism more fiercely, wherever it exists—and this fight, in turn, is crucial in order to win a just and liberated world.

"[Jews are] like a lot of people who are from recent immigrant families, who are probably dealing with ancestral traumas . . . What would that positionality look like if passport peoples were in solidarity with one another?" asks Weintraub. The experience of trauma, and the resiliency many of us gained in proximity to it, becomes a strength Jews hold in concert with others fighting oppression. And by tracing the connections between different forms of oppression we face, we can deepen our solidarity.

TWELVE

INTERSECTING OPPRESSIONS:
CONNECTING THE THREATS WE FACE

A s a young Black organizer in the 1980s, Eric Ward didn't think much about antisemitism or white nationalists— he was focused on issues like mass incarceration and racist police violence. But living in the mostly white state of Oregon, in the wake of racist skinhead attacks and the neo-Nazi killing of Ethiopian student Mulugeta Seraw in 1988, his thinking shifted.

With the growth of an increasingly volatile paramilitary far-right as well as the hard edge of Christian fundamentalism, Oregon had become a flash point in racist violence as well as anti-abortion, anti-LGBT radicalism. "What I learned when I got to Oregon," Ward wrote in his influential 2017 essay "Skin in the Game,"

> as I began to log untold hours trying to understand
> White nationalists and their ideas, was that antisemi-
> tism was the lynchpin of the White nationalist belief
> system . . . antisemitism, I discovered, is a particular
> and potent form of racism so central to White suprem-
> acy that Black people would not win our freedom with-
> out tearing it down.[1]

In 1991, after a Portland neo-Nazi was arrested with a flyer for the punk band Fugazi in his back pocket, fears spread that Nazis would swarm an upcoming Fugazi show in nearby Eugene. This led Ward to form the group Communities Against Hate, which took an intersectional approach, he told us, "before intersectionality was a thing." He became part of a movement to confront the white nationalist scene, alongside groups like the Center for Democratic Renewal, the Coalition for Human Dignity, the Northwest Coalition Against Malicious Harassment, and the emerging Anti-Racist Action (the older cousin to today's antifa groups).

With the rise of Trumpism, Ward saw the movements and ideologies he once fought in Portland storm center stage in American political life. Since then, he has worked with groups like Southern Poverty Law Center and Western States Center to counter these threats—and fighting antisemitism remains central. "[White] nationalist or other politically violent movements . . . don't bring antisemitism or other forms of bigotry to our community. They merely organize the bigotry that already exists," Ward told us. "Antisemitism exists in American society. White nationalists are tapping into it in order to build political power. It means we have to understand antisemitism, and one of the things we should understand about antisemitism is it doesn't just impact Jews." In an era where antisemitic conspiracy theories motivate violence against a range of marginalized groups, Ward said, "non-Jews are just as vulnerable to the violence of anti-Semitism as the Jewish community."[2]

When antisemitism is separated from all other forms of oppression—which, as we discussed, is too often the case in public discourse—it can appear eternal, unchanging, and unique unto itself. Not only does this perpetuate a falsehood about how antisemitism works, it also dissolves our ability to build alliances across our identities, and to create a culture of mutual safety in solidarity. It blurs the strategic focus needed to challenge the power that threatens all of us.

To reclaim this we have to look at how antisemitism relates to other types of oppression, giving us the clear picture needed to fight for a world of freedom, safety, and equality for Jews and all people.

"THE CONDITIONS OF OUR LIVES"

One important model to help trace these connections was offered by the Combahee River Collective, a Black socialist, feminist, and queer organization with a brief but influential life from 1974 to 1980. The Combahee River Collective carved out space in the overwhelmingly white feminist movement, and the male-dominated Black Power movement, to address the complex identities they held as Black, queer, working-class women.

They theorized that their own liberation, since it had to break at multiple axes, would have ramifications far beyond their own lives: it could free all people. By expanding our vision of who was oppressed and where the power to liberate came from, they insisted, movements for justice could more thoroughly understand how systems like capitalism operate, who the working class actually are, and how linked up our experiences are with those of other marginalized people, even if the direct points of oppression are not identical.

"[We] are actively committed to struggling against racial, sexual, heterosexual, and class oppression," they wrote in "A Black Feminist Statement," "and see as our particular task the development of integrated analysis and practice based upon the fact that the major systems of oppression are interlocking. The synthesis of these oppressions creates the conditions of our lives."[3]

In 1989, legal scholar Kimberlé Crenshaw coined the term "intersectionality" in an essay analyzing the inability of preexisting legal frameworks to address what she called the "multidimensionality of Black women's experience" of discrimination in the workplace. "Because the intersectional experience is greater than the sum of racism and sexism," she wrote, "any analysis that does not take intersectionality into account cannot sufficiently address the particular manner in which Black women are subordinated."[4] Today, activists use an intersectional framework across a variety of contexts to understand the interlocking systems of oppression that structure the world we live in, and the experiences faced by marginalized individuals and groups working to navigate and transform that world.

In this chapter we will analyze some of the interlocking connections between antisemitism and anti-Blackness, anti-immigrant xenophobia, anti-LGBTQ bigotry, and Islamophobia. "Systems of oppression are not distinct separate entities that interact with one another," wrote anarchist author Zoe Baker. Rather, they "interlock and intersect with one another to form a totality which is greater than the sum of its parts . . . inter-twinned to such an extent that one cannot be separated from the other."[5] By tracing these connections, we can help illuminate a shared horizon for Jews and other groups to pursue justice work side by side, conscious of the differences we hold as well as the solidarity that can bind us together.

"The Right, and supremacist movements, are very intersectional," Alex DiBranco, executive director at the Institute for Research on Male Supremacism, told us. "They know that all of these causes are interrelated, but *we* on the Left have been very siloed." DiBranco reminded us that the work of tracing these connections carries important lessons for building justice movements, too. "It's really important that we work on these issues as interconnected," she told us. "Part of that means making the connection that, no, if we're going to work on misogyny, then you can't have a [movement] partner who is antisemitic. You can't have partners who are transphobic, or racist—any form of supremacism opens the door for other forms."

We cannot pluck antisemitism out of its intersectional context since it does not exist autonomously, and it rarely spikes solo. The rise of the far-right, the crisis of conspiracism, and the explosive political, economic, and ecological instability underneath are giving all types of bigotries and oppressive systems free rein. The strength to fight comes from the ability to grow our ranks, which means offering everyone a stake in crushing antisemitism.

"[As] much as I draw inspiration from the Jewish community," wrote Eric Ward, "and as much as I adore my Jewish partner and friends, it was my organizing against antisemitism as a Black antiracist that first pulled me to the Jewish community, not the other way around. I developed an analysis of antisemitism because I wanted to smash White supremacy; because I wanted to be free."[6]

ANTISEMITISM AND ANTI-BLACKNESS

When an eighteen-year-old white nationalist walked into Tops Friendly Markets in Buffalo, New York, on May 14, 2022, and murdered ten souls, his target was Black America. In the lead-up to his carefully planned attack, he scoped out a high-density Black neighborhood. Most of his victims were Black and elderly, later eulogized as beloved pillars of their community.

The shooter's manifesto pivoted around the white nationalist "great replacement" conspiracy theory—the notion that the "white race" is on the route to "extinction" in the United States and Europe due to non-white immigration and birth rates. The text is a grab bag of racist memes and tropes alleging Black cultural, intellectual, and moral inferiority, using pseudoscientific "race realist" claims pushed by a handful of disgraced academics and championed in forums like 4chan, to bolster its claims.

Antisemitism helped sharpen and clarify the shooter's anti-Blackness with the support of an ideological scaffolding. "The real war I'm advocating for," he explained, "is the gentiles vs the Jews . . . the Jews are the biggest problem the Western world has ever had."[7]

Taking a line from the GOP's reigning moral panic, he explained that "currently the Jews are spreading ideas such as Critical Race Theory and white shame/guilt to brainwash Whites into hating themselves and their people."[8] After wondering aloud why he did not attack Jews, he answered that "they can be dealt with in time, but the high fertility replacers will destroy us now, it is a matter of survival we destroy them first."[9]

White nationalists believe that throughout the twentieth century, Jews promoted racial equality to weaken white dominance and, ultimately, to destroy the "white race." Jews have been "instrumental," wrote white nationalist thought leader Kevin MacDonald in 1998, "in organizing African Americans as a political force that served Jewish interests in diluting the political and cultural hegemony of non-Jewish European Americans."[10] They believe Jews today have engineered Black Lives Matter, "Critical Race Theory," and more in pursuit of the same ends.

In the mid-twentieth century, a time when many white Jewish activists supported Black-led freedom struggles, groups like the National States' Rights Party and Christian Anti-Jewish Party claimed Jews were behind the growth of the civil rights movement in the Jim Crow South.[11] When white vigilantes firebombed dozens of Black churches in the waves of violence and terror, a number of synagogues were burned as well.

As the Cold War escalated, the Right's anti-communist hysteria blended anti-Black and antisemitic overtones, and conservative leaders stereotyped Jews as outside agitators behind militant, integrated labor unions and pro-worker, antiracist messages in Hollywood, music, and media.[12] In the 1950s, McCarthyist persecution helped sunder ties between white Jewish and Black non-Jewish organizers, amplifying division between the communities, which persists today.

During the 2020 George Floyd uprising MAGA leaders spread the conspiracy theory that George Soros was the hidden orchestrator behind the uprising, and that shadowy antifa "outside agitators" were coming for the white suburbs.[13] In the years since, they have doubled down on these conspiracy theories, claiming that Soros is orchestrating the destruction of the criminal justice system by installing progressive district attorneys in majority-Black cities, and that an elite cabal of "Cultural Marxists" is spreading "anti-white hatred" through promoting "Critical Race Theory" in media, educational, and governmental institutions.

The goal of all this is to delegitimize vital movements for racial justice by convincing millions that they do not arise from the legitimate grievances of Black folks, but instead are imposed on the nation by the shadowy machinations of sinister, foreign elites. The Right uses antisemitism to protect and reinforce the foundations of structural white supremacy in the United States, helping to confuse the public so they cannot see the agency of Black communities demanding justice. Not only are these conspiracy theories antisemitic, they are also deeply anti-Black, asserting that non-Jewish Black folks are not capable of leading their own movements. They also erase the existence of Black Jews, who live within both communities.

As long as systemic anti-Blackness continues to exist—convincing millions of white Americans to fear the Black freedom struggle—antisemitism will continue to be useful to demagogues, providing a reservoir of tropes to draw upon that lend a paranoid voice to this fear. We can't fully dismantle anti-Blackness without also ending antisemitism, which remains a durable part of its ideological scaffolding.

It's no surprise we find these forms of oppression so deeply intertwined today—they draw from similar wellsprings in the modern era. Beginning in the nineteenth century, European anthropologists, writers, and scholars developed pseudoscientific racial taxonomies in order to subdivide humanity into distinct biological, cultural, and/or spiritual racial essences. Eager to provide intellectual scaffolding for European dominance, many claimed the so-called Aryan race was superior to the "Semitic" race (Jews) as well as the "Hamitic" and "Negroid" races (Black people), among many other categories. Variations of these specious schemas were used by generations of European elites to justify slavery, colonialism, modern antisemitism, and eventually, Nazism.[14]

Countless modern commentators have drawn attention to these deep linkages. "It was my philosophy teacher from the Antilles," wrote Afro-Caribbean Marxist Frantz Fanon, one of the most influential anti-colonial intellectuals of the twentieth century, "who reminded me one day: 'When you hear someone insulting the Jews, pay attention; he is talking about you.' And I believed at the time he was universally right, meaning that I was responsible in my body and my soul for the fate reserved for my brother. Since then, I have understood that what he meant quite simply was the anti-Semite is inevitably a negrophobe."[15]

As we will discuss, this means that any strategy to fight antisemitism by mobilizing anti-Blackness—or to fight anti-Blackness by relying on antisemitism—is doomed to fail. " Anti-Black racism and antisemitism are mutually supporting structures," tweeted Black Jewish activist Chanda Prescod-Weinstein in November 2022, calling out the racist reactions some white Jews displayed after rapper Kanye West doubled down on antisemitism. "You cannot invest in or uphold the one and expect to escape the other."[16]

"NONE IS TOO MANY"

When mass shooter Robert Bowers entered the Tree of Life synagogue in October of 2018, ultimately murdering eleven congregants in the largest antisemitic attack in American history, he wasn't acting alone. In the week leading up to his attack, far-right politicians and pundits were championing the conspiracy theory that George Soros was orchestrating a migrant caravan to pierce the United States' southern border, in order to undermine American sovereignty.[17] By the day of the shooting, according to one analysis, the conspiracy theory had a potential reach of over 670 million on Facebook and Twitter alone. This helped create the scapegoating climate in which Bowers knew he had to act.

What drew him to this synagogue in particular was that they were holding a service to support the Hebrew Immigrant Aid Society (HIAS). "HIAS likes to bring in invaders that kill our people," Bowers posted online before entering their Refugee Shabbat. "I can't sit by and watch my people get slaughtered."

The history of HIAS is, in part, the history of American Jewishness. The organization was formed in 1881 to support the resettlement of Jewish refugees escaping persecution in Eastern Europe. Today, drawing upon that memory, it supports mainly non-Jewish refugees from around the world, such as those fleeing the Syrian civil war.

In the early twentieth century, around 15 million immigrants from Eastern and Southern Europe arrived in the United States. Among them were around 2 million Ashkenazi Jews, fleeing antisemitic persecution from ultranationalist forces and hoping to find, in America, a refuge of tolerance.

Anglo-American elites warned that these new immigrants would unravel social cohesion, degrade public cleanliness and virtue, dilute racial purity, and bring the foreign disease of communism to factory floors across the country.

This nativist backlash led to scapegoating, discrimination, and violence, and before long, Rightist movements were determined to maintain an Anglo-Saxon demographic majority. The 1924 Immigration Act codified limits on nationalities entering the United States, establishing a series of national origins quotas that, along with racial laws across the Jim Crow South, were admired by the Nazis as they crafted their Nuremberg Laws a decade later.[18]

By 1938, the year of the infamous Kristallnacht pogrom, around one-fourth of Germany's Jewish population had fled the country. As the crisis of European Jewry escalated and Jewish refugees demanded to be allowed to escape the horrors rising on all sides, the American far-right coalesced around America First nativism. By January 1939, a polled 67 percent of Americans were against a bill that would have permitted entry into the United States for ten thousand German Jewish children. Boats packed with Jews looking for safe harbor were turned around, sent back to a Europe that was on fire.

The Roosevelt administration and the State Department (which itself included antisemites) made little effort to help, and by June, the list of those waiting for asylum was upward of three hundred thousand people.[19] In Canada, too, the attitude toward Jewish immigration was summarized by a 1939 quote, popularly attributed to Prime Minister William Lyon Mackenzie King, that "none is too many."[20] These leaders refused to provide the shelter that could have saved millions of lives, and Jews remember this. This memory binds us to refugees and immigrants around the world, reminders of how anti-immigrant nativism can collaborate with genocide.

Our memory is longer, too. For millennia, Jews have been a diasporic people, making our home in nearly every civilization around the world. For this reason, our very existence has long unsettled those who seek to carve the world into discrete nation-states or territories for separate peoples. A world where Jews are free to live as we please must of necessity be a world where walls and borders no longer limit full human flourishing.

Today, our world has seen the worst crises of migrants and refugees since the end of World War II, brought on by the horrors of war, the exploitative cruelties of neoliberal globalization, and the mounting catastrophes of human-made climate change. Growing ethnonationalist movements around the world are blending anti-immigrant xenophobia with thinly veiled antisemitic conspiracy theories, claiming that George Soros, a "globalist" cabal, or some other shadowy elite is weaponizing migration in order to undermine national borders and sovereignty, dissolve organic communities, exploit "native" workers and families, and entrench global control.

As anti-immigrant xenophobia continues to ramp up, politicians and pundits will continue to rely on antisemitism to keep people divided and afraid. Meanwhile, the companies, political leaders, and organizations at the helm of the anti-immigrant movement continue to reap profits and maintain their grip on power. A shared story can form, situating the fight against antisemitism within a shared vision of migrant justice.

"The United States is running concentration camps on our southern border, and that is exactly what they are—they are concentration camps," exclaimed progressive congresswoman Alexandria Ocasio-Cortez in an Instagram Live story on June 17, 2019. Conditions at the Trump administration's immigrant detention centers at the US-Mexico border were unbearable, with mounting reports of freezing-cold temperatures, torture through sleep deprivation, severe overcrowding, rotting food, starvation, and lack of access to showers and basic medicine. "And if that doesn't bother you . . . I want to talk to the people that are concerned enough with humanity to say . . . that 'never again' means something."[21]

For right-wing leaders and some Jewish establishment organizations, however, the biggest problem was not the existence or conditions of these camps, but the fact that AOC chose to call them "concentration camps"—a word choice that, according to the Jewish Community Relations Council of New York (JCRC), "diminishes the evil intent of the Nazis to eradicate the Jewish people."[22] Republican leader Liz Cheney tweeted that "6 million Jews were exterminated in the Holocaust. You demean their memory and disgrace yourself with comments like this,"[23] while then–vice president Mike Pence, speaking at a Christian Zionist conference, claimed AOC had "cheapened" the memory of the Holocaust "to advance some left-wing political narrative."[24]

Progressive Jews knew they had to redirect the narrative by standing boldly, as Jews, for immigrant justice. "All of a sudden," Alyssa Rubin, an organizer in Boston, remembered,

> the conversation about immigration in this country was "do the Jews think that it's bad enough to compare it to the Holocaust?'—which was an infuriating conversation to be having . . . and it was a complete mask off of the way that the Right weaponizes Jewish trauma to shut down really legitimate and powerful moments of confrontation, when the symptoms of racial capitalism and xenophobia are on full display.

Within two weeks, Rubin and others took to the streets, holding confrontational protests to shut down ICE detention centers across the country under the banner Never Again Action, an organization that continues to mobilize Jews to fight for immigrant justice today. "I remember standing side by side with a lot of white Jews and a lot of non-white immigrants," Rubin told us, recalling an action to shut down ICE headquarters in Washington, D.C.,

> and seeing some actual real confusion and fear in the faces of the police officers and security forces—I think they had not really seen a lot of that solidarity before! . . . We talk a lot, especially in white organizing spaces, about leveraging our privilege to put our bodies on the line and throw down in ways that are too risky for people who are undocumented or not white . . . Having a truly multiracial, cross-class, cross-identity group of people showing up, I was like, "Wow, this is truly the Right's worst nightmare!"

GENDER REBELS

In the first three months of 2022, the Right sent waves of anti-LGBTQ legislation pummeling statehouses across the country, escalating as if to outpace each other in ferocity. Nearly 240 such bills were introduced in this time,[25] such as the Idaho law that could hand out life sentences to doctors who provided trans youth with gender-affirming care.[26]

"Across the country, GOP lawmakers have waged a legislative crusade targeting queer and trans kids, smearing opponents as 'groomers,' language that rhymes with the 'pedophile' claims that inspired the attack on Comet Ping Pong," described journalist Melissa Gira Grant in a piece for *The New Republic*. "And where once the targets of these conspiracy theories were largely confined to a select group of Democratic lawmakers and their allies, the fearmongering—amplified by Fox News and prominent conservative social media accounts—is now targeted at all LGBTQ people, from national figures to members of your local community. The stage is set for a Pizzagate in any city."[27]

This far-right crusade is focused on the LGBTQ community, and they're using this as a starting point for an even wider assortment of grievances. That summer, a bevy of far-right groups, inspired by transphobic pundits like Matt Walsh and social media accounts like Libs of TikTok, showed up to harass and confront participants in Pride, Drag Story Hour, and other events promoting LGBTQ equality and acceptance across the country. Among these were white nationalist groups like Nationalist Social Club and the America First/groyper movement that hold antisemitism at the center of their worldview. The "biggest threat to America is Jewish domination over the world," claimed one member of Patriot Front, a group whose members were arrested for planning to attack a Pride parade in Coeur d'Alene, Idaho.[28]

White nationalists believe Jews are the hidden masterminds behind the increasing normalization and acceptance of feminism, LGBTQ rights, and changing gender norms across parts of US society and popular culture. They believe Jews weaponize Hollywood, mass media, and other culture indus-tries in order to emasculate men, destroy heterosexuality, and warp "natural" gender roles as part of a broader plot to cause "white genocide."

The neofascist militant accelerationist movement, wrote re-searcher Blyth Crawford in a 2022 report for the London-based International Centre for the Study of Radicalisation, "regard[s] 'deviant' sexualities as being pushed or forced on to society by Jewish people," who are "often framed as 'turning' vulnerable white children gay or trans in order to attack the traditional nuclear family structure." They also believe Jewish elites en-gineer pornography as a tool "to keep white men weak and distracted from their racial replacement," and feminism to "encourag[e] white women not to have children, which there-fore threatens the continuation of the white race."[29]

On October 12, 2022, a nineteen-year-old Slovakian white nationalist murdered two people outside a gay bar in the Slo-vakian capital of Bratislava. The shooter's manifesto opened with "It's the Jews; it's the Jews; it's the Jews." Jews, he claimed, "organize and spearhead everything related to 'LGBT rights,' pushing degenerate propaganda onto our Race." Like the Buf-falo shooter's anti-Blackness, antisemitism was the scaffolding for his virulent hatred of queer folks; by attacking a gay bar, he imagined, he was simultaneously striking at a deeper enemy.[30]

Across the Right, these conspiracy theories are echoed in code. Conservatives and trans-exclusionary radical femi-nists, or TERFs, spread the lie that George Soros, "globalists," "Cultural Marxists," or some other shadowy cabal is pushing "gender ideology," feminism, and LGBTQ acceptance on an unsuspecting public, all in pursuit of some nefarious agenda. "I don't think it's an accident that you see QAnon conspirac[y theories] that Jews are running a pedophile ring, and [right-wing discourse that] trans people are groomers," Max Strass-feld, a scholar of both rabbinic literature and transgender studies, told us. "When they rhyme so closely, you have to think there's some kind of relationship."

Like the anti-immigrant movement, the contemporary anti-LGBTQ movement depends on conspiratorial narratives that powerful, malevolent elites are conspiring to overwhelm sacred borders—in this case, the boundaries and binaries of traditional Western gender and sexuality. Pundits falsely insist that Jewish billionaires like George Soros and the Pritzker family are pushing what anti-trans activists call "synthetic sex identities" as a way of undermining sexual integrity.

"The current anti-trans movement owes everything to the political project of antisemitism," Rosza Daniel Lang/Lev-itsky, a trans Jewish cultural worker and organizer, told us. Both ideologies invariably require "the conspiratorial enemy that is outside of all human society, has its own internal structure, and specifically goes after innocent children."

These conspiracy theories didn't pop up overnight. For decades, the global Christian Right has insisted that demonic secular humanists are hell-bent on destroying conservative Christian gender roles, in a plot to disintegrate the moral fabric of the West. For centuries before that, Jews themselves have been understood as gender rebels in their own right: in European Christian society, Jewish women were often stereotyped as too pushy, aggressive, and "masculine," while Jewish men were "feminized" to the point that, in the Middle Ages, it was not uncommon to believe Jewish men menstruated.[31] Even now, white nationalists focus on stories of perceived Jewish sexual deviance as a way of presenting their dangerous alienness.

Transphobia and antisemitism have been at the forefront of history's most violent fascist movements. One of the most iconic images of the Nazi era shows a group of smiling German youth throwing books into a massive bonfire, epitomizing the fascist assault on truth. The Institute of Sexology in Berlin, headed by Jewish activist Magnus Hirschfeld, was the target of the flames. The institute had pioneered early research into trans health care, which epitomized, for the Nazis, the destabilizing effect of Jewish ideologies on the German body.[32]

When we talked to Ada-Rhodes Short, an organizer with the trans-led direct action and advocacy group Tear It Up, she was adamant that "it's really hard not to see how all of our oppressions are linked and how all the violence we experience is the same violence . . . It's the same people attacking us. It's the same structures oppressing us. It's the same struggles that we're all pushing against."

Right-wing pundits and politicians insist their anti-trans activism is in defense of "Judeo-Christian values," citing Genesis 1:27, when God created humans "male and female," to claim that their favored gender norms are not social constructs but rooted in immutable, divinely ordained biological reality. In actuality, these norms reflect the fundamentalist Christianity favored by the Christian nationalist movement, as well as deep-rooted Euro-Christian gender binaries that differ from those found in classical Jewish thought. As discussed earlier, Christian nationalists claim to speak for the "authentic religious worldview," but they are bent on enforcing their exclusionary "virtues" on other communities, including Jews, that rarely agree with their interpretation.

Across the country, many Jewish activists are joining others at the front lines of defending LGBTQ communities from attack, driven to oppose what one activist called the "very clear link between antisemitism and transphobia that is increasing at a terrifying rate."[33] But establishment Jewish organizations are lagging behind. In November 2022, for example, one speaker at the general assembly of the Jewish Federations of North America, the country's leading umbrella Jewish organization, suggested Jewish communities should grant a platform to transphobic speakers in the name of "viewpoint diversity."[34]

"Our job, as Jews, is to build a world where all people can thrive," protested Rabbi Becky Silverstein, a queer and trans rabbi based in Boston. "Who thrives when our federations don't stand up to transphobia and other forms of oppression?"[35]

ANTISEMITISM AND ISLAMOPHOBIA

As discussed previously, if you listen to popular discourse to-day, especially on the Right, you might think it is an impossible fantasy that Jews and Muslims should band together to fight a common enemy. And yet, this alliance is an absolute necessity in an era when antisemitism and Islamophobia are deeply connected, and the far-right is using both oppressions to divide communities and enshrine white Christian supremacy.

Across the Western world, the Right has demonized Muslim immigrants and refugees as a demographic and civilizational threat, fueling nativist policy, vigilante street violence, and white nationalist mass shootings like the 2019 Christchurch massacre. Islamophobia is now afforded its own "cultural code" by which Rightists express their perceived loss of identity, and locate a new agent of influx that is stripping them of their history and culture.

For the open fascists of the movement, the connection to antisemitism is simple: Jews weaponize Muslim immigration to dilute the purity and attack the strength of an ethnically homogeneous people. "I originally planned to storm a mosque or an antifa 'culture' center, which are way less defended," stated the white nationalist who attempted a mass shooting against a synagogue in Halle, Germany, on Yom Kippur in October 2019, "but even killing 100 golems won't make a difference, when on a single day more than that are shipped to Europe. The only way to win is to cut of[f] the head of ZOG, which are the kikes."[36] This narrative is present in the United States as well. The Pittsburgh synagogue shooter, days before his October 2018 attack, shared content on Gab railing against "the filthy EVIL jews Bringing the Filthy EVIL Muslims into the Country!!"[37]

In the United States, both groups are targeted by the radical Right. In spring 2022, a Portland synagogue found "Die Juden" scrawled across its side, while another synagogue across town had its windows smashed. In the same week a man attempted to torch a local mosque.[38] A local far-right reporter, known for propagating COVID-19 denialism and conspiracy theories, was found responsible for the attacks.

In a now-familiar pattern, these conspiracy theories are echoed in code across the broader Right. The Right casts George Soros or "globalists" as the "enemy within," weakening the borders of the West for the Muslim hordes to swarm from without. The "Eurabia" conspiracy theory, common across the European far-right, claims that a cabal, made up of Arab and Muslim leaders and liberal Western elites, is working to undermine "Judeo-Christian" civilization, just as *The Protocols of the Elders of Zion* alleged a Jewish cabal pulling the strings a century earlier.

"These [Islamophobic and antisemitic] conspiracy theories not only Other the Jew or the Muslim," writes historian Reza Zia-Ebrahimi, "but also aim to demonstrate their profound enmity towards us . . . This is very much a process of racialization: it defines a group, it describes its presumed psychological and moral essence and, on that basis, it proclaims its unbridgeable opposition between us and them."[39] In this way, Islamophobia and antisemitism are interconnected components of a broader conspiratorial ideology, bound together in a shared story of supposed enmity.

In liberal European discourse, too, the religious practices of both Muslims and Jews come under fire, in campaigns to cleanse the secular public square of any trace of religious expression. Centrist, liberal, and right-wing politicians in countries like Belgium seek to ban kosher and halal meat slaughter, framed as liberal concern for animal welfare. Movements to end circumcision have often reproduced bigoted narratives against both communities.[40]

Right-wing politicians have moved to ban Muslim face veils such as burka or niqab, and French National Rally leader Marine Le Pen has repeatedly proposed banning the kippah as well, expressing the hope that Jews would "sacrifice" the kippah as a sign of commitment to the "joint struggle" to "stamp out radical Islam in France."[41]

Since the Middle Ages, Jews and Muslims both faced persecution under Christian Europe.[42] Both groups faced the sword during the medieval-era Crusades, when marauding Christian armies traversed Europe to recapture the Holy Land from Muslim infidels, and bands of angry peasants brought death and destruction to Ashkenazi Jewish communities across the Rhineland in the process. In the fifteenth and sixteenth centuries, both groups faced compulsory conversion from Christianizing Spain, which maintained an air of distrust surrounding these "New Christians." Judeoconversos (Jewish converts) and moriscos (Muslim converts) were confronted by the Office of the Inquisition, leading to state-sponsored scapegoating, discrimination, and eventual expulsion.

In the modern era, antisemitism and Islamophobia are intertwined in what historian Ethan Katz called "an entangled history of Othering." As Christian Europe adopted Enlightenment discourses, Judaism and Islam were seen as little more than archaic relics, a set of irrational practices destined to be swept aside in the steady march of humanity toward liberal secularism. "Jews and Muslims, long seen as foils and conversion targets for Christianity," wrote Katz, "also became symbols of the challenges in the Enlightenment quest for human perfectibility."[43] With the rise of racist pseudoscience, Orientalism, and nationalism in the nineteenth century, Jews, Muslims, and the Arab world were labeled as backward and threatening "Semites" by the Euro-Christian elite, who thought of themselves, by contrast, as superior "Aryans" in a tidy civilizational binary.[44]

At the same time, European states adopted a divide-and-conquer strategy in their overseas colonies, to prevent Jews and Muslims from uniting to overthrow colonial rule. In the French settler-colony of Algeria, for example, the Crémieux Decree granted French citizenship rights to Algeria's native Jewish population, but denied these privileges to the Muslim and Berber populations. As a result, the Algerian Jewish community, with roots in the region dating back to the first century C.E., came to be resented by many Muslim neighbors as the "face" of colonial occupation. This helped antisemitism spread among Algerian Muslims in the decades to follow, with the enthusiastic support of the French far-right.[45]

Jews and Muslims often forged powerful alliances within anti-colonial struggles across the region. Nonetheless, when countries like Algeria won national independence, their new national identities left little room for Jews, one factor contributing to the gradual exodus of most Jews from countries across the Middle East and North Africa.

Today, Europe's divide-and-conquer strategy continues to entrench deep-seated tensions. "The state grants privileges to the Jews in France," explained Houria Bouteldja, French Algerian decolonial activist and author, in a 2019 interview,

> which makes the Muslims jealous and provokes a spirit of conspiracy: "Why are the Jews so privileged? Look, the Jews control everything." It seems as if the Jews have a lot of power, but this is a manipulation of the state. We are currently in a phase in which the philosemitic state is protecting the Jews. I don't know when, but I think this will change soon, and they will not be protected anymore.[46]

Far-right parties like Alternative für Deutschland in Germany and National Rally in France have used Islamophobia to recruit Jews into their nationalist coalition. "I do not stop repeating it to French Jews," stated Marine Le Pen in 2014, "not only is the

National Front not your enemy, but it is without a doubt the best shield to protect you . . . [from] the only real enemy, Islamist fundamentalism."[47] That same year, a survey showed that National Front supporters—a party that included many Vichy supporters in its ranks, and carried a history of Holocaust revisionism—were at least twice as likely as the broader French population to believe in a "global Zionist conspiracy" and that Jews were "responsible for the current economic crisis" and hold too much power in the economy, media, and politics.[48]

"For those radical right parties for whom Islamophobia is central, they have moved very much towards a pro-Israel position," historian Cas Mudde told us. "In the world of Islamophobia, Israel is seen as the future of Europe, as a democratic state embattled by Islam." The Israeli Right shares this narrative. "Israel is on the forefront of the global war on terror," far-right leader Naftali Bennett, standing on a West Bank hilltop, proclaimed in a 2015 video entitled "Israel: Fighting for Your Freedom." "This is the front line between the free and civilized world and radical Islam . . . When we fight terror here, we are protecting London, Paris, and Madrid."[49]

Meanwhile mainstream antisemitism institutes, pro-Israel NGOs, and right-wing politicians, armed with the "new antisemitism" thesis, insist that Islam itself has developed into an intractable force of Jew hatred, encoded in sharia (Islamic law) and rooted in entrenched bigotry in Muslim-majority societies. This harmful falsehood has fueled the "counter-Jihad" movement of far-right loudspeakers like David Horowitz, and has helped nativist parties in Europe garner Jewish support based on opposition to the "Islamization of the West." It also reinforces the misconception that the crisis in Israel/Palestine is caused by some perennial hostility between Jews and Muslims, rather than by modern political oppression, which can be dismantled to build a just and flourishing shared society.

In the United States, pro-Israel organizations like the Anti-Defamation League and Simon Wiesenthal Center have slammed Muslim leaders and organizations under the guise of fighting antisemitism, all while claiming to speak on behalf of the Jewish community.[50] As we discuss later, this activism makes our communities complicit in broader Islamophobia in the "War on Terror" era. Just like the racist obsession with so-called Black antisemitism, this Islamophobia harms the mainstream Jewish community's ability to create allegiances against the shared threats we face. Yesterday and today, these divide-and-conquer strategies have helped undercut the possibility of powerful alliances between Jews and other marginalized groups. As we discuss in the next chapter, untangling these knots, and building meaningful safety through solidarity, is more important than ever.

THIRTEEN

CONTAINING MULTITUDES: ANTISEMITISM AND THE DIVERSITY OF JEWISH EXPERIENCE

On January 21, 2017, the day after President Trump's inauguration, an estimated 3 million to 5 million people took the streets in hundreds of rallies across the country. Joined by millions more protesters worldwide, the Women's March was a galvanizing display of solidarity and resistance against MAGA misogyny and bigotry in a frightening and uncertain moment. "You are what democracy looks like," Palestinian American march leader Linda Sarsour told the nearly half-million people packed into the National Mall in Washington, D.C. "[You] are my hope for my community."[1]

By early 2018, the movement was mired in controversy. The Women's March faced a barrage of politicized antisemitism accusations when it was revealed that one of its leaders, Tamika Mallory, attended a rally and expressed support for Nation of Islam leader Louis Farrakhan—a reactionary Black nationalist leader with a history of antisemitic, anti-LGBTQ, and misogynist statements. Critics also demonized Sarsour for her unapologetic support for Palestinian liberation.

March organizers quickly insisted that Farrakhan's "statements about Jewish, queer, and trans people are not aligned with the Women's March Unity principles," but many criticized Mallory for not severing ties with Farrakhan himself. Before long, reports of a few additional antisemitic incidents surfaced, and a toxic media narrative congealed casting Women's March as a den of Jew hatred, and its leaders of color, in particular, as angry, unrepentant antisemites.

Mallory remained resistant to disavow Farrakhan, and it's easy to see why. The Nation of Islam has provided services and been a supportive presence in Black communities, and "where my people are is where I must also be," Mallory wrote. "I go into difficult spaces."[2]

Writing in *The Atlantic*, Black Jewish writer Adam Serwer noted that "many Black people come into contact with the Nation of Islam as a force in impoverished Black communities—not simply as a champion of the Black poor or working class, but of the Black underclass: Black people, especially men, who have been written off or abandoned by white society."[3] The Nation of Islam had supported Mallory herself decades earlier, after the murder of her son's father.

"In that most difficult period of my life," she wrote, "it was the women of the Nation of Islam who supported me and I have always held them close to my heart for that reason."

White Jewish activist Sophie Ellman-Golan, then a staffer at the Women's March, knew her close, personal relationship with Mallory, built over years of side-by-side racial justice work, would be crucial in bridging the gap. "Anti-Semitism can be unlearned and addressed," she said in a 2019 interview. "[It's] not an immutable characteristic to anyone. There is a better chance of addressing that on the left when you have Jewish leftists working closely with non-Jewish leftist leaders."[4]

But the climate of accusations from the Right raised the stakes, and made public reconciliation that much harder. "We have to be able to hold at once that people and movements are imperfect and that people can be really racist in their reactions to those imperfections," Ellman-Golan said.

These racist, Islamophobic, and misogynist attacks continued for over a year, and helped the Right fracture a powerful resistance movement to Trumpism. Endless ink was spilled lamenting the supposed breakdown of the "Black-Jewish alliance," the threat of Palestinian Jew-hatred, and the abandonment of the Jews by the Left, and of the Left by the Jews. Some coalition partners and celebrity endorsers, Jewish and non-Jewish, withdrew support, and the movement lost crucial momentum, all while Trumpism ravaged our communities.

"[Antisemitism is] a real, serious problem," Mallory explained in a January 2019 appearance on *The Breakfast Club*, a popular national radio show, "and it's one that Black folks particularly need to pay attention to—because there are forces that want to be able to use anti-Black racism and antisemitism within the Jewish and Black communities to keep us apart. Because God forbid we ever pooled our power together and really, really started working together."[5]

Public accusations of antisemitism against high-profile progressive leaders of color, and the oversaturated media cycles they generate, have become a mainstay in our political discourse. Antisemitism and racism feed off each other in a vicious cycle, deepening resentment and defensiveness all around and undercutting the powerful alliances we need to fight white supremacy in all its forms.

The work of building and maintaining coalition across communities is knotty, tangled, and difficult. Antisemitism, racism, and other forms of oppression don't just confront us out there, on the other side of the barricades—they also tear groups apart from one another, and even divide our communities from within. We can trace connections between these systems of oppression we face, but this does not mean our experiences facing those systems are the same. Different individuals and groups hold greater access to resources, and real differences in privilege, power, and positionality. The Right, meanwhile, is eager to exploit these tensions to weaken movements that threaten its agenda.

In this chapter we will explore how these knots became so tangled over the last century, and how we can break them. We'll look at how white Jews "became white folks," as one popular book on the subject puts it,[6] and how white Jewish racism can harm folks of color within and beyond the Jewish community. We'll look at how antisemitism within non-Jewish communities of color, in turn, deepens division between potential allies, and weakens liberation movements. We'll widen our frame to look at how Jews of color and Orthodox Jews we've engaged with experience antisemitism, uplifting voices that are often marginalized as we deepen our vision of a liberated society where difference, in all its forms, is celebrated and cherished.

JEWS AND WHITENESS

Most accounts of how Jews became white focus on the years after the Second World War, when many Ashkenazi communities, along with other "white ethnics" like the Italians and Irish, moved up the ladder of American race and class privilege. The same policies that ushered these communities into the waiting arms of the "American dream," such as the GI Bill and its accessible housing and education loans, were de facto denied to Black families, part of the structural discrimination that reinscribed racist hierarchies.[7] White Christian America welcomed many Jews into its neighborhoods, but the "no Blacks allowed" signs remained or de facto persisted through redlining.

In fact, from the early days of white settlement and colonization in continental America light-skinned Jews had long been granted legal acceptance, if not full inclusion, in the dominant white caste. The 1705 Virginia Slave Codes forbade Jews, Muslims, and other "infidels" from having white Christian servants—marking their difference vis-à-vis the Christian majority—but not from owning Native or African-descended slaves. "The intermingling of racial and religious discrimination," wrote scholar Mark Tseng-Putterman, "is noteworthy: the central function of the Slave Codes was to create a Black and Native underclass[,] whom European Jews were granted access to exploit."[8] The Naturalization Act of 1790 barred Black and Indigenous people, Asian migrants, and many other groups from the "free white persons" eligible for citizenship, but not Jews as a group.[9]

While white, Christian, landowning men remained atop the racial and class pyramid, long before the twentieth century, many of America's Jews, hailing largely from Sephardic and German immigrant communities, were reasonably well integrated, and even prospered within white American society. Some Jews, like their Christian counterparts, owned slaves, and some, like Confederate Secretary of State Judah Benjamin, enthusiastically fought to protect that privilege during the Civil War.

Jews were not free from persecution in white Christian America, however. Jews faced de jure and de facto discrimination in areas ranging from housing and education to employment and political office until the mid-twentieth century, as well as other forms of bigotry, scapegoating, and violence. Jews "were accepted as white, but their precise racial place was not fixed," wrote Leonard Rogoff, historian of Jews in the American South.[10] Early twentieth century eugenicists, who pushed the United States to adopt exclusionary immigration laws in 1924 that would shut the country's doors to Jews fleeing fascism one decade later, and advanced a taxonomy of European races with Jews at the bottom, with Madison Grant insisting "the cross between any of the three European races and a Jew is a Jew."[11]

The rise of fascism in the 1930s saw organized antisemitism reach a crescendo in the United States, with groups like Father Coughlin's Christian Front violently attacking and terrorizing Jews and holding fascist rallies across the country. As the horrors of the Holocaust became widely known, the postwar embrace of whiteness was, for many US Jews, a scramble for safety in a world which, they realized, could snatch it away in an instant.[12]

The story of Jewish whiteness is a story of persecution on one side, and complicity in persecution on the other. It illustrates how Jews, like any group, can hold both oppressed and oppressor roles, often simultaneous and overlapping, within a social order. Today, faced with antisemitism's resurgence, some white Jews rush to disavow their whiteness. If white nationalists insist we are not white, they reason, why not take their claims at face value? If we are truly white, why do we still face antisemitism?

"I want white Jews to acknowledge that they are white," Chanda Prescod-Weinstein, cosmologist and Black Jewish activist, told the *Forward* in 2019. "White Jews may not live at the center of the tent of whiteness, but they are still white. When white Jews refuse to acknowledge that they benefit from and participate in white supremacy, they are wasting time that could otherwise be spent upending that white supremacy."[13]

Some non-Jewish Leftists err in the opposite direction. If most Jews are white, they reason, then antisemitism can't be taken seriously—why devote valuable resources to "white people issues"? But antisemitism is harmful to Jews, and should be fought for that reason alone—and as we have discussed, it works in tandem to uphold white supremacy and other forms of oppression. It threatens us all, and we need to fight it all, together.

Race, of course, is ultimately a construct—albeit a very real construct, with direct impacts across practically every area of our society. "Whiteness" is not a biological fact, a kind of Euro-Aryan racial essence, as white nationalists claim. It is a social relation whose boundaries shift, depending on context, to include or exclude different communities based on the distribution of power and privilege across society at any given moment. "White Jews are white, now, because of the confluence of social and economic factors across the twentieth century," Dania Rajendra, a Jewish Indian American organizer, told us:

And, we're in a very different economic and social time today. Part of what's so interesting about Christian nationalism is the way that it seems to extend whiteness to others who previously have been considered not white. At a time when whiteness is unstable, it can be both extended and rescinded. It's entirely possible that it will be extended and rescinded along a combination of religious and political lines.

"BLACK ANTISEMITISM": A RACIST FANTASY

Whenever controversies like that surrounding the Women's March erupt, you're sure to see media headlines screaming an unending refrain of "Black antisemitism."

Antisemitism should be condemned on its own terms, wherever it occurs. We should also reject racist narratives, epitomized in media buzzwords like "Black antisemitism," suggesting that non-Jewish communities of color are somehow inherently antisemitic, any more so than their white counterparts. "It is a racialized fantasy, a projection of white anxieties about dark horrors lurking just beyond the horizon," explained Black Marxist scholar Adolph Reed. "Any Black anti-Semite is seen not as an individual but as a barometer of the Black collective mind; belief in Black antisemitism, therefore, is itself a form of racialist thinking."[14]

But these racist narratives sit atop deep fault lines in American history. During the mid-twentieth century, white Jewish and Black non-Jewish communities found themselves living in close proximity, yet on opposite sides of fast-widening racial divisions. Similar patterns played out in city after city—many (though not all) white Jewish families moved to the suburbs, and some became landlords over their old properties, into which Black families moved as tenants. Some white Jews became small business owners at groceries, department stores, or other businesses in predominantly Black neighborhoods, getting a leg up while their neighbors remained entrenched in generational poverty.

"It is bitter," James Baldwin wrote in a 1967 essay elucidating these tensions, "to watch the Jewish storekeeper locking up his store for the night, and going home. Going, with your money in his pocket, to a clean neighborhood, miles from you, which you will not be allowed to enter . . . He is playing in Harlem the role assigned him by Christians long ago: he is doing their dirty work."[15] Some white Jews became schoolteachers, social workers, and benefits administrators in low-income Black neighborhoods.

The result is that white Jews appeared as visible faces of larger structures of racial and economic injustice. "Jews in the United States," as Puerto Rican Jewish activist Aurora Levins Morales put it,

> have collaborated in the exploitation of urban people of color, trading an illusion of safety for the powerful alliances we could have built, and often becoming one of the local faces of oppression: landlords, pawnbrokers, public school teachers and administrators, doctors, and the social workers of the welfare machine, implementing policies that serve others, and collecting rents for the shareholders of the Bank of America.[16]

In a sense, Morales continued, this reestablished the "middle agent" position of the feudal era, where European peasants attacked the local Jews collecting heavy taxes for the nobility, while leaving actual ruling elites untouched. Antisemitism served, for some non-Jewish communities of color, as a means to lash out at white Jews positioned in proximity above them in race and class hierarchies, leaving the roots of the system—and the overwhelmingly white and Christian leaders on top—shielded.

The megacorporations dotting the American landscape, Baldwin noted, were *not* controlled by Jews. Instead they were "controlled by Americans, and the American Negro situation is a direct result of this control." White Christians, he explained, formed the bulk of America's ruling elite, and "the root of anti-Semitism among negroes is, ironically, the relationship of colored peoples—all over the globe—to the Christian world," which white Jews now seem to embody when participating in this supremacist system.[17]

This antisemitism originated in white Christian Europe— but it didn't remain there. Through colonialism, chattel slavery, and its other systems of global violence, Europe exported its antisemitism to communities around the world, and it is now part of the American (and global) folk narrative, appearing wherever people are fed up and looking for answers. "Illuminati theory helps oppressed people to explain our experiences in the hood," explained *How to Overthrow the Illuminati*, a popular 2013 radical pamphlet unpacking the fight against conspiracy theories in BIPOC communities.[18]

> Society throws horrible stuff in our faces: our family members get locked up for bullshit. Our friends kill each other over beefs, money or turf. Our future is full of dead-end jobs that don't pay shit. We struggle to pay bills while others live in luxury . . . Why does this occur? We start looking for answers, and Illuminati theory provides one.

When far-right Black nationalist leaders like Louis Farrakhan scapegoat Jews as prime architects of the slave trade (which is untrue, although there were some Jewish slave owners) or as special urban exploiters of Black communities, to name two oft-cited examples, they are using a narrative first fashioned in Christian Europe. Much like it was used in Europe, they are using this narrative to misdiagnose the root causes of subjugation and offer a dead-end "cure." Instead of analyzing the transcontinental accumulation of European capital and colonial conquest that enabled slavery—or tracing the neoliberal policies shredding social safety nets—blame is displaced onto a shadowy, racialized cabal. This both makes Jews less safe and social movements less effective.

Conspiracy theories in communities of color tap into real grievances against injustices of structural racism, and can sometimes appear as what scholar Patricia Turner calls "tools of resistance."[19] Nonetheless, these intimate expressions of discontent ultimately serve as faulty guides for analysis and action. This is challenging because so many actual conspiracies have occurred in US history, particularly against communities of color. For instance, because the US government literally has a history of intentionally infecting Black communities with lethal pathogens, it was easier for many to believe in the 1980s that HIV/AIDS was manufactured by a government laboratory to attack Black communities. As a result, conspiracy theories spread that hampered health interventions and social services.[20]

Like other right-wing movements, some POC-led movements that push antisemitism, such as the Nation of Islam, also propagate misogyny, anti-LGBTQ bigotry, and reactionary forms of nationalism. The base of today's far-right movements remains majority white, but people of color are drawn to groups like the Proud Boys, Oath Keepers, and America First/groyper movement as well. "To some on the Far Right, building a broader coalition that includes people of color is self-evidently part of their project to redefine nationalism," explained antifascist researchers and organizers Cloee Cooper and Daryle Lamont Jenkins in 2019. "Above all, what the multiracial Far Right demonstrates is how much their movement can and will continue to change form, at times coalescing within communities more often associated with the Left, and along axes other than [explicit white nationalism]."[21]

The conviction that nationalists of different races should

unite to defeat the shared enemy of Jewish power has even aligned some unlikely political partners. In the early 1960s, George Lincoln Rockwell's American Nazi Party was welcomed at multiple Nation of Islam rallies, and once even addressed the crowd.[22] Holding up a distorted mirror to the Left's promise of true solidarity, these alliances underscore the dangerous appeal antisemitism, with its illusory "punching up," can hold across diverse communities—even while it upholds the white Christian supremacist status quo harming all of us.

In truth, there is no specifically "Black" antisemitism—"it's American antisemitism, as it can manifest in Black communities," explained Rebecca Pierce, a Black Jewish filmmaker and activist, in a November 2022 podcast. "But it's still worth, as Black folks, us having a conversation about where and how this does come up because it does matter."[23]

THE RICH DIVERSITY OF JEWISH LIFE

In 2019, the Women's March set off on a new footing. A cohort of over one hundred Jewish women of color led the march in Washington, D.C., carrying Torah scrolls down the streets of the nation's capital. They released an open letter before the march, stating that "as Jewish women of color who live at the intersection of racism, sexism and anti-Semitism, and who are committed to standing against white supremacy, patriarchy and religious oppression in all its forms, we will play an integral role in the healing and unification of our communities and in the work of securing greater justice and freedom for us all."[24]

These intersections are only highlighted by the racism that many Jews of color face in the majority-white American Jewish community. "Entering Jewish spaces often means entering white spaces and being subjected to anti-Blackness," wrote culture critic Soraya Nadia McDonald in 2020, "and questions about whether I truly belong, an experience that's common among Jews of color . . . Jews of color often face a burden to publicly prove their Jewishness while white counterparts can take that part of themselves for granted."[25]

A 2021 survey found 80 percent of Jews of color experience discrimination in Jewish spaces, and nearly two-thirds believed community leaders are inadequately addressing racism and white supremacy within the American Jewish community.[26] Living at the intersection of multiple communities, Jews of color often find their Jewish identity erased, particularly when people assume they are not Jews, and likewise face racism and antisemitism as overlapping phenomena.

"I've been called the N-word and the K-word at the same time," Robin Washington, a Black Jewish journalist who helped found the Alliance of Black Jews in 1995, told us. Washington grew up in a civil rights activist family, noticing that the Chicago school system he attended was de facto segregated along multiple axes, separating Black students from white as well as Jewish students from Gentiles.

In 1963, at the age of six, he participated with his family in a multiday sit-in at the Chicago Board of Education. It was planned in his living room as part of a campaign to pressure the city to abolish its racist school district maps. ("The article could have also described us as Jewish children," Washington wrote decades later in the *Forward*, reflecting on an article at the time that described him and his brother Glen as "two Negro children.") The school board refused to make meaningful changes until forced by the Justice Department in 1980, and today, deep de facto educational segregation and inequality remain the norm in Chicago.[27]

Awqasisa Friedman, an Indigenous Peruvian Jewish woman living in Louisiana, recounted the antisemitism she often faced from non-Jewish communities growing up in Peru. Her first boyfriend told her that Jews controlled the world, for example, while people often made fun of her father's nose. Moving to the United States, she found her experiences with antisemitism differed from white Jews. "Our identity comes into question a lot more often," she told us. "A lot of times, when I go into [Jewish] spaces and people have found out that I'm Jewish, they have sort of tried to pull my identity apart."

Israeli Mizrahi scholar Smadar Lavie, of mixed Yemeni and Ashkenazi heritage, told us that when she went hiking outside of Charlottesville, Virginia:

> I would stop my car, knock on doors, and ask for directions. The first thing I heard was, "Are you Muslim?" And I would say, "I am an Israeli," and they would say, "Oh, you don't look Jewish!" Sometimes it was very blatant: "You don't have the nose" . . . Other times, like in Utah or Nevada, people would talk to me, a short, dark woman, in Spanish . . . I was afraid of those people, so I would say, "I am Israeli," and they would sing the praises of the Israeli army, and leave me alone.

When Jews of color lead the way in fighting antisemitism, they can build profound bridges, and deepen collaboration between communities. "When you have Black Jews talking to other non-Jewish Black people, and Arab Jews talking to other non-Jewish Arabs, the whole vibe is going to be different," Leo Ferguson, a Black Jewish organizer and director of special projects at Jews for Racial and Economic Justice (JFREJ), told us. "The shared histories, the shared understandings, because of those overlapping, intersectional identities, are going to be different."

For example, in 2017, JFREJ's Mizrahi caucus organized with Arab Muslim and Christian communities against Trump's Muslim ban, building on a shared stake in fighting anti-Muslim and anti-Arab racism and bigotry. The long-standing close relationships between Jewish and non-Jewish Arab organizers, built upon shared centuries-long legacies of language, culture, and memory in the Middle East and North Africa, created a foundation to move intersectional movement work forward. When the Tree of Life shooting happened in October 2018, Ferguson remembered:

> All of those relationships were there and there wasn't any question about "are these folks we can turn to? Are we in this together?" It was like, "Obviously!" . . . We held a gathering, and all of our partners across New York City showed up, not because we even asked them to but because they were going to whether we wanted them or not, because they wanted to be there for us. And similarly, when the Muslim ban first came down, we had all of these rabbis and other Jews showing up at JFK [Airport] . . . There were just so many people who recognized our shared stake in this.

Mizrahi, Sephardi, and other non-Ashkenazi Jews have also organized to combat Ashkenazi dominance in American Jewry. Too often, certain Ashkenazi religious practices and cultural narratives—such as Yiddishisms like "oy," the Lower East Side immigrant story, food like lox and bagels, and shows like *Seinfeld*—are portrayed as universal Jewish experiences. This obscures the rich diversity of Jewish life, and it often reflects a stale, assimilated version of Ashkenazi culture as well.

As we have discussed, mainstream antisemitism analysis often defaults to Eurocentric narratives, projecting intense legacies of Christian European persecution as the universal Jewish experience. By contrast, until the mid-twentieth century, many Jews across Southwest Asia and North Africa lived alongside their non-Jewish neighbors with relatively greater coexistence and stability.

The persecution of Jews in the region "was of a different nature than [European] antisemitism," Lavie told us. "The same way that Israel hijacks Judaism into a Zionist framework, the US and European pro-Israel lobby hijacks Mizrahi experience and reformulates it historically inaccurately" to portray Israel as the "savior" of Mizrahi Jews. These narratives are then used to break any potential solidarity between Mizrahim and Palestinians, and thus bolster the Israeli Right.

Today, the antisemitism developed in Europe forms the backbone of far-right conspiracism and threats to Jews worldwide. "Of course it makes sense for us to be digging into the history of antisemitism in [the context of] European Christian white supremacy," Keren Soffer-Sharon, an Iraqi Jewish community organizer said, "because we still live in a Christian white supremacist country . . . [It] is the best shot we have to figure out how our own power structure is working."[28] But by remaining clear that it is not the whole story, we can remain attentive to the diversity of Jewish life and history.

THE EXPERIENCES OF "VISIBLE" JEWS

In June 2010, activists were gearing up to confront the G20 summit, a gathering, held that year in Toronto, where heads of state from around the world would be discussing global financial policy. As Avi Gross-Grand was doing reconnaissance for the upcoming protest, a man pulled up next to him on the road and yelled, "You're a fucking Jew!" "My first reaction was, oh, he's making a joke or something," Avi, who was wearing a kippah, told us. After Avi challenged him and tried to move on, the man emerged from his car and took a swing at him, forcing Avi to fight him off. Regular experiences of harassment "certainly, over time, started to wear down my desire to wear a kippah," he told us.

Those who are "visibly" Jewish—wearing clothing like a kippah, tzitzit,[29] *tichel*,[30] or the black hat and suit characteristic of Haredim—are frontline targets for antisemitism. By publicly marking their Jewishness, visible Jews are vulnerable to the everpresent possibility of harassment and violence that can be hard for many non-Jews, or less visibly marked Jews, to understand.

For Haredi Jews especially, antisemitic attacks in places like New York City are not uncommon,[31] and a 2023 study shows that these communities remain the most likely to face antisemitic assaults globally.[32] Most Haredim have been attacked themselves, or know someone who has.

"I've gotten [antisemitism] from so many different nationalities and ethnicities in New York," Asher Lovy, an observant Jew who grew up in Boro Park, told us. Data shows that 60 percent of individuals arrested in 2019 for antisemitic hate crimes in NYC were white, while one-third were African American, echoing a similar ratio in 2018.[33] Sometimes, it is what Lovy called "harmless"—like the time a man approached him and very earnestly, respectfully asked him for a job. "[He] said, 'come on, I know you own buildings up here' . . . Never once did he say anything mean—he just seemed to really believe if he saw an Ashkenazi Jew with a yarmulke on in Harlem, he would be there to collect the rent."

Other incidents are more brutal. Passersby, Lovy told us, have yelled "kike" out of cars, and he has been harassed on trains on multiple occasions. "One person even followed me from Manhattan onto New Jersey Transit, harassing me because he was panhandling and I didn't have any cash. He was hounding me, saying 'I know you have property' . . . I didn't have a job, I didn't have anything. If I had money I would've given it to him." Lovy recalls once walking through Boro Park, and "a guy points at me and says to his little kid, 'look at that— that's a fucking Jew.' And I thought to myself—your kid doesn't even know what hate is, who Jews are, what antisemitism is."

Nesha Abramson told us that when taking her Hasidic son to an early-morning doctor's appointment, "this man started screaming at us, telling us how we're devils, we're stealing money . . . no one said anything. And I realized that in that moment, I was grateful he was *just* yelling at us." Street harassment can feel so routine, Abramson told us, that many Haredim implicitly accept it as normal.

I was walking with my son the other day and he said to me, "How many times have you been spit on, Mommy? I've been spit on two times." And I thought—this is not normal, that my child can talk about how much he's been spit on. And I've also been spit on. And I responded, "Yeah, I've been spit on once or twice" . . . That struck me how normal it was. People will honestly say, "Well, it's not that bad, we only got spat on, we only got yelled at."

Abramson works at Community Counter, a nonprofit focused on public health advocacy in Orthodox communities, and tracks cases of medical discrimination against Haredi patients. In the first months of the COVID-19 pandemic in 2020, Haredim were scapegoated as prime carriers of the disease, along with Asian Americans, leading to heightened discrimination and assaults.[34] This mobilized long-standing antisemitic tropes casting Jews as disease carriers, prevalent during the Black Death in medieval Europe, and it diverted widespread anger away from the failed systems and leaders (such as Trump) responsible for mismanaging the pandemic, and onto a vulnerable and familiar target.

Haredim faced vitriol from hospital staff who lambasted them, saying "you're dirty," "you're bringing COVID here," "you're the reason why we all have COVID now," or "you people aren't vaccinated anyway," as Abramson told us. Nurses tightened their face masks when administering care to Orthodox Jewish patients, but left the masks loose otherwise. Hospitals that typically allowed doulas to accompany patients in labor consistently required doulas with "Jewish-sounding" last names to fill out disproportionate paperwork or take prohibitive COVID precautions, or barred them from entering the hospital entirely.

Haredi Jews often face a different set of antisemitic tropes from those most featured in this book. Right-wing conspiracy theories blame Jews as supposed agents of liberal modernity and Left movements for equality, and fixate mostly on assimilated, secular white Jews, who "blend in" to subvert white society from within. The antisemitism levied against Haredim, by contrast, scapegoats them as *opponents* of liberal modernity, and chastises them for *refusing* to blend in. Haredi communities are slandered as fanatically patriarchal, clouded by religious superstition and hatred of science, and motivated by total disregard for children, animals, and the environment—all qualities deemed inherent to Haredi culture. Religious practices like circumcision are misrepresented to portray Haredi Jews as barbaric and uncivilized, alien, and excessively legalistic.

These reflect accusations leveled at Jews for centuries, and are similar to bigotry directed against other marginalized groups as well. "Certain sects of Jews are much like illegal immigrants," posted a New Jersey resident in 2019, incensed that Haredim were moving to their neighborhood. "They have their own language and customs and refuse to become part of the Greater Community. Instead they expect the community to tolerate their bizarre way of life."[35]

In places like Rockland County, New York, or Lakewood, New Jersey, complex tensions over housing and education generate deep resentment between newly arrived Haredim and their non-Haredi neighbors, and xenophobia is often in the mix. Neighbors have warned of an "Orthodox invasion," depicted growing Haredi populations as an "infestation," and placed signs on their lawns as barricades against the feared onslaught. This rhetoric sounds indistinguishable from any right-wing radio host fearmongering about the purported Latinx *reconquista* of the American Southwest. "Last time I drove through I thought I was in a different country," lamented one Facebook comment, "[with] buildings and billboards all in Hebrew . . . They control everything . . . [It's] changing the landscape of our lives and our culture."[36]

Much of the rhetoric scapegoating Haredim as backward and fanatical also mirrors Islamophobia. One Haredi woman told Abramson that, shortly after she had given birth in the hospital on a hot Brooklyn summer day, she complained to the nurse that it was too hot in the room, and she couldn't breathe. The nurse replied, "If you didn't wear that *turban* on your head, you wouldn't be so hot." The slippage was revealing—the nurse mistakenly referred to the *tichel*, the headscarf worn by married Orthodox women, using the word for the wrap commonly worn by Muslim men.

Anti-Orthodox bias remains prevalent in the United States. Shows like *Unorthodox* and *My Unorthodox Life* dramatize salvation narratives of individuals who choose to leave behind the strictures of a cultlike Haredi world.[37] In popular culture, "you see the Jerry Seinfeld, totally secular [character] kind of mocking their heritage," Allison Josephs, founder of Jew in the City, a nonprofit which counters negative perceptions of religious Jews in the media, said in a 2021 interview, "or you see the crazy Hasidic Jew who hates women and is judgmental and extreme," with nothing in the middle.[38]

Non-Haredi Jews can be complicit in this, too—by spreading narratives that Haredim are uniquely powerful or malicious, for example, that in other contexts would be rightly recognized as antisemitic. People "are much less tolerant of others than we believe we are," Motti Seligson, media director at Chabad, reminded us.

These narratives rob complex communities of depth, texture, and diversity, in favor of flat, unidimensional portrayals tinted with Christian anti-Judaism. They can be especially appealing for liberals who are understandably concerned with progressive issues, like women's rights and education. And, indeed, progressives shouldn't compromise our values—we should support a range of progressive leaders from both inside and formerly inside the Haredi world who genuinely respect *Hasidishe* ways of life.

We should also practice humility and curiosity, especially toward Haredim who challenge our worldview. "There will be real differences in values and culture," Jonah Boyarin, a Jewish activist who works closely with Haredim targeted by antisemitism in New York City, reminded us. "We [progressives] don't need to change who we are, or attempt to impose a change on who they are—*that they're not asking for*. We need to figure out—what are shared points of values and shared points of interest?"

Boyarin reminded us that liberal non-Haredi Jews, especially, should avoid distancing themselves from Haredi communities or blaming them for the oppression they face. "Whenever there's an attack on Hasidim," Boyarin told us, "I hear from other Jews, 'Why can't they just dress more like us? Why can't they sound, look, eat, pray differently?' etc. And that's respectability politics—it's a safety strategy that the more conforming [Jewish] group uses."

REACHING ACROSS DIFFERENCE

For decades, while Leftists have largely overlooked Orthodox communities as potential movement partners, the Christian Right has prioritized outreach, enlisting Orthodox Jews as culture war crusaders against reproductive choice and LGBTQ rights, despite real theological differences around these issues, to lend a pluralist veneer to their Christian nationalism. The result is that today, many (though certainly not all) Haredi communities and leaders are currently aligned with the Christian Right and MAGA movement.

Some Orthodox leaders even excuse MAGA antisemitism against non-Orthodox liberal Jews on the problematic grounds that these Jews "aren't really Jewish" or that their liberal activism warrants demonization. But yesterday and today, this is a shortsighted and regrettable safety strategy. In 1933, some German Orthodox leaders wrote a letter to Adolf Hitler, then the new German chancellor, assuring Nazi leadership that "Marxist materialism and Communist atheism share not the least in common with the spirit of the positive Jewish religious tradition, as handed down through Orthodox teachings obligatory on the Jewish People . . . We seek a *Lebensraum* within the *Lebensraum* of the German people."[39] The Nazi Holocaust, of course, targeted Orthodox and non-Orthodox Jews alike with genocide.

In places like New York City, complex tensions between Haredi communities and non-Jewish communities of color inform a simmering brew of antisemitism, racism, and class resentment. Deep estrangement from non-Jewish neighbors and progressive movements, as well as the kind of anti-Black racism that can be found in any white community, lead many Haredim to conclude that the only way to keep their communities safe is by supporting anti-Black measures like increased police funding and harsh criminal sentencing.

Shulim Leifer grew up in the Nadvorna and Bobov Hasidic communities in the 1980s and '90s, the grandchild of concentration camp survivors and the son of a Jewish Defense League member. He told us that antisemitism was a constant presence hanging over the community's consciousness. "The [persistence of] European, old-fashioned antisemitism was very much ingrained into us as children," Leifer told us, which is why "fifth-generation American Jews can't shake that feeling that the government is persecuting them when they're just trying to pull you over for speeding."

But over time, Leifer worried this became a self-fulfilling prophecy, as conflict with neighbors over any issue was recast as simply one more manifestation of an age-old hatred. The conviction that theirs is the only authentic Jewishness, Leifer explained, helps predispose many Haredim to define "antisemitism" simply as whatever obstacles their community might face vis-à-vis the non-Jewish world. "That's how you end up having visibly Orthodox Jews storming the Capitol together with [people wearing Camp Auschwitz shirts]," pointed out Leifer, who told us that even many Haredim who fight against real systemic barriers faced by their communities lapse into antisemitic conspiracy theories targeting George Soros or "globalists" in their analysis of broader political issues.

But Haredim are not a far-right monolith, and by finding overlap around issues like poverty, we can cut through entrenched feelings of isolation, take back the narrative from the Right, and build a shared stake in fighting antisemitism with solidarity. Organizations like Chochmat Nashim are fighting against overbearing patriarchy from within the Haredi world, while a small, but meaningful, progressive presence is growing inside of Haredi communities in both the United States and Israel. This is not a new phenomenon. In the twentieth century, Jewish anarchists like Shmuel Alexandrov and Yehuda Ashlag emerged from Hasidic communities and brought this tradition of mysticism and *mitzvot*-centered living into their confrontation with imperialism and capitalism.[41] "Haredi Jewish communities are frontline targeted communities when it comes to antisemitism," Jonah Boyarin explains. "We [on the Left] have a commitment to supporting frontline communities and valuing their voices. So how can we live out that commitment when it comes to Haredi communities?"

"IT'S NOT WALKING AWAY"

For Megan Black, an organizer countering antisemitism with the pro-democracy group Western States Center, fighting for a world where Jews can fully thrive means fighting for one where she, as a Black biracial Christian woman, can thrive as well. "I need people to be committed to a multiethnic, multiracial, pluralist society," she told us, "because that's the only one in which I can live. And if people don't invest in the skills and understanding needed to reduce inequities between communities and negotiate with each other, there is no place for people like me."

Black reminded us that this work is easier said than done. "On the Left, there is this very 'kumbaya' idea that we can all get along and we all are the same at the end of the day," she told us. But while helping one predominantly white Reform synagogue and a Black Baptist church build a relationship with each other, she saw that "they kept running into these extraordinarily deep chasms of difference between them." The work, she realized, is much messier on the ground:

> This ["kumbaya" vision] completely ignores the true depth of the ways in which we're almost incomprehensibly different from each other—and the realities of what it looks like for us to negotiate, not necessarily as friends but as distinct parties committed to finding a common ground so that we can each thrive fully as who we are.

Stosh Cotler, former CEO of Bend the Arc, a national progressive Jewish organization, told us that during the Trump years, Jewish and non-Jewish social movement leaders were able to navigate complex, and often difficult, tensions surrounding the fight against antisemitism primarily because of the strength of close, genuine relationships, forged over years of side-by-side struggle across a range of issues. The "vulnerable and truthful conversations" that are often required, she explained, "happen when there is real relationship." That way, "if and when hard things come up over time, everyone is invested in working it out."

Chabad rabbi Mordechai Lightstone shared his optimism that progressives and Haredi communities can find common ground around the issue of prison reform. "Fundamentally, from a Torah point of view," Lightstone told us, "prison is almost unethical." The punitive model of incarceration clashes with Jewish ideas of *teshuvah*, human growth and repentance, and so there "has been a lot of activism on the part of many Hasidic Jews" to envision reform, and alternatives to incarceration:

If we can say, "Yeah, we disagree on a lot of things. But when it comes to the question of prison reform, we both see eye to eye on that. Let's work on that together" . . . That also [helps combat] antisemitism because now when you're working on the shared issue, even when you see all these other problems [between communities] . . . it's much harder to hate. It's much harder to "Other" [each other].

Tracing intersections between the oppressions we face, and naming shared interests and experiences is the beginning, not the end, of creating safety through solidarity. "Real coalitions are hard," wrote Jewish scholar and organizer April Rosenblum in 2020. "They are built with people who are interested in working with us but may start out distrustful. They are forged through a thousand different errors, failures and disappointments, with people who are still there when the dust clears, perhaps also disappointed in us, but willing to try again to get it right."[41]

RESISTING ASSIMILATION

One of the core struggles faced by marginalized groups is the demand to assimilate: to become as similar as possible to the dominant group. While Nazi eliminationism is often cited as the epitome of anti-Jewish persecution, it hasn't always been the dominant way that Jews are targeted. Centuries before Jewish racialization, the demand was typically that European Jews convert, to blend in to the Christian majority and voluntarily eradicate their difference. This pressure erased a great number of Jewish communities, a tragedy expressed in the gaps we hold in family histories and memories. Our ancestry was spread like wildflowers beneath towns and cities across Europe, usually remembered as a historical footnote to whatever population we were part of. With the advent of DNA tests like 23andMe many people discover that their ancestry carries traces of Jewish communities lost to history.

Following the French Revolution, European Jews faced tremendous pressure to abandon deeply held religious and cultural traditions, and communal structures of self-governance, in order to prove their full integration as upstanding citizens of the modern, secular nation-state. While this process of "emancipation" was complex and multilayered—and enthusiastically embraced by adherents of the *Haskalah*, or Jewish Enlightenment, across Europe—it also carried a coercive edge. It was experienced by Jewish communities as "a matter of life and death," wrote sociologist Zygmunt Bauman, across a continent in which "strangers had either to stop being strangers—or stop being."[42] Once twentieth-century ethnonationalist movements decided the attempt at Jewish assimilation had failed, they chose the latter option.

After World War II, state socialist projects intensified their own assimilationist demands. Drawing upon Enlightenment and left-wing traditions of universalism, reason, and anti-clericalism, they mistakenly concluded that in order to combat entrenched social divisions among their citizen populations, they needed to use coercive state power to suppress the distinct religious and cultural structures, institutions, and identities held by Jews and many other religious and ethnic communities. For decades, vibrant Jewish life in the U.S.S.R. and across the Eastern Bloc was largely extinguished or driven underground, contributing to a lasting hostility toward socialism held by many of today's descendants of those communities, who continue to carry the scars.

Remnants of this harmful framework still exist in pockets of today's Left. Years ago, a white, Christian-raised activist attempted to dissuade Ben from getting involved with a Jewish activist group by insisting, "I would never form a group like 'White Boys from Iowa for Justice!'" The message was clear—Jews shouldn't form organizations, caucuses, or initiatives in

Left movements because Jews are merely a subcategory of white oppressors, with no distinct identity or political expression worth articulating of their own. Thankfully, this attitude has receded in recent years in the US Left, thanks in part to the activism of the Jewish Left and the growing acceptance of identity-based organizing.

In the West, whiteness carries its own risk of assimilation. White racialization homogenizes a group's evolving history and culture, in exchange for privilege in a racialized class structure ultimately built to benefit the rich. White Jews share in this experience, particularly in the United States, where they face less systemic antisemitism than in Europe and have enjoyed most privileges granted other "ethnic whites" since the 1950s. Jewish assimilation can come both from living in a Christian-hegemonic culture and from white Jewish complicity in white supremacy, both of which are aimed at minimizing Jewish difference.

At its core, a culture of equality allows people to be themselves, but together as part of a more egalitarian partnership. Since we became a diaspora community, Jewish peoplehood has always spoken to the way tradition and particularity can be maintained while sharing space with different communities. Our ability to live a liberated life does not demand us to drop identities, but to find a way to share, respect, and coexist.

In the 1970s, as the activists of the Combahee River Collective developed their intersectional theory and practice, the Jewish feminist movement, too, was emerging, and groups like the Jewish lesbian feminist collective Di Vilde Chayes incorporated an intersectional lens to parse out the sexism, class oppression, and antisemitism they faced, including their erasure as Jews on the Left. They acknowledged that non-Jewish women of color set the groundwork and helped inspire them to reclaim a proud Jewish identity.[43]

"Assimilation promises that if Jews give up their Jewishness, we can belong to the dominant culture, escape anti-Semitism, be safe," said Jewish feminist trailblazers Melanie Kaye/Kantrowitz, Irena Klepfisz, and Bernice Mennis in their classic 1989 handbook on fighting antisemitism and reviving Jewish pride, *In Gerangl/In Struggle*.[44]

> The Jew becomes afraid of associating with identified Jews, of defending other Jews. This "promise" is based on: 1) anti-Semitism is perpetual and impossible to resist or overcome; 2) there is nothing of value in Jewishness to make Jewhating worth resisting; 3) assimilation is possible. But complete assimilation takes generations, involves rejection of Jewishness; and one is then left bland and rootless.

Part of fighting antisemitism with solidarity involves reclaiming and deepening our own intersectional, expansive Jewish identities. "What we have to win is regaining the beauty of our tradition, regaining the connection to the earth, regaining our families and our cultural structures," Ami Weintraub, a rabbinic student and founding member of both the radical project Rebellious Anarchist Young Jews (RAYJ) and Ratzon: Center for Healing and Resistance, told us. "Part of how we fight antisemitism is reengaging in our traditions right now because that's what we're losing. And it's been happening for two thousand years."

To just live as who we are is itself a blow against the forces that have been trying to smother us for millennia. And to build a world where everyone can thrive as who they are is the ultimate goal of building safety through solidarity. We now turn, finally, to look again at ways in which the dominant approaches to fighting antisemitism fall short of this goal—and the ways in which the Jewish Left, by contrast, is putting this vision into practice.

FOURTEEN

TWO TRADITIONS OF FIGHTING
ANTISEMITISM: STRATEGIES OF
SOLIDARITY, PAST AND PRESENT

We see the Right acting appalled at antisemitism, and
think of it as a Right-wing issue. We don't realize, the
Right got to take it because the Left was silent.

April Rosenblum, "The Past Didn't Go Anywhere:
Making Resistance to Antisemitism
Part of All of our Movements"[1]

"We Jews have maintained a dignified silence. We refuse
to dignify the Nazi falsehoods with denials," thundered David Robinson. The year was 1939 and Robinson, an
organizer with the Portland, Oregon chapter of the Anti-Defamation League (ADL), addressed a community meeting of
Jews as the Nazi-supporting German American Bund rallied
nearby. "But we have felt, and still feel, that as it has occurred
throughout history, anti-Semitism is the entering wedge, not
only of intolerance, but to terror and Fascism." Calling for the
Jewish community to go on the offense, Robinson charged
that "Anti-Semitism is not a Jewish problem. It is a Christian
problem, an indictment of Christian civilization."[2]

Following the Great Depression, the rise of global fascist
movements ushered in a period of open Jew hatred then unprecedented in the United States. Portland, like many other
places across the country, was swarming with antisemitic and
pro-Nazi organizing. Robinson often prepared stage-managed

confrontations: he made fascist leaders answer for their words, and he recorded their responses.

He did this with one particularly eccentric figure of the antisemitic Right, a popular Indigenous grifter named Elwood A. Towner, who adopted the title "Chief Red Cloud." Towner frequented meetings of the fascist Silver Legion, arguing that Indigenous people in the United States were, in fact, Aryans. "The lines are being drawn throughout the world for a final showdown on this Jewish communism," declared Towner. "Indians and all Christian people will be united in one cause against Jewish communism and all the other isms of Satan."[3]

Robinson had set his sights on Towner, acting as a thorn in the fascist leader's side after several of Towner's antisemitic claims had circulated. "David Robinson's body may be found some day floating in the Willamette River," Towner was alleged to have said, and Robinson called him on it. He arranged a meeting with Towner and had the confrontation recorded with a Dictaphone in an adjacent room, later adding the transcript to the historical record.

Towner insisted Robinson's accusations of antisemitism were hyperbolic, but Robinson would not allow for Towner's trademark obfuscation. Robinson opened up a July 12 newspaper and quoted verbatim from a speech by Towner where he blamed abuses by the Indian Bureau as the fault of a "half-baked, half-witted Jew" and then read from the antisemitic forgery *The Protocols of the Elders of Zion*.

"I'll say this for you. Everybody says you are a good speaker," said Robinson. "The Indians have been very ashamed and renounce you as their representative, as you know. They came to Portland apologetic over your claims and insisted Elwood Towner does not represent them."

Robinson was prepared, demanding Towner acknowledge his friendship with local fascists. Did he know German American Bund leader Fritz Kuhn? How about Hermann Schwinn, former Pacific Coast leader for the Bund? What about William Dudley Pelley, the founder of the Silver Legion?

"I am an American. I am of Jewish faith and I believe in my religion. You are preaching a doctrine of hate. You are doing everything you can to destroy this country," said Robinson. "You are carrying on Hitler's program. The American people will not stand for it. You and I understand each other. We are adversaries. You have made threats against my life but I do not fear you or those with whom you work." Towner eventually conceded, muttering, "I guess I did some wrong talking," a partial admission of guilt.[4]

The state of Oregon, itself founded as a white ethnostate in 1859, had been a hub for far-right recruitment since the second-era Ku Klux Klan in the 1920s. In the 1930s, the Friends of New Germany organized pro-Nazi German immigrants in the area, and their newspaper, the *Nachrichten*, became a mouthpiece for antisemitism. In 1935 they posted flyers around Portland demanding their neighbors boycott Jews and "Buy Gentile!" In 1936, the Friends gave way to the German American Bund, among the most notorious fascist groups in American history. Simultaneously, a homegrown fascist figure, William Dudley Pelley, formed the Silver Legion (nicknamed the Silver Shirts) after a decades-long career as a far-right Christian mystic, prophesying a massive revolutionary cataclysm that would eradicate the Jews and establish an authoritarian Christian theocracy. Both the legion and the Bund grew around the Pacific Northwest, and the former established 125 neighborhood councils across Portland, where fascists railed against the Federal Reserve and the threat of Godless "Jewish" communism, insisted that President Roosevelt was in fact "President Rosenfeld," and warned that the United States had been captured by Zionists hell-bent on dragging the country into war.[5]

The ADL took a leading role in fighting back against this sweeping domestic fascist movement, both in Portland, where members of the Jewish community who could pass as

Gentile did reconnaissance work for the organization, and around the country, where it established itself as a front line in the fight against the fascist menace. "We gave [the ADL] information that we picked up, and they in turn would share with us. We had a pretty good idea of who the Nazis were and what they were up to," said Arthur Markewitz, a Portland Jewish resident who organized with the ADL in the 1930s and whose sister-in-law attended German Bund meetings covertly to spy (her blonde hair made her appear particularly German).[6]

While the ADL seemed to be on the right side of history, they have spent decades fighting Palestinian rights and against the left. all while presenting their centrist vision as the only appropriate vehicle for fighting antisemitism. In this chapter, we'll look at what happened to the ADL, and how so much of the mainstream conversation around antisemitism follows its mistaken path. And we'll look, finally, at some of the new strategies the Jewish Left is developing to build safety through solidarity.

"HAVE YOU TRIED REPORTING IT TO THE ADL?"

It was November 2022. The news media was captivated by antisemitic comments rapper Ye (formerly Kanye West) had recently made. In a New York City conference hall, a host of celebrity and corporate CEO speakers had gathered at what the ADL called the largest conference in the world against antisemitism: their annual summit on antisemitism and hate, Never Is Now. Audience members around the world watched as an Adidas executive drew rounding accolades for canceling Ye's multimillion-dollar contract, with no mention of the company's use of supply chains rife with worker exploitation, forced labor, and other human rights violations.

Panel after panel hinged on defense of Israel as central to fighting antisemitism, with no mention of that country's long-standing human rights violations against Palestinians and rapid slide into outright fascism. "'Free Palestine, from the river to the sea' [is] as we all know, a call for genocide," said one speaker during the opening session, misrepresenting a common phrase in Palestine rights activism, which demands freedom for Palestinians across their native land, as an attack on Jews. The speaker then ludicrously claimed that "no other group on campus is getting directly targeted like [Jews] are," citing Palestine solidarity activism during Israeli Apartheid Week—a week of action, held on college campuses in the United States and around the world to draw attention to Israel's apartheid policies.[7]

"Zionism is a Jewish value," insisted Matt Berger, executive director of the Foundation to Combat Antisemitism, equating Zionism to kashrut (kosher) laws in an egregious conflation of *halacha* with political ideology. "So when you attack Zionism or Zionists, you are attacking Jews for believing in Judaism. That is fundamentally antisemitic." Marie van der Zyl, president of the Board of Deputies of British Jews, even claimed it would be antisemitic for elected officials to vote against a bill providing additional funding for Israel to purchase weaponry. For her, at least, the military-industrial complex is also apparently a Jewish value.[8]

Earlier that spring, ADL CEO Jonathan Greenblatt released a video that barely mentioned the antisemitic Right, but demonized Palestinian rights activists at length in no uncertain terms. "Anti-Zionism is antisemitism," announced Greenblatt, staring into the camera with characteristic earnestness, before turning his criticism toward Students for Justice in Palestine, Jewish Voice for Peace (JVP), and the Council on American-Islamic Relations: groups that he alleged "epitomize the radical left, the photo inverse of the extreme right."[9] Soon after his video Greenblatt doubled down, boosting a Twitter thread attacking the progressive Jewish organization Jews for Racial and Economic Justice (JFREJ) as a "far-left scam."[10]

And in October 2023, as groups like JVP and IfNotNow mobilized to demand an end to Israel's massive bombardment of Gaza, Greenblatt went further, calling them "hate groups" and claiming Palestine solidarity activists are "like the Hitler Youth" and "want a final solution."[11]

Even in the fight against the antisemitic Right, the ADL has made serious missteps. In October 2022, Greenblatt praised tech CEO Elon Musk, shortly before Musk's takeover of Twitter, as "an amazing entrepreneur and extraordinary innovator— he's the Henry Ford of our time."[12] Seemingly oblivious to Ford's rabidly antisemitic legacy, Greenblatt's comparison was perhaps not so far off—Musk's disastrous leadership of Twitter would soon open the floodgates for far-right antisemitism and disinformation to run rampant. Ironically, in September 2023 Musk joined antisemitic white nationalist Twitter campaigns attacking the ADL, and in November, Musk embraced explicit white nationalist antisemitism, endorsing a tweet that accused Jews of "pushing . . . dialectical hatred against whites."[13]

Still, Greenblatt continued to provide cover for Musk's blatant antisemitism. While he initially criticized Musk, just one day later, when Musk promised to crack down on pro-Palestine speech on Twitter—a key priority for the ADL as Israel continued its bombardment—Greenblatt reversed course, thanking Musk for the "important and welcome move."[14]

So what happened? If the mission of the ADL is "to stop the defamation of the Jewish people, and to secure justice and fair treatment to all," as they claim, why are they getting the fight against antisemitism so wrong?[15]

The deeper story is that the ADL has long played a role in repressing social justice movements. As Jewish scholar and activist Emmaia Gelman describes, the ADL was founded in 1913 as part of a wave of Jewish organizations, preceded by the American Jewish Committee (AJC) in 1906, intending not simply to defend Jews against trenchant antisemitism, but to provide an alternative to the Jewish socialist Left.[16] The

Jewish Left had more successfully organized the community than establishment groups like B'nai B'rith had, and organizations like the Workmen's Circle and the Yiddish-speaking Jewish Federations in both the Communist and Socialist Parties were avenues for newly arriving poor Eastern European Jewish immigrants to find safety and empowerment through working-class solidarity. These Leftist Jews were inspired by groups like the Jewish Labor Bund in Europe and the Jewish Defense Association in the United States, who mobilized a massive march of 125,000 Jews in 1905 by specifically appealing to socialist radicalism.[17]

The earlier generation of Jewish immigrants, many of them middle-income immigrants from Germany, did not like these new rabble-rousers, whose presence, they worried, might damage earlier Jewish immigrants' carefully cultivated image of respectability. They wanted Jews to be viewed as another type of white American, and these radicals were tarnishing that image by inculcating them with a distinctly unassimilated ethnic flavor and revolutionary politics. "The ADL's mission of anti-defamation was, from the outset, also a mission to reshape U.S. Jewry as distinctly white and capitalist in orientation," writes Gelman.

The ADL always had little tolerance for the Left. They mounted scant opposition to far-right figures like Joseph McCarthy and Roy Cohn in the 1950s, and even shared their files with the House Committee on Un-American Activities (HUAC), along with the AJC.[18] When Julius and Ethel Rosenberg were prosecuted, and later executed, as part of the McCarthyist witch hunts, the ADL pushed back on the Left's view that antisemitism was afoot, eager, like much of the liberal assimilationist Jewish establishment, to dispel any associations of Jews with communism in the public imagination.

In the 1970s, as the occupation of the West Bank and Gaza became more entrenched and the global Left threw its support behind the Palestinian cause, the ADL focused more heavily on attacking critics of Israel. While congressional conservatives spurred an aggressive interventionist US foreign policy, the ADL played a leading role popularizing the "new antisemitism" thesis, which sees the primary manifestation of Jew hatred today as criticism of Israel from the Left, Black nationalism (and radical people of color–led movements more broadly), and the Muslim world. Today this analysis remains popular in antisemitism scholarship, and deeply influences the ADL's orientation.

A bombshell 1993 investigation revealed that for over three decades, a ring of undercover informants contracted by the ADL had surveilled a dizzying array of progressive groups, in a spy network involving collaboration with police departments in California and nationwide. Groups targeted included NAACP, ACLU, Greenpeace, ACT UP, National Lawyers Guild, Asian Law Caucus, Arab American Anti-Discrimination Committee (ADC), United Auto Workers, United Farm Workers, and even left-wing Jewish groups like New Jewish Agenda, as well as journalists and politicians.[19] "The right-wing isn't the problem. The left-wing is the problem," the ADL's chief fact finder, Irwin Suall, reportedly explained to a progressive researcher in 1993. "It's the American left that is the biggest threat to American Jews."[20]

In 1979, the ADL began to publish annual audits on antisemitism, which quickly became the standard for governmental agencies, journalists, Jewish institutions, and other advocates. Today, the ADL is a go-to source of expertise around issues of antisemitism and far-right "extremism" in public discourse. In one measure of their influence, more than two-thirds of the forty-six thousand articles published on white nationalism in 2019 alone referenced the ADL, according to Gelman.[21]

The centrality given to the ADL makes their capitulation with power and participation in the subjugation of Palestinians all the more troubling, and part of this problem emerges directly from how they track antisemitism. In spring 2021, as Israeli settlers, police, and military escalated their long-standing

attempt to expel Palestinian residents from the Sheikh Jar-
rah neighborhood of East Jerusalem and Israel subsequently
bombed Gaza, a wave of worldwide protest began. Amidst
powerful displays of solidarity across the country, videos of
reported antisemitic incidents in Los Angeles and New York
City spurred widespread condemnation, including from leading Palestine solidarity activists. But when the ADL released
data asserting a spike in antisemitism across the United States
during this time, there were some issues with the numbers.
As *Jewish Currents* reported, the ADL lumped everything from
online trolling to physical attacks on Jews and statements criticizing Zionism, many of which are not antisemitic, on the
other in the same dataset of antisemitic incidents. This methodology makes it nearly impossible to get a clear picture of the
contours and scope of the threat.[22]

But it isn't just a methodological shortcoming—the organization wields its problematic "new antisemitism" ideology
as a weapon against the movement for Palestinian rights.
The ADL supported proposed Trump-era federal legislation
like the Antisemitism Awareness Act and Israel Anti-Boycott
Act, Trump's 2019 executive order on antisemitism, and state
legislation that uses the problematic IHRA definition of antisemitism. These efforts unconstitutionally restrict, and even
criminalize, speech critical of Israel or support for the BDS
movement, and the ADL's support for them has continued under the Biden administration.[23]

The ADL supported far-right policy moves like the Trump
administration's opening of the US embassy in Jerusalem,
which it celebrated as a "historic milestone 2000 years in the
making." Greenblatt personally attended the opening ceremony, and tweeted a selfie sporting sunglasses and an embassy hat, saying he was "deeply moved to be here." At the
ceremony, leading antisemitic Christian Zionist pastors John
Hagee and Robert Jeffress—who each previously claimed Hitler's Holocaust was part of God's plan to send the Jews back to

Israel, and that "you can't be saved being a Jew," respectively—delivered opening benedictions.[24]

In recent years the ADL has led pile-ons against progressive Muslim leaders of color like Linda Sarsour and Ilhan Omar, and advocacy organizations like the Council on American-Islamic Relations (CAIR). The organization's "eagerness to tar political opponents as antisemites," wrote reporters Jacob Hutt and Alex Kane, "fell particularly hard on Muslim and Arab leaders . . . undermining the ADL's universalist, anti-bigotry mission."[25] This, too, is not new—in previous decades, the ADL held intel files on thousands of members of the Arab American Anti-Discrimination Committee, and circulated blacklists targeting Arab American academics.[26] In the wake of Israel's genocidal assault on Gaza in late 2023, the ADL advocated more fiercely for repression than ever before, calling on university administrators, the FBI, and the IRS to investigate Students for Justice in Palestine chapters for material support for terrorism—a groundless charge, heavily criticized by civil rights groups, that bolstered the unconstitutional and McCarthyite attacks on free speech.[27]

In the post-9/11 era of the "War on Terror," the ADL joined a right-wing chorus opposing the opening of a mosque and Islamic community center near Ground Zero, once called the Islamic declaration of faith an "expression of hate," and justified calls for blanket surveillance against Muslim Americans.[28] The ADL has long supported state-backed Islamophobic approaches to fighting antisemitism,[29] such as Countering Violent Extremism (CVE) programs, a series of civil society grants by federal law enforcement institutions that, in their attempt to combat "radicalization," bolster biased policing, surveillance, and criminalization against Muslim Americans as well as other marginalized communities and activists.[30]

As Hutt and Kane have documented, the ADL's approach is inconsistent with its professed support for civil rights and antiracism.[31] In the 1980s, the ADL sent an informant to infiltrate anti-apartheid activists, who later sold that intel to the apartheid South African government.[32] In recent years, the ADL has attacked Black progressive leaders like Marc Lamont Hill and Michelle Alexander for principled criticism of Israel.[33] In 2016, the ADL attacked the Movement for Black Lives platform, a comprehensive policy proposal to uproot racist systems like housing and wealth disparities, policing, mass incarceration, and US imperialism, because it condemned the "genocide taking place against the Palestinian people" and included strident calls for Palestinian liberation. Greenblatt patronizingly lectured activists to "keep [y]our eyes on the prize," appropriating a civil rights anthem from the Black church.[34]

The ADL proudly touts its close collaboration with law enforcement, has handed awards to police chiefs who pioneered anti-Black "stop-and-frisk" and "broken windows" policing initiatives in New York City, and organized "deadly exchange" delegations for US and Israeli police officers to share repressive tactics. In these and other ways, the ADL cultivates what Palestinian organizer Celine Qussiny called "longstanding relationships with institutions that target and criminalize our communities."[35]

Many ADL staffers contribute valuable research and advocacy combating the far-right. But as an institution, the ADL has worked against antifascists, even briefly advising police to use infiltrators and surveillance to arrest antifascists in advance of the deadly Unite the Right rally in 2017.[36] In the lead-up to Unite the Right, as antifascist coalitions organized to defend their community, the ADL broadcast statements from the Charlottesville mayor to a national audience, suggesting the rally should be "ignore[d]."[37] Jewish activist Ben Doernberg remembers working with other radical groups to build the on-the-ground counterprotest. Inspired by the messages of "never again" that were a touchstone of his upbringing in the Charlottesville Jewish community, he reached out to local Jewish organizations to get them involved. To his surprise, one leading Jewish institution told him, as he remembers it, that "the ADL is working behind the scenes to keep the Jewish community safe" and that they would not be encouraging Jews to attend the counterprotest.

The advice from the ADL seemed to be not to link up with other targeted communities in community self-defense and defiance, but instead to rely on civic leadership and Charlottesville law enforcement—who unsurprisingly had their own history of anti-Black racism.[38] "I just thought that people had actually learned the same lessons from the Holocaust that I had, but it became very quickly clear that that was not the case," Doernberg told us. "[The violence at Charlottesville] only happened because [many thousands more] people didn't show up." After Unite the Right, the ADL released statements suggesting that antifascists who confront fascists forcefully in the streets only increase the likelihood of violence and play into the Right's game.[39] The ADL used the violence in Charlottesville to cultivate support: their donations spiked 1,000 percent higher than average in the week after the rally.[40]

The reality of what happened in Charlottesville weighed on Doernberg. That November, at the Union for Reform Judaism's annual conference, Greenblatt spoke at a panel called "Acting Against Hate" and Doernberg confronted him, expressing his outrage that when he and others from Charlottesville had reached out to the ADL for support, they heard only crickets in response. Doernberg told us that Greenblatt became agitated, showing "zero curiosity, remorse, [or] interest," and became so rude that a volunteer had to intervene.

In August 2020, dozens of progressive groups, including trailblazers like Dream Defenders, Mijente, and United We Dream, and Jewish groups like IfNotNow, Jewish Voice for Peace, and JFREJ, launched the #DroptheADL campaign. They demanded that "[communities] say no to the Anti-Defamation League in our schools, coalitions and movements," citing the organization's "history and ongoing pattern of attacking social justice movements led by communities of color, queer people, immigrants, Muslims, Arabs, and other marginalized groups, while aligning itself with police, right-wing leaders, and perpetrators of state violence."[41]

THE JEWS MOVED RIGHT—RIGHT?

The ADL isn't the only conservatizing force in American Jewish politics today. Within many establishment communal institutions, a small but influential pool of major funders has set a center-right political agenda that doesn't reflect the rest of us.[42] Rich donor power isn't unique here—it reflects a troubling antidemocratic trend occurring across civil society, and a broader drop-off of grassroots political engagement decades in the making.

Meanwhile, a small but active minority of American Jews have cast their lot squarely with the Right. Groups like the Republican Jewish Coalition are active players in conservative politics, while many Orthodox and Haredi communities are solidly aligned with the Christian Right and the MAGA movement. Institutions like AIPAC, rooted largely in and widely seen as representing the Jewish community, lobby for a reactionary pro-Israel consensus on both sides of the aisle, and increasingly launch full-frontal attacks against progressive Democratic candidates critical of Israel's policies.[43]

While a solid majority of American Jews support liberal causes, this does not mean they are in the trenches, deeply involved in social movements. Decades of privilege left large parts of our community relatively quiescent—voting Democrat, donating to charities, and carrying much of the baggage of normative, white suburbia. Jews did show up in large, disproportionate numbers in Left movements in the 1960s and after, but until recently, many Jews in social movements were not connected to Jewish civic life, and did not foreground their Jewish identity.

After the 1967 Six-Day War, tensions around Israel's mounting oppression of Palestinians drove the wedge deeper between social justice movements and the mainstream Jewish consensus. Organizations like the ADL forcefully criticized the New Left over its solidarity with Palestinians. In the decades that followed, even as the majority of American Jews did not support the deepening of Israel's occupation and the growth of the Israeli Right, this was not reflected in communal leadership, which folded squarely into the pro-Israel consensus.

Today, growing movements of progressive Jews are taking to the streets as part of powerful, vibrant justice movements. But establishment Jewish organizations lag behind, offering little more than tepid liberalism and often participating in antisemitism accusation pile-ons against justice movements. Because the Right uses these accusations to delegitimize their political enemies, when we simply repeat them uncritically we can play into the Right's strategy. "The Democrats," then–House Republican chair Liz Cheney said on *Meet the Press* in 2019, "have become the party of anti-Semitism, the party of infanticide, the party of socialism."[44]

Meanwhile, instead of offering a meaningful social movement strategy to combat antisemitism, the American Jewish establishment has turned to the state. As we will discuss, Jewish organizations tout close collaboration with law enforcement in a top-down approach to community safety, utilizing federal grant programs that employ policing, militarized surveillance, and "domestic terrorism" statutes to combat "hate crimes" or "extremism." Aligning with racist, Islamophobic forces of state repression betrays the intersectional principles we need—and labeling antisemitism merely as "hate" or "extremism" doesn't get at the roots of the problem. It misleadingly portrays antisemitism as a pathological deviation found at the fringes of society, rather than as a system of oppression baked into the same white Christian supremacist status quo the state seeks to uphold.

This is a frustratingly familiar pattern to activists across many marginalized communities, where conservative communal leaders collaborate with ruling authorities, and seek access to power, in pursuit of a self-serving agenda of narrowly defined "communal interests." The Jewish Left has for years watched our community's self-appointed leaders seek a "vertical alliance" of proximity to power, whether in a misguided strategy to keep Jews safe, or to protect their own interests as members of the one percent. But for over a century, many Jews have fought for a different vision entirely.

REBUILDING THE JEWISH LEFT

There's perhaps a kernel of truth in the claim voiced by antisemites that Jews are fiery radicals. Our experiences fighting against marginalization have long put us in line with other oppressed communities who saw a better future through the collective action of working people, and Jews have long been well represented within the ranks of justice movements. The history of the Jewish Left is simultaneously the history of a particular strategy to fight antisemitism: the struggle to build safety through solidarity.

Over a century ago, across Russia and Eastern Europe, the revolt against capitalism saw heavy Jewish participation. The Jewish Labor Bund, founded in 1897, had a unique approach to socialism. Instead of fighting for a supposedly homogenous working class, or seeking an escape from Europe (or turning to Zionism) as the solution to antisemitism, some of them had a vision they called *doikayt*, or "here-ness," that Jews should be able to maintain distinctiveness, true to their culture and history, yet in a multicultural confederation with other working people. The Bund believed the fight for Jewish safety was essential to the Jewish Left, and they recognized that safety could not be achieved by simply dissolving Jews into the larger working class. Not only did Jews face unique struggles not shared by non-Jewish coworkers on the factory floor—sometimes, they also recognized, antisemitism set their fellow workers at their throats.

Along with trade unions, Yiddish schools, and newspapers, they organized *zelbst-shuts*, self-defense units, to fight back against antisemitic attacks. In 1905, these units pushed back against violent ultranationalist, antisemitic pogroms spreading across the Pale of Settlement. There, Bundists, packing revolvers, positioned themselves around *shtetls* to scare off would-be attackers. As antisemitic violence escalated, the Bund used mass tactics, such as general strikes after four Jews were killed in a Przytyk, Poland, pogrom in 1936 and after the Polish government began segregating Jewish students in 1937. These organizers became partisans as the war intensified and were key leaders, alongside other factions, in the Warsaw Ghetto Uprising.[45]

In the United States, heavily immigrant areas like the Lower East Side in New York City or the East End in London were hotbeds of the industrial labor movement, rejecting the conservatism of the "craft-unionist" American Federation of Labor in favor of the strike-ready Congress of Industrial Organizations. Jews made up a large portion of these Eastern European immigrants, well represented among communists and anarchists who were organizing on shop floors. Jews fought during the Great Depression and against rising fascist movements, and were so central to social movements that some saw the Communist Party as a secular synagogue.

Meanwhile, Jews played important roles within socialist and national liberation movements across the Middle East and North Africa. Jewish activists like Abraham Serfaty in Morocco, Daniel Timsit in Algeria, and Henri Curiel in Egypt helped lead national movements to shake off the yoke of European colonialism and fight for pluralistic societies. Like their Jewish Left counterparts in the West, they opposed Zionism for its false promise of liberation through separatism, placing their hope instead in fighting antisemitism, and building a just society, alongside their Muslim, Christian, and other Arab neighbors. Jewish organizations like the Anti-Zionist League in Iraq insisted, as they put it in their 1945 founding petition, that "the Jewish problem [i.e., antisemitism] is deep-rooted in the social system . . . Jews have fallen a sacrifice to a parasitic class that want to maintain their privileges by turning people's fury toward the Jews . . . the Jewish problem cannot be resolved except by resolving the Jewish problem of a country where Jews are living."[46]

In the mid-twentieth century, many American Jews joined the civil rights movement, supporting organizations like the NAACP and participating in the Freedom Rides and action against Jim Crow.[47] Jews were a core constituency of New Left groups like Students for a Democratic Society.[48] They rediscovered Jewish tradition in ways that broke with the conservatism of the Jewish establishment and the stilted consumerism of suburban synagogue life.

Zionism divided Jews on the Left, particularly after the 1967 Six-Day War. Some embraced anti-Zionism, while others maintained what they called a "radical Zionism" that saw the potential for a liberatory type of socialist Israel and supported Palestinian rights.[49] Groups like the Brooklyn Bridge Collective and the Jewish Liberation Project went after both America's capitalist class and the capitulation of Jewish civic leaders, all while keeping the fight against antisemitism as a centerpiece of their work as Jewish Leftists.[50]

The large confluence of radical Jewish groups led to the first conference of what would become the New Jewish Agenda (NJA) in 1980, bringing together activists from the religious Havurah movement with collectives like Chutzpah and the Boston Committee to Challenge Anti-Semitism. They built a platform and structure to go after issues like nuclear proliferation, reproductive rights, Reaganism, and international human rights with a distinct Jewish lens. Fighting antisemitism remained in the mix—it was part of what NJA addressed that the rest of the Left seemed unable to.[51] "We are especially conscious that as Jewish activists we have encountered anti-

Semitism not only in the Right, but in the Left," NJA wrote in a 1991 pamphlet.

> To us this is a cause for pain, disappointment and alarm and we refuse to ignore it or erase it. But we also refuse to be pushed towards isolationism or backlash. We know that we cannot wait for a hatred-free world before we commit ourselves to action. We must challenge anti-Semitism and, at the same time, organize in coalition with other groups to fight against racism, poverty, and unemployment, homophobia, sexism, and forced cultural assimilation. We believe these struggles are as much the concern of Jews as anti-Semitism is the concern of non-Jews.[52]

NJA's work also emerged from the Jewish feminist movement, which offered an early intersectional approach to identity and movement work. They formed magazines like *Lilith*, and published books like *Nice Jewish Girls: A Lesbian Anthology* and *The Tribe of Dina*, which took an unflinching look at antisemitism on the Left. These feminists stressed the interconnectedness of Jewish and women's liberation and demanded the reclamation of Jewish pride, the rejection of the bargains offered by whiteness, and the end of Jewish self-hate that blamed Jews for antisemitism.

"[The] racism of many white Jewish women discourages many non-Jewish women of color from strongly confronting Jewish oppression; the anti-Semitism of many non-Jewish women of color discourages many white Jewish women from being strongly anti-racist," wrote Elly Bulkin in the 1984 dialogue *Yours in Struggle*, advancing an intersectional approach. "Each is the inevitable by-product of the society in which we live."[53]

With New Jewish Agenda's 1992 dissolution, a gap widened in left-wing approaches to antisemitism. Until the Trump era, many Jewish Left organizations focused on other pressing issues like poverty, anti-Black racism, immigrant justice, gender, and voting rights. While this work was vital, the lack of a sustained focus on antisemitism helped keep the issue largely unacknowledged among radicals.

"I think for a lot of Jews growing up [during this time] who then became politicized and were part of movements, a focus on antisemitism would feel like a focus on the past and not a focus on the future," Dove Kent explained to us.

"There has also been this binary setup where Jews are either allies [to others] or fighting for ourselves, and not this idea that those fights are deeply intertwined," Sophie Ellman-Golan, communications director with JFREJ, told us. "When you don't have an analysis of how those things are actually deeply connected to each other, we almost adopt a scarcity mindset, where we can't take on [antisemitism] and if we do, maybe we're centering ourselves when the plight of others is so great."

During the Trump presidency, progressive Jewish organizations like Bend the Arc, JFREJ, IfNotNow, and Jewish Voice for Peace took the fight to the Right. They held protests targeting far-right operatives like Steve Bannon and Christian Zionist groups, and launched national projects like Jews Against White Nationalism (JAWN), which exposed the pervasive white nationalist rhetoric, and far-right relationships, of dozens of Republican politicians and leaders.[54] "The Right had done such an effective job of tarring the Left as antisemitic," Ellman-Golan told us, "that it was really blinding people to the reality of how much the very antisemitic Right was growing, and finding a home in the Republican Party. And the Republican Party was using the energy of that antisemitic base to build a right-wing populist movement."

In recent years, groups like JFREJ, Jewish Community Action in Minnesota, and many others have led the way by developing antisemitism political education materials and implementing trainings within progressive movement spaces.

These trainings open up space for dialogue, and trainers and participants alike are often surprised by what they learn and encounter. "Our progressive partners were incredibly eager for this," Leo Ferguson, director of special projects at JFREJ, told us.

> From a genuine place, they wanted to know how to support Jews . . . Did people say antisemitic things [during question-and-answer sessions] in the trainings? Absolutely. And almost invariably they said them out of ignorance, not because they had any animosity towards Jews in any kind of coherent way . . . What I was seeing was the product of a lack of a progressive intersectional antisemitism analysis on the Left. I guarantee you that if we went back to 1975 or '85 and had conversations in progressive spaces about the LGBT community, we'd be seeing the exact same kinds of things—people that weren't hateful, but had a lot of yucky myths and things that they just didn't understand, and hadn't had a context and a liberatory framework in which to process them.

If the Left is going to improve in fighting antisemitism, it will be in no small part due to the efforts of Jews, organized *as* Jews and from a radical, antiracist perspective, showing up to make it happen. Unlike the Right—where antisemitism, whether in explicit or coded form, is central to the ideology of reaction and exclusion—antisemitism on the Left is ultimately something that, when confronted, can be undone with commitment and perseverance, since it runs in the face of the Left's core values of equality and justice.

Jews on the Left have a crucial role to play in making the Left as a whole a weapon against rising antisemitism. But Jews can't do it alone—antisemitism is a problem of the non-Jewish world, and it also takes non-Jewish comrades who are willing to learn and grow and challenge antisemitism whenever it emerges. This means intentionally looking at where the Left needs to grow around antisemitism. It means embedding an analysis of antisemitism that reflects the continued role it plays in our social systems. And it means learning from movements that have done this well, such as antifascist organizations that have always centered antisemitism as a central component of insurgent fascism.

SAFETY THROUGH SOLIDARITY

When the Tree of Life synagogue shooting happened in Pittsburgh in October 2018, "a lot of Jews were scared and panicked," Hannah Freedman, an organizer and member of Kavod, an independent collective of young Jews in Boston that bridges spirituality and activism, told us. "And our non-Jewish comrades were like, 'What's up? Are you guys okay? How can we help?'" Non-Jewish activists from Muslim and white antiracist communities "came through and held grief space and ritual space" for Jews processing the trauma of what had just occurred. "It felt really powerful for me, to see and feel non-Jewish friends at our backs and with us as we were going through the whole range of emotions."

In Kavod's first Shabbat service after the shooting, hundreds of Jews gathered inside, while over twenty non-Jewish community safety volunteers kept watch outside the building. "It was very scary to gather as Jews at that time," Alyssa Rubin, another Kavod member, recalls. "I felt moved to tears by seeing that many allies outside."

In moments of heightened antisemitic violence, establishment Jewish institutions typically advocate for increased police and private security at synagogues and Jewish spaces. "The top priority likely by any standard is the safety and security of the Jewish community," said Eric Fingerhut, CEO of the Jewish Federations of North America, at the federation's annual general assembly in October 2022. Fingerhut was touting the Secure Community Network, a national initiative collaborating with law enforcement to provide synagogues access to armed security and surveillance. "This week is the fourth *yahrzeit* [anniversary of the death] of those we lost at Tree of Life in Pittsburgh . . . Since then we've continued to see the violent attacks. And there is an organized effort led by the Jewish Federations of North America to ensure that every Jewish community in North America has a professional security program."[55]

But putting more police and militarized security in synagogues can make these spaces less safe for Black Jews, in an era when racist policing puts Black folks across the United States at risk of profiling, incarceration, violence, and murder, as well as other Jews of color and disabled and queer Jews. "My heart already clenches each time I walk into a shul because of fear of an anti-Semitic attack," wrote Bentley Addison, a Black Jewish activist, one week after the Tree of Life shooting. "I don't need to also be terrified of the possibility of the police violence that's become all too normal. Instead of throwing guns at the problem, let's work to eradicate the problems of antisemitism and white supremacy that allow these massacres to happen."[56]

When the 2020 George Floyd uprising began, Chava Shervington, a Black Orthodox Jewish woman, remembered seeing warnings on her WhatsApp[57] thread that presented the protests as threatening, and some would suggest that they "go thank every police officer" in response to the presence of the protests. There was often a distance that white Jews in her community had from issues of police violence because they had moved through the world without having to experience the racist victimization by law enforcement that many Black people have experienced. "It's a reflection on the fact that in America [white] Jews and Black people have had very different experiences of safety and community at the hands of the police," Shervington told us. "So when [white] Jewish communities feel harm they rely on policing and other forms of armed security, which makes me feel less safe, makes my family feel less safe." Fear, and a sense of the exceptional nature of antisemitism, drives many of these responses from white Jews. But there is a "different level of fear that Black Jews . . . [are] walking around with," Shervington continued. "There's always a lack of safety in my personhood because I'm a Black person in America."

This reality has driven a core resiliency: a determination to survive and thrive despite the threats. "I would love to see . . . the resilience that Black Jews have acquired due to the other oppression they face, . . . seen as a tool worth acquiring by the larger Jewish community," Shervington told us. But to achieve this, she acknowledged, white Jews have to confront the racism in their own institutions and the privileges many enjoy. These are some of the issues that she wanted to address when she cofounded Kamochah, which supports Black Orthodox Jews, advocates for diversity in *yeshtvot* (Jewish religious schools), and prepares Orthodox communities to interrupt racism.

The federal security grants championed by communal leaders like Fingerhut can also undercut the principled, intersectional approach to fighting antisemitism we need. Many federal funding initiatives designed to provide faith groups with access to these resources, such as the Nonprofit Security Grants or Countering Violent Extremism (CVE) programs, have long been used "to increase state surveillance of Muslim organizations under the guise of protecting them," as *Jewish Currents* reporter Mari Cohen said in 2021. Some programs mandate collaboration and intelligence sharing with law enforcement, while others work closely with federal agencies like the Department of Homeland Security known for biased surveillance against Muslims, detaining and deporting migrants at the border, and crackdowns on Leftists.[58]

For organizations like the Council on American-Islamic Relations (CAIR) and the Boston-based Muslim Justice League, the "counterterrorism" frame underlying these initiatives plays on long-standing Islamophobic post-9/11 narratives. "Expanding the counterterrorism complex is not the answer to white supremacist violence—in fact, these measures often wind up reinforcing systemic white supremacy," wrote organizer Fatema Ahmad and legal advocate Azadeh Shahshahani in 2022.[59]

Moreover, even for white Jews, police are not inherently a source of safety. Many police themselves are part of or sympathize with antisemitic radical Right groups. A 2020 report by Michael German of the Brennan Center for Justice calculated that since 2000, law enforcement officials in at least fourteen states have been outed as members or supporters of groups like the Ku Klux Klan, Proud Boys, Oath Keepers, and militias.[60] At a time when police officers, sheriffs, military members, and other law enforcement agents are increasingly embracing MAGA conspiracism and white nationalism, even white Jews used to feeling safe around law enforcement might think again.

Activists across the country are developing alternative models to defend protests, religious centers, and other marginalized community spaces from bigoted violence without relying on racist policing or the national security state apparatus. After Unite the Right, Mimi Arbeit—who helped organize the counterprotest in Charlottesville—traveled to Boston and shared stories during Shabbat services with Kavod.[61] "They really challenged a lot of us to think more about how we were organizing around anti-fascism and protecting our communities without relying on state violence," Nadav David, an organizer and member of Kavod's Jews of Color, Indigenous Jews, Sephardim, and Mizrahim Caucus, told us.

For the High Holy Days that year and in following years, Kavod organized and trained a community safety team of mostly non-Jewish volunteers from the local Showing Up for Racial Justice (SURJ) chapter and other local movement groups, such as the Democratic Socialists of America (DSA), to guard their services. "It was a really important step," Nadav David told us, "that set the foundation for many more years of building community safety infrastructure." SURJ, a national antiracist group for white activists, has long trained its members on preparedness, de-escalation, and defense to provide community safety for demonstrations and marginalized faith communities. "In Appalachia, the South, we have a long lineage of both abolition and opposition to the Klan, the cops, and the state," Shawn Fischer, a non-Jewish member of SURJ's Faith Committee who helps run these trainings, told us. "And I think that's really important for me to understand that I'm part of this much longer tradition."

Community solidarity after the Pittsburgh shooting, Freedman told us, "was a big turning point for people to believe that we could be doing this work, and that folks could be showing up for us." In the years since, Kavod built an active community safety team, working with partners to anticipate possible threats, build safety plans, deploy dozens of volunteers, and collaborate with groups like JFREJ and Jewish Voice for Peace doing similar work across the country. These skills have also been put to use during community mobilizations, such as the 2020 George Floyd uprising, following highly visible antisemitic attacks, or when preparing for possible unrest during the 2020 presidential election.

Activists witnessed firsthand the transformative power of seeing community safety teams in action. "One of the results of antisemitism for Jews in the US," Hannah Freedman told us,

is this experience of isolation, and not totally knowing how to build solidarity relationships . . . A lot of Jews have never experienced other people actually showing up in that way, and actually having our backs. The only stories that we get from the Holocaust and generations of Jewish oppression are times in which our neighbors have sold us out, or not had our backs . . . I've seen and witnessed when people [encounter a community safety crew] for the first time as they're entering services; it's really powerful.

Dozens of synagogues and Jewish centers across the United States use community safety models as a values-based approach to fighting antisemitism with solidarity, while also supporting local or national abolitionist campaigns. Kavod has built bridges to introduce this approach into the larger Boston Jewish community with some stories of success and transformation, but has also faced resistance from congregations that support the principles, but fear the risks of divesting from police protection. "Helping white (and sometimes wealthy) Jews recognize that they experience safety differently than other folks in their communities, or folks in non-Jewish communities, is a big hurdle," Nadav David told us. "How do you bring someone to a shared stake or a shared struggle, when they actually haven't had the same experience of negative interactions with policing and surveillance?"

"I think we on the Left are at the very beginning of figuring out our approach to threats to Jewish spaces," Jewish scholar and activist April Rosenblum told us.

Most Jews in the US don't know what it's like to live with violent authoritarianism. We're just beginning to grapple with how to protect ourselves in a time like this . . . I think for many US Jews, who grew up with relative privilege and safety, there is a comfort in sticking to abstract ethical ideals. We want to express our liberatory and abolitionist principles by focusing on having open doors and broad networks of solidarity. And that solidarity is essential. It's the only way forward for the long term. But we have to also have a plan for the short term. We have to figure out concrete ways of actually preventing

attacks in our spaces, while also protecting and priori-
tizing Jews and allies who would be made unsafe by the
mainstream methods of policing and surveillance that
we are trying to undo . . . It will take creativity to figure out how we can really block physical attacks on our
community in a liberatory way. But when we figure it
out, I think we'll gain a lot of momentum and we'll see
many more people start to join us in our larger vision.

There were spikes of anti-Jewish violence in 2019, many targeting Orthodox and Haredi Jews across New York City and the
surrounding suburbs. Jews were beaten and harassed on their
way to synagogue, or simply while living their lives, while
assailants carried out shooting and knife attacks targeting a
kosher grocery store in Jersey City and a rabbi's home in Monsey, New York. In the aftermath, the NYPD, police unions,
and right-wing and centrist politicians clamored for increased
funding for police, harsher tough-on-crime legislation, and
tougher penalties for sentencing, often with the support of
Jewish establishment organizations.

Progressives knew that "a carceral, pro-cop, pro-prosecu-
tion approach to public safety," as Leo Ferguson put it, does
little to keep Jews safe, or get at the root of bias-motivated violence. All it would do was bolster the racist policing, incarceration, and state repression that already made the city unsafe
for Black and brown New Yorkers. In a national climate where
President Trump and the Right attacked the Black Lives Matter movement with racist rhetoric and policy proposals, "incidents of hate violence against Jews," Ferguson told us, "were
being used to tear down our hard-fought wins around bail
reform in NY, and other progressive criminal justice reform
measures . . . It was just a quick way [for politicians] to score
political points."

In response, activists formed NYC Against Hate—a coalition of Asian American, Black, Arab American, immigrant,

Indo-Caribbean, LGBTQ, and Jewish groups united to advance grassroots organizing and community-based models of safety. They centered preventive anti-bias education, community-based transformative and restorative justice programs, rapid-response community infrastructure, and public policy to address root causes of hate violence. They campaigned for redirecting police funding into mental health services and community programs, held anti-bias and "upstander" trainings, and created a model of education, counseling, and relationship building in affected neighborhoods.

Often, after an attack has occurred, JFREJ and other groups will partner with local organizations and hold a public training in the neighborhood, then pamphlet the surrounding streets in Yiddish, Arabic, and other languages, engaging passersby in conversations about preventing violence through solidarity. The "sense of victimization and isolation" felt in communities after an attack is often flipped on its head by this direct, face-to-face connection.

For Rabbi Dev Noily, leader of Congregation Kehilla in the San Francisco Bay area, the Jewish holiday of Sukkot offers a "safety through solidarity" model in action. During Sukkot, Jews around the world build small huts outside their homes and eat, sleep, welcome guests, and otherwise live in them, embodying the desert wanderings of the ancient Israelites after their exodus from Egypt. "In Sukkot we live, and have joy, in the fragility," Rabbi Noily told us.

> We don't build little fortresses with locks and gates on Sukkot, and a guard outside—we're out, we're exposed, we have no roof over our head, we're in the world—and the world is uncertain, and sometimes dangerous. But if you don't open yourself to the uncertainty and the possibility of danger, you also don't open yourself to the possibility of joy and connection, love and community. And I want our communities to have the joy, and the love,

and the celebration, and the community, and the rich-
ness that comes from being in relationship with people
outside of Jewish communities

It is that joyous life that ultimately determines whether or not
we've won the future we are fighting for. The prophetic Jewish
tradition has always been threatening to authoritarians seeking to subjugate and eradicate those who deviate from their
preferred norm. "If we can find a way to create a shared language of a moral vision . . . [of] creating a better society for
everyone," Eli Rubin, a writer at Chabad.org, told us, "that's
more productive than fighting about antisemitism."

Our ability to persevere determines our efficacy. Instead of
letting Jewish identity be defined by antagonism, we should
embody our history as one of ecstatic survival. "We can't just
shut the place down or shut everyone out including the people who need to be there" after an attack, Motti Seligson, a
member of Chabad, affirmed. "We need to make sure we have
warm faith environments, not just garrisons or citadels and
fortresses . . . We need to remember as Jews we have a message
to share to the world."

On October 18, 2023, a striking image went viral across
social media: a sea of Jewish activists in black shirts, em-
blazoned with "Jews Say Ceasefire Now," overwhelming the
rotunda of a congressional office building in Washington D.C.
Protesters blocked the roads surrounding the busy capitol and
staged a sit-in on the floor of the cavernous, pillar-lined lobby,
their chants echoing across the domed ceiling as they demanded politicians stop using their tax dollars to fund a genocide in Gaza. More than this, they wanted their names left out
of it: don't say you are supporting mass murder, displacement,
and dispossession of Palestinians in the name of Jewish safety
and the fight against antisemitism.

The action was organized by the twenty-two-thousand-
member anti-Zionist organization Jewish Voice for Peace
(JVP) and the anti-occupation group IfNotNow, both established players on the Jewish Left who are mobilizing Jewish
identity to end Israeli apartheid. This crowd, including many
rabbis wearing *kippah*, *tallit*, and *tzitzit*, arrived at the capitol
just eleven days after Hamas's October 7 attack into mainland
Israel, which included the brutal murder of over 1,200 Israelis,
mostly civilians, and the kidnapping of over 200 more. Understanding that the overall attack was part of a decades-long
struggle by Palestinians against their dispossession, these activists already knew what would happen next: an all-out collective punishment by the state of Israel on Gaza, which has

resulted in over fifteen thousand murdered Palestinians, and the displacement of nearly 2 million at the time of writing. As Israel began its relentless bombardment, and called in reservists for a ground invasion of one of the most densely populated regions on Earth (where almost half the residents are children), activists mobilized disruptive actions across the country, demanding a ceasefire. In the weeks that followed, JVP and IfNotNow participated in countless mass actions from Los Angeles to Portland to New York, where JVP amassed some five thousand people to shut down "business as usual" at Manhattan's Grand Central Station, and staged historic demonstrations at iconic locations like the Statue of Liberty.

Ben helped organize a grassroots coalition of activists from JVP, IfNotNow, and the Jewish immigrant justice group Never Again Action to blockade the Midwest Israeli consulate in Chicago, where over one hundred Jews were arrested. In Portland, Jobs With Justice, where Shane is a board member, organized actions where labor activists demanded a ceasefire, working closely with Jewish activists in JVP and other groups.[1] This was a historic upsurge of the Jewish Left, a glimpse of a spiking generation of activism grounded firmly in a revival of Jewish identity.

At the same time, this resurgent Jewish Left faced a fraught movement landscape. In the hours after Hamas's attack, voices at Palestine solidarity rallies minimized Hamas's civilian massacres, or even celebrated them—such as in New York City, where an activist cheered the sight of Hamas militants on hang gliders taking "at least several dozen hipsters" hostage before opening fire on civilians. Similar sentiments were voiced on social media—one scholar, for example, tweeted "what did y'all think decolonization meant? vibes? essays? Losers,"[2] while others derided anyone who voiced criticism, or despair, at the sight of hundreds of Israeli civilians mercilessly murdered or whisked into captivity. National Students for Justice in Palestine called October 7 a "historic win" in which "our people are actualizing revolution," while some student activists maintained that "Israel bears full responsibility for this tremendous loss of life," as one law student leader at NYU put it, erasing Hamas's responsibility for its massacres.[3] In the weeks that followed, videos surfaced of people tearing down posters calling for the release of kidnapped Israelis, and conspiracy theories abounded in some circles, claiming that Hamas's massacres were entirely a Zionist "false flag." Antisemitic incidents spiked in the United States and around the world, with mobs storming through a Russian airport looking for "Jewish refugees," vandalism of Jewish sites and synagogues, threats against Jewish students, and even attacks on Jews on the streets.

In a predictable pattern, the Zionist Right, and Israeli state leaders, immediately capitalized on the few problematic responses from activists, expanding their definition of antisemitism to include basically anyone demanding a ceasefire and launching a McCarthyite attack on activists. Student leaders were sanctioned by administrators, had job offers rescinded and were put on hiring blacklists, and were targeted by vicious doxing and smear campaigns led by off-campus pro-Israel organizations, while multiple SJP chapters were banned, had events canceled, and were unjustly disciplined on campuses across the country. Elected officials and groups like the ADL called for federal investigations of activists for providing material support to terrorism, a groundless and dangerous charge. The wave of firings and disciplining of speech hit media, tech, and other industries, leading to a widespread climate of fear. Predictably, many activists became less willing to address antisemitism because of the disingenuous accusations.

This wave of repression rebounded within the Jewish community as well. The Boston Workers Circle, a secular progressive community center and organizing hub, was kicked out of Boston's Jewish Community Relations Council, the city's umbrella Jewish coalition, for cosponsoring a ceasefire event with anti-Zionists.[4] Anti-Zionist Jews were targeted with a special fury: how dare they break rank. Many were fired from jobs and leaders of multiple national Jewish establishment organizations and publications released op-eds, statements, and social media posts declaring that these Jews deserved excommunication from the Jewish people.[5]

Islamophobic incidents skyrocketed alongside antisemitism, with Muslim, Arab, and Palestinian figures targeted in workplaces and schools. Muslim students had their hijabs torn off, were spat on, and labeled terrorists, and mosques were vandalized with racist graffiti. In Chicago, six-year-old Palestinian American Wadea al Fayoume was stabbed twenty-six times in a racially motivated attack, while in Burlington, Vermont, three Palestinian students, wearing keffiyehs and speaking Arabic, were shot while walking to dinner at a relative's house over Thanksgiving weekend. Palestinians were demonized across mainstream media, and saber-rattling politicians like Marjorie Taylor Greene used the moment to revive the Islamophobic "counter-Jihad" movement, rhapsodizing about a war to defend Western civilization, with Jewish Israelis as necessary frontline sacrifices. Christian Zionist leaders like Pastor John Hagee rapturously spread antisemitic End Times prophecy as they clamored for the United States and Israel to attack Iran—a dramatic escalation that, to their sure glee, would likely have sparked a world war.

Many white Christian nationalists sought to play Islamophobia and antisemitism off each other. Rightists like Elon Musk and Charlie Kirk began "naming the Jew" to a previously unparalleled degree, attacking American Jews directly for their alleged role in fomenting the forces of mass immigration, liberalism, and "anti-white racism" which, they claimed, fueled Palestine solidarity protests.[6] Others, like Tucker Carlson and Candace Owens, leaned into America First isolationism, peddling dog-whistle conspiracy theories about supposed Zionist lobbies dragging the U.S. into their latest Middle East war. At the same time, street-level white nationalists from across the country opportunistically claimed they were against Israel's crimes as an extension of the same Jewish conspiracy they were convinced is crucifying whites. Two-dozen masked neo-Nazis from Blood Tribe, a new player on the white nationalist scene, marched at Wisconsin's capital chanting "Israel is not our friend,"[7] and racist podcaster Mike "Enoch" Peinovich led a Washington D.C. rally with his National Justice Party demanding "no more Jewish wars."[8] The fear was palpable, and the Anti-Defamation League was choosing to target Jewish anti-Zionists, and Palestine solidarity activists writ large, rather than Twitter's trending conspiracy theories or these emerging threats from the Right.

"We are unflinching: antisemitism is wrong, it is unacceptable, and it has no place in any struggle for liberation," wrote IfNotNow in a public statement on November 1, 2023, acknowledging both rising antisemitism and Islamophobia and disingenuous actors who want to manipulate the crisis to push bigoted ideas. "We are not alone in our fear of being recognized for our religion and attacked, or massacred as we pray. Our Palestinian, Arab, and Muslim neighbors share it too." They, like so many organizations on the Jewish Left, demanded a ceasefire, a rallying cry that became a roar as millions joined in. The ceasefire movement had the potential to build a game-changing kind of unity because it was founded on the notion that all life is precious, each life contains a whole world, as the Talmud teaches and as the slogan "everyone for everyone," championed by the families of Israeli hostages, embodies: the starting point for acknowledging, and building, a shared humanity.[9] During this moment of Jewish Left unity, the ranks of organizations like JVP and INN swelled, spilling out into the streets. That growth likely signaled an exodus as well, as Jews were walking away from establishment organizations for whom demands for ceasefire were maligned, as Jewish history professor Derek Penslar described, as the "new BDS." A whole generation is looking to build not just a new Jewish community, but a new approach to fighting antisemitism.

The year 2023 ended with more questions than answers. How do we build movements big and bold enough to embrace our shared humanity; to fight antisemitism, Islamophobia, and anti-Palestinian bigotry together; to demand a future where all people can live in true safety, dignity, and full flourishing across Israel/Palestine? How do we hold difficult conversations across our movement spaces, recognizing our differences while remaining in relationship? How do we block the continued rise of fascism in the United States and around the world, and resist its ceaseless attempts to divide our communities from each other, and from within? While the path forward feels unclear, one thing is certain: isolation, militarism, and appealing to power won't save us. Only solidarity can.

"I'm very skeptical of the security story, that has also given rise to a very profitable industry of security consultants who tell people how to harden their perimeters," Mark Oppenheimer, former host of the *Unorthodox* podcast, told us.

> To me, the more interesting story is, given that we live in a world that has violence, which was true even before there were mass killings in America and even before Columbine, how that changes those of us who aren't shot. The human condition is one that has violence and unexpected death. We should always be asking how people move through it and come together again. How they endure.

The Jewish story has been told with what Magda Teter calls a "limited vocabulary," where too often, only our suffering is deemed worthy to recall. But our resistance, indistinguishable from our worship, our family and community, and our passionate love, is part of how we live out the world we want to see now. "Even if there may be many antisemitic people out there, that's not the latent state of nature," Rabbi Mordechai Lightstone told us, noting that this is part of the foundational brokenness of a world that needs to be healed. "It exists because there is a lack [of recognition] of a divine commonality that we all share."

It is through this combined work, of building community and organizing a mass movement, that we can build safety through solidarity, and win a just world. "At the core of why I do antisemitism work, and Left work in general," Jonah Boyarin told us, "is love of my people . . . as a people in diaspora along with other peoples, seeing what we can make of it all, together."

To find safety in solidarity, it takes a leap of radical imagination. "No one who is alive today has ever lived in a world that didn't have antisemitism, anti-Blackness, white supremacy, or Christian hegemony," Leo Ferguson told us.

> And we have no idea whether it's possible to get rid of it—once you mix the dye into the water, can you take the dye back out of the water? It's much easier to do the one than the other. And so all of us, in the Left, are engaged in a project of trying to figure out if it is possible to rebuild a society that is not fundamentally characterized by these oppressions . . . But I do know that our best chance as Jews is to be doing that work alongside all of the other work, fighting all the other oppressions that we know we have to defeat, alongside all the other communities that are implicated.

The alternative to the lachrymose story of Jewish history is not just Jewish survival, but the joy of a Jewish life, lived in defiance to those who want us snuffed out. We, understandably, focus on the antisemites as the dangerous ones. But, to them, we are the frightening ones, the strangers in their midst strapped with the unnerving ability to tear their world apart. So let's do it. Let's become the frightful creatures from their nightmares by ripping out the roots of a capitalist, white Christian supremacist system that serves none of us.

ACKNOWLEDGMENTS

After years of working on this book, we feel lucky that our names appear on the cover and that you get to read it. But it would be malpractice if we were to take full credit because the analysis presented on these pages is the work of generations of leaders who have fought for these ideas in the streets, developed them in social movements, and debated them across the pages of lefty magazines, social media and scholarship. We stand on the shoulders of giants, and have inherited everything worth saying from those who came before, just as we draw sustenance and inspiration from those fighting with solidarity today.

Since beginning this process in 2020, we have been backed by a global village of comrades who offered support so substantive, that we consider them our unindicted co-conspirators. We have received crucial feedback from scholars, journalists, and activists who reviewed portions of the text, including Mimi Arbeit, Sina Arnold, Jonah Ben Avraham, Benjamin Balthaser, Jonah Boyarin, Nadav David, Ben Doernberg, Sophie Ellman-Golan, Hannah Freedman, Emily Gorcenski, Dove Kent, Kim Kelly, Jacob Labendz, Ilana Lerman, Matthew Lyons, Shaul Magid, Moishe Ben Marx, Alexander Reid Ross, Emma Saltzberg, Spencer Sunshine, and others. We'd like to give special thanks to April Rosenblum, who provided vital feedback and editorial comments.

We also want to thank the people we interviewed for this book, whose open-ended, generous and generative conversation helped sharpen and guide us in so many ways. In addition to many listed above, these folks include Nesha Abramson, Fatema Ahmad, Megan Black, Joan Braune, Ari Brostoff, Benjamin Case, Stosh Cotler, Tobita Chow, Hadar Cohen, Alex DiBranco, Rev. Anne Dunlap, Leo Ferguson, Avi Gross-Grand,

Rabbi Tom Gutherz, Michael Harrington, Liz Jackson, Jo Kent Katz, Margaret Killjoy, Daryle Lamont Jenkins, Rosza Daniel Lang/Levitsky, Smadar Lavie, Rev. Dr. Jacqui Lewis, Mordechai Lightstone, Asher Lovy, Cassandra Mae, Shahanna McKinney-Baldon, Carin Mrotz, Rabbi Dev Noily, Mark Oppenheimer, Dania Rajendra, Penny Rosenwasser, Rabbi Eli Rubin, Rabbi Danya Ruttenberg, Rabbi Rachel Schmelkin, Motti Seligson, Keren Soffer-Sharon, Rabbi Ariel Stone, Max Strassfeld, Emily Tamkin, Eric Ward, Ami Weintraub, Simone Zimmerman, and many more.

We're grateful to our editor, Carl Bromley, for his invaluable insight and guidance, and to the entire team at Melville House for shepherding us through this process.

Finally, Shane wants to thank his wife and partner Alexandra, whose love is the heart of everything that makes this struggle worth winning. He is also blessed for the compassionate relationships of friends and collaborators during the process of pulling this book together; every person he met in the aisles of shul or the streets of mass demonstrations has had a hand in building this vision of a new kind of world. Ben would like to thank his wife and best friend Carrie for being his rock, right there by his side, every step of the way, in all matters head and heart, serious and silly; his parents and grandparents, ancestors and elders for teaching him to be gentle, to try, and to care; his dear comrade Benjamin Balthaser, for his enduring thought partnership through the turns and trials of these times; his many communities of love and struggle through the years; his colleagues at Political Research Associates, for helping him to explore and to grow; Hashem; and the angel of history, wreckage and all.

ENDNOTES

INTRODUCTION. BUILDING SAFETY THROUGH SOLIDARITY

1   "Breaking the Antisemitism Cycle Through Solidarity," speech by Dove Kent, Avodah, video, May 23, 2018, 21:57, youtube.com.

2   Annalise E. Glauz-Todrank, *Judging Jewish Identity in the United States* (Blue Ridge Summit, PA: Lexington Books, 2022).

ONE. WHAT IS ANTISEMITISM? THE STRUGGLE TO UNDERSTAND 2,000 YEARS OF OPPRESSION

1   Stosh Cotler, *All of Us: Organizing to Counter White Christian Nationalism and Build a Pro-Democracy Society* (Kairos Center and MoveOn Education Fund, 2023); interview with author.

2   Emily Tamkin, *Bad Jews: A History of American Jewish Politics and Identities* (New York: Harper, 2022), 6.

3   David Nirenberg, *Anti-Judaism: The Western Tradition* (New York: W. W. Norton, 2013).

4   Brian Klug, "The Collective Jew: Israel and the New Antisemitism," *Patterns of Prejudice* 37, no. 2 (March 1, 2003): 124.

5   Keith Kahn-Harris, *Strange Hate: Antisemitism, Racism, and the Limits of Diversity* (London: Repeater Books, 2019), 46–47.

6   Mauricio J. Dulfano, "Antisemitism in Argentina: Patterns of Jewish Adaptation," *Jewish Social Studies* 31, no. 2 (1969): 124.

7   The term "Semitic" was initially used (and is still used today) in the field of modern linguistics to denote a family of languages spoken by millions across Africa and Asia, before it was misappropriated as a pseudoscientific racial category.

8   See David Engel, "Away from a Definition of Antisemitism: An Essay in the Semantics of Historical Description," in *Rethinking European Jewish History*, ed. Jeremy Cohen and Moshe Rosman (Liverpool: Liverpool University Press, 2008), 30–53.

9   Ben Gidley, Brendan McGeever, and David Feldman, "Labour and Antisemitism: A Crisis Misunderstood," *The Political Quarterly* 91, no. 2 (April 1, 2020): 416. We use the term "reservoir" repeatedly in this book, and are indebted to Gidley, McGeever, and Feldman for the formulation.

10 Bernard Harrison, *Blaming the Jews: Politics and Delusion* (Bloomington: Indiana University Press, 2020), 116.

11 Moishe Postone, "Anti-Semitism and National Socialism: Notes on the German Reaction to 'Holocaust,'" *New German Critique*, no. 19 (January 1, 1980): 106.

12   The work of scholar and activist April Rosenblum has been foundational in popularizing this Left analysis of antisemitism as a mechanism of populist misdirection, a false power analysis that leaves real oppressive systems and actors unscathed. See April Rosenblum, *The Past Didn't Go Anywhere: Making Resistance to Antisemitism a Part of All of Our Movements* (pamphlet, 2007).

13   Postone, "Anti-Semitism," 115.

14   Shulamit Volkov, "Antisemitism as a Cultural Code: Reflections on the History and Historiography of Antisemitism in Imperial Germany," *Year Book* 23, no. 1 (January 1, 1978): 25–46.

15   Quoted in Cassie Miller, "Social Media and System Collapse: How Extremists Built an International Neo-Nazi Network," in *Antisemitism on Social Media*, ed. Monika Hübscher and Sabine von Mering (Abingdon, VA: Routledge, 2022), 97.

16   Mike Rothschild, *The Storm Is upon Us: How QAnon Became a Movement, Cult, and Conspiracy Theory of Everything* (Brooklyn: Melville House, 2021), 54.

17   Dan Berger, "The Fools of National Socialism: Thoughts on Antisemitism and the Fight Against Trumpism," *Abolition: A Journal of Insurgent Politics*, November 21, 2016.

18   Sharon Goldtzvik and Ginna Green, "Messaging Training: How to Fight Anti-Semitism in Solidarity" (presentation, Netroots Nation, Pittsburgh, PA, August 18, 2022).

19   "Jewish Population Rises to 15.3 Million Worldwide, with Over 7 Million Residing in Israel," The Jewish Agency for Israel, news release, September 25, 2022, jewishagency.org.

20   Today, Sephardim are sometimes understood as one subset of Jews within the Mizrahi umbrella. In other cases, especially in Israel, the term "Sephardim" is used interchangeably with "Mizrahim."

21   Leo Ferguson, Dove Kent, and Keren Soffer-Sharon, *Understanding Antisemitism: An Offering to Our Movement* (New York: Jews for Racial and Economic Justice, 2017), 8.

22   "Population of Jews of Color Is Increasing in U.S., Despite Undercounting in Population Studies," *EJewish Philanthropy*, May 15, 2019, ejewishphilanthropy.com.

23   Sam Kestenbaum, "Jews of Color Speak Out on Racial Divides," *Forward*, April 6, 2017, forward.com.

24   Taylor Orth, "From Millionaires to Muslims, Small Subgroups of the Population Seem Much Larger to Many Americans," YouGov, March 15, 2022, yougov.com.

25   *Audit of Antisemitic Incidents 2021* (New York: ADL Center on Extremism, April 2022).

26   *Supplemental Hate Crime Statistics, 2021* (Clarksburg, WV: Federal Bureau of Investigation, Criminal Justice Information Services Division, 2023), 9.

27   Mari Cohen, "A Closer Look at the 'Uptick' in Antisemitism," *Jewish Currents*, May 27, 2021, jewishcurrents.org; Mari Cohen, "The Numbers Game," *Jewish Currents*, April 28, 2022, jewishcurrents.org; Mari Cohen, "The State of An-

tisemitism Reporting," *Jewish Currents*, January 19, 2023, jewishcurrents.org.

28   Micah Lee, "Anti-Defamation League Maps Jewish Peace Rallies With Antisemitic Attacks," *The Intercept*, November 11, 2023, theintercept.com; Anti-Defamation League, "Slogan: 'From the River to the Sea Palestine Will be Free'," October 26, 2023, adl.org; Yousef Munayyer, "What Does 'From the River to the Sea' Really Mean?," *Jewish Currents*, June 11, 2021, jewishcurrents.org.

29   *Antisemitic Attitudes in America: Topline Findings* (New York: Anti-Defamation League, 2023).

30   *Jewish Americans in 2020* (Washington, D.C.: Pew Research Center, 2021), 28.

31   *The State of Antisemitism in America 2021: Insights and Analysis* (New York: American Jewish Committee, 2021), 19.

32   *Jewish Americans in 2020*, 197–205. This Pew study was cited in an essay by Arielle Angel, executive editor at *Jewish Currents*, that raises many of the questions we raise here. See Arielle Angel, "Beyond Grievance," *Jewish Currents*, September 6, 2022.

33   Jacob Labendz, "The Jewish National Minority and the 'Globalists' of Donald Trump's America," in *Four Years After: Ethnonationalism, Antisemitism and Racism in Trump's America*, ed. Stefanie Schüler-Springorum et al. (Heidelberg, DE: Universitätsverlag Winter, 2020), 109. This "shared culture of anti-antisemitism," it should be remembered, is historically contingent and may be eroding in our era.

34   Peter Beinart, "How To Oppose Pro-Palestinian Antisemitism," *The Beinart Notebook*, November 7, 2023, peterbeinart.substack.com.

35   *J Street National Jewish Voters Survey* (Washington, D.C.: GBAO Strategies, 2022), 8.

36   Avi Mayer, *The State of Antisemitism in America 2020* (New York: American Jewish Committee, 2020), 23–24.

37   "1 in 4 Hiring Managers Say They Are Less Likely to Move Forward with Jewish Applicants," *Resume Builder*, January 19, 2023, resumebuilder.com.

38   Rachel C. Schneider et al., "How Religious Discrimination Is Perceived in the Workplace: Expanding the View," *Socius* 8 (January 1, 2022).

TWO. NEITHER ETERNAL NOR INEVITABLE: NEW PERSPECTIVES ON "THE OLDEST HATRED"

1   Edward S. Shapiro, "Interpretations of the Crown Heights Riot," *American Jewish History* 90, no. 2 (January 1, 2002): 97.

2   Cornel West, "Black Anti-Semitism and the Rhetoric of Resentment," *Tikkun* 7, no.1 (January/February 1992): 16.

3   Quoted in William Saletan and Avi Zenilman, "The Gaffes of Al Sharpton," *Slate Magazine*, October 7, 2003, slate.com.

4   Quoted in Edward S. Shapiro, *Crown Heights: Blacks, Jews, and the 1991 Brooklyn Riot* (Waltham, MA: Brandeis University Press, 2006), 145.

5   A. M. Rosenthal, "Pogrom in Brooklyn," *The New York Times*, September 3, 1991.

6   Quoted in Shapiro, *Crown Heights*.

7   See Shaul Magid, "Judeopessimism: On Antisemitism and Afropessimism," *Ayin One: Tardema* 1, no. 1 (March 2021).

8   Quoted in Henry Goldschmidt, "The Voices of Jacob on the Streets of Brooklyn: Black and Jewish Israelites in and around Crown Heights," *American Ethnologist* 33, no. 3 (August 1, 2006): 384.

9   Quoted in Martin Lockshin, "*Sinyat Yisrael* (Hatred of Jews)," in *Key Concepts in the Study of Antisemitism*, ed. Sol Goldberg, Scott Ury, and Kalman Weiser (New York: Palgrave Macmillan, 2020), 273.

10 Henry Goldschmidt, *Race and Religion Among the Chosen Peoples of Crown Heights* (New Brunswick, NJ: Rutgers University Press, 2007), 208.

11 Ibid, 199–217.

12 Avigdor Bonchek, "Esau and Jacob," *Aish*, accessed September 10, 2023, aish.com.

13 Leon Pinsker, *Auto-Emancipation* (New York: The Maccabaean Publishing Company, 1906), 3.

14 Theodor Herzl, *The Complete Diaries of Theodor Herzl*, Vol. 1, trans. Harry Zohn (New York: Herzl Press, 1960), 6.

15 Shaul Magid, *Meir Kahane: The Public Life and Political Thought of an American Jewish Radical* (Princeton: Princeton University Press, 2021), 29.

16 Shaul Magid, "Anti-Semitism as Colonialism: Meir Kahane's 'Ethics of Violence,'" *Journal of Jewish Ethics* 1, no. 2 (2015): 208.

17 Ibid, 222.

18 Deborah Lipstadt, *Antisemitism: Here and Now* (New York: Schocken Books, 2019), 16.

19 Benjamin Epstein and Arnold Forster, *The New Anti-Semitism* (New York: McGraw Hill, 1974).

20 This move by the ADL was widely denounced on the Jewish Left. See Shane Burley and Ben Lorber, "The ADL's Crazily Irresponsible Crusade Against anti-Zionism," *Haaretz*, May 11, 2022, haaretz.com; Joshua Leifer, "The ADL Goes Full Bully," *The Nation*, May 6, 2022, thenation.com; Mari Cohen and Isaac Scher, "The ADL Doubles Down on Opposing the Anti-Zionist Left," *Jewish Currents*, May 1, 2022, jewishcurrents.org.

21 Alex Kane, "A 'McCarthyite Backlash' Against Pro-Palestine Speech," *Jewish Currents*, October 20, 2023, jewishcurrents.org; Murtaza Hussain, "The Senate Condemns Student Groups As Backlash to Pro-Palestinian Speech Grows," *The Intercept*, October 27, 2023, theintercept.com.

22 Kate Brady, Anthony Faiola, Emily Rauhala, Karla Adam, and Beatriz Ríos, "European Bans on Pro-Palestinian Protests Prompt Claims of Bias," *The Washington Post*, October 26, 2023, washingtonpost.com.

23 "What is antisemitism?," International Holocaust Remembrance Alliance, accessed October 20, 2023, holocaustremembrance.com.

24 Zvika Klein, "More Than 1,000 Global Entities Adopted IHRA Definition of Antisemitism," *The Jerusalem Post*, January 17, 2023, jpost.com.

25 Radhika Sainath, "The Anti-Palestinian Censorship Machine Runs on Racism," *Jacobin*, April 1, 2023, jacobin.com.

26 Kenneth Stern, "I Drafted the Definition of Antisemitism. Rightwing Jews Are Weaponizing It," *The Guardian*, December 13, 2019, theguardian.com.

27 Emily Tamkin, "Who won the battle over the White House antisemitism strategy?," *+972 Magazine*, August 8, 2023, 972mag.com.

28 *The Jerusalem Declaration on Antisemitism* (Jerusalem: JDA, May 25, 2021), jerusalemdeclaration.org.

29 "Our Approach to Zionism," Jewish Voice for Peace, accessed October 20, 2023, jvp.org.

30 "Statement of Principles: Jewish Alliance Against Zionism," Jewish Alliance Against Zionism, Anti-Zionism Collection at the Freedom Archives, 1.

31 Shmuel Alexandrov quoted in Hayyim Rothman, *No Masters but God: Portraits of Anarcho-Judaism* (Manchester: Manchester University Press, 2020), 123.

32 Irena Klepfisz, "Anti-Semitism in the Lesbian/Feminist Movement," in *Nice Jews Girls: A Lesbian Anthology: Second Edition*, ed. Evelyn Torton Beck (Trumansburg, NY: The Crossing Press, 1982), 46–47.

33 April Rosenblum, *The Past Didn't Go Anywhere: Making Resistance to Antisemitism Part of All of Our Movements* (pamphlet, 2007), 15, aprilrosenblum.com.

34 Genesis Rabbah 65:1, quoted in Malka Z. Simkovich, "Why Rome Is Likened to a Boar," *TheTorah.com*, accessed September 10, 2023.

35 Menahem Nahum, *The Light of the Eyes: Homilies on the Torah*, trans. Arthur Green (Stanford: Stanford University Press, 2021), 280.

36 Rothman, *No Masters but God*, 119–120.

THREE. THE CABAL: ANTISEMITISM AND CONSPIRACY THEORIES

1 Yair Rosenberg, "Elon Musk Among the Anti-Semites," *The Atlantic*, May 16, 2023, theatlantic.com; Tori Otten, "Republicans' Only Defense Against the Trump Indictment: George Soros," *The New Republic*, March 31, 2023, newrepublic.com; Melissa Gira Grant, "Why the Right Can't Quit Its Antisemitic Attacks Against George Soros," *The New Republic*, August 11, 2022, newrepublic.com.

2 Brain Stelter, "Glenn Beck's Attacks on Soros Draw Heat," *The New York Times*, November 11, 2010.

3 "Hungarian Prime Minister Orban Attacks 'Enemy' Who 'Speculates with Money' in Election Rally Speech," Jewish Telegraphic Agency, March 16, 2018, jta.org.

4 Zack Beauchamp, "Hungary Just passed a 'Stop Soros' Law that Makes It Illegal to Help Undocumented Migrants," *Vox*, June 22, 2018, vox.com.

5 ATL Antifascists (@afaintl), "These antisemitic flyers were found strewn around the Capitol—likely from yesterday's big rally there," Twitter, November 22, 2020, 12:42 p.m.

6   Alex Kaplan, "Here Are the QAnon Supporters Running for Congress in
        2020," *Media Matters for America*, January 7, 2020.

7   Alex Kaplan, "Here Are the QAnon Supporters Running for Congress in
        2022," *Media Matters for America*, June 2, 2021.

8   *National Politics Survey September 2020* (Oakland: Civiqs, 2020), 17.

9   Norman Cohn, *Warrant for Genocide: The Myth of the Jewish World Conspiracy
        and The Protocols of the Elders of Zion* (London: Eyre & Spottiswoode
        Ltd., 1967), 118–126.

10   Leonard Dinnerstein, *Antisemitism in America* (Oxford: Oxford University
        Press, 1995), 81.

11   Winston Churchill, "Zionism Versus Bolshevism: A Struggle for the Soul
        of the Jewish People," *Illustrated Sunday Herald*, February 8, 1920, 5.

12   Randall L. Bytwerk, "Believing in 'Inner Truth': *The Protocols of the Elders of
        Zion* in Nazi Propaganda, 1933–1945," *Holocaust and Genocide Studies* 29, no.
        2 (August 1, 2015): 214–15.

13   *The International Jew: The World's Foremost Problem* (Dearborn, MI: The
        Dearborn Publishing Company, 1920), 115.

14   *The Jewish Peril: Protocols of the Learned Elders of Zion* (London: Eyre & Spot-
        tiswoode, 1920), 40.

15   Ibid, 7.

16   Ibid, 2, 17.

17   *The International Jew*, 118.

18   Ibid, 122.

19   Donna Rachel Edmunds, "Qatari Children Taught Protocols of Zion, Other
        Antisemitic Tropes as Fact," *The Jerusalem Post*, August 26, 2020, jpost.com.

20   "Citing 'Protocols,' Jordanian TV Tells Viewers Jews Are an 'Abhorred'
        People," *The Times of Israel*, May 2, 2017, timesofisrael.com.

21   Ely Karmon, "Aum-Shinrikyo, the Anti-Semitic Doomsday Cult: A Dan-
        gerous Comeback," in *Anti-Semitism Worldwide 1998/1999* (Tel Aviv: Stephen
        Roth Institute for the Study of Contemporary Anti-Semitism and Racism,
        2000), 5–15.

22   Morgan Halvorsen, "Not Every QAnon Believer's an Antisemite. But
        There's a Lot of Overlap Between Its Adherents and Belief in a Century-Old
        Antisemitic Hoax," *Morning Consult*, June 28, 2021, morningconsult.com.

23   Jesse Walker, *The United States of Paranoia: A Conspiracy Theory* (New York:
        Harper Perennial, 2013), 23–45.

24   Richard Hofstadter, "The Paranoid Style in American Politics," *Harper's
        Magazine*, November 1964.

25   Anna Merlan, *Republic of Lies: American Conspiracy Theorists and Their Sur-
        prising Rise to Power* (New York: Metropolitan Books, 2019), 7.

26   Michael Barkun, *A Culture of Conspiracy: Apocalyptic Visions in Contemporary
        America* (Berkeley: University of California Press, 2003), 3–4.

27   Hofstadter, "The Paranoid Style in American Politics."

28   Barkun, *A Culture of Conspiracy*, 26–28.

29   Christina E. Farhart et al., "Vax Attacks: How Conspiracy Theory Belief

Undermines Vaccine Support," *Progress in Molecular Biology and Transla-tional Science* 188 (December 2021): 137.

30   Lord Mann of Holbeck Moor and Lewis Arthurton, *From Anti-vaxxers to Antisemitism: Conspiracy Theory in the COVID-19 Pandemic* (London: The Office of Her Majesty's Government's Independent Adviser on Antisemitism, 2020).

31   *Public Support for Social Media Reform* (London: Center for Countering Digital Hate, 2023), 13.

32   Robert O. Paxton, *The Anatomy of Fascism* (New York: Vintage Books, 2004), 41.

33   Spencer Sunshine, "The Right Hand of Occupy Wall Street," *Political Research Associates*, February 24, 2014, politicalresearch.org.

34   Will, Chino, Saudade, and Mamos, *How to Overthrow the Illuminati* (pamphlet, 2013), 1.

35   Ibid, 15.

36   Ibid, 14.

FOUR. A CHRISTIAN HISTORY:
ANTISEMITISM IN CHRISTIAN EUROPE

1   David Horowitz quoted in Diana Krusman, "Conservative Writer David Horowitz Visits Campus," *Daily Trojan*, March 24, 2016, dailytrojan.com.

2   Bat Ye'or, "Antisemitism/Anti-Zionism: Primal Pillars in Europe's Decay," in *Anti-Judaism, Antisemitism, and Delegitimizing Israel*, ed. Robert S. Wistrich (Lincoln: University of Nebraska Press, 2016), 37.

3   Bat Ye'or, *Eurabia: The Euro-Arab Axis* (Vancouver, BC: Fairleigh Dickinson University Press, 2005), 9, 20; quoted in Sindre Bangstad, "Bat Ye'or and Eurabia."

4   Shane Burley, "There's Something Dangerous in 'Antisemitism Studies,'" *Full Stop*, May 10, 2022, full-stop.net.

5   John Kelsay, "Antisemitism in Classical Islamic Sources," in *Not Your Father's Antisemitism: Hatred of the Jews in the 21st Century*, ed. Michael Berenbaum (St. Paul: Paragon House, 2008), 101–115.

6   David Nirenberg, *Anti-Judaism: The Western Tradition* (New York City: W. W. Norton, 2013), 17–31.

7   Pieter van der Horst, "The Egyptian Beginning of Anti-Semitism's Long History," Jerusalem Center for Public Affairs, October 10, 2007, jcpa.org.

8   Dan Cohn-Sherbok, *Antisemitism: A World History of Prejudice* (Gloucestershire: The History Press, 2022), 12.

9   Martin Goodman, *A History of Judaism* (Princeton: Princeton University Press, 2018), 192–198.

10   Nirenberg, *Anti-Judaism*, 79.

11   Ibid, 109.

12   Augustine of Hippo, *Reply to Faustus the Manichaean*, trans. Richard Stoth-

ert (Bedford, PA: Lighthouse Publishing, 2018), Book 12, Chapter 12.

13   Parallel processes of proto-racialization in medieval Christian Europe
     were also directed against Muslim, African, Native American, Mongol, Ro-
     mani, and even fellow European Christian communities. Geraldine Heng,
     "Race and Racism in the European Middle Ages," in *Outcasts: Prejudice &
     Persecution in the Medieval World* (Los Angeles: Getty Center, 2018). Thanks
     to Noah Schoen for directing our attention to this source.

14   Ben Gidley, Brendan McGeever, and David Feldman, "Labour and An-
     tisemitism: A Crisis Misunderstood," *The Political Quarterly* 91, no. 2 (April
     1, 2020): 413–21, doi:10.1111/1467-923x.12854.

15   Quoted in Joshua Trachtenberg, *The Devil and the Jews: The Medieval Con-
     ception of the Jew and Its Relation to Modern Anti-Semitism* (Philadelphia: The
     Jewish Publication Society, 1993), 18.

16   For a deeper look see Ezra Rose, *FYMA: A Lesser Key to the Appropriation of
     Jewish Magic & Mysticism* (2022), accessed September 10, 2023.

17   These tropes, too, persisted into the modern era, from Soviet leader Joseph
     Stalin's paranoid fantasies that a "Doctors' Plot" of Jewish doctors sought
     to poison him, to the lurid memes blaming Jews for COVID-19. Religious
     and cultural parades in towns and villages across Europe still feature an-
     tisemitic themes, a testament to the enduring legacy of these myths.

18   Debra Kaplan, "Martin Luther and the Reformation," in *The Cambridge
     Companion to Antisemitism*, ed. Steven Katz (Cambridge: Cambridge Uni-
     versity Press, 2022), 273.

19   "Nazi Propaganda Depicting Martin Luther," *Facing History and Ourselves*,
     last updated June 30, 2022.

20   Leonard Dinnerstein, *Antisemitism In America* (Oxford: Oxford University
     Press, 1994), x.

21   *The 2020 Census of American Religion* (Washington, D.C.: Public Religion Re-
     search Institute, 2021), 7–8.

22   Paul Kivel, *Living in the Shadow of the Cross: Understanding and Resisting the
     Power and Privilege of Christian Hegemony* (Gabriola, BC: New Society Pub-
     lishers, 2013), 144.

23   Benjamin Balthaser, "Lessons on Anti-Semitism from Growing Up in Ru-
     ral America," *Jewschool*, November 30, 2016, jewschool.com.

24   Ibid.

25   According to 2020 census data, the Twin Cities population stands at 3.16
     million. According to a 2019 Brandeis study, there are 64,800 Jews in the
     Twin Cities. Janet Krasner Aronson et al., *Portrait of Our Community: 2019
     Twin Cities Jewish Community Study* (Waltham, MA: Brandeis Cohen Cen-
     ter for Modern Jewish Studies, August 2020), 1; "Twin Cities Population is
     Growing and Diversifying," Metropolitan Council, August 12, 2021, metro-
     council.org.

26   Kivel, *Living in the Shadow of the Cross*, 3.

27   Chrissy Stroop, "One Year After 1/6, Media Still Refuse to Recognize Authori-
     tarian Christianity," *Religion Dispatches*, January 4, 2022, religiondispatches.org.

28   "What Is Christian Supremacy?," Soulforce, 2019, accessed September 11, 2023, soulforce.org.

29   Magda Teter, *Christian Supremacy: Reckoning with the Roots of Antisemitism and Racism* (Princeton: Princeton University Press, 2023), 4.

30   Elizabeth Moraff, "'To Dismantle White Supremacy, Christians Must Confront Antisemitism," *Christians for Social Action*, July 26, 2021, christiansfor-socialaction.org.

FIVE. THE SOCIALISM OF FOOLS: ANTISEMITISM AND ANTI-CAPITALISM

1   A pseudonym.

2   Dania Rajendra, "Anti-Semitism and White Nationalism" (lecture, Jewish Community Action, Minneapolis, January 6, 2019).

3   This phrasing first appeared in Ben Lorber, "Attacking Antisemitism," *Jacobin*, November 1, 2018, jacobin.com.

4   "Donald Trump's Argument For America," Team Trump, video, 2:00, November 6, 2016, youtube.com; for analysis on the ad, see Josh Marshall, "Trump Rolls Out Anti-Semitic Closing Ad," *Talking Points Memo*, November 5, 2016, talkingpointsmemo.com.

5   Kerice Doten-Snitker, "Debunking the Myth of 'Elite Jews' in Medieval Europe," Stroum Center for Jewish Studies at the University of Washington, May 31, 2019, jewishstudies.washington.edu.

6   Julie Mell, "Jews and Money: The Medieval Origins of a Modern Stereotype," in *The Cambridge Companion to Antisemitism*, ed. Steven Katz (Cambridge: Cambridge University Press, 2022), 213–231.

7   In recent years, some Jewish progressives have proposed what has been called the "middle agent theory" of antisemitism, suggesting that this position of Jews is the fundamental cause of antisemitism across time and place. This theory has faced heated criticism for erasing non-Ashkenazi Jewish history and obscuring important dynamics of power and agency in other situations where the label is applied. See Tallie Ben-Daniel, "Antisemitism, Palestine and the Mizrahi Question," in *On Antisemitism: Solidarity and the Struggle for Justice*, ed. Jewish Voice for Peace (Chicago: Haymarket Books, 2017), 75–78.

8   April Rosenblum, *The Past Didn't Go Anywhere: Making Resistance to Antisemitism a Part of All of Our Movements* (pamphlet, 2007), 9.

9   Aurora Levins Morales, "Latin@s, Israel and Palestine: Understanding Anti-Semitism," *AuroraLevinsMorales.com* (blog), March 15, 2021.

10   See Yosef Hayim Yerushalmi, "'Servants of Kings, Not Servants of Servants': Some Aspects of the Jewish Political History," *Raisons Politiques* 7, Issue 3 (2002): 19–52.

11   Quoted in Leo Ferguson, Dove Kent, and Keren Soffer Sharon, *Understanding Antisemitism: An Offering to Our Movement* (New York: Jews for Racial and Economic Justice, 2017), 17.

12 Karl Marx and Friedrich Engels, "The Communist Manifesto," in *Karl Marx: Selected Writings*, ed. Lawrence H. Simon (Indianapolis: Hackett Publishing Company, 1994), 161–2.

13 Michel Winock, *Nationalism, Anti-Semitism, and Fascism in France*, trans. Jane Marie Todd (Stanford: Stanford University Press, 1998), 98. Originally cited in John Ganz, "The Socialism of Fools?," *Unpopular Front*, Substack, November 7, 2022, johnganz.substack.com.

14 Hannah Arendt, *The Origins of Totalitarianism* (New York: Harcourt, Inc, 1976), 15–20.

15 Quoted in Hal Draper, *Karl Marx's Theory of Revolution: Volume IV: Critique of Other Socialisms* (New York: Monthly Review Press, 1990), 293–296.

16 Pierre-Joseph Proudhon, "On the Jew," trans. Mitchell Abidor, Marxists. org, accessed September 11, 2023. Originally quoted in Pierre-Joseph Proudhon, *Carnets de P.J. Proudhon* (Paris: M. Rivière, 1960).

17 Mike Rothschild, *Jewish Space Lasers: The Rothschilds and 200 Years of Conspiracy Theories* (New York: Melville House, 2023), 41–58.

18 Ben Sales, "Congresswoman Says Rothschild-Funded Space Lasers Caused Deadly California Fire," Jewish Telegraphic Agency, January 28, 2021, jta.org.

19 Andrew Porwancher, "Alexander Hamilton and American Paranoia," *Marginalia*, November 19, 2021, marginalia.lareviewofbooks.org.

20 Steve Cohen, *That's Funny, You Don't Look Anti-Semitic: An Anti-Racist Analysis of Left Antisemitism* (London: No Pasaran! Media, 2019), 16.

21 Werner Bonefeld, "Notes on Antisemitism," *Common Sense*, no. 21 (1997): 64.

22 Werner Bonefeld, "Critical Theory and the Critique of Antisemitism: On Society as Economic Object," *Journal of Social Justice* 9 (2019): 3.

23 John Ganz, "The Socialism of Fools," *Unpopular Front*, Substack, November 7, 2022.

24 "Page from the Antisemitic Children's Book *The Poisonous Mushroom*," United States Holocaust Memorial Museum, accessed December 5, 2022.

25 V. I. Lenin, "Anti-Jewish Pogroms," March 1919. Republished at Marxists Internet Archive, marxists.org.

26 Brendan McGeever, *Antisemitism and the Russian Revolution* (Cambridge: Cambridge University Press, 2019), 120.

27 Brendan McGeever, "Red Antisemitism: Anti-Jewish Violence and Revolutionary Politics in Ukraine, 1919," *Quest: Issues in Contemporary Jewish History* 15 (August 2019).

28 Quoted in Enzo Traverso, *The Jewish Question: History of a Marxist Debate* (Chicago: Haymarket Books, 2018), 148.

29 Quoted in Leonard Zeskind, *Blood and Politics: The History of the White Nationalist Movement from the Margins to the Mainstream* (New York: Farrar Straus Giroux, 2009), 75.

30 Vladimir Bolshakov, "Zionism in the Service of Anti-Communism," *Novosti Press Agency*, 1972. Quoted in "The Stalinist Roots of 'Left' Anti-semitism," *Workers' Liberty*, April 28, 2011, workersliberty.org.

31 Alex Jones quoted in Spencer Sunshine, "20 on the Right in Occupy," Po-

litical Research Associates, February 13, 2014, politicalresearch.org.

32   Ibid.

33   Mear One quoted in Dave Rich, "Not Sure Why That Mural Is Antisemitic? Let Me Explain . . . ," *The Jewish Chronicle*, March 28, 2018, thejc.com.

34   Heather Stewart and Sarah Marsh, "Jewish leaders demand explanation over Corbyn book foreword," *The Guardian*, May 1, 2019, theguardian.com.

35   While there was real antisemitism in the Labour Party, the controversy was driven opportunistically by the Right, Center and many liberals as a way of delegitimizing the left-wing of the party. For more on antisemitism and the UK Labour Party, see David Renton, *Labour's Antisemitism Crisis: What the Left Got Wrong and How to Learn From It* (Abingdon: Routledge, 2021).

36   Quoted in Chip Berlet, "Interview: G. William Domhoff," *The Public Eye*, September 2004, publiceye.org.

37   Rajendra, "Anti-Semitism and White Nationalism."

SIX. THE RED MENACE:
ANTISEMITISM AND ANTI-COMMUNISM

1   A pseudonym

2   This phrasing is featured heavily in Paul Hanebrink's influential book *A Specter Haunting Europe: The Myth of Judeo-Bolshevism*, from which this section draws upon. See Paul Hanebrink, *A Specter Haunting Europe: The Myth of Judeo-Bolshevism* (Cambridge: Harvard University Press, 2018).

3   Vivian Gornick, *The Romance of American Communism* (New York: Basic Books, 1977), 29.

4   Hannah Arendt, *The Origins of Totalitarianism* (New York: Harcourt, Inc, 1976), 45.

5   Hanebrink, *A Specter Haunting Europe*, 27.

6   Norman Cohn, *Warrant for Genocide: The Myth of the Jewish World Conspiracy and* The Protocols of the Elders of Zion (London: Eyre & Spottiswoode Ltd., 1967), 122.

7   Quoted in Cohn, *Warrant for Genocide*, 121.

8   Winston Churchill, "Zionism Versus Bolshevism: A Struggle for the Soul of the Jewish People," *Illustrated Sunday Herald*, February 8, 1920.

9   Hanebrink, *A Spectre Haunting Europe*, 6.

10   Quoted in Leonard Dinnerstein, *Antisemitism in America* (Oxford: Oxford University Press, 1994), 80.

11   Adam Serwer, "White Nationalism's Deep American Roots," *The Atlantic*, April 2019, theatlantic.com.

12   Max Horkheimer, "The Jews and Europe," in *The Frankfurt School on Religion: Key Writings by the Major Thinkers*, ed. Eduardo Mendieta (New York: Routledge, 2005), 226.

13   Quoted in Ronald Grigor Suny, "The Left Side of History: The Embattled

Pasts of Communism in the 20th Century," *Perspectives on Politics* 15, No. 2 (June 2017), 459.

14 Joseph Goebbels quoted in Ellen Engelstad and Mimir Kristjansson, "The Return of 'Judeo-Bolshevism,'" trans. Ashild Lappegard Lahn, *Jacobin*, February 16, 2019, jacobin.com.

15 Thanks to Jacob Labendz for this point. See Hanebrink, *A Specter Haunting Europe,* 127–130.

16 Dinnerstein, *Antisemitism In America*, 109–121; Charles R. Gallagher, *Nazis of Copley Square: The Forgotten History of the Christian Front* (Cambridge: Harvard University Press, 2021), 12–46.

17 Charles Coughlin quoted in "Charles Coughlin," *Americans and the Holocaust* (Washington, D.C.: United States Holocaust Memorial Museum, accessed September 11, 2023).

18 Dinnerstein, 118–122.

19 Joseph McCarthy, "Speech Delivered Before Senate on June 14th, 1951," Internet Modern History Sourcebook, Fordham University, accessed Sep. 10, 2023, sourcebooks.fordham.edu.

20 Lawrence Bush, "May 2: McCarthyism and the Jews," *Jewish Currents*, May 2, 2011, jewishcurrents.org.

21 "Hunting Communists? They Were Really After Jews," *The Jewish Chronicle*, August 6, 2009, thejc.com; Stuart Svonkin, *Jews Against Prejudice: American Jews and the Fight for Civil Liberties* (New York: Columbia University Press, 1997), 114, 121.

22 Yotam Marom, "Towards the Next Jewish Rebellion," Medium, August 9, 2016, medium.com.

23 Matthew Dallek, *Birchers: How the John Birch Society Radicalized the American Right* (New York: Basic Books, 2022), 27.

24 April Rosenblum, "Offers We Couldn't Refuse: The Decline of Actively Secular Jewish Identity in the 20th Century US," *Jewish Currents* (May/June 2009), 8–28.

25 Ben's grandfather, Irving Lorber, was also targeted with suspicion during this time after the government discovered that, while in the army during the Second World War, Irving had attended a dance held by the Industrial Workers of the World (IWW), a militant labor union, and signed his name on a document in order to buy insurance. Irving was not, in fact, involved with the IWW.

26 Clive Webb, "Counterblast: How the Atlanta Temple Bombing Strengthened the Civil Rights Cause," *Southern Spaces*, June 22, 2009, southernspaces.org.

27 David B. Green, "This Day in Jewish History | 1958: White Supremacists Bomb Atlanta Congregation," *Haaretz*, October 12, 2012, haaretz.com.

28 Quoted in Ben Lorber, "The Resurgence of Right-Wing Anti-Semitic Conspiracism Endangers All Justice Movements," *Religion Dispatches*, May 1, 2019, religiondispatches.org.

29 William Lind, "Who Stole Our Culture?," in *The Culture-Wise Family: Upholding Christian Values in a Mass Media World*, ed. Ted Baehr and Pat Boone

(Ada, MI: Baker Books, 2012), 178–85.

30 Mike Gonzalez and Katharine C. Gorka, "How Cultural Marxism Threatens the United States—and How Americans Can Fight It," *Heritage Foundation*, November 14, 2022, heritage.org.

31 A. G. Gancarski, "Ron DeSantis Vows to Stamp Out the 'Vicious Ideology' of 'Wokeness,'" *Florida Politics*, January 29, 2022, floridapolitics.com.

32 Jana Winter and Elias Groll, "Here's the Memo That Blew Up the NSC," *Foreign Policy*, August 10, 2017, foreignpolicy.com.

33 William Lind quoted in "Ally of Christian Right Heavyweight Paul Weyrich Addresses Holocaust Denial Conference," Southern Poverty Law Center, September 20, 2002, splcenter.org.

34 Gavin McInnes quoted in Andy Campbell, *We Are Proud Boys: How a Right-Wing Street Gang Ushered in a New Era of American Extremism* (New York: Hachette Books, 2022), 31.

35 Barnaby Raine, "Jewophobia," *Salvage*, January 7, 2019, salvage.zone.

36 Julia Carrie Wong, "Facebook Reportedly Discredited Critics by Linking Them to George Soros," *The Guardian*, November 14, 2018, theguardian.com.

SEVEN. A RACE APART: ANTISEMITISM AND THE WHITE NATIONALIST MOVEMENT

1 Blocked by a court injunction, the city's Robert E. Lee statue was not removed until April 2021. Ben Paviour, "Charlottesville Removes Robert E. Lee Statue That Sparked A Deadly Rally," *NPR*, July 10, 2021, npr.org.

2 Many of those same DSA members, now with the Jewish Solidarity Caucus, returned a year later to commemorate the anniversary of Unite the Right with Charlottesville's Jewish community. Jewish Solidarity Caucus, "Jewish Solidarity in Charlottesville," *Jewish Currents*, August 24, 2018, jewishcurrents.org.

3 Diane D'Costa, quoted in Nora Neus, *24 Hours in Charlottesville: An Oral History of the Stand Against White Supremacy* (Boston: Beacon Press, 2023), 63.

4 "Full text: Trump's Comments on White Supremacists, 'Alt-Left' in Charlottesville," *Politico*, August 15, 2017, politico.com.

5 Matthew N. Lyons, *Insurgent Supremacists: The U.S. Far-Right's Challenge to State and Empire* (Oakland: PM Press and Kersplebedeb, 2018), x–xvii.

6 Daniel de Visé, "America's White Majority Is Aging Out," *The Hill*, August 7, 2023, thehill.com.

7 Francis Parker Yockey, *Imperium: The Philosophy of History and Politics* (London: Wermod and Wermod Publishing Group, 2013) , 57.

8 Leonard Zeskind, *Blood and Politics: The History of the White Nationalist Movement from the Margins to the Mainstream* (New York: Farrar Straus Giroux, 2009), 22.

9 See Eric Ward, "Skin in the Game: How Antisemitism Animates White Nationalism," *Political Research Associates*, June 29, 2017, politicalresearch.org.

10 Alex Haley, "Alex Haley Interviews George Lincoln Rockwell (Republish),"
    Alex Haley, alexhaley.com. These views weren't held by Rockwell alone—
    they were championed by white reactionaries across the country, desper-
    ate to beat back Black-led challenges to the supremacist racial order.

11 Jeffrey Kaplan and Leonard Weinberg, *The Emergence of a Euro-American
    Radical Right* (New Brunswick, NJ: Rutgers University Press, 1998), 118–120.

12 Zoe Hyman, "Transatlantic White Supremacy: American Segregationists
    and International Racism After Civil Rights," in *Global White Nationalism:
    From Apartheid to Trump*, ed. Daniel Geary, Camilla Schofield, and Jennifer
    Sutton (Manchester, UK: Manchester University Press, 2020), 192–204.

13 Elinor Langer, *A Hundred Little Hitlers: The Death of a Black Man, the Trial of
    a White Racist, and the Rise of the Neo-Nazi Movement in America* (New York:
    Metropolitan Books, 2003), 9–35.

14 Dylan Weir, "Displacement and Replacement: The Political History of
    David Duke, Patrick Buchanan, and Racial Resentment," *Journal of Hate
    Studies* 18, no.1 (2023), 1–15.

15 Pat Buchanan quoted in John Ganz, "The Year the Clock Broke: How the
    World We Live in Already Happened in 1992," *The Baffler*, November 2018,
    thebaffler.com.

16 Howard Kurtz, "Pat Buchanan the Jewish Question," *The Washington
    Post*, September 20, 1990; Heidi Beirich, "Pat Buchanan Pens Exclusive for
    Anti-Semitic Publication," Southern Poverty Law Center, April 29, 2015,
    splcenter.org. In chapter 9, we distinguish this antisemitic conspiracy from
    a principled critique of US support for Israel and its unjust oppression of
    Palestinians.

17 Joseph Sobran, "'For Fear of the Jews,'" *Institute for Historical Review*, ac-
    cessed September 11, 2023; "The Jewish Question Redux," Southern Pov-
    erty Law Center, August 11, 2006, splcenter.org.

18 "Sam Francis," Southern Poverty Law Center, accessed September 11, 2023,
    splcenter.org.

19 Deborah Lipstadt, *Denying the Holocaust: The Growing Assault on Truth and
    Memory* (New York: Plume, 1994), 183–201.

20 Ibid, 179–181.

21 José Pedro Zúquete, *The Identitarians: The Movement Against Globalism and
    Islam in Europe* (Notre Dame, IN: Notre Dame Press, 2018), 146–56; Mathias
    Hee Pedersen, "Identitarianism in Denmark," in *Global Identitarianism*, ed.
    Jose Pedro Zuquete and Riccardo Marchi (London: Routledge, 2023), 39.

22 Kevin MacDonald, *A People That Shall Dwell Alone: Judaism as a Group Evolu-
    tionary Strategy, with Diaspora Peoples* (New York: Writers Club Press, 2002), 95.

23 Quoted in Ben Lorber, "'America First Is Inevitable' Nick Fuentes, the
    Groyper Army, and the Mainstreaming of White Nationalism," Political
    Research Associates, January 15, 2021, politicalresearch.org.

24 Robert A. Pape, *Understanding American Domestic Terrorism: Mobilization
    Potential and Risk Factors of a New Threat Trajectory* (Chicago: University of
    Chicago Project on Security and Threats, 2021).

25 "Views on Great Replacement Theory | YouGov Poll: June 1–5, 2022," You-Gov, June 7, 2022, yougov.com.

26 Eitan D. Hersh and Laura Royden, "Antisemitic Attitudes across the Ideological Spectrum," *Political Research Quarterly* 76, no. 2 (June 25, 2022): 697–711.

EIGHT. A CHRISTIAN NATION:
ANTISEMITISM AND THE CHRISTIAN RIGHT

1 Michael Flynn quoted in Brad Bull, "Michael Flynn Says America Needs 'One Religion Under God,'" *Baptist News Global*, November 15, 2021, baptistnews.com.

2 Sean Quinn, "Hard Support vs. Soft Support," *FiveThirtyEight*, July 15, 2008, fivethirtyeight.com.

3 Sarah Pulliam Bailey, "White Evangelicals Voted Overwhelmingly for Donald Trump, Exit Polls Show," *The Washington Post*, November 9, 2022. This polling puts the white evangelical support for Trump 2 percent higher than for George W. Bush, who was himself a white evangelical, and loudly proclaimed his faith during his campaign.

4 Randall Balmer, "The Real Origins of the Religious Right," *Politico*, May 27, 2014, politico.com.

5 See Andrew Gow, "The Myth of the Jewish Antichrist: Falwell Stumbles Badly," *Origins: Current Events in Historical Perspective*, February 1999, origins.osu.edu; Martin Schram, "Jerry Falwell Vows Amity with Israel," *The Washington Post*, September 12, 1981; James Warren, "Nixon, Graham Anti-Semitism on Tape," *Chicago Tribune*, March 1, 2002; Jacob Heilbrunn, "His Anti-Semitic Sources," *The New York Review of Books*, April 20, 1995; Shane Burley, "A Friend of the Jews," *The Maiseh Review*, July 31, 2023, maiseh-review.ghost.io; Jeffrey Goldberg, "I, Antichrist?", *The Atlantic*, November 5, 1999, theatlantic.com.

6 Bailey Smith quoted in David E. Anderson, "Head of Moral Majority Says God Hears Jewish Prayers," *United Press International*, October 10, 1980.

7 Megan Rosenfeld, "The New Moral America and the War of the Religicos," *The Washington Post*, August 24, 1980.

8 *In U.S., Decline of Christianity Continues at Rapid Pace* (Washington, D.C.: 2019), 9.

9 Frederick Clarkson, "Christian Nationalism and Donald Trump," Political Research Associates, April 6, 2018, politicalresearch.org.

10 Rachel Tabachnick, "The Christian Right, Reborn: The New Apostolic Reformation Goes to War," *Public Eye* 75 (Spring 2013): 8.

11 Liz Rutan Ram quoted in "Tennessee Jewish Couple Discriminated Against by Foster Care Agency Sues Tenn. Dept. of Children's Services," Americans United for Separation of Church and State, January 19, 2022, au.org.

12 Robert P. Jones et al., *Increasing Support for Religiously Based Service Refusals* (Washington, D.C.: Public Religion Research Institute, 2019), 11–12. Most of

these percentages are a marked increase from the same survey in 2014.

13 Ephraim Sherman, "Striking Down *Roe v. Wade* Will Violate Jewish Religious Liberty," *Forward*, May 3, 2022, forward.com. This is why, in June 2022, Congregation L'Dor Va-Dor in Palm Beach County sued the State of Florida, after the state shortened its cutoff date for abortion procedures from twenty-four weeks to fifteen following the overturning of *Roe v. Wade*. Eliza Fawcett, "Synagogue Sues Florida, Saying Abortion Restrictions Violate Religious Freedoms," *The New York Times*, June 16, 2022.

14 Dania Rajendra, "Anti-Semitism and White Nationalism" (lecture, Jewish Community Action, Minneapolis, January 6, 2019).

15 *A Christian Nation? Understanding the Threat of Christian Nationalism to American Democracy and Culture* (Washington, D.C.: Public Religion Research Institute and The Brookings Institution, 2023), 5, 8, 19.

16 Paul A. Djupe and Jacob Dennen, "Christian Nationalists and Qanon Followers Tend to be Anti-Semitic. That Was Seen in the Capitol Attack," *The Washington Post*, January 26, 2021.

17 Aila Slisco, "Marjorie Taylor Greene Defends Nationalist Speech as 'She Is a Nazi' Trends," *Newsweek*, July 25, 2022, newsweek.com; Thomas Kika, "Marjorie Taylor Greene to GOP: 'We Should be Christian Nationalists,'" *Newsweek*, July 24, 2022, newsweek.com.

18 Steven Gardiner, "End Times Antisemitism: Christian Zionism, Christian Nationalism, and the Threat to Democracy," Political Research Associates, July 9, 2020, politicalresearch.org.

19 "A Night to Honor Israel - LIVE from Cornerstone Church - Sunday October 22nd 2023," OfficialCUFI, video, 38:21-45, 35:38-58, 48:38-56, October 22, 2023, youtube.com.

20 "Watch: 'March for Israel' rally held at National Mall, Washington D.C.," USA Today, video, 2:23:37-55, November 14, 2023, youtube.com.

21 Jonathan Brenneman, quoted in "Building Broad Coalitions: A Roundtable on Confronting Christian Zionism," Political Research Associates, July 6, 2022, politicalresearch.org.

22 Joel C. Rosenberg, *Evangelical Attitudes toward Israel Research Study* (New York: Chosen People Ministries, 2017), 3. Cited in Gardiner, "End Times Antisemitism." Support for Israel may be slipping for younger Evangelicals—one 2021 survey found that support for Israel among young evangelicals dropped to 34 percent, from 75 percent in 2018. Shibley Telhami, "As Israel Increasingly Relies on US Evangelicals for Support, Younger Ones Are Walking Away: What Polls Show," The Brookings Institution, May 21, 2021, brookings.edu.

23 Jerry Falwell quoted in Sean Durbin, *Righteous Gentiles: Religion, Identity, and Myth in John Hagee's Christians United for Israel* (Leiden, NL: Brill Publishers, Studies in Critical Research on Religion, 2018), 39.

24 S. Jonathon O'Donnell, "Antisemitism Under Erasure: Christian Zionist Anti-Globalism and the Refusal of Cohabitation," *Ethnic and Racial Studies* 44, no. 1 (2021): 44.

25   Rachel Tabachnick, "Hagee vs. Hagee—In His Own Words," Talk2Action, May 21, 2010, talk2action.org.

26   Thomas C. Fox, "Lefebvre Movement: Long, Troubled History with Judaism," *National Catholic Reporter*, January 26, 2009, ncronline.org; Heidi Beirich, "Radical Traditionalist Catholics Spew Anti-Semitic Hate, Commit Violence Against Jews," Southern Poverty Law Center, January 16, 2007, splcenter.org.

27   Mark Weitzman, "Antisemitism and the Radical Catholic Traditionalist Movement," in *Deciphering the New Antisemitism*, ed. Alvin H. Rosenfeld (Bloomington: Indiana University Press, 2016), 242–274; Heidi Beirich, "Radical Powerhouse," Southern Poverty Law Center, 2015, splcenter.org.

28   Michael Warren, "Catholic group disrupts Kristallnacht ceremony in Argentina," *The Times of Israel*, November 14, 2013, timesofisrael.com.

29   Annika Brockschmidt, "The White Nationalist Fringe Just Took a Giant Step Closer to the Center of the GOP," *Religion Dispatches*, March 31, 2022, religiondispatches.org.

30   Michael Barkun, *Religion and the Racist Right: The Origins of the Christian Identity Movement* (Chapel Hill: The University of North Carolina Press, 1996), 149–190.

31   James Ridgeway, *Blood in the Face: The Ku Klux Klan, Aryan Nations, Nazi Skinheads, and the Rise of a New White Culture* (New York: Basic Books, 1995), 140–149.

32   Alex DiBranco, "The Long History of the Anti Abortion Movement's Links to White Supremacists," *The Nation*, February 3, 2020, thenation.com.

33   "Anti-Semitism Evident Among Anti-Abortion Extremists," Feminist Majority Foundation, November 3, 1998, feminist.org.

34   See Mattias Gardell, *Gods of the Blood: The Pagan Revival and White Separatism* (Durham: Duke University Press, 2003).

35   Gil Hochberg, "'Remembering Semitism' or 'On the Prospect of Re-Membering the Semites,'" *ReOrient* 1, No. 2 (2016): 196.

36   Shalom Goldman, "What Do We Mean by 'Judeo-Christian'?," *Religion Dispatches*, February 15, 2011, religiondispatches.org.

37   *The 2020 Census of American Religion* (Washington, D.C.: Public Religion Research Institute, 2021), 42.

38   *A Christian Nation? Understanding the Threat of Christian Nationalism to American Democracy and Culture* (Washington, D.C.: Public Religion Research Institute and the Brookings Institution 2023), 6.

39   Josh Mandel quoted in Martin Pengelly, "Trump Ally Michael Flynn Condemned Over Call for 'One Religion' in US," *The Guardian*, November 15, 2021, theguardian.com. Incidentally, Mandel himself, months earlier, was the target of an antisemitic attack ad from another GOP candidate, Mike Pukita, which asked "Are we seriously supposed to believe the most Christian-values Senate candidate is Jewish? I am so sick of these phony caricatures." Shira Hanau, "Candidate Mark Pukita Defends Ad Calling Out Opponent Josh Mandel's Jewishness," *The Jewish Chronicle*, November 17, 2021, thejc.com.

40 Eliyahu Stern, "Anti-Semitism and Orthodoxy in the Age of Trump," *Tablet*, March 12, 2019, tabletmag.com. See also David H. Schraub, "Liberal Jews and Religious Liberty," *New York University Law Review* 98 (March 2023).

41 Rudy Giuliani quoted in Veronica Stracqualursi, "Giuliani Claims He's 'More of a Jew' than Holocaust Survivor George Soros," CNN, December 25, 2019, cnn.com.

42 April Rosenblum, "Trump and Giuliani's Crude, Coercive and Conditional 'Love' for Jews," *Haaretz*, January 26, 2020, haaretz.com.

43 Julia Mueller, "Trump Blasted for Telling American Jews to 'Get Their Act Together,'" *The Hill*, October 16, 2022, thehill.com.

44 Tzvi Joffre, "GOP Candidate Doug Mastriano's Wife: 'We Love Israel More Than Jews,'" *The Jerusalem Post*, October 30, 2022, jpost.com.

NINE. LOOKING AT ANTISEMITISM
AND ISRAEL/PALESTINE

1 Fayez Sayegh, "Zionist Colonialism in Palestine (1965)," *Settler Colonial Studies* 2, no.1 (2012): 206–225.

2 Kenneth W. Stein, *The Land Question in Palestine, 1917–1939* (Chapel Hill: University of North Carolina Press, 1984); Geoffrey Wheatcroft, "Zionism's Colonial Roots," *The National Interest*, no. 125 (2013): 9–15; Joseph Massad, "Jewish National Fund: A Century of Land Theft, Belligerence and Erasure," *Middle East Eye*, February 1, 2023, middleeasteye.net.

3 For a discussion of the exclusionary character of the early Zionist labor organization the Histadrut, see Haim Hanegbi, "The Histadrut: Union and Boss" in *The Other Israel: The Radical Case Against Zionism*, ed. Arie Bober (New York: Doubleday & Co, 1972); Steven A. Glazer, "Language of Propaganda: The Histadrut, Hebrew Labor, and the Palestinian Worker," *Journal of Palestine Studies* 36, no. 2 (Winter 2007): 25–38.

4 Abe Silberstein, "A Logic of Elimination," *Jewish Currents*, January 11, 2022, jewishcurrents.org.

5 Ramzy Baroud, "How Britain Destroyed the Palestinian Homeland," *Al Jazeera*, April 10, 2018.

6 Peter Beinart, "Palestinian Refugees Deserve to Return Home. Jews Should Understand," *The New York Times*, May 12, 2021.

7 Nathan Citino, Ana Martín Gil, and Kelsey P. Norman, "Generations of Palestinian Refugees Face Protracted Displacement and Dispossession," Migration Policy Institute, May 3, 2023, migrationpolicy.org.

8 "Policy on the Right of Return: Treatment and Rights in Arab Host States," Human Rights Watch, hrw.org.

9 "The Discriminatory Laws Database," Adalah: The Legal Center for Arab Minority Rights in Israel, September 25, 2017, adalah.org.

10 "Israel's Apartheid Against Palestinians: A Look Into Decades of Oppression and Domination," Amnesty International, February 2022, amnesty.

org; "A Regime of Jewish Supremacy from the Jordan River to the Mediterranean Sea: This Is Apartheid," B'Tselem, January 12, 2021, btselem.org.

11   "Gaza: Israel's 'Open-Air Prison' at 15," Human Rights Watch, June 14, 2022, hrw.org.

12   Ella Shohat, "Sephardim in Israel: Zionism from the Standpoint of its Jewish Victims," *Social Text* 19/20 (1988): 2.

13   Ella Shohat, "Rupture and Return: Zionist Discourse and the Study of Arab Jews," *Social Text* 21 no.2 (2003): 50, 62.

14   "Senate Session," CSPAN, video, 1:27:15, June 5, 1986, c-span.org; "US President Joe Biden: 'If There Were Not an Israel, We'd Have to Invent One,'" *Middle East Eye*, October 28, 2022, middleeasteye.net.

15   Theodor Herzl, *The Jewish State* (New York: American Zionist Emergency Council, 1946) 96.

16   *The Palestine Exception to Free Speech* (New York: Palestine Legal and the Center for Constitutional Rights, 2015); *Stifling Dissent: How Israel's Defenders Use False Charges of Anti-Semitism to Limit the Debate Over Israel on Campus* (Oakland: Jewish Voice for Peace, 2015).

17   Alex Kane, "The FBI Is Using Unvetted, Right-Wing Blacklists to Question Activists About Their Support for Palestine," *The Intercept*, June 24, 2018, theintercept.com; "The Firing of Steven Salaita: Palestine Solidarity & Academic Freedom," Center for Constitutional Rights, January 29, 2015, ccrjustice.org; Ed Pilkington, "University Denies Tenure to Outspoken Holocaust Academic," *The Guardian*, June 12, 2007, theguardian.com; Colleen Flaherty, "Another Broken Promise," *Inside Higher Ed*, March 21, 2022, insidehighered.com.

18   Hebh Jamal, "Germany Just Took a Drastic Step Toward Criminalizing Palestine Activism," +972 *Magazine*, December 21, 2022, 972mag.com; Alex Kane, "What the Fossil Fuel Industry Learned from Anti-BDS Laws," *Jewish Currents*, April 4, 2022, jewishcurrents.org.

19   Kate Brady, Anthony Faiola, Emily Rauhala, Karla Adam and Beatriz Ríos, "European bans on pro-Palestinian protests prompt claims of bias," *The Washington Post*, October 26, 2023, washingtonpost.com.

20   Elad Nehorai, "The Right's Selective Outrage on Antisemitism is a Scam," *The Daily Beast*, March 14, 2022, thedailybeast.com.

21   Benjamin Balthaser, "The New Anti-Dreyfusards: Zionism and State Antisemitism in the West," *Spectre Journal*, April 16, 2023, spectrejournal.com.

22   Talia Lavin, "When Non-Jews Wield Anti-Semitism as Political Shield," *GQ*, July 17, 2019, gq.com.

23   "John McDonnell: Labour Treatment of Jewish Group Brutal," BBC News, July 27, 2022, bbc.com.

24   Tareq Baconi, "A Colonized Palestine Isn't the Answer to the World's Guilt," +972 *Magazine*, June 20, 2022, 972mag.com.

25   Peter Beinart, "How to Oppose Pro-Palestinian Antisemitism," *The Beinart Notebook*, November 7, 2023, peterbeinart.substack.com.

26   Brian Klug, "The Collective Jew: Israel and the New Antisemitism," *Pat-*

terns of Prejudice 37, no. 2 (2003).

27 Izabella Tabarovsky, "Demonization Blueprints: Soviet Conspiracist Antizionism in Contemporary Left-Wing Discourse," *Journal of Contemporary Antisemitism* 5, no.1 (August 2022): 1–20.

28 Of course, the U.S.S.R. dissolved over a decade before most college students today were even born, and older generations may hear echoes of Soviet anti-Zionism that Gen-Z and millennials don't notice or intend.

29 Rashmee Kumar, "The Network of Hindu Nationalists Behind Modi's "Diaspora Diplomacy" in the U.S.," *The Intercept*, September 25, 2019, theintercept.com.

30 Aparna Gopalan, "The Hindu Nationalists Using the Pro-Israel Playbook," *Jewish Currents*, June 28, 2023, jewishcurrents.org.

31 Daniel Randall, "Do not "defend David Miller"," *Workers' Liberty*, October 12, 2021, www.workersliberty.org.

32 Daniel Randall, "David Miller's Antisemitic Ideology," *The Social Review*, August 21, 2023, thesocialreview.co.uk.

33 John Mearsheimer and Stephen Walt, "The Israel Lobby," *The London Review of Books*, March 23, 2006, lrb.co.uk.

34 "Noam Chomsky—Why Does the U.S. Support Israel?," Chomsky's Philosophy, video, July 2, 2016, youtube.com.

35 Balthaser, "The New Anti-Dreyfusards."

36 Josh Reubner, Salih Booker, and Zaha Hassan, "Bringing Assistance to Israel in Line with Rights and U.S. Laws," Carnegie Endowment for International Peace, May 12, 2021, carnegieendowment.org.

37 David Duke, "Dr Duke & Dr Slattery—The Zionist Treason of ZOG driving America into the Ultimate Catastrophe of War for Israel Against Iran!," DavidDuke.com, January 8, 2020.

38 Shane Burley, "How the far right is trying to manipulate the crisis in Gaza," *Waging Nonviolence*, November 1, 2023, wagingnonviolence.org.

39 Alison Weir, "The History of US-Israel Relations—Against Our Better Judgment: The Hidden History of How the United States Was Used to Create Israel," If Americans Knew, February 28, 2014, ifamericansknew.org.

40 "Israel Lobby Organizations," If Americans Knew, accessed September 11, 2023, ifamericansknew.org.

41 "Statement on Complaint Filed Regarding Alison Weir and If Americans Knew," US Campaign for Palestinian Rights, uscpr.org.

42 Jonah Boyarin, "AIPAC Isn't the Whole Story," *Jewish Currents*, March 4, 2019, jewishcurrents.org.

43 Gilad Atzmon, *The Wandering Who?: A Study of Jewish Identity Politics* (Winchester, UK: Zero Books, 2012), 121.

44 "Granting No Quarter: A Call for the Disavowal of the Racism and Antisemitism of Gilad Atzmon," US Palestinian Community Network, March 13, 2012, uspcn.org.

45 Using Jewish religious and cultural iconography, such as the Star of David or a menorah, as stand-in symbols for Israel, without qualification, when criticizing the state is never a good idea—even while Israel uses this imag-

ery in its own self-representation, from its flag to its coinage.

46 Daniel Randall, "Challenging Anti-Semitism on Gaza Demonstrations," *Workers' Liberty*, July 28, 2014, workersliberty.org.

47 Brian Klug, "The Collective Jew: Israel and the New Antisemitism," *Patterns of Prejudice* 37, no. 2 (2003): 18–19.

48 Shiryn Ghermezian, "Swastika, 'Free Palestine' Graffiti Spray-Painted on Door of UK Synagogue," *Algemeiner*, May 14, 2021, algemeiner.com; Shawna Chen and Gigi Sukin, "Latest Gaza Conflict Fuels Anti-Semitism, Islamophobia Across U.S., Europe," *Axios*, May 21, 2021, axios.com.

49 Jen Mills, "Convoy Drives Through London Shouting 'F**k the Jews, Rape Their Daughters,'" *Metro*, May 16, 2021, metro.co.uk; Shane Burley, "The Left Feels Palestinian Pain. It Must Also Recognize Jewish Fears," *Haaretz*, May 30, 2021, haaretz.com.

50 Isaac Deutscher, "On the Israeli-Arab War," *New Left Review* 1, no.44 (July/August 1967).

51 Smadar Lavie, "Mizrahi Feminism and the Question of Palestine," *Journal of Middle East Women's Studies* 7, no. 2 (Spring 2011): 57; Clare Louis Ducker, "Jews, Arabs, and Arab Jews: The Politics of Identity and Reproduction in Israel," *Institute of Social Studies* 421 (2006).

52 Waleed Shahid, "What We Talk About When We Talk About Gaza," *The Forge*, October 24, 2023, forgeorganizing.org.

53 Natasha Roth-Rowland, "Is the 'Antisemitism Crisis' on US College Campuses Real?," +972 *Magazine*, June 28, 2023, 972mag.com; Ben Sales, "Jewish Students Dismiss Claims Hunter College 'Pervasively Hostile' to Them," *The Jerusalem Post*, November 18, 2021, jpost.com; Ari Kelman et al., *Safe and On the Sidelines: Jewish Students and the Israel/Palestine Conflict on Campus* (Stanford: Stanford University Graduate School of Education, 2017); Graham Wright, Michelle Shain, Shahar Hecht, and Leonard Saxe, *The Limits of Hostility: Students Report on Antisemitism and anti-Israel Sentiment at Four US Universities* (Waltham, MA: Cohen Center for Modern Jewish Studies, 2017).

54 *The Jerusalem Declaration on Antisemitism* (Jerusalem: JDA, May 25, 2021), jerusalemdeclaration.org.

55 Lara Sheehi, "On Targeting an Arab Woman," *Jadaliyya*, February 12, 2023, jadaliyya.com.

56 Michael Richmond, "Anti-Racism as Procedure," *Protocols* 8 (2020).

TEN. A SAFETY OF NATIONALISM?
ANTISEMITISM AND THE HISTORY OF ZIONISM

1 Karl Marx, "The Eighteenth Brumaire of Louis Bonaparte," in *Karl Marx: Selected Writings*, ed. Lawrence H. Simon (Indianapolis: Hackett Publishing Company, 1994), 188.

2 Quoted in Jeremy Sharon, "The Rage of Anti-Zionism: When Jews Are Targeted for Israel's Actions," *The Jerusalem Post*, May 27, 2021, jpost.com.

3   Keith Kahn-Harris (@KeithKahnHarris), "All right I'll bite: Even if you assume that antisemitism is simply a reaction to things Jews do and believe—which, rest assured, I do not—no social phenomenon is simply 'reversible'. Racism has its own dynamic that persists beyond its origins . . . ," Twitter, May 22, 2021, 1:55 p.m.

4   Alain Badiou, Eric Hazan, and Ivan Segré, *Reflections on Anti-Semitism* (New York: Verso, 2013), 13.

5   "American Jewish Committee Surveys French Jewish, Muslim, and General Populations' Perspectives on Antisemitism," American Jewish Committee, February 2, 2022; Gunther Jikeli, "Antisemitism Among Young European Muslims," in *Resurgent Antisemitism: Global Perspectives*, ed. Alvin Rosenfeld (Bloomington: Indiana University Press, 2013), 272, 278–288.

6   Jeffrey Herf, "Nazi Propaganda to the Arab World During World War II and the Emergence of Islamism," in *Global Antisemitism: A Crisis of Modernity, Volume IV*, ed. Charles Asher Small (Miami Beach: Institute for the Study of Global Antisemitism and Policy, 2013), 82.

7   Matthias Küntzel, "Nazi Propaganda in the Middle East and its Repercussions in the Postwar Period," in *Comprehending Antisemitism Through the Ages: A Historical Perspective*, ed. Armin Lange, Kerstin Mayerhofer, Dina Porat, Lawrence H. Schiffman (Berlin: De Gruyter, 2021), 263–7.

8   Ella Shohat, "Rupture and Return: Zionist Discourse and the Study of Arab Jews," *Social Text* 21, no. 2 (2003): 57.

9   "Hamas: Charter (August 1988)," in *The Israel-Arab Reader: A Documentary History of the Middle East Conflict*, ed. Walter Laqueur and Barry Rubin (New York: Penguin Random House, 2001), 344. In 2017, Hamas revised its charter. The revised charter claimed that their struggle is against the "Zionist project . . . not with the Jews because of their religion." Joshua Mitnick and Rushdi Abu Alouf, "A Revised Hamas Charter Will Moderate Its Stance Toward Israel—Slightly," *Los Angeles Times*, May 1, 2017. The Palestinian liberation movement has often rebuked these ideas. In 1970, the Palestine Liberation Organization (PLO) commissioned a study on the Talmud, publishing an Arabic-language monograph defending it against antisemitic slander. Initiatives like these asserted that their struggle lay not against Jews or Judaism, but against the policies of expulsion and disenfranchisement carried out by Israel against Palestinians. Jonathan Marc Gribetz, "The PLO's Defense of the Talmud," *AJS Review—The Journal of the Association for Jewish Studies* 42, no. 2 (November 1, 2018): 293–314.

10   Moishe Postone, "History and Helplessness: Mass Mobilization and Contemporary Forms of Anticapitalism," *Public Culture* 18, no. 1 (January 1, 2006): 93–110, 101.

11   Ibid, 102.

12   Peter Beinart, "There Is a Jewish Hope for Palestinian Liberation. It Must Survive," *The New York Times*, October 14, 2023, nytimes.com.

13   James Baldwin, "Negroes Are Anti-Semitic Because They're Anti-White," *The New York Times*, April 9, 1967.

14 Quoted in Joseph Telushkin, *Jewish Literacy: The Most Important Things to Know About the Jewish Religion, Its People, and Its History* (New York: Harper Collins, 2001) 261.

15 Hayyim Bialik, "In The City of Slaughter," in *Complete Poetic Works of Hayyim Nahman Bialik Translated From the Hebrew, Volume 1*, trans. Israel Efros (New York: Histadruth Ivrith of America, Inc, 1948), 129–43.

16 Hayyim Bialik quoted in Daniel Gordis, *Israel: A Concise History of a Nation Reborn* (New York: Harper Collins, 2016), 50. Gordis goes on to say that "the exile of the Jew from his own land, Bialik claimed, has more than robbed the Jew of his strength and his courage. It has eroded his capacity to feel. Exile has destroyed them . . . The Jewish tradition, Bialik essentially says, is a cancer that has destroyed the Jew's humanity." Bialik's charge also reflects the antisemitic notion of Jewish men as effeminate.

17 Leon Pinsker, *Auto-Emancipation* (New York: The Maccabaean Publishing Company, 1906), 3, 7, 10.

18 Theodor Herzl, "Mauschel," *Die Welt*, October 15, 1897, in *Zionist Writings and Addresses: January 1896–June 1898*, Volume 1, trans. Harry Zohn (New York: Herzl Press, 1973), 163.

19 Susie Linfield, *The Lions' Den: Zionism and the Left from Hannah Arendt to Noam Chomsky* (New Haven: Yale University Press, 2019,) 87. Before Herzl settled on political Zionism, one of his first ideas for the solution of the "Jewish question" in Europe involved mass Jewish conversion to Christianity. In his diary, he outlined a proposal to assemble the Jews "in broad daylight . . . with festive processions" outside St. Stephen's Cathedral in Vienna, in a ceremony "sealed," as author Jacques Kornberg put it, "by a historic alliance with the Pope." Jacques Kornberg, *Theodore Herzl: From Assimilation to Zionism* (Indianapolis: Indiana University Press, 1993), 116.

20 James Horrox, *A Living Revolution: Anarchism in the Kibbutz Movement* (Chico, CA: AK Press, 2009), 26.

21 Daniel Boyarin, *Unheroic Conduct: The Rise of Heterosexuality and the Invention of the Jewish Man* (Berkeley: University of California Press, 1997), 271–313.

22 Theodore Herzl, *The Complete Diaries of Theodor Herzl Vol 1*, trans. Harry Zohn (New York: Herzl Press, 1960), 6, 84.

23 Quoted in Derek J. Penslar, "Anti-Semites on Zionism: From Indifference to Obsession," *Journal of Israeli History* 25, no. 1 (March 2006): 16.

24 Brian Klug, "The Collective Jew: Israel and the New Antisemitism," *Patterns of Prejudice* 37, no. 2 (2003): 8–11.

25 Enzo Traverso, *The Jewish Question: History of a Marxist Debate* (Chicago: Haymarket Books, 2019), xvii.

26 Hannah Rose, *The New Philosemitism: Exploring a Changing Relationship Between Jews and the Far-Right* (London: International Centre for the Study of Radicalisation, 2020).

27 Barnaby Raine, "Jewophobia," *Salvage* 6 (November 2018): 96, 100. Emphasis in original.

28 Amar Tibon, "Steve Bannon to Speak at Annual Zionist Organization of America Gala: 'He's So Pro-Israel,'" *Haaretz*, August 28, 2017, haaretz.com.

29 AFP, JTA, and Jeremy Sharon, "Musk tours Gaza border kibbutz with PM, says 'no choice' but for Israel to destroy Hamas," *The Times of Israel*, November 27, 2023, timesofisrael.com.

30 Zack Beauchamp, "Benjamin Netanyahu blames the Holocaust on a Palestinian mufti. That's ludicrous.," *Vox*, October 21, 2015, vox.com.

31 Matt Lebovic, "'Alien Reptile' and Cloaked Figure in Yair Netanyahu's Meme Have Old-New Origins," *The Times of Israel*, September 11, 2017, timesofisrael.com.

32 Ts. Lakhman, "Oy, Ir Narishe Tsionistn/Oh, You Foolish Little Zionists," collected by Moshe Beregovsky, republished in *Old Jewish Folk Music: The Collections and Writings of Moshe Beregovski*, ed. Mark Slobin (Syracuse: Syracuse University Press, 2000). This song was brought to our attention from the album *The Unternationale*. Daniel Kahn, Psoy Korolenko, Oy Division, "Oy Ir Narishe Tsienistn," track 2 on *The Unternationale: The First Unternational*, Auris Media, 2008, compact disc.

ELEVEN. GENERATIONS OF TRAUMA:
HEALING FROM ANTISEMITISM'S SCARS

1 Jo Kent Kaz, "Unpacking Trauma," Transcending Jewish Trauma, accessed December 4, 2023, transcendingjewishtrauma.com.

2 Arielle Angel, "Beyond Grievance," *Jewish Currents*, September 6, 2022, jewishcurrents.org.

3 Quoted in Katz, "Unpacking Trauma."

4 Angel, "Beyond Grievance."

5 This refrain, heard regularly in some Palestine solidarity circles, mixes disdain for Jews with an uncritical acceptance of the categories of discredited European colonial race science. As discussed, "Semitic" is a name for a family of languages, including Hebrew and Arabic. The term "Semites" was misleadingly crafted as an imagined racial category by nineteenth-century European elites, as a contrast to the superior (and similarly imaginary) "Aryans." These elites coined the term "antisemitism" to express a new form of modern Jew hatred. There is no such thing as a "Semitic people," and it remains appropriate to use the term "antisemitism" to refer to hatred of Jews specifically.

6 Arielle Angel, "'We Cannot Cross Until We Carry Eachother'," *Jewish Currents*, October 12, 2023, jewishcurrents.org.

7 Yotam Marom, "Toward the Next Jewish Rebellion: Facing Anti-Semitism and Assimilation in the Movement," Medium, August 9, 2016. Accessed October 12, 2022, medium.com.

TWELVE. INTERSECTING OPPRESSIONS: CONNECTING THE THREATS WE FACE

1   Eric Ward, "Skin in the Game: How Antisemitism Animates White Nation-alism," Political Research Associates, June 29, 2017, politicalresearch.org.

2   Eric Ward quoted in "Exploring Hate: How Antisemitism Fuels White Na-tionalism," PBS, October 24, 2021, pbs.org.

3   Combahee River Collective, "From 'A Black Feminist Statement' (1977)," in *Remaking Radicalism: A Grassroots Documentary Reader of the United States, 1973–2001,* ed. Dan Berger and Emily K. Hobson (Athens: University of Georgia Press, 2020), 27.

4   Kimberlé Crenshaw, "Demarginalizing the Intersection of Race and Sex: A Black Feminist Critique of Antidiscrimination Doctrine, Feminist Theory and Antiracist Politics," *University of Chicago Legal Forum* 1989, no. 1 (1989): 140.

5   Zoe Baker, "'Identity Politics Divides The Left'—A Response," *Anarchopac,* anarchopac.com.

6   Ward, "Skin in the Game."

7   Payton Gendron, *What You Need to Know* (self-published, 2022), 24.

8   Ibid, 53.

9   Ibid, 12.

10 Kevin MacDonald, *The Culture of Critique: An Evolutionary Analysis of Jewish Involvement in Twentieth Century Intellectual and Political Movements* (West-port, CT: Praeger Publishers, 1998), 254.

11 Clive Webb, "Counterblast: How the Atlanta Temple Bombing Strengthened the Civil Rights Cause," Southern Spaces, June 22, 2009, southernspaces.org.

12 "Hunting Communists? They Were Really After Jews," *The Jewish Chroni-cle,* August 6, 2009, thejc.com.

13 Shane Burley, "The Great 2020 Antifa Scare," Political Research Associ-ates, July 13, 2021, politicalresearch.org; "Right-Wing Conspiracists Pull From Old Playbook: Blame George Soros for Riots," *Forbes,* March 30, 2020, forbes.com.

14 Hannah Arendt, "Race-Thinking Before Racism," *The Review of Politics* 6, no. 1 (January 1944): 36–73. Scholar Magda Teter has claimed that antisemi-tism and racism share a common root in the origins of European Christian theology. See Magda Teter, *Christian Supremacy: Reckoning with the Roots of Antisemitism and Racism* (Princeton: Princeton University Press, 2023).

15 Frantz Fanon, *Black Skin, White Masks,* trans. Richard Philcox (New York: Grove Press, 1952), 101.

16 Chanda Prescod-Weinstein (@ibjiyongi), "Anti-Black racism and antisemi-tism are mutually supporting structures. You cannot invest in or uphold the one and expect to escape the other.," Twitter, November 5, 2022, 9:58 p.m.

17 Ben Lorber, "Taking Aim at Multiracial Democracy: Antisemitism, White Nationalism and Anti-Immigrant Racism in the Era of Trump," Political Research Associates, October 22, 2019, politicalresearch.org.

18 These quotas remained in place until the passage of the Immigration and Nationality Act of 1965. Today, white nationalists, as well as prominent anti-immigrant organizations and former Trump administration officials like Attorney General Jeff Sessions, cite the 1924 laws as a blueprint for the draconian immigration restrictions they wish to impose. See Alex Ross, "How American Racism Influenced Hitler," *The New Yorker*, April 23, 2018, newyorker.com; Adam Serwer, "Jeff Sessions's Unqualified Praise for a 1924 Immigration Law," *The Atlantic*, January 10, 2017, theatlantic.com.

19 Erika Lee, *America for Americans: A History of Xenophobia in the United States* (New York: Basic Books, 2019), 144–145.

20 Irving Abella and Harold Troper, *None Is Too Many: Canada and the Jews of Europe 1933–1943* (New York: Random House, 1983).

21 Caroline Kelly, "Ocasio-Cortez Compares Migrant Detention Facilities to Concentration Camps," CNN, June 18, 2019, cnn.com.

22 Jewish Community Relations Council of New York (@JCRCNY), "We urge @AOC to refrain from using terminology evocative of the Holocaust to voice concerns about contemporary political issues, as per our letter below," Twitter, June 18, 2019, 5:11 p.m.

23 Morgan Gstalter, "Liz Cheney Hits Ocasio-Cortez for Concentration Camp Comments: You 'Disgrace Yourself,'" *The Hill*, June 18, 2019, thehill.com.

24 Joseph Wulfsohn, "Pence Rips AOC's 'Concentration Camp' Remarks to Pro-Israel Group, Says They're 'Slander of Law Enforcement," Fox News, July 8, 2019, foxnews.com. Immigrant rights groups, historians, and others insisted that "concentration camps" was a legitimate descriptor of Trump's camps. Andrea Pitzer, "How the Trump Administration's Border Camps Fit into the History of Concentration Camps," *GQ*, June 18, 2019, gq.com.

25 Matt Lavietes and Elliot Ramos, "Nearly 240 Anti-LGBTQ Bills Filed in 2022 so Far, Most of Them Targeting Trans People," NBC News, March 20, 2022, nbcnews.com.

26 Anne Branigin, "An Idaho Bill Would criminalize Medical Treatments for Trans Youths. It Echoes Abortion Bans," *The Washington Post*, March 11, 2022.

27 Melissa Gira Grant, "A Pizzagate in Every City," *The New Republic*, June 8, 2022, newrepublic.com.

28 Chris Schiano and Dan Feidt, "Patriot Front Fascist Leak Exposes Nationwide Racist Campaigns," *Unicorn Riot*, January 21, 2022, unicornriot.ninja; Odette Yousef, "31 Members of the White Nationalist Patriot Front Arrested Near an Idaho Pride Event," NPR, June 12, 2022, npr.org.

29 Blyth Crawford, *Sleeping With the Enemy: Sex, Sexuality and Antisemitism in the Extreme Right* (London: International Centre for the Study of Radicalisation, 2022), 5–6.

30 Hannah Rose, "The Bratislava Attacks: Insights from the Shooter's Manifesto," Global Network on Extremism and Technology, October 14, 2022, gnet-research.org.

31 Irven M. Resnick, "Medieval Roots of the Myth of Jewish Male Menses," *Harvard Theological Review* 93, no. 3 (July 1, 2000): 241–63.

32 Joni Alizah Cohen, "The Eradication of 'Talmudic Abstractions': Anti-Sem-
    itism, Transmisogyny and the National Socialist Project," Verso, Decem-
    ber 19, 2018, versobooks.com.

33 Jacob Henry, "These Jews are defending Drag Queen Story Hour against
    far-right protestors. Here's why," Jewish Telegraphic Agency, January 6,
    2023, jta.org.

34 Ben Sales, "At JFNA GA, Attendees Confront Division Amid Calls for
    Unity," EJewish Philanthropy, November 2, 2022, ejewishphilanthropy.com.

35 Rabbi Becky Silverstein (@rabbibecky), "Whose lives are made better by
    platforming hate? Our job, as Jews, is to build a world where all people can
    thrive. Who thrives when our federations don't stand up to transphobia
    and other forms of oppression?," Twitter, November 1, 2022, 11:09 a.m.

36 Thomas Escritt, "Alone Before an Invisible Audience: German Gunman
    Lived Online," Reuters, October 10, 2018, reuters.com.

37 Lois Beckett, "Pittsburgh Shooting: Suspect Railed Against Jews and Mus-
    lims on Site Used by 'Alt-Right,'" The Guardian, October 27, 2018, theguard-
    ian.com.

38 "Freelance Journalist Connected to Vandalism at Two Synagogues and
    Mosque, Portland Police Say," KGW8, May 7, 2022, kgw.com.

39 Reza Zia-Ebrahimi, "When the Elders of Zion Relocated to Eurabia: Con-
    spiratorial Racialisation in Antisemitism and Islamophobia," Patterns of
    Prejudice 52, no. 4 (2018): 314–337.

40 Dana Ionescu, "A 'Serious Attack on Jewish Life': Antisemitic Stereotypes
    in the Public Debate About Ritual Male Circumcision in Germany in 2012,"
    in Contending with Antisemitism in a Rapidly Changing Political Climate, ed.
    Alvin H. Rosenfeld (Bloomington: Indiana University Press, 2022), 267–285.

41 Daniel J. Solomon, "Marine Le Pen Says Jews Should 'Sacrifice' Kippah to
    Fight Radical Islam," Forward, February 6, 2017, forward.com; Adam Chan-
    dler, "Marine Le Pen Calls for Kippah Ban," Tablet, September 21, 2012,
    tabletmag.com.

42 Ivan Davidson Kalmar, "Anti-Semitism and Islamophobia: The Formation
    of a Secret," Human Architecture: Journal of the Sociology of Self-Knowledge 7, no.
    2 (Spring 2009): 135–143.

43 Ethan B. Katz, "An Imperial Entanglement: Anti-Semitism, Islamopho-
    bia, and Colonialism," The American Historical Review 123, no. 4 (October 1,
    2018): 1193.

44 Kalmar, "Anti-Semitism and Islamophobia," 135–8. These parallels led
    Palestinian intellectual Edward Said to note, in the introduction to his
    groundbreaking work Orientalism, that "by an almost inescapable logic, I
    have found myself writing the history of a strange secret sharer of Western
    anti-Semitism. That anti-Semitism, and as I have discussed it in its Islamic
    branch, Orientalism resemble each other is a historical, cultural, and po-
    litical truth that needs only be mentioned to an Arab Palestinian for its
    irony to be perfectly understood." Edward W. Said, Orientalism (New York:
    Verso, 1978), 27–28.

45   Katz, "An Imperial Entanglement." The Crémieux Decree was rescinded
      by France's Nazi-allied Vichy regime in 1940, which subjected Jews in the
      French mainland to escalating persecution, and eventual deportation to
      Nazi death camps.

46   Isabel Frey, "The Price of Living Together," *Jewish Currents*, June 26, 2019,
      jewishcurrents.org.

47   Ethan Katz, "How Marine Le Pen Relies on Dividing French Jews and Mus-
      lims," *The Atlantic*, April 19, 2017, theatlantic.com.

48   Dominique Reynié, *Anti-Semitic Attitudes in France: New Insights* (Paris: Fon-
      dation pour l'innovation politique, 2015), 21, 29.

49   "Israel: Fighting for Your Freedom," Naftali Bennett, video, 0:20–0:42, Feb-
      ruary 17, 2015. Israel functions here as what historian Gil Anidjar called "the
      clear continuation of Western Christendom's relation to Islam." Nermeen
      Shaikh, "The Jew, the Arab: An Interview with Gil Anidjar," Asia Society,
      accessed December 4, 2023, asiasociety.org.

50   Elly Bulkin and Donna Nevel, "How Pro-Israel Forces Drove Two Virulent
      Anti-Muslim Campaigns," *Alternet*, September 20, 2013, alternet.org.

THIRTEEN. CONTAINING MULTITUDES: ANTISEMITISM AND THE DIVERSITY OF JEWISH EXPERIENCE

1   Linda Sarsour, "Speech at the Women's March On Washington—Jan. 21,
      2017," Iowa State University Archives of Women's Political Communica-
      tion, January 17, 2017, awpc.cattcenter.iastate.edu.

2   Tamika Mallory, "[EXCLUSIVE] Tamika Mallory Speaks: 'Wherever My
      People Are Is Where I Must Be,'" *Newsone*, March 7, 2018, newsone.com.

3   Adam Serwer, "Why Tamika Mallory Won't Condemn Farrakhan," *The
      Atlantic*, March 11, 2018, theatlantic.com.

4   Sophie Ellman-Golan quoted in Mairav Zonszein, "Women's March Jew-
      ish outreach director: 'Anti-Semitism can be unlearned,'" *+972 Magazine*,
      January 29, 2019, 972mag.com.

5   "Tamika Mallory on Her Appearance on *The View*, the Women's March &
      Tangible Change Within Communities," Breakfast Club Power 105.1 FM,
      video, 11:20–11:45, January 16, 2019. Thanks to Sophie Ellman-Golan for
      sharing this interview with us.

6   Karen Brodkin, *How Jews Became White Folks and What That Says About Race
      in America* (New Brunswick, NJ: Rutgers University Press, 1998).

7   Eric L. Goldstein, *The Price of Whiteness: Jews, Race, and American Identity*
      (Princeton: Princeton University Press, 2006), 189–208.

8   Mark Tseng-Putterman, "More Than a Feeling: Jews and Whiteness in
      Trump's America," *Unruly*, February 23, 2017, jocsm.org. Note: We added
      a comma to the quote from Tseng-Putterman because the text, as it was
      originally written, could easily be misunderstood to indicate that the Slave
      Codes were specifically created to empower European Jews to exploit

Black slaves, rather than granting that privilege to whites as a broad category that, in its formulation, included white Jews.

9   Shari Rabin, "American Jews: How 1789 Created 2019," *The Panorama*, November 4, 2019, the panorama.shear.com.

10 Leonard Rogoff, "Is the Jew White?: The Racial Place of the Southern Jew," *American Jewish History* 85, no 3 (September 1997): 195.

11 Madison Grant, *The Passing of the Great Race, or the Racial Basis of European History* (New York: Charles Scribner's Sons, 1923), 18.

12 "In the post-Holocaust, anti-communist era," writes scholar and activist April Rosenblum, "Jews had compelling reasons to want to blend into the crowd. Both the 'carrot' of upward mobility and the 'sticks' of antisemitic violence and red-baiting motivated American Jews to avoid seeming too foreign, too visible, too 'ethnic.'" April Rosenblum, "Offers We Couldn't Refuse: The Decline of Actively Secular Jewish Identity in the 20th Century US," *Jewish Currents* (May/June 2009): 8–28.

13 Bentley Addison, "Roundtable | White Jews: Here Is What Black Jews Need from You in 2019," *Forward*, December 28, 2018, forward.com.

14 Adolph Reed Jr, "What Color Is Anti-Semitism?" in *Class Notes: Posing as Politics and Other Thoughts on the American Scene* (New York: The New Press, 2001), 34–5.

15 James Baldwin, "Negroes are Anti-Semitic Because They're Anti-White," *The New York Times*, April 9, 1967.

16 Aurora Levins Morales, "Latin@s, Israel and Palestine: Understanding Anti-Semitism," AuroraLevinsMorales.com, March 15, 2012.

17 Baldwin, "Negroes are Anti-Semitic Because They're Anti-White."

18 Will, Chino, Saudade, and Mamos, *How to Overthrow the Illuminati*, (pamphlet, 2013), 1.

19 Patricia A. Turner, *I Heard It Through the Grapevine* (Berkeley: University of California Press, 1994), xvi.

20 William Paul Simmons and Stephen Parsons, "Beliefs in Conspiracy Theories Among African Americans: A Comparison of Elites and Masses," *Social Science Quarterly* 86, no. 3 (September 1, 2005): 582–98.

21 Cloee Cooper and Daryle Lamont Jenkins, "Culture and Belonging in the USA: Multiracial Organizing on the Contemporary Far Right," Political Research Associates, September 3, 2019, politicalresearch.org.

22 Sam McPheeters, "When Malcom X Met the Nazis," *Vice*, April 15, 2015, vice.com.

23 Rebecca Pierce, "'The Jews,'" *On the Nose: A Jewish Currents Podcast*, November 23, 2022, 41:40–55.

24 Shoshana Brown, "Jewish Women of Color Open Letter," JWOCmarching, Medium, January 11, 2019.

25 Soraya Nadia McDonald, "I'm a Jew of Color. I Won't be Quiet About Anti-Semitism.," *Andscape*, July 17, 2020, andscape.com.

26 Tobin Belzer et al., *Beyond the Count: Perspectives and Lived Experiences of Jews of Color* (Berkeley: Jews of Color Initiative, August 12, 2021), ii–vii.

27　Robin Washington, "I Was a Child at a Civil Rights Sit-In. 60 Years Later, What's Changed?," *Forward*, July 19, 2023, forward.com.

28　Quoted in Ben Lorber, "Where Did the Past Go?," *Jewish Currents*, August 26, 2019, jewishcurrents.org. This article inadvertently attributed middle agent theory's popularization to April Rosenblum, who has stated her disagreement with middle agent theory.

29　Fringes that hang below a person's shirt, worn as part of Jewish ritual observance.

30　Yiddish word meaning "hair wrap," typically worn by married Orthodox women.

31　They have also seen some reasonably sharp increases, such as a 41 percent increase in 2022. Haley Cohen, "Hate in New York: Antisemitic Attacks Increased 41% in 2022," *The Jerusalem Post*, January 11, 2023, jpost.com.

32　Yonat Shimron, "Haredi Jews Bear the Brunt of Antisemitic Attacks, Global Report Finds," *Religion News*, April 17, 2023, religionnews.com.

33　Jeremy Sharon, "33% of Those Arrested for Antisemitic Crimes in NYC Were Black, 60% White," *Jerusalem Post*, January 1, 2020, jpost.com.

34　Matt Katz, "Jewish Americans Say They Are Scapegoated for the Coronavirus Spread," NPR, May 13, 2020, npr.org.

35　Ben Lorber, "'Primitive, Diseased Invaders' Threatening America: How Scapegoating Ultra-Orthodox Jews for Coronavirus Mirrors Islamophobia," *Haaretz*, May 5, 2020, haaretz.com.

36　The Hate of Rise Up Ocean County," Rise Up Ocean County Hate, May 17, 2019, ruochate.blogspot.com.

37　Shaina Hammerman, "'My Unorthodox Life' Joins a Long History of Depicting, and Distorting, Orthodox Jews on Stage and Screen," Jewish Telegraphic Agency, August 12, 2021, jta.org.

38　Abrar Al-Heeti, "Netflix's *My Unorthodox Life* Perpetuates Harmful Jewish Stereotypes, Some Say," *CNET*, October 19, 2021, cnet.com.

39　Eliyahu Stern, "Anti-Semitism and Orthodoxy in the Age of Trump," *Tablet*, March 12, 2019, tabletmag.com.

40　Hayyim Rothman, *No Masters but God: Portraits of Anarcho-Judaism* (Manchester, UK: Manchester University Press, 2021), 101–150.

41　April Rosenblum, "Trump and Giuliani's Crude, Coercive and Conditional 'Love' for Jews," *Haaretz*, January 26, 2020, haaretz.com.

42　Zygmunt Bauman, "Jews and Other Europeans, Old and New," *European Judaism: A Journal for the New Europe* 42, no.1 (Spring 2009): 122.

43　Joyce Antler, *Jewish Radical Feminism: Voices from the Women's Liberation Movement* (New York: New York University Press, 2020), 281, 304–305.

44　Melanie Kaye/Kantrowitz, Irena Klepfisz, and Bernice Mennis, "In Gerangl/In Struggle: A Handbook for Recognizing and Resisting Anti-Semitism and for Building Jewish Identity and Pride," in *The Tribe of Dina: A Jewish Women's Anthology: Revised and Expanded Edition*, ed. Melanie Kaye/Kantrowitz and Irena Klepfisz (Boston: Beacon Press, 1989), 336.

FOURTEEN. TWO TRADITIONS OF
FIGHTING ANTISEMITISM: STRATEGIES OF
SOLIDARITY, PAST AND PRESENT

1 April Rosenblum, *The Past Didn't Go Anywhere: Making Resistance to Antisemitism Part of All of our Movements* (pamphlet, 2007), 14, aprilrosenblum.com.

2 Quoted in "Bund Rally Scored by Jewish Leader," *Seattle Post-Intelligence*, February 22, 1939.

3 Letter to John Bird Earrings, December 27, 1938, George E. Rennar papers [manuscript], 1922–1959, MSS 2918, Oregon Historical Society.

4 "Conference in Office of David Robinson," April 24, 1941, 2:30 p.m., police recording transcription, George E. Rennar papers [manuscript], 1922–1959, MSS 2918, Oregon Historical Society.

5 Burley, Shane, and Alexander Reid Ross, "From Nativism to White Power: Mid-Twentieth-Century White Supremacist Movements in Oregon," *Oregon Historical Quarterly* 120, no. 4 (2019): 564–87.

6 Arthur Markewitz, "Arthur Markewitz 1908–1984: Oral History," Oregon Jewish Museum and Center for Holocaust Education, 1977.

7 "ADL's 2022 Never Is Now | Opening Session," Anti-Defamation League, video, 1:18:20–1:19:10, November 10, 2022.

8 "ADL's 2022 Never Is Now | Anti-Israel? Anti-Zionism? Antisemitism? How to Identify and What to Do," Anti-Defamation League, video, 23:30, 34:00, November 10, 2022.

9 Jonathan Greenblatt, "Remarks by Jonathan Greenblatt to the ADL Virtual National Leadership Summit," Anti-Defamation League, May 3, 2022, adl. org.

10 Brian Robinson quoted in Jacob Henry, "ADL Condemns NY Progressive Group Jews for Racial & Economic Justice as 'Out of Touch,'" Jewish Telegraphic Agency, July 29, 2023, jta.org. An ADL spokesperson later called JFREJ "out of touch" with American Jews, despite the organization's decades-long history of progressive advocacy, sizeable Jewish base, and established record of tracking and fighting antisemitism.

11 Ben Lorber, "The ADL Is Making It Less Safe to Be a Progressive Jew," *In These Times*, November 21, 2023, inthesetimes.com; "Taking Action Against Campus Antisemitism | Fighting Hate From Home," Anti-Defamation League, video, 43:48, youtube.com. Thanks to Jenni Olson for the latter source.

12 Ron Kampeas, "ADL's Jonathan Greenblatt Praises Elon Musk as a Modern Henry Ford, Then Reconsiders," *Jewish Telegraphic Agency*, October 7, 2022, jta.org.

13 Ron Kampeas, "Elon Musk Amplifies Call by Antisemites to Ban the ADL from X," *The Times of Israel*, September 4, 2023, timesofisrael.com; Lora Kolodny, "TECH. Elon Musk boosts antisemitic tweet, claims ADL and other groups push 'anti-white' messaging," *CNBC*, November 16, 2023, cnbc.com.

14 Miranda Nazzaro, "ADL chief defends praise of Musk following X owner's

apparent embrace of antisemitic conspiracy theory," *The Hill*, November 21, 2023, thehill.com.

15   "Our Mission," Anti-Defamation League, adl.org, accessed November 26, 2023.

16   Emmaia Gelman, "The Anti-Democratic Origins of the Jewish Establishment," *Jewish Currents*, March 12, 2021, jewishcurrents.org.

17   Arthur Gorenstein, "A Portrait of Ethnic Politics: The Socialists and the 1908 and 1910 Congressional Elections on the East Side," *Publications of the American Jewish Historical Society* 50, no. 3 (1961): 213.

18   Stuart Svonkin, *Jews Against Prejudice: American Jews and the Fight for Civil Liberties* (New York: Columbia University Press, 1997), 134.

19   Jim McGee, "Jewish Group's Tactics Investigated," *The Washington Post*, October 9, 1993; Mark Ames, "The Kings of Garbage, or, The ADL Spied On Me and All I Got Was this Lousy Index Card," *Pacific Standard*, March 10, 2014, psmag.com; Richard C. Paddock, "New Details of Extensive ADL Spy Operation Emerge," *Los Angeles Times*, April 13, 1993; Al Miskin, "ADL's Spy Ring," *Middle East Research and Information Project* 183 (July/August, 1993). Many far-right groups were surveilled as well.

20   Ames, "The Kings of Garbage."

21   Emmaia Gelman, "The Anti-Defamation League Is Not What It Seems," *Boston Review*, May 23, 2019, bostonreview.net.

22   Mari Cohen, "A Closer Look at the 'Uptick' in Antisemitism," *Jewish Currents*, May 27, 2021, jewishcurrents.org.

23   Jacob Hutt and Alex Kane, "How the ADL's Israel Advocacy Undermines Its Civil Rights Work," *Jewish Currents*, February 8, 2021, jewishcurrents. org.

24   "ADL Celebrates 'Historic Milestone' as U.S. Embassy Opens in Jerusalem," Anti-Defamation League, May 14, 2018, adl.org; Jonathan Greenblatt (@ JGreenblattADL), "So many challenges in MidEast. Need to end bloodshed in Syria; to push back on Iranian terror & militarism; defeat Islamism; achieve I/P peace; create hope+oppty for next gen across region. But today, opening of US Embassy in JLM, is moment to celebrate. Deeply moved to be here.," Twitter, May 14, 2018, 7:00 a.m.; Matthew Haag, "Robert Jeffress, Pastor Who Said Jews Are Going to Hell, Led Prayer at Jerusalem Embassy," *The New York Times*, May 14, 2018.

25   Hutt and Kane, "How the ADL's Israel Advocacy Undermines Its Civil Rights Work."

26   Paddock, "New Details of Extensive ADL Spy Operation Emerge"; Gelman, "The Anti-Defamation League Is Not What It Seems."

27   Alex Kane, "The Push to 'Deactivate' Students for Justice in Palestine," *Jewish Currents*, November 21, 2023, jewishcurrents.org.

28   "ADL Opposes Ground Zero Mosque," Associated Press, July 31, 2010; Ori Nir, "Muslim Students Get Apology in a Tiff over 'Shahada' Scarf," *Forward*, July 2, 2004, forward.com; Ali Gharib, "Abe Foxman Rationalizes Blanket

Spying on American Muslims," *The Daily Beast*, April 29, 2013, thedaily-beast.com. The organization later offered apologies for their opposition to the Ground Zero mosque, and for their expressed hostility to the *shahada*, the Islamic declaration of faith.

29   Elly Bulkin and Donna Nevel, "How the Anti-Defamation League Fuels Islamophobia," *AlterNet*, February 1, 2013, alternet.org.

30   Amber Michel, "Countering Violent Extremism: Islamophobia, the De-partment of Justice and American Islamic Organizations," *Islamophobia Studies Journal* 3, no. 1 (2015): 127–137; "#StopCVE Now," Muslim Justice League, May 2020, muslimjusticeleague.org.

31   Hutt and Kane, "How the ADL's Israel Advocacy Undermines Its Civil Rights Work."

32   McGee, "Jewish Group's Tactics Investigated"; Ames, "The Kings of Gar-bage, or, The ADL Spied On Me and All I Got Was this Lousy Index Card."

33   Isaac Stanley-Becker, "CNN Fired Him for Speech Some Deemed Anti-Se-mitic. But His University Says the Constitution Protects Him," *The Wash-ington Post*, December 12, 2018; "Michelle Alexander's 'Time to Break the Silence on Palestine' Omits Key Facts, Puts Entire Onus for Conflict on Israel," Anti-Defamation League, January 29, 2019, adl.org.

34   Mazin Sidahmed, "Critics Denounce Black Lives Matter Platform Accusing Israel of 'Genocide,'" *The Guardian*, August 11, 2016, theguardian.com; Jon-athan Greenblatt, "Eyes on the Prize: In Pursuit of Racial Justice, Stick to the Facts and Avoid the Fiction," Medium, August 4, 2016, medium.com.

35   Hutt and Kane, "How the ADL's Israel Advocacy Undermines Its Civil Rights Work"; Alex Kane and Sam Levin, "Internal ADL Memo Recom-mended Ending Police Delegations to Israel Amid Backlash," *Jewish Cur-rents*, March 17, 2022, jewishcurrents.org; "ADL Honors Former Police Commissioner Ray Kelly for Lifetime of Public Service & Keeping New Yorkers Safe," Anti-Defamation League, March 26, 2014, adl.org; "Top Cop William Bratton Honored by ADL for His Vision and Service," Anti-Defa-mation League, August 16, 2013, adl.org.

36   Josh Nathan-Kazis, "ADL Suggests Cops Infiltrate, Film Antifa Protests—Then Takes It Back," *Forward*, August 31, 2017, forward.com.

37   "'Unite the Right' Rally Could Be Largest White Supremacist Gathering in a Decade," Anti-Defamation League, August 7, 2017, adl.org.

38   Holly Yan and Dana Ford, "Black UVA Student Bloodied During Arrest: 'How Could This Happen?,'" CNN, March 19, 2015, cnn.com.

39   "Who are Antifa," Anti-Defamation League, August 30, 2017, adl.org.

40   Timothy Sandoval, "How the Anti-Defamation League Rallied Support After Charlottesville," *The Chronicle of Philanthropy*, August 24, 2017, philan-thropy.com.

41   "Open Letter to Progressives: The ADL Is Not an Ally," Drop the ADL, August 2020, droptheadl.org.

42   Ben Sales, "Mega-Donors Are Taking Over Jewish Philanthropy, New

Study Says," *Jewish Telegraphic Agency*, March 26, 2018, jta.org.

43   Chris McGreal, "Pro-Israel Lobbying Group AIPAC Secretly Pouring Millions into Defeating Progressive Democrats," *The Guardian*, May 17, 2022, theguardian.com.

44   Liz Cheney quoted in Tim Hains, "Liz Cheney: Democrats Have Become the Party of Anti-Semitism, Infanticide, and Socialism," RealClearPolitics, March 10, 2019, realclearpolitics.com.

45   Marvin S. Zuckerman, *The Jewish Labor Bund: On the Occasion of its 100th Anniversary 1897–1997* (Los Angeles: Capra Publishing, 2020), 6–28.

46   Quoted in Akira Usuki, "Jewish National Communist Movement in Iraq: A Case of Anti-Zionist League in 1946," Mediterranean Studies Group at Hitotsubashi University, 2006.

47   Jews in this period did not only show up as white accomplices to the Black-led freedom struggle. Charles McDew, a Black leader of the Student Nonviolent Coordinating Committee, was Jewish. See Charles McDew, "Telling the Story: The Most Important Jewish Civil Rights Leader You May Not Have Heard Of," *Forward*, January 30, 2022, forward.com. Thanks to Rebecca Pierce for drawing our attention to McDew.

48   Benjamin Balthaser, "Exceptional Whites, Bad Jews: Racial Subjectivity, Anti-Zionism, and the Jewish New Left," *Shofar: An Interdisciplinary Journal of Jewish Studies* 41, no. 2 (2023): 32–55.

49   Joyce Antler, *Jewish Radical Feminism: Voices from the Women's Liberation Movement* (New York: New York University Press, 2022), 250. This corner receded over the subsequent decades.

50   Ibid, 244–277.

51   See Ezra Berkley Nepon, *Justice, Justice Shall You Pursue: A History of New Jewish Agenda* (Philadelphia: Thread Makes Blanket Press, 2012).

52   *Awareness and Action: A Resource Book on Anti-Semitism* (New Jewish Agenda, October 1991).

53   Elly Bulkin, "Hard Groups: Jewish Identity, Racism, and Anti-Semitism," in *Yours in Struggle: Three Feminist Perspectives on Anti-Semitism and Racism*, ed. Elly Bulkin, Minnie Bruce Pratt, and Barbara Smith (Ithaca, NY: Firebrand Books, 1984), 142.

54   Shane Burley, "How the Left Is Reclaiming the Fight Against Antisemitism," *Waging Nonviolence*, September 2, 2021, wagingnonviolence.org; "Jewish Protesters March Into D.C. Building Hosting Trump Team Against Bannon's Appointment," *Haaretz*, November 18, 2016, haaretz.com; "Faith Leaders Disrupt U.S. Vice President Mike Pence During CUFI Summit," Religion News Service, July 10, 2019, religionnews.com.

55   Eric Fingerhut on "Generally Assembled," *Unorthodox Podcast*, November 2, 2022.

56   Bentley Addison, "Arming Synagogues Will Make Them Less Safe—for Black Jews. Stop Erasing Us," *Forward*, November 5, 2018, forward.com.

57   WhatsApp is a popular text messaging app, especially common in Orthodox Jewish communities.

58 Mari Cohen, "Fears of Government Surveillance Complicate Muslim Groups' Access to Federal Security Funding," *Jewish Currents*, March 30, 2021, jewishcurrents.org.

59 Fatema Ahmad and Azadeh Shahshahani, "The Surveillance State Can't Solve White Supremacy," *The Progressive*, September 6, 2022, progressive. org.

60 Michael German, *Hidden in Plain Sight: Racism, White Supremacy, and Far-Right Militancy in Law Enforcement* (New York: Brennan Center for Justice, 2020).

61 Mimi Arbeit, "Call Out White Supremacy: For Pittsburgh, for Charlottes-ville and for the Jewish Community of Boston," *Jewish Boston*, November 5, 2018, jewishboston.com.

CONCLUSION: THE WORLD TO COME

1   Shane Burley, "The International Labor Movement Is Mobilizing for a Free Palestine," Truthout, November 29, 2023, truthout.org.

2   Najma Sharif (@najmamsharif), "what did y'all think decolonization meant? vibes? papers? essays? losers.," Twitter, October 7, 2023, 12:12 p.m.

3   Ben Lorber, "Toward a Sober Assessment of Campus Antisemitism," *Jewish Currents*, November 28, 2023, jewishcurrents.org.

4   Miles Meth, "The Boston Workers Circle was expelled from a major Jewish coalition. As a board member, I'm heartbroken — and so proud," *Forward*, October 27, 2023, forward.com.

5   Ben Lorber, "The ADL Is Making It Less Safe to Be a Progressive Jew," *In These Times*, November 21, 2023, inthesetimes.com.

6   Matt Shuman, "Right-Wing Figures Go All In On Antisemitism," HuffPost, November 17, 2023, huffpost.com.

7   Tyler Katzenberger and Thao Nguyen, "'Repulsive and disgusting': Wisconsin officials condemn neo-Nazi group after march in Madison," *USA Today*, November 21, 2023, usatoday.com.

8   Shane Burley, "How the far right is trying to manipulate the crisis in Gaza," *Waging Nonviolence*, November 1, 2023, wagingnonviolence.org; Ben Lorber, "The Right is Deeply Divided Over Support for Israel—Though It's Not About Justice for Palestinians," *Religion Dispatches*, October 19, 2023, religiondispatches.org.

9   Dan Berger, "The Abolitionist Logic of 'Everyone for Everyone,'" *Jewish Currents*, December 1, 2023.

INDEX

296–97, 302–3; the 2014 war on Gaza, 230; the 2021 war on Gaza, 202, 209. See also Israel-Gaza war (October 2023)

Israel Anti-Boycott Act, 298

Israel Defense Forces (IDF), 178–79

"Israel lobby," 195–99

Israel-Gaza war (October 2023), 5, 31, 41, 45, 168, 183, 190, 219–20, 299, 319–23; ceasefire movement and anti-war movements, 29, 41, 319–23; Hamas's October 7 attack, 5, 46, 168, 206, 214, 238, 319–21

Israeli Apartheid Week, 6, 294

Israeli Black Panthers, 184

Jackson, Liz, 186–87, 189–90

January 6th Capitol insurrection (2021), 57, 58, 65, 158–59, 283–84

Jeffress, Robert, 298

Jenkins, Daryle Lamont, 157, 272

Jerusalem Declaration on Antisemitism (JDA), 43–44, 207

Jew in the City, 281

Jewish Alliance Against Zionism, 44

Jewish Community Action in Minnesota, 87, 308–9

Jewish Community Relations Council of New York (JCRC), 251

Jewish Defense Association, 296

Jewish Defense League (JDL), 37–38, 283

Jewish Federations of North America, 195, 256, 296, 310–11

Jewish Labor Bund, 221, 296, 304–5

Jewish Liberation Project, 306

Jewish Right, 24, 84, 175–77, 219, 302–4; Israeli Right, 38, 167–68, 184–85, 208, 219–20, 261, 271, 303. See also Anti-Defamation League (ADL)

Jewish Solidarity Caucus of the Democratic Socialists of America (DSA), 141

Jewish Voice for Peace (JVP), 6, 44, 294–95, 301, 308, 314, 319–20, 323–24

Jews Against White Nationalism (JAWN), 308

Jews for Racial and Economic Justice (JFREJ), 26, 44, 275, 294, 301, 308–9, 314, 317

Jews of color, 16, 27, 247, 273–77, 311–12. See also Mizrahi Jews

Jobs With Justice, 320

John Birch Society, 129

Johnson, Greg, 174

Johnson, Mike, 168

Jones, Alex, 110, 160–61

Josephs, Allison, 281

"Judeo-Bolshevism," 22, 55, 107, 117–31, 134–35

"Judeo-Christian values," 25, 162, 174–77, 256

Justice Is Global, 108

Kahane, Meir, 37–38

Kahn-Harris, Keith, 18, 209

Kamochah, 312

Kane, Alex, 299–300

Kaplan, Morriah, 39

Katz, Ethan, 259

Katz, Jo Kent, 225–27

Kavod (collective), 310, 313–14, 315

Kaye-Kantrowitz, Melanie, 289

Kent, Dove, 1–2, 8, 39, 45, 235, 236, 239, 308

Kessler, Jason, 139

King, Steve, 158

King, William Lyon Mackenzie, 250

Kirk, Charlie, 322

Kishinev pogrom (1903), 59, 215–16

Kivel, Paul, 88

Klepfisz, Irena, 46, 289

Klug, Brian, 18, 192, 201–2

Knights Templar, 97

Koch brothers, 55

Koestler, Arthur, 217

Kopp, James Charles, 173

Kristallnacht (1938), 35, 127, 171, 250

Krushevan, Pavel, 59

Ku Klux Klan, 130, 139, 140, 148, 149, 171–72, 292, 313, 314

ABOUT THE AUTHORS

BEN LORBER is Senior Research Analyst at Political Research Associates, a social movement think tank, where he studies and publishes on antisemitism and white Chritsian nationalism. He previously worked as national campus organizer with Jewish Voice for Peace, supporting justice-driven young Jewish communities across the country, and has written extensively on antisemitism, Israel/Palestine and Jewish identity.

SHANE BURLEY is the author of several books on the far-right and social movements, and has contributed to places such as *NBC News*, *Jewish Currents*, *Al Jazeera*, *The Baffler*, *The Daily Beast*, *Haaretz*, *In These Times*, *Yes! Magazine*, *Tikkun*, and *The Oregon Historical Quarterly*.